Canada Revisited 7
Concept Map

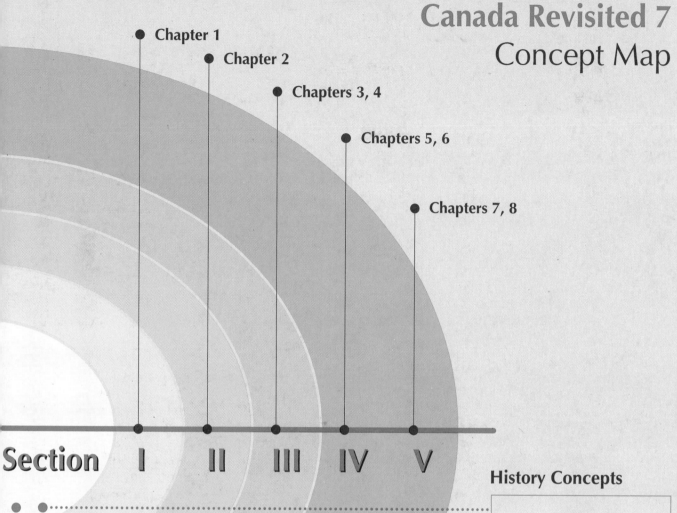

Chapter 1

Chapter 2

Chapters 3, 4

Chapters 5, 6

Chapters 7, 8

Section   I   II   III   IV   V

Section Structure

Section Story
Chapter Overview
Chapter Focus
Chapter Preview/Prediction
Chapter Content
Chapter Review
  Understanding Concepts
  Developing Research Skills
  Developing Communication Skills
  Applying Concepts
  Challenge Plus

History Concepts

Power

Co-operation

Decision-making

Conflict

Canada 7 Revisited

New France, British North America, Conflict and Change

Penney Clark

Phyllis Arnold

Roberta McKay

with

Lynn Soetaert

ARNOLD PUBLISHING LTD.

For more information contact
Nelson
1120 Birchmount Road
Scarborough, Ontario
M1K 5G4

Or you can visit our Internet site at
http://www.nelson.com

Canadian Cataloguing in Publication Data

Clark, Penney, 1950–
    Canada revisited 7

Includes index.
ISBN 0-919913-70-9

1. Canada—History—Juvenile literature.
I. Arnold, Phyllis A. II. McKay, Roberta, 1951–
III. Soetaert, Lynn. IV. Title.
V. Title: Canada revisited seven.
FC172.M285 1999 j971   C99-910245-1
F1008.2.C52 1999

Arnold Publishing Project Team

Project Managers: Lynn Soetaert, Betty Gibbs
Project Coordinators: Judi McIntyre, Christina Barabash,
    Jill Murrin, Kathleen Vanderlinden
Educational Editors: Phyllis A. Arnold, Lynn Soetaert
Editors: Betty Gibbs, Philippa Fairbairn, Christina Barabash,
    Kathleen Vanderlinden, Tim Heath
Proofreaders: Christina Barabash,
    Barbara Demers, Carole Howrish
Design: Marcey Andrews, Jill Murrin, Linda Tremblay
Illustrators: Marcey Andrews, Jill Murrin, Shelah Ruth
Production: Marcey Andrews, Judy Bauer, Anna Singkhone,
    Leslie Stewart, Linda Tremblay, Colette Howie, Tracy Suter,
    Pauline Herms, Jill Murrin, Michael Burgess

Assisted by

Maps: Johnson Cartographics Inc., Wendy Johnson
Indexer: Philippa Fairbairn
Cover Design: Marcey Andrews

Printed and bound in Canada
3 4 5 6 7 8 9   07 06 05 03

Cast of Characters

Ms. Ito	Urara Kobayashi
Erin	Jonez Durham
Roberto	Marcos Vargas
Dakota	Pierre Dumont
Ken	Ryosuke Yamaki
Brenda	Erin Unterschute

See page **254–255** for Other Contributions.

The following is referred to throughout this book:
Ordinary People in Canada's Past, Second Edition, by Nancy Sellars Marcotte, published by Arnold Publishing, Ltd., ISBN 0-919913-46-6

Support Materials:

Canada Revisited 7 Teacher's Resource Package,
IBSN 0-919913-78-4

Canadian Historical Images ClipArt CD-ROM,
Macintosh, ISBN 0-919913-41-5
Windows, ISBN 0-919913-71-7

Throughout this book, various websites are mentioned. Due to the changing nature of internet sites Arnold Publishing cannot guarantee that they will continue to be in existence, nor can we assume responsibility for content on these sites.

Cover photographs:

Front: tc Photo: Brian Morin, Parks Canada, Ontario; tr Photo Courtesy of Lower Fort Garry National Historic Site (W. Lynch), Reproduced with permission; br Photo Courtesy of Lower Fort Garry National Historic Site, Reproduced with permission; mc Phyllis A. Arnold; bl Phyllis A. Arnold; tl Courtesy of Old Fort William, Thunder Bay, Ontario

Back: tc Photo Courtesy of Sainte-Marie among the Hurons, Midland, ON, Canada; tr Photo: Brian Morin, Parks Canada, Ontario; mr EDUTECH/Arnold Publishing Ltd.; c Photo Courtesy of Lower Fort Garry National Historic Site (LSGtemp 1), Reproduced with permission; bl Phyllis A. Arnold; ml Phyllis A. Arnold; tl EDUTECH/Arnold Publishing Ltd.

Acknowledgements

We would particularly like to express our gratitude to our publisher, Phyllis A. Arnold, who has provided us with support, advice, and friendship through the many years it has taken this project to come to fruition.

We would like to extend our thanks as well to the talented members of the editorial, design, and production team at Arnold Publishing. Their creativity and resourcefulness were greatly appreciated.

Finally, our thanks go to our husbands, without whom we would not have seen the humour in the often frustrating and always demanding task of writing a textbook.

Penney Clark
Roberta McKay
March 1999

Dedicated to Hugh Clark

Consultants
HISTORICAL CONSULTANT
Dr. David Mills ●
Department of History
University of Alberta
Edmonton, Alberta

EDUCATIONAL CONSULTANTS
Elaine Chalus ●
Department of History
University of Alberta
Edmonton, Alberta

Ken Osborne ●
Faculty of Education
The University of Manitoba
Winnipeg, Manitoba

Validators
FIELD VALIDATORS
George Adams ●
History Department Head
Notre Dame Secondary School
Brampton, Ontario

Angelo Bolotta ● ●
Program Coordinator of Social Sciences
Toronto Catholic District School Board
Toronto, Ontario

Tony Burley ●
Coordinator of Instruction
Red Deer Public School District #104
Red Deer, Alberta

Dr. Bryan Connors ●
Supervisor, Consultant Services
Edmonton Public Schools
Edmonton, Alberta

John Johnston ●
Vice Principal
Central Junior High School
Red Deer Public School District #104
Red Deer, Alberta

FIELD TESTING
Olga Curtis ●
Teacher
(1992: Grade 8–4, 8–5, 8–7)
Vernon Barford Junior High School
Edmonton, Alberta

Terry Gerling ●
Teacher
(1992: Grade 8–1, 8–3, 8–6)
Vernon Barford Junior High School
Edmonton, Alberta

Pat Shields ●
Teacher
(1992: Grade 8–2 and 8–8)
Vernon Barford Junior High School
Edmonton, Alberta

EDUCATIONAL VALIDATORS
Bill Larkin ● ●
Consultant, Social Studies, Geography & History
Programme Department
Toronto District School Board
Toronto, Ontario

Elspeth Deir ●
Instructor, Faculty of Education
Queen's University
Kingston, Ontario

Bill Alexander ●
Curriculum Coordinator (Retired)
Geography and History Global Education
Toronto District School Board
Toronto, Ontario

Jack MacFadden ●
Teacher/Researcher
W.H. Day Elementary School
Bradford, Ontario

Bernie Rubinstein ●
Program Advisor
Social Sciences, Social Studies
Toronto District School Board
Toronto, Ontario

CONTENT VALIDATORS
Dr. Barry Gough ● ●
Professor of History
History Department
Wilfrid Laurier University
Waterloo, Ontario
(Chapters 1–3, 6)
Native Validation

Jeffrey L. McNairn ●
Postdoctoral Fellow
Department of History
York University
Toronto, Ontario

Bias Reviewers
John M. Smith ●
Principal
Green Glade Senior Public
Mississauga, Ontario

Ken Ramphal ●
Toronto, Ontario

Special Thanks
National Archives of Canada
Ottawa, Ontario

Parks Canada

We acknowledge the financial support of the Government of Canada through the Book Publishing Industry Development Program for our publishing activities.

●=*Canada Revisited* (1992)
●=*Canada Revisited 7* (1999)

Table of Contents

To the Student

Revisiting Canada's Past

These students and Ms. Ito from the Passport Tour School are featured in Section stories and on various activity pages. You are invited to join them as they tour Canada to revisit its past.

Ms. Ito

Erin

Brenda

Ken

Dakota

Roberto

Focus of the Text

By looking at history we can often examine the roots of events and issues of today. Methods of preventing problems or facing today's issues may be built upon ideas and methods used in our past. People in history faced situations that relate to those of today. Many fascinating individuals who had impact on the history of Canada appear throughout this text.

Canada Revisited 7 begins with a brief review of First People and European explorers. The remaining five sections trace Canada's history from early colonization to the time just prior to Confederation, when Canada became a country. Wherever possible the information is arranged chronologically—in the order in which the events happened.

An understanding of history can prepare you for addressing and resolving with more confidence the issues that we face today.

Learning How to Learn

Canada Revisited 7 focuses on the way you learn. Activities for "revisiting" Canadian historical eras are provided in the textbook prior to discussion of major political changes. Predicting outcomes, then reading further to confirm your prediction and add to your knowledge, will help you learn.

You will be involved in building thinking and learning skills as you increase your knowledge of Canada's past. Photo essays, works of art, original narratives (stories), and excerpts from historical documents will give you the feeling of "revisiting Canadian history." Role-plays, simulations, debates, critical thinking exercises, and decision-making exercises will draw you into historical situations.

Challenge Plus, problem-solving, research projects, and Review activities encourage you to apply and extend your skills and knowledge of Canadian history to related topics. Activities are provided in a variety of types to suit your interests and learning style. Challenge yourself by selecting a range of different activities.

An understanding of the way you learn can allow you to become more confident, involved, and responsible for your own learning.

The pages that follow provide more detail about the features of this text and how you can best use them to understand and experience Canada's past.

Have fun and enjoy revisiting Canada's past!

About the Text

The more involved you become in reliving history through *Canada Revisited 7*, the more meaningful and enjoyable your study can be.

Preview

Section stories relate to students' lives and introduce the Section theme. See page 18 for an example.

Questions to Talk About relate each Section story to the type of government to be covered. See page 19 for an example.

An **Overview** at the beginning of each chapter (except Chapter 1) shows the main ideas of the chapter. See page 52 for an example.

The **Chapter Focus** points out which of the four Social Studies concepts (described on page viii) will be emphasized. See page 88 for an example.

A **Chapter Preview/Prediction** activity helps you make predictions about the main ideas to be covered in that chapter. See page 23 for an example.

Visual Cues and Features

This textbook has been designed in ways that assist you to understand, organize, and remember information.

Graphics present information in visual ways. Read the illustrations, charts, maps, and graphs for information. See pages 16 and 224 for examples.

Titles in each chapter are coded by size and colour so you can tell when a new idea begins. As the title size decreases, the idea is explained in more detail. There are four main heading sizes:

Level I headings are used to show the main ideas of the chapter. See the heading "The Atlantic Colonies" on page 237 for an example. All Level I headings are listed in the Table of Contents under each chapter title.

Level II headings show the subtopics of the main ideas. See the heading "Government" on page 237.

Level III headings show the subtopics of Level II headings. See the heading "Establishing Responsible Government" on page 238.

Level IV headings show the subtopics of Level III headings. See the heading "In Nova Scotia" on page 238 for an example.

Narratives have a coloured border and a row of dots along the top of the page. Section stories introduce a theme of the chapter. Other narratives portray fictional people in stories based on actual events. See page 156 for an example.

Focus On sections appear on a tabbed divider page with a tan background colour. They offer more detailed information about people, places, and events. See page 93 for an example.

Eyewitness Accounts are written in *italics*. They are quotations of people who were present at the time of the events described. (Unusual words and spellings found in them were used in the original.) Quotations can help you gain an understanding of the times and the people who wrote about them. See page 202 for examples.

Individual Biographies highlight people who are recognized as having contributed to events in Canada's past. A photograph or illustration is provided where available. See page 106 for examples.

Vocabulary words or expressions in **bold** print are explained at the bottom of that page. They also appear in the glossary at the end of the text (pages 248–253). Check for unfamiliar words in the Glossary.

Footnotes are marked by asterisks (*). They signal that something on the page is explained in more detail at the bottom of the page. See page 114 for examples.

Political Acts show changes made to government throughout our history. The example below is part of the Proclamation shown on page 114.

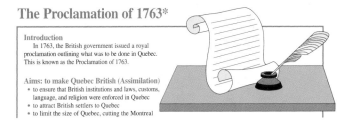

The Proclamation of 1763*

> **Introduction**
> In 1763, the British government issued a royal proclamation outlining what was to be done in Quebec. This is known as the Proclamation of 1763.
>
> **Aims: to make Quebec British (Assimilation)**
> • to ensure that British institutions and laws, customs, language, and religion were enforced in Quebec
> • to attract British settlers to Quebec
> • to limit the size of Quebec, cutting the Montreal

Canada Revisited sections highlight and revisit archeological or historic sites, people, and events. See page 171 for an example.

Timelines are a visual way of showing a series of events in chronological order. The numbers in the dots correspond to sections of the text that describe events in more detail. See page 172 for an example.

Numbered dots also relate other kinds of information to each other: text and pictures (see page 4), and text and map locations (see page 167).

The **Mini-atlas** inside the back cover of the textbook provides 10 maps that show the changes in territory lived in or claimed by different groups or countries.

Icons

Learning How to Learn Icons appear in black and white at the beginning of exercises and Review questions. Some examples are shown below. A complete list appears inside the front cover of the text.

Look for the **icons** in the Appendix (pages 256–271) to find ideas and information related to activities they appear beside.

 The **Research Model Icon** reminds you to look on pages x and xi to find information about completing a research project.

The **Ongoing Project Icon** signals three ongoing projects—Passport to the Past (introduced on pages 20 and 21), a timeline project (introduced in Question 8 on page 48), and a website or magazine project for each text section (see Question 34, page 85).

History Icons are used to cue which of the following four **concepts** are being emphasized in a chapter. They appear in colour if they are a particular focus. If an icon appears with a title, at the beginning of a paragraph, or in an exercise, the concept is a focus of that section.

Power

- being chosen to lead by people who trust you to make life better or easier
- commanding people's obedience with or without their agreement
- using superior strength and authority

Co-operation

- sharing ideas, trusting, and working with others to achieve a common goal
- using the strengths of different individuals to complement each other
- recognizing that the team, as well as the individual, matters

Decision-making

- finding a solution for a problem or issue
- involves considering a variety of alternatives, making a choice, and acting on that choice

Conflict

- a tense situation, a struggle between forces, a battle or war
- a clash between individuals, groups, or societies holding opposing ideas, interests, or ways of life

Icon—pictorial representation
Concept—a general idea or thought (e.g., colonization, nationhood)

Activities

Critical Thinking activities ask you to think about various points of view. Some are identified with the heading Point of View and by a "talking head" style. See page 31 for an example. Others are indicated with a heading like the example below.

An Exercise in Critical Thinking

Problem Solving activities ask you to become involved in an historic event by solving a related problem. These are indicated with a heading like the example below.

An Exercise in Problem Solving

Simulations are meant to help you experience life as a person in a particular time period would. See page 196 for an example.

Research Projects ask you to find and present materials related to history. See page 20 for an example.

Many of the special projects include opportunities for you to share what you have learned with others (parents, classmates). See page 55 for an example.

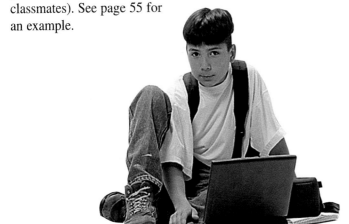

Decision-making activities require you to make a choice related to an historical event. These are indicated with a heading like the example below.

An Exercise in Decision-Making

Learning Skills

The **Learning How to Learn (SKIMM™) Appendix** is on pages 256 to 271. When working on exercises and Review activities, the icons are your cue to turn to the Appendix for ideas to help you complete the activity.

For Your Notebook questions ask you to understand and work with information you have read.

Exploring Further questions ask you to extend your learning beyond the information in the chapter.

A **Review** section is found at the end of each chapter. This includes a chance to check the predictions you made at the beginning of the chapter. Review questions and activities are designed to help you understand concepts, and develop research and communication skills (reading, writing, listening and speaking, viewing and presenting). You can also apply and extend what you have learned in Applying Concepts and Challenge Plus activities. See page 82 for an example of a Review.

Concept Map

A Concept Map to *Canada Revisited 7* is included inside the front cover. It is a visual summary of the organization and features of the book. The coloured rings show the five Sections of the book. Chapters found within each Section are also identified. For example, Section III (light green ring) contains Chapters 3 and 4. The Section Structure box on the lower right page lists regular features of each Section and Chapter. Icons (pictorial representations) on the far bottom right are cues to material throughout the textbook that focuses on these four history concepts. The icons on the left page are cues to learning strategies used in the book (see Appendix pages 256 to 271).

A Research Model

Research means locating useful information on a topic by following an organized procedure. In various activities in *Canada Revisited 7* you are asked to do research and solve problems or make decisions about issues. The research model shown below is provided to help you. You may decide to modify the model or design your own research model to suit your particular needs.

This model divides research into three parts: Gathering Information, Examining and Organizing Information, and Communicating the Information.

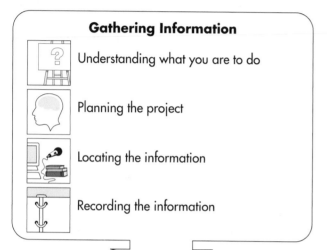

Gathering Information

 Understanding what you are to do

 Planning the project

 Locating the information

 Recording the information

Examining and Organizing Information

Examining the information

Organizing the information

Communicating the Information

 Preparing the presentation

Sharing the presentation

Assessing what you've done

Criteria—standards by which something is judged or categorized

Gathering Information

1. **Understanding what you are to do**
   Focus on the topic you are researching.

   - Read your topic several times and think about what you are being asked to do.
   - Examine the topic by asking what, why, which, where, when, who, and how.
   - Rewrite the topic in your own words or explain the topic to another student.

2. **Planning the project**
   Make a list of what you need to know and do before you start solving the problem.

   - Develop questions to guide your research:
     –What type of information is needed?
     –What key terms do you have to define?
     –What are possible sources of information?
   - Decide on the steps to follow in locating your information.
   - Think about the **criteria** that will be used to assess your project and decide how best to fulfil the requirements. See Appendix page 267 for Self-assessment ideas.
   - Decide on an Action Plan to outline how you are going to do your research. (See page 57 for a sample Action Plan.)
   - Set target dates for stages of completion.
   - Remember your plan of action must be flexible. Review it often and revise it if it isn't working.
   - Think about how you will present your research project later on.

3. **Locating the information**
Use a variety of information sources:

–almanacs	–maps
–charts and graphic	–monuments
organizers	–museum displays and
–cartoons	artifacts
–CD-ROMS	–newspapers and
–data bases	magazines
–diaries and journals	–photographs
–dictionaries	–posters and banners
–encyclopedias	–radio and television
–fiction and non-	programs
fiction material	–re-enactments
–government records	–reference books
–graphs (circle, bar,	–scrapbooks
line)	–scripts and transcripts
–reconstructed	–songs
historical sites	–speeches
–internet	–statistics
–interviews and	–textbooks
surveys	–videos and films
–legal documents	

- Do surveys.
- Interview a variety of people about your topic.
- Contact experts.
- Skim read; use the table of contents, the index, the glossary.
- Keep a record of reference materials you use by following this format: author's last name, first name, book title, place of publication, date of publication (e.g., Marcotte, Nancy Sellars, *Ordinary People in Canada's Past*, Second Edition, Edmonton, AB, Arnold Publishing Ltd., 1997).

4. **Recording the information**
Record only information related to your project.

- Use one of the following or a combination:
  –make graphic organizers and notes (See Appendix pages 257 and 264)
  –draw pictures, maps, and create graphs
  –make diagrams and charts
- Record definitions that relate to your topic.
- Write the information in your own words.

Examining and Organizing Information

5. **Examining the information**

6. **Organizing the information**
Steps 5 and 6 are difficult to separate and are often done at the same time.

- Go through all the information you have collected. Organize it into groups of similar types using graphic organizers such as charts, webs, diagrams, and maps. (See Appendix pages 257–259 and 264–266.)
- Decide if you need to do more research.

Communicating the Information

7. **Preparing the presentation***

- Ask yourself if you really have done what you were assigned to do.
- Decide how you wish to communicate your research findings to others by choosing a presentation idea from the Appendix on page 267.
- Prepare your presentation.

8. **Sharing the presentation**
Practise sharing your presentation. Show it to a friend before you share it with others.

9. **Assessing what you've done**

- Judge the effectiveness of your project based on the criteria you determined when planning the project. See Appendix page 267 for Self-assessment ideas.
- Record in your History Journal what you would do differently next time. Record what you would do again.

---

*Presentation, as used in this book, refers to the communication of information in visual, oral, or written forms.

Ms. Ito and the Passport Tour students, carrying backpacks, cameras, and the laptop computer, paused at the large totem pole in the Vancouver Airport arrival area. Then they proceeded to the briefing room.

The group will be visiting the Museum of **Anthropology** at the University of British Columbia to view the displays of Northwest Coast First Peoples culture and tour the grounds. They will see the Haida houses and totem poles and spend some time with an Elder. After a full day in Vancouver they will fly to Alberta to see Head-Smashed-In Buffalo Jump, then go on to points east to visit sites where explorers like Cabot and Cartier landed. The students are on an extended study tour. They have just spent several weeks in Japan. During the coming months they will visit special sites in Canada where they will learn about Canada's past—from **pre-history** to about 1850.

In the briefing room at the airport, Ms. Ito attached some photographs of historical places and objects to the bulletin board. "The photographs on this bulletin board act as a review of Canada's earliest history," she said. "Over the next few weeks we will be visiting these sites to refresh our memories about Canada's early history. Later we'll examine the other topics—New France, British North America, and Conflict and Change."

Anthropology—study of customs, beliefs, and ways of life of different groups of people
Pre-history—before events were recorded or written down

Section I

Connecting to Prior Learning

The group crowded around the bulletin board. They discussed each of the photographs.

"Wow," exclaimed Ken. "We know more than I thought about Native culture and early explorers and our early history."

"Next, you will have an opportunity to actually experience history when you visit the museum displays," Ms. Ito reminded them.

"I'm really looking forward to meeting the Haida Elder," Dakota added.

There was a chorus of "Me too's" from the rest of the group.

"Great!" said Ms. Ito. "Please keep in mind that we will be relating all of these people, places, and events to our study of Canadian history. Now, before we find our van, are there any questions?"

No one spoke out or raised a hand, but Erin was frowning. "I get the impression you have something you want to ask, Erin," Ms. Ito prompted. Somewhat reluctantly, Erin said, "I can understand visiting the museum displays, the Haida Elder, and also why we're going to Head-Smashed-In Buffalo Jump. They make sense. I mean, the Haida are real people. The Buffalo Jump is a real place. It's just all the other stuff I don't get."

Ms. Ito nodded to encourage Erin to continue.

"Well, it's just that, not everything we are learning about is real. So much of this history stuff doesn't seem to relate to today or real life at all. It doesn't relate to us. So...," Erin hesitated and then plunged on, "what's the point?"

Ms. Ito looked at her seriously. "Erin," she began, "I could tell you many reasons for studying history, and you could probably predict some of my answers."

"Like understanding and appreciating where we come from?" Brenda suggested.

"That's right! But saying it and believing it are two different things. Sometimes, you need more proof, right?"

"Our next trip isn't going to be on a time machine, is it?" Ken asked, grinning.

"No, but the people, places, and events from the past can be as real and important to us as the people that we meet on this trip. What we have to do is make connections between history and our lives."

No one reacted for a moment, then Dakota asked, "But how? How do we figure that out?"

"Did you know that many of the ideas, decisions, beliefs, and issues we experience in our day-to-day lives are directly related to, or are similar to, those of the past? By looking from the present to the past

1. Viking settlement at L'Anse aux Meadows, Newfoundland
2. Model Huron village
3. Stretched fur pelts
4. Totem pole of Northwest Coast People
5. Model of Jacques Cartier's ship

and back to the present again, we can sometimes make better sense of our world today—as well as the past. It helps us avoid mistakes and repeat successes."

"I know what you mean," said Roberto. "I've learned from my big brother's past. He told me about running the spoon under the warm water before scooping ice cream, and I haven't bent a spoon since!" Roberto had a way of connecting everything with food!

"Too bad the connections to the past aren't always that obvious!" Ken suggested hesitantly. "After all, your brother is only nineteen, but history is really OLD stuff!"

"I have an idea," said Ms. Ito. "We'll begin each section of your study of Canadian history by sharing something from the modern day. This modern-day story will show us issues and events in our world today that are similar to or a result of events from the past. This will help us revisit and connect to our history."

The students shrugged and nodded, willing to give it a try.

"Too bad we can't actually meet the people from Canada's past, like we can the Haida Elder!" said Brenda.

Ms. Ito smiled. "Oh, just wait until I tell you about another activity I have planned for later—it's called Passport to the Past..."

"Would it be okay if we ate lunch first?" Roberto asked.

For Your Notebook

1. To help you connect to your prior learning, create two webs to summarize what you know about the history of Aboriginal people and European explorers before 1670. As you read through Chapter 1, add additional details to your webs in another colour of ink.

Chapter 1 *Review*

First People and European Explorers

This chapter provides a short review of what you studied last year in History. The circled numbers on the pictures, maps, and other visuals relate to the text material labelled with the same number.

First People

Origins

Who were the First People?* How did they get to the Americas? Many theories have been developed to explain this mystery.

Ice Age and Beringia

❶ The Beringia theory suggests that ocean levels dropped about 65 to 138 metres during the ice age that occurred in the last million years. The large masses of land that were exposed formed a continent-sized land bridge joining Siberia and North America. Scientists have named this land bridge Beringia.

*Visit SchoolNet's First People website to learn more about Native people of Canada. The address is http://www.schoolnet.ca/aboriginal/

Some scientists and scholars believe that Asian people travelled across Beringia and down the central ice-free corridor following game animals that were seeking new pastures in North America. These Asian explorers are believed to have spread across the continent and become the ancestors of the Native peoples.

❷ Many Native people believe that the North American First People were created here by the Great Spirit. The following legend presents one version of the Creation.

On the great waters created by Manitou, Old Man was sitting. Nearby was the first woman. They were trying to decide what substance Manitou used to hold up the water. "I will send down some creatures to find out," declared the woman. She sent a fish, an otter, and a beaver. None returned. Finally she sent a muskrat. The muskrat reappeared. In his forepaw he clutched a sticky brown substance, mud. When the woman rolled it in her hands, it grew so large that she could not hold it, so she cast it into the water. It quickly spread and formed the land where we live.

Ways of Life

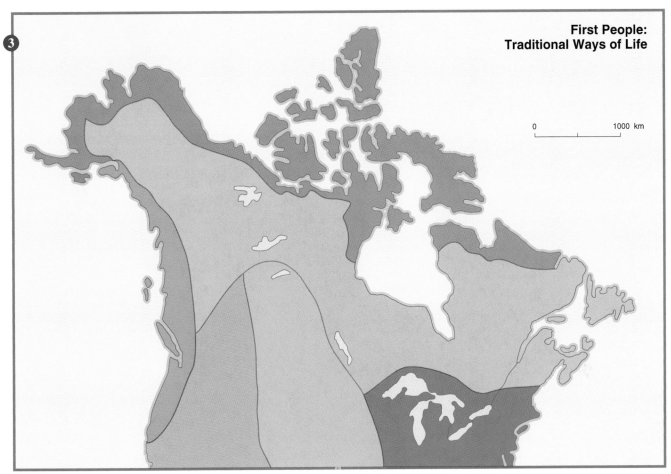

**First People:
Traditional Ways of Life**

❸

0   1000 km

Algonquian Nations

- Algonquin
- Cree
- Montagnais
- Naskapi
- Ojibwa/Chippewa
- Malecite
- Micmaq
- Beothuk

Iroquoian Nations

- Mohawk
- Oneida
- Onondaga
- Huron/Wendat
- Tobacco/Petun
- Tuscarora
- Cayuga
- Seneca
- Neutral
- Erie

Legend

❹

- Hunters (Northern Hunters and some Algonquian Peoples*)
- Fishers (Northwest Coast Peoples)
- Hunters and farmers (Iroquoian and some Algonquian Peoples)
- Hunters and gatherers (Plains Peoples)
- Gatherers (Plateau Peoples)
- Hunters and fishers (Arctic Peoples)

* Refers to Algonquian-speaking peoples

❸ The map divides the First People into six groups according to their **traditional** way of life. These ways of life were closely related to the land where they lived. Different **cultures** developed depending on the resources available. Boundaries as we know them today did not exist for the First People and groups ranged widely in order to obtain enough food. The boundaries on the map indicate the general territorial areas of these groups.

❹ **Native peoples** lived throughout Canada's different regions and were well adapted to their environments. Groups that settled near the oceans concentrated on fishing. Forest people were hunters. Other groups made use of the good agricultural land and became farmers. Over thousands of years, complex and distinct cultures developed. The First People were made up of different **nations** with different ways of life. These people are often referred to as the First Nations.

Traditional—following customs handed down for a long time
Culture—the way of life of a specific group of people
Native peoples—includes all Aboriginal peoples (Indians, Inuit, Metis) in Canada. Native peoples means more than one Native group is involved. In this book, Native peoples may also be called First People, First Nations, or Aboriginal People.

Nation—a group of people who live in a certain area, speak the same language, have the same way of life, have the same system of decision-making (government), and usually belong to the same group

Same/Different

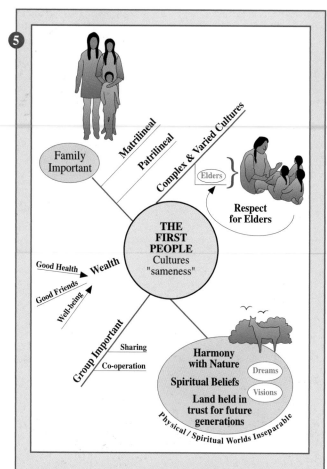

5

Nation

A nation is a group of people who:

- live in a certain area
- speak the same language(s)
- have the same way of life
- have the same system of decision-making (government)
- belong to the same group

5 The First People developed cultures that were appropriate for their environments and the natural resources available to them. The Iroquoian peoples used the rich soil to become farmers; the Algonquian peoples hunted and fished; the Plains peoples used the buffalo to supply their needs; the Northwest Coast peoples used products from the sea and the forests to satisfy their needs.

Native cultures were not all the same. It is important to not over-generalize about the First People. Groups were often as different as nations are today. Yet, although the First People formed different nations and developed different ways of life, their cultures shared many of the same characteristics.

6 Native cultures were complex and varied. Traditions, customs, and history were handed down orally to the children. Elders were highly respected because of their important role in society. Children learned by watching and helping adults. They also listened to their people's history and beliefs in stories told by Elders.

Most Native cultures emphasized the well-being of the group over individual gain. Thus, sharing and co-operation were more important than accumulating personal wealth. Wealth generally meant good health, good friends, and well-being for the First People. It was not always measured by possessions.

Native cultures were based on a family unit and **kinship**. Some tribes were matrilineal: they traced their relationships through their mothers. Other tribes were patrilineal: they traced their relationships through their fathers.

Although this chapter has been written in the past tense, as the generalizations refer to the historical period under study, many Native people today hold the beliefs and values described.

Kinship—having some of the same ancestors or being related by marriage

Jules by Carl Fontaine

8 Decisions were made by **consensus** after long discussions and debates. Chiefs and leaders were chosen by their **clans** and could act only as representatives. They had no power of their own.

9 Native spiritual beliefs centered on living in harmony with nature. Spiritual beliefs touched every facet of ordinary life. The physical and spiritual worlds were considered to be inseparable. Nature was respected. Dreams and visions formed an important part of the spiritual beliefs.

7 Conservation and living in harmony with nature were essential parts of the Native way of life. For thousands of years before Europeans came to what is now modern-day Canada, the Aboriginal people lived here. During this time they took and used wisely what they needed from nature. They interacted with nature, but they were careful not to destroy the natural **ecosystem**. The land was held in trust for future generations.

Ecosystem—the system formed by the interaction of all living things in a particular environment with one another and their environment
Consensus—general agreement among all people consulted
Clan—a group of related families that claim to be descended from common ancestors

Northwest Coast Peoples

People Who Fished

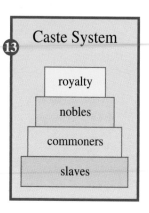

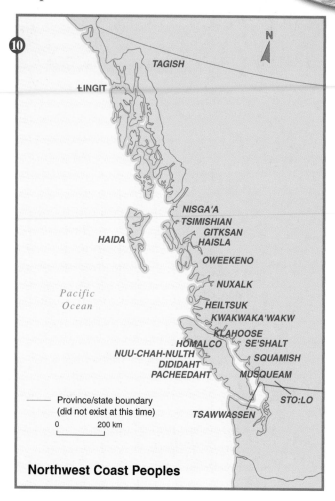

Northwest Coast Peoples

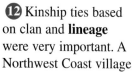

Caste System

royalty

nobles

commoners

slaves

⑩ Northwest Coast peoples lived along the western coast of the North American continent between what is now Alaska/northern British Columbia and the American states of Washington and Oregon. This area is composed of many islands and deep, narrow coastal inlets.

⑪ The Northwest Coast peoples had a much more abundant food supply than other Native groups. They obtained most of their food from the sea, which was full of fish (such as salmon, cod, and halibut), mammals (such as whales, seals, porpoises, sea otters, and sea lions), and shellfish (such as clams, mussels, and crabs). Edible seaweed was also available.

For meat, these people hunted deer and other land animals. The land also provided fern roots, berries, and the inner bark of hemlock and other trees.

The main role of men was hunting, fishing, and gathering food; the main role of women was preparing the food.

⑫ Kinship ties based on clan and **lineage** were very important. A Northwest Coast village could contain one or more lineages. Neighbouring villages were not linked together in a tribal organization, although they would join together in times of need, such as war.

A typical village might contain 30 houses built along the beach. The houses were made of cedar planks. Among the Northwest Coast people, relatives, or people of one lineage, lived together in one house. Inside, the space was divided into individual family areas by planks or woven mats of cedar bark. Each family usually had its own fire for cooking and warmth. A raised wooden platform for sleeping and for storage of family possessions extended around the walls of the house. The Northwest Coast people were able to accumulate far more furniture and possessions than other Native groups because they had permanent villages.

Many of the Coastal peoples developed very sophisticated art forms. Carvers created elaborate ceremonial face masks, canoe prows, wooden chests, and bowls from cedar trees. Totem poles often stood at the front of a house and depicted the history of the families living in the house.

⑬ The Northwest Coast peoples had a complex **caste system.** Their society had royalty, who were the chiefs, at the top, then nobles, commoners, and slaves. Native people of the West Coast believed in the existence in the non-human world of one supreme being and lesser spirits.

Lineage—a person's descent or place in a line of ancestors
Caste system—social system with distinct classes based on differences of birth, rank, position, or wealth

The Plains Peoples

Buffalo Hunters

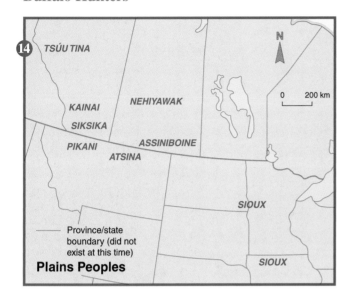

⓮ TSÚU TINA

KAINAI

SIKSIKA

PIKANI

ATSINA

NEHIYAWAK

ASSINIBOINE

SIOUX

SIOUX

N

0   200 km

— Province/state boundary (did not exist at this time)

Plains Peoples

⓱

⓲

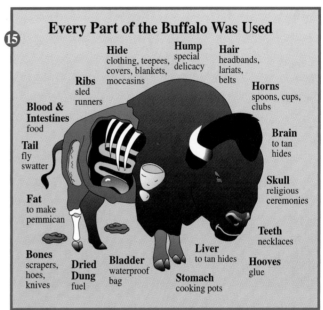

Every Part of the Buffalo Was Used

⓯

Hide clothing, teepees, covers, blankets, moccasins

Hump special delicacy

Hair headbands, lariats, belts

Ribs sled runners

Blood & Intestines food

Tail fly swatter

Fat to make pemmican

Bones scrapers, hoes, knives

Dried Dung fuel

Bladder waterproof bag

Stomach cooking pots

Liver to tan hides

Horns spoons, cups, clubs

Brain to tan hides

Skull religious ceremonies

Teeth necklaces

Hooves glue

⓮ The Plains peoples were hunters and gatherers. Food was plentiful on the plains. Buffalo (bison), deer, elk, and antelope roamed in abundance. Wild berries and plants completed the diet.

⓯ The buffalo provided the Plains peoples with almost everything they needed. Hunting buffalo was the men's most important role, as the well-being of the group depended on their skill. In Plains societies, the main role of women was to prepare food, make clothing, build and care for the home, and look after the children.

⓰ The teepee was the main form of shelter for the Plains peoples. Teepees could be moved to different places as the seasons changed. Each family normally had its own teepee. Teepees were the property of the women.

⓱ Plains peoples were governed by councils consisting of both men and women. Group decisions were reached by consensus after the opinions of the adults had been heard. This often involved much discussion, debate, and persuasion.

⓲ The Circle was sacred to the Plains peoples. They perceived that many things in their lives were based on

⓰

the Circle: the cycle of the day, the four great winds, the phases of the moon, the seasons, and the cycle of life and death. The Plains peoples viewed life as a cycle of events from birth to death.

Children were very important because they were the ones who continued the culture. Children spent a large part of their time with their grandparents and the Elders. The Elders were highly respected for their knowledge of the band's history, customs, and traditions.

The Plains peoples believed in the importance of sharing and generosity. Their survival depended on group co-operation. They did not believe in private ownership of land. The land had been made by the Great Spirit (the Creator) for all to use. It could not be bought or sold, for it did not belong to them individually.

The Plains peoples honoured the Great Spirit. They believed that everything on earth was sacred and was to be respected. They believed that rocks, trees, lakes, rivers, animals, and people had all been given spirits and special roles by the Great Spirit. Hunters and trappers thanked the animals they killed for giving up their lives to provide the people with food, clothing, and shelter. Women thanked the plants they used in the same way.

Iroquoian Peoples

Planters of Corn

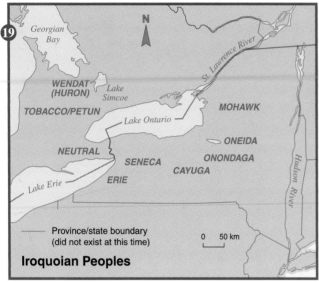

Iroquoian Peoples

19 The Iroquoian peoples lived near the Great Lakes and the St. Lawrence River on forest-covered rolling hills that contained many lakes. This area provided enough food for a large population.

20 The people were farmers who lived in villages of 20 to 350 families. Land was cleared by the men, using stone-bladed axes. Shrubs and stumps were burned. When the land was cleared, the women used their digging sticks to loosen the soil, and then made holes with their stone-tipped hoes. They put fish into the holes for fertilizer, said a prayer, and then added the seeds. Almost all of the agricultural work was done by women. The men recognized the women's contributions to the group by acknowledging their status to be equal with that of the men.

The main crops grown were maize (corn), beans, and squash. These were so important to the Iroquoian peoples' diet that they were called "the three sisters." Late in the summer the women also picked berries, nuts, wild plants, onions, pumpkins, cabbages, and sunflowers to add to their winter food supply. Tobacco was grown and harvested in the fall. Maple syrup and sugar were made in late winter. The men contributed to the food supply by hunting and fishing. Women did the cooking.

Spirituality was part of everyday life for the Iroquoian peoples. Corn was believed to be the holy gift of the Creator. The Creator was consulted through prayers at all feasts and ceremonies.

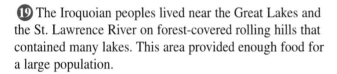

21 There was normally plenty of food, so large groups of people were able to live together and find food nearby. Iroquoian villages were made up of 30 to 75 lodges each. The lodges were called longhouses, as they were long enough for several related families.

22 The Iroquoian social system reflected the importance of women. The society was matrilineal. Kin relationships were traced through the mother, not the father. Families were very important to the Iroquoian people. At birth, children became part of their mother's clan. A clan was made up of the female leader, her sisters, their children, and their daughters' children, as well as their husbands. The women chose the leader of the clan from amongst themselves. The leader was highly respected by all the members of the clan.

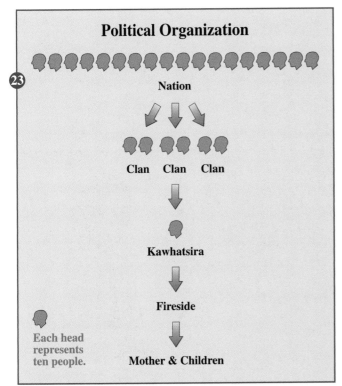

Political Organization

Nation

Clan   Clan   Clan

Kawhatsira

Fireside

Mother & Children

Each head represents ten people.

and power in decision-making. Decisions that affected the entire group, however, had to be made by a council of the clans' representatives. The female clan leader chose a man to act as representative. He was chosen for his wisdom and skill in dealing with others. It was his job to speak for the clan and follow its instructions at the larger council meetings and in the Iroquois Peace League (also called the League of Five Nations or the Iroquois **Confederacy**). If either the clan mother or the clan was not pleased with his work, he could be replaced at any time. This ensured that representatives respected their clan's wishes.

24 The Iroquois Confederacy dates from the 1400s. An **alliance**, called the League of Five Nations, was created to bring peace to the Mohawk, Oneida, Onondaga, Cayuga, and Seneca Nations.

The Five Nations' territories formed a symbolic longhouse, which reinforced the kinship ties among the groups. Thus, the Confederacy was a spiritual as well as a **political** organization. The Confederacy Council was made up of 50 representatives. It met once a year in the fall around the central fire of the Onondaga Nation. The fire was both real and symbolic.

When making decisions, the representatives of each of the Five Nations continued discussions until they arrived at a consensus. Once consensus had been reached among the representatives of each nation, the people of the Five Nations also had to agree. Achieving this consensus required time, tact, and diplomacy. Decisions were reached only after long discussions and debates. All of the adults had a say.

23 Iroquoian society was based around the fireside, which was a group made up of a mother and her children. The firesides were part of a larger group of matrilineally related families known as a *kawhatsira*. The *kawhatsira* was part of a clan, and the clan formed part of a nation.

Each village held council meetings to settle its own problems. Men and women took part in this decision-making process. The men respected women's equal status

Confederacy—people joined for a common purpose; an alliance
Alliance—union formed between nations or groups of people based on an agreement that benefits those in the union
Political—providing direction, order, and security to meet group needs

Algonquian Peoples

Wild Game Hunters

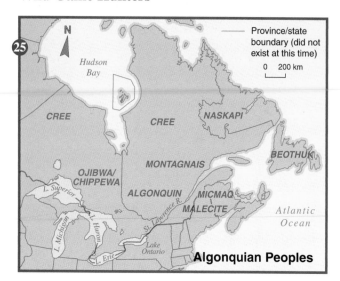

25 The Algonquian peoples lived in Canada's northern forest, an area of rocks, lakes, and trees. Their homelands extended from the Atlantic coastal area to the area north and west of the Great Lakes.

26 The forested area in which they lived had an abundance of wild game (moose, caribou, deer, bear, rabbit, beaver, birds, and fish). The men were skilful hunters and fishers. The women added to the food supply by gathering wild berries and roots. They collected maple syrup. Some groups harvested wild rice.

27 The Algonquian peoples lived in small groups of about 25 to 50 people. Everybody in the group had kinship ties. Children became part of the father's clan at birth.

The leaders were adults who were respected for their important skills, such as hunting. All the adults in a group helped to make important decisions.

Sometimes several groups got together for celebrations or to make decisions that affected them all. In the summer, much larger groups of people would live together and camp near a river or lake. They speared fish or caught them on hooks or in nets. In the winter, they lived in the woods, in small groups of just a few people.

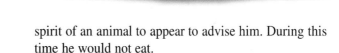

28 Because they were nomadic, the Algonquian people had few possessions. They had to be able to take everything with them when they travelled. In the winter, they carried their goods on toboggans or on their backs. They used snowshoes to make walking on snow easier. In summer they travelled in canoes or walked, carrying their goods on their backs.

29 Each group would camp in a different place in the area. Their homes, called wigwams, consisted of a frame made from tree branches and covered with sheets of bark or animal skins. They moved to another area if game was becoming scarce rather than kill all the animals in an area.

30 The Algonquian peoples believed that they were surrounded by spirits. Before they killed an animal, they would ask for permission from its spirit.

When a boy became a man, he would go on a vision quest. Going alone to a quiet place, he would wait for the spirit of an animal to appear to advise him. During this time he would not eat.

A person who had many spirit guides might become a **shaman**. A shaman advised people and told them about the future. Some shamans were also medical experts. They often cured sick people using herbs, roots, and other parts of plants, many of which are used today.

Elders were men and women who knew the history, traditions, and beliefs of their groups. They played an important part in teaching children and they also advised adults.

Changes

The First People met their economic, political, social, and spiritual needs for thousands of years through lifestyles and cultures suited to their environment. Changes were gradual. Interaction with European explorers would bring many new changes.

Shaman—a Native spiritual leader

European Explorers

Exploration

This part of the review focuses on the early exploration of Canada by the Europeans. The terms *exploration* and *discovery*, in this book, refer only to Europeans. Although what is now Canada was new to the European explorers, the Aboriginal people had already discovered and explored the land.

Exploration
Seeking new lands and new routes.

1 Vikings (approximately 900–1000 AD): Norse sagas spoke of Bjarni Herjulfsson reaching the coast of a new land when he was blown off course sailing from Iceland to Greenland. A few years later, Leif Eriksson explored the new land he called Vinland. This was part of what we now call North America. The Vikings made some attempts at settlement at L'Anse aux Meadows in Newfoundland, but did not settle permanently.

2 Over the next 500 years, Portuguese, Spanish, French, Basque, and English ships came to North America's rich fishing grounds.

3 During the latter part of the 1400s, explorers from many European countries began searching for new water routes to the Spice Lands of the Far East (India and China) in order to obtain goods such as silks and spices, and to find out more about the world. These voyages led to the European exploration of lands in the Americas.

From 1450 to 1600 there was an "age of exploration" in Europe. New ideas, combined with improved methods of building sailing ships, allowed mariners to sail on longer voyages of exploration. These voyages were risky and they cost a great deal of money. As a result, voyages

of exploration depended on European kings and queens for financial backing. Fortunately, European monarchs were not only eager to find out more about the world, they also wanted to gain power and the riches of the Far East. They hired mariners to search for a water route to the Far East. Portugal and Spain were the first European countries to seek a route to the Far East by going west across the Atlantic; England and France sent explorers soon after.

In 1492, the Italian sea captain Christopher Columbus was sent by Spain to find a short route to the riches of the Far East by sailing west. He landed on islands in the West Indies and explored the Caribbean and the South American coast.

4 In 1497, the Italian explorer Giovanni Caboto (John Cabot) was financed and sent by the English to look for a short route to the Far East. He reached Newfoundland, and established England's claim there.

Mercantilism

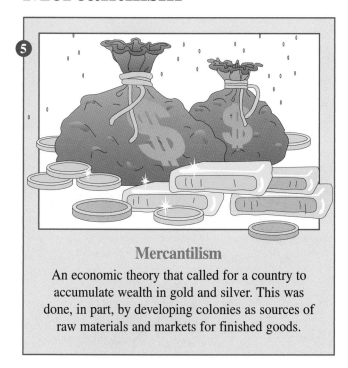

Mercantilism

An economic theory that called for a country to accumulate wealth in gold and silver. This was done, in part, by developing colonies as sources of raw materials and markets for finished goods.

5 During the 1500s and 1600s, many European countries wanted to be wealthy and powerful. Colonies were central to the practice of mercantilism because of their importance as places for European countries to obtain raw materials and to sell finished goods.

6 The theory of mercantilism was a major reason behind European exploration and **colonization** of the world. The kings and queens of Europe encouraged overseas exploration, the establishment of colonies for trade, and **missionary** efforts among the First People. Before colonies could be established, lands that were unknown to the Europeans had to be explored. (More detail about colonization is found on page 17.)

7 As lands in the Americas were explored, European rulers would claim ownership over them. By claiming these lands, the European rulers believed they also had the right to control all the trade in the area. This was known as a **monopoly**. They believed their control also extended beyond the land and its resources to include its people, even though the people had been living there for thousands of years and already had their own government, laws, customs, and traditions.

Colonization—settling and controlling new lands
Missionary—bringing one's religious teachings to others who do not share them
Monopoly—a right granted for one person or group to control buying and selling

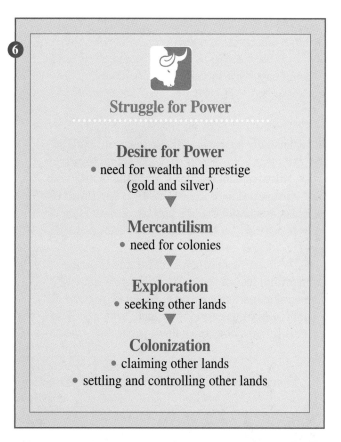

6

Struggle for Power

Desire for Power
• need for wealth and prestige (gold and silver)
▼
Mercantilism
• need for colonies
▼
Exploration
• seeking other lands
▼
Colonization
• claiming other lands
• settling and controlling other lands

The explorers would plant a huge cross and/or flag of their home country into the earth of the land being claimed. This claim was recognized by other European countries. In this painting, Jacques Cartier is claiming the land for the King of France in 1534.

In 1535, Francis I sent Cartier to explore farther up the St. Lawrence for the vast riches of the Kingdom of Saguenay. Sailing as far as present-day Montreal, he and his crew spent the winter in the New Found Land. In 1541, Francis I sent Cartier to the St. Lawrence once again to establish a permanent French settlement. After two harsh winters, the settlement failed.

Exploration and Mercantilism

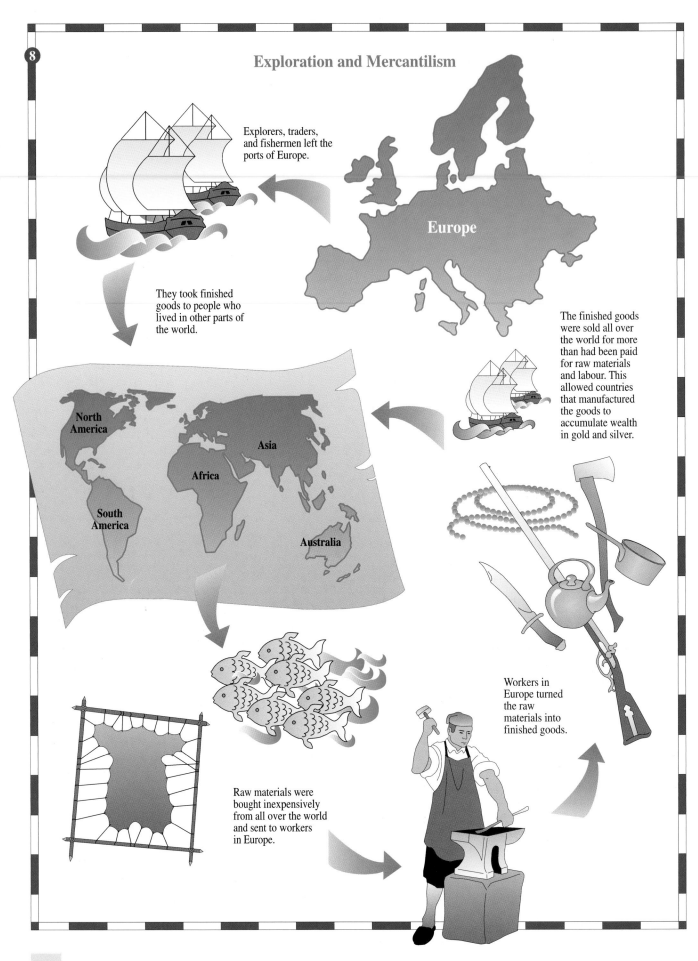

Explorers, traders, and fishermen left the ports of Europe.

Europe

They took finished goods to people who lived in other parts of the world.

The finished goods were sold all over the world for more than had been paid for raw materials and labour. This allowed countries that manufactured the goods to accumulate wealth in gold and silver.

North America

Asia

Africa

South America

Australia

Workers in Europe turned the raw materials into finished goods.

Raw materials were bought inexpensively from all over the world and sent to workers in Europe.

Colonization

8 **9** As pages 14–16 show, exploration, mercantilism, and colonization are closely related. To control the newly claimed lands, colonization was essential. Colonization refers to one country (historically called the mother country) bringing another separate region under its direct control. This was often accomplished by establishing permanent settlements in the new region. These new settlements were expected to develop the region's resources and supply the European country with inexpensive raw materials or products. Colonies were also expected to provide a **market** for manufactured products. Raw materials were shipped to the European country to be **manufactured** into goods. Manufactured goods were shipped back to the colony to be sold at a higher price. Thus, colonies were an important part of the European trading theory of mercantilism.

The French and the English were impressed with the wealth the Spanish gained from their colonies in Central and South America. They also wished to become wealthy, so they began to colonize the area of North America they had claimed.

10 Early colonization attempts were slowed by the fact that, unlike the Spanish colonies, North America did not immediately yield precious metals and jewels. The first prosperous industry in North America was the fishing industry. Later the fur trade became an important industry. Although these two industries supplied important raw materials, they did not necessarily require permanent settlements. However, many Europeans recognized that these lands were a source of potential wealth which colonization would increase. This led to further development of what is now Canada.

Market—an environment or place where trade, buying, and selling take place
Manufacture—to make raw materials into finished goods

Section II

European Colonization 1600s

Ms. Ito and her Passport Tour students got out of the van in front of the Space Center. They were excited about actually seeing a rock from the surface of the moon. They would also see scenes of NASA's Mars probe and the rover *Sojourner* exploring the surface of the planet, and get an update on the progress of the International Space Station. The highlight of the day was going to be a lecture by Roberta Bondar, Canada's first woman astronaut. They hoped to get her autograph.

Ms. Ito gave them some direction before they entered the displays. "Today, we will be focusing on space exploration.While viewing the displays write down reasons modern-day countries are involved in space exploration."

"I'll bet our study of the story of modern-day space exploration is supposed to help us make the connections between today and the past," said Erin.

"They didn't explore outer space in the 1600s, so the real connection must be the exploration part," Dakota suggested.

"Right. We are going to be touring actual historical sites where the European explorers visited Eastern Canada during the 15th and 16th centuries—Newfoundland, Percé Rock, Port Royal in Nova Scotia, and Quebec City. While visiting these sites we will examine the reasons these people were exploring

An artist's version of the International Space Station shows the Earth below.

the eastern coast of Canada. Were they just searching for adventure, or was it about prestige, or were there business reasons behind exploration? Then, we will compare modern-day space exploration with exploration and colonization of planet Earth."

Everyone was anxious to start viewing the displays, so Ms. Ito quickly finished. "Let's meet back at the exhibit of the International Space Station at 4:00 PM."

The First Era

The students saw exhibits of the early milestones of space exploration.

1957: The Soviet Union launches *Sputnik I*, the first satellite to circle the earth, starting the "space race" with the United States.

1961: Soviet cosmonaut, Yuri Gargarin, becomes the first person into space. Alan Shepard is the first American in space.

1962: John Glenn is the first American to orbit the earth.

1969: *Apollo–II* astronauts Neil Armstrong and Edwin Aldrin walk on the moon, plant the American flag, and collect rock samples and moon dust to bring back to earth.

1977: The American *Voyageur* space probes are sent to Saturn and Jupiter to gather data on the solar system.

1981: The first American space shuttle, *Columbia*, is launched.

1984: Marc Garneau, on the shuttle *Challenger*, is the first Canadian in space.

1980s & 1990s: Satellites are launched to monitor the weather, observe military actions, and improve world communication.

1999: Mars mission is sent to research climatic changes on Mars.

"The museum has a free internet link!" exclaimed Ken. "Let's search for more information about Canadians in space."

"Search under Roberta Bondar and Marc Garneau...and let's find out more about the Canadarm!" added Erin excitedly.

The Next Era

The Passport Tour students gathered at the display about the International Space Station, a collaborative effort of 16 nations. This orbiting laboratory is being developed as a base for further exploration of the solar system. It is the first step on the way to possible colonization of space.

Ms. Ito and the students reviewed what they had seen and considered their day. Ms. Ito began, "The first era focused on the question *is it possible?*"

"I'll bet European explorers felt the same way," said Erin. "They were travelling to unknown places just like the space explorers. Their countries were investing a lot of

The American flag is planted on the moon in 1969.

money to send them; it was financially risky *and* dangerous."

"But they might find resources and opportunities that were very valuable," said Brenda. "That's why they went."

"Yeah," said Roberto, "but the early explorers must have wondered if they would get back home safely!"

Ken read aloud from a pamphlet in his hand, "After his second trip

in space in 1998, John Glenn said, '...we are only at the beginning of our space quest...there is so much more to explore and learn.' That seems to sum it up."

"Hopefully, the world will really benefit from space research in some way," said Roberto.

"From what I've seen today," said Dakota, "almost anything seems possible."

Questions to Talk About

As a class, discuss the following questions. Keep these questions in mind as you read Chapter 2 on French and English colonies. At the end of the chapter, you will be asked to think about them again.

1. Why do you think it would be important which country reached newly discovered areas first?

2. Why do you think claiming newly discovered areas would be important?

3. What part does a country's flag play in exploration and colonization?

4. Why do you think setting up permanent settlements in new areas (colonizing) would be important?

5. Why do you think explorers would bring back samples of materials from newly discovered areas?

6. What similarities do you see between space exploration/ colonization and early European exploration/colonization of other lands?

To find out more about space exploration, visit NASA's website at http://www.nasa.gov/

19

Research Project

Passport to the Past

The research model shown on pages x and xi may be used to guide you through the steps for completing this project.

Understanding what you are to do
(See steps on page x.)

While studying *Canada Revisited 7* you are going to have the chance to "meet" a number of individuals who have played important roles in Canada's past. This will help you learn about Canada's people, places, and events. You will have the opportunity to step into the shoes of one historical figure. By getting to know this individual, you will be able to make connections between his or her world and your own.

At some time during your study your teacher will assign a figure from Canadian history for you to investigate. You are to become an expert on this individual. You can imagine that you are a close friend, ally, partner, fellow worker, or acquaintance of the person, or you may even choose to "become" him or her. To do so, you will need to find out more about the person through background research using this textbook and other resources.

People from Canada's History*

William Alexander	Pierre La Vérendrye
Madeleine d'Allonne	Jean-Louis Le Loutre
Robert Baldwin	Chevalier de Lévis
Juan Bodega y Quadra	Louis XIV of France
Charles de Boishébert	Alexander Mackenzie
Hélène Boullé	William Lyon Mackenzie
Marguerite Bourgeoys	Paul de Maisonneuve
Jean de Brébeuf and other	Jeanne Mance
Jesuit martyrs	Paul Mascarene
Isaac Brock	Membertou
Étienne Brûlé	Louis-Joseph de Montcalm
Guy Carleton	Pierre Du Gua de Monts
Samuel de Champlain	James Murray
Charles II of England	Jean Nicollet
Jean-Baptiste Colbert	Louis-Joseph Papineau
James Cook	Marie de la Peltrie
Mathieu Da Costa	Thomas Peters
Adam Dollard	Peter Pond
Lord Durham	Jean de Poutrincourt
Lord Elgin (James Bruce)	Pierre-Esprit Radisson
Simon Fraser	Egerton Ryerson
Comte de Frontenac	Michel Sarrazin
Garakontié	Laura Secord
Robert Gourlay	Sir John Graves Simcoe
Médard Chouart des Groseilliers	John Strachan (Bishop)
Frederick Haldimand	Jean Talon
Sir Francis Bond Head	Tecumseh
Samuel Hearne	Kateri Tekakwitha
Louis Hébert	Thanandelthur
Marie Hébert	Thayendanegea (Joseph Brant)
Anthony Henday	David Thompson
Joseph Howe	Catherine Parr Traill
Marie de l'Incarnation	Harriet Tubman
Henry Kelsey	George Vancouver
King's Daughters	Pierre de Rigaud de Vaudreuil
Robert La Salle	Madeleine de Verchères
Charles de La Tour	James Wolfe
Marie de La Tour	Philemon Wright
François de Laval	Marguerite d'Youville
Marc Lescarbot	
Noël Levasseur	

Planning the project
(See steps on page x.)

Locating the information
(See steps on page xi.)

As you progress through *Canada Revisited 7* you will find information on these people. In addition you should be using other sources to locate information.

---

*You may wish to suggest additional names for this project.

When gathering information for a history book, researchers often rely on **primary sources**. People mentioned in journals and other sources from the time were often those who were most well known— usually prominent men of noble status. Sources with references to women, Aboriginal people, and "common" people are far fewer in number. People of "noble" status were more likely to be educated and therefore able to write about their ideas and experiences.

Nowadays, because of computers and greater access to education, more people have opportunities to publish stories about their families and **ancestors**—on the internet, for example. Perhaps you have a story about one of your ancestors that should be told.

Recording the information
(See steps on page xi.)

Examining the information
(See steps on page xi.)

Organizing the information
(See steps on page xi.)

Preparing the Presentation
(See steps on page xi.)

Once you have researched your historical figure, prepare his or her passport. Include information about the topics shown on the easel. A historical person of European background will require a written passport. Most Native individuals would present this type of information orally, so prepare a script for presenting your identification. (Native cultures had a spoken and visual history, rather than a written one.)

Primary source—an account of an historical event by someone who witnessed it or lived during the time of the event; historical evidence from the time
Ancestor—a person from whom one is descended

Historical passport should include
- Personal Information
- Personality
- Important Life Events
- Accomplishments
- Challenges and Difficulties
- Impact/Importance to Future Canadians

On your trip to the past, you may present your historical figure in a variety of ways (see page 267). For example, in addition to creating a passport, you might wear an appropriate costume, read to the class several diary entries about important events in the person's life, and have someone help videotape the presentation. Another person might record on audio tape a speech his or her historical individual might have made, and plot important life events on a map.

You will get to know many important individuals from the past, as your classmates introduce their historical figures to you. For example, during your study of Chapter 3, someone may present Louis XIV to the class and during Chapter 6 someone else could present Laura Secord.

Your teacher will let you know when it is time to make your presentation.

Sharing the presentation
(See steps on pages xi and 267.)

Assessing what you've done
(See steps on page xi.)

Enjoy your trip to the past!

Chapter 2
French and English Colonies (1600s)

Overview

Use this Overview to predict the events of this chapter.

Colonization involves one country bringing another separate region under its direct control. Usually permanent settlements were established.

1604
Pierre Du Gua de Monts established a settlement in Port Royal (Acadia) for France. A mapmaker named Samuel de Champlain was with him.

Port Royal

When two cultures meet they affect each other.

1607
The English established a colony, Jamestown, in Virginia. Other colonies along the east coast of North America followed.

Jamestown   **American Colonies**

1608
Champlain founded the colony of Quebec for France and had a habitation built. The fur trade was developed. Settlers arrived in Acadia.

Quebec

Port Royal   **Acadia**

The Roman Catholic Church was involved in the religious life of the French colonies. They started the first schools and hospital.

Chapter 2 Focus

This book uses four concepts—power, co-operation, decision-making, and conflict—to organize the ideas about Canada's history. An icon at the beginning of a paragraph is your cue that the paragraph focuses on that concept. Refer to page viii for an explanation of the concepts.

Chapter 1 reviewed some early history of Native peoples and European exploration of Canada. Native peoples have lived in North America for thousands of years. Chapter 2 is about early colonization by European people, who have been permanent residents for the last 300 years. The concepts of power, co-operation, decision-making, and conflict underlie the events of this chapter. The concept of power is the special focus of Chapter 2.

Power   **Co-operation**   **Decision-making**   **Conflict**

Other Concepts and Main Topics

- French and English exploration and colonization
- Acadia and New France
- fur trade
- Native/European interaction
- role of the Roman Catholic Church

Notebook Organization

 Set up a binder for your study of Canadian history.

Create a title page: Look through the textbook. Use the headings and pictures to gather ideas.

Prepare dividers and sections:

- a section called Activities for your notes, activities, maps, charts, and illustrations
- a section called WordBook to record vocabulary (chapter content and learning words) and concept charts
- a section called History Journal for your thoughts and ideas about Canadian history
- a section called Tools of Learning for information on how to learn and think

Organize your notes: Go through the notes you already have for this unit. Decide, as a class, in which section each set of notes belongs. Add to these sections throughout your study of Canadian history. The notebook icon shown above is a reminder to organize your notes.

Prediction—to think about and/or state ideas and events you believe will occur

Chapter Preview/Prediction

Research about how one learns and remembers shows that making **predictions** can increase your understanding of new information by helping you make connections between what you already know and what you will learn. You will be asked to make predictions at the beginning of each chapter and to check your predictions at the end (see Making Predictions on page 48 for an example).

Several methods of making predictions will be introduced throughout this textbook, beginning with the Prediction Chart shown here.

Before making your predictions

- Look through the chapter; note headings and captions.
- Examine the chapter's visuals, including the chapter Overview (Chapter 2 Overview is on page 22).
- Read the Chapter Focus (Chapter 2 Focus is on this page).
- Think about what you already know about this chapter/topic.

Use the above information to predict answers to the questions on the Prediction Chart that follows. Create a similar chart in your notebook. Put your predictions in the "My Predictions" column.

Once you have finished the chapter

- Complete the column "What I Found Out" to help you review and summarize what you have learned.

Prediction Chart—What Do You Think?		
Questions	**My Predictions** (fill out now)	**What I Found Out** (fill out at end of chapter)
1. What might be the major events?		
2. Who might be some of the important people or groups?		
3. Who might hold power?		
4. What conflicts might occur?		
5. How might the conflicts be resolved?		
6. How might decisions be made?		
7. What might be some examples of co-operation?		
8. Questions you have.		

Colonization

To control newly claimed lands, colonization was essential. Colonization involves one country (historically called the mother country) bringing another separate region under its direct control. This was often accomplished by establishing permanent settlements in the new region. These new settlements were expected to develop the region's resources and supply the European country with inexpensive raw materials or products. **Colonies** were also expected to provide a market for manufactured products. Raw materials shipped to the European country were manufactured into goods. These and other manufactured products were shipped back to the colony to be sold at a profit. Thus colonies were an important part of mercantilism.

The French and the English were impressed with the wealth the Spanish were gaining from their colonies in Central and South America. They also wished to become wealthy, so they began to colonize the area of North America they had claimed.

Early colonization attempts were slowed by the fact that, unlike the Spanish colonies, North America did not immediately yield precious metals and jewels. The first prosperous industry in North America was the fishing industry. Later the fur trade became an important industry. Although these industries supplied important raw materials, Europeans felt they did not necessarily require permanent settlements. As the fishing industry prospered and fur trade developed in North America many Europeans came to recognize these lands as a source of potential wealth.

In European societies, wealth and power were tied to land ownership. Since only royalty or nobility could own land, it was a mark of social status. Many settlers moved to the new colonies because land was plentiful and inexpensive. As landowners, settlers gained status. The colonists believed so strongly in their right to hold their own land (private property) and in the agricultural way of life that these beliefs became a basis of Canadian society.

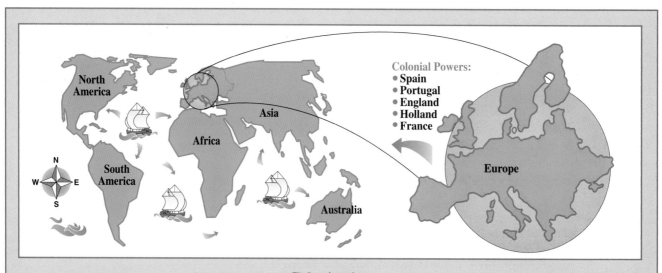

Colonization
Settling and controlling other lands

Places That Were Colonized

- had lands that Europeans needed to explore before they could establish colonies
- provided raw materials, as well as cheap labour needed to obtain raw materials and get them to ports from where they could be shipped to Europe
- bought finished goods manufactured in the European countries to be sold for a profit

Countries in Europe

- claimed territory, settled, and controlled colonies in North America, Africa, Asia, and Australia
- had direct influence over the running of the colonies and decided on the types of government for them
- believed that the colonies should be patterned after the mother country
- manufactured finished goods from raw materials

Colonies—new lands settled and controlled by citizens of a distant country

French Colonization

 Prior to the 1660s, France had colonized very little territory compared to other European nations. France had been too busy with European wars. Also, the French mercantile economy was directed by the state (the French government) under the leadership of the king and his ministers. The money that funded colonization and expansion came from the **aristocracy** and the Roman Catholic Church. Developments were slow and cautious.

The French government granted trading monopolies to trading companies that promised to invest a portion of their profits in colonization and to support missionaries. But these merchants were not interested in colonization. Thus, few settlers immigrated to **New France** before the French government took over the colony in the 1660s.

Rule by Trading Companies

Trading companies controlled the French fur trade in North America, playing an important role in mercantilism. The traders were the merchants who obtained raw materials (furs) from Native peoples and shipped them to France to be processed, then sold for higher prices. They also sold or traded European manufactured goods to Native peoples.

New France was not colonized until the early 1600s. Then the French king realized that colonies were necessary to protect the riches of the fur trade from other European powers. Mercantilism would not work without colonies. Between 1603 and 1645, the French state granted trading monopolies to individuals and companies that were supposed to help in the colonization of New France.

Settlement in Acadia

In 1603, Pierre Du Gua de Monts was granted a monopoly on the fur trade in Canada. His goal was to protect his land from illegal fur traders by establishing a permanent settlement near the mouth of the St. Lawrence River. In 1604, de Monts and his mapmaker/manager, Samuel de Champlain, established a French settlement on Ste. Croix Island in **Acadia**. This settlement was moved to Port Royal in 1605. Unfortunately, Port Royal was poorly located. The settlement did not keep other French fur traders from establishing trading posts and trading for furs.

Aristocracy—the ruling class; the nobles of a country
New France—area along the St. Lawrence River, in what is now Canada, which was colonized by France
Acadia—included present-day Nova Scotia, Prince Edward Island, and parts of New Brunswick and Quebec

The Trading Room. A Native person has brought furs to the French at a trading post to trade for European goods.

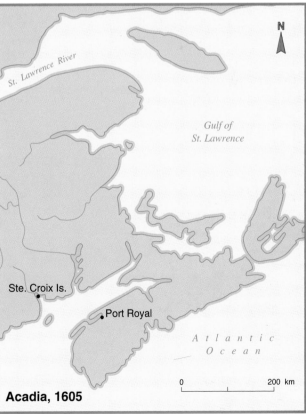

Acadia, 1605

Pierre Du Gua de Monts is recognized as founder of Port Royal.

Pierre Du Gua de Monts (1558–1628)

Pierre Du Gua de Monts is remembered as an early explorer and fur trader and especially for establishing Port Royal in Acadia—the first permanent European settlement in what is now Canada. In 1603, de Monts was given a monopoly on the fur trade in New France, with the authority to seize any illegal traders. In return for this monopoly, de Monts became governor of Acadia. His duties were to maintain control of the area, Christianize the Native peoples, explore, and locate precious metals.

Others involved in the colonization of Port Royal included Jean de Poutrincourt, Samuel de Champlain, Marc Lescarbot, Mathieu Da Costa, and Louis Hébert. Several others were not identified by name in the historical records.

The colonists planted and harvested crops and built a mill to grind flour. The Micmaq were friendly and traded the few surplus furs they had with the French.

Even though the colony seemed successful, the business part of the venture was not. The French king cancelled the monopoly and de Monts was forced to abandon the settlement at Port Royal in 1607. He helped Champlain build Quebec in 1608. De Monts helped to prove that the country could support agriculture and that Europeans could live in North America on a permanent basis.

Jean de Poutrincourt (1557–1615)

In 1604, Poutrincourt accompanied Pierre Du Gua de Monts and Champlain to Acadia to look for a suitable location for a colony. Poutrincourt paid for the soldiers, guns, and ammunition that were taken to protect the new settlement.

While in the Bay of Fundy area, Poutrincourt asked de Monts for and was granted a certain piece of land (shown as Port Royal on the map on page 25). He agreed to colonize it in return for fur trading and fishing rights.

As winter approached, some members of the expedition continued to search for a suitable campsite while others traded for furs. After the site known as Ste. Croix Island had been located, Poutrincourt left for France with a large cargo of furs.

In 1606, Poutrincourt returned with new settlers and supplies from France. He discovered that de Monts had moved the colony across the Bay of Fundy to Port Royal. Among the Port Royal settlers were Mathieu Da Costa, Louis Hébert, and Marc Lescarbot.

Under Poutrincourt's instruction the settlers began to clear the land of trees and prepare the field for seeding. The first water-driven mill for grinding grain in North America was constructed. The fur trade with the local Micmaq continued. Due to the number of illegal traders in the area, it was impossible to obtain furs in large numbers.

The king cancelled their trading monopoly and the colony was abandoned.* In 1610, Poutrincourt once again returned to Acadia with his sons and Father Fléché, Claude de Saint-Étienne de La Tour, and La Tour's son Charles. Because of the special care and protection of Membertou, chief of a band of Micmaq, the **habitation** at Port Royal and its contents were much as they had been left. The colonists once again tilled and planted the soil. Father Fléché focused his efforts on converting the Micmaq to Christianity.

Supplies and more colonists, including Poutrincourt's family and Fathers Biard and Massé, two Jesuits who planned on establishing missions in North America, arrived at Port Royal the next year. The next few years were a struggle for Poutrincourt as he tried to raise money for the Port Royal colony, keep the monopoly, and continue to Christianize the Native people.

In 1613, while Poutrincourt was in France, Port Royal was attacked and most of its buildings were destroyed by the English sea captain Samuel Argall. Poutrincourt arrived in the late winter of 1614 to find the area in ruins. He returned to France and was unable to obtain further investors. Acadia, as a European settlement, almost disappeared.

---

*Although the French had claimed title to this area in treaties they had with other European countries, the area was too vast for the French to patrol from Port Royal. Ships from other countries were also trading for furs and fishing in the area. Eventually, the people in France who paid for the expedition to Port Royal felt their profits were too small, so the expedition was declared unsuccessful.

Habitation—place to live

A dramatic performance created by Lescarbot greeted Poutrincourt in Port Royal in 1606.

Marc Lescarbot (1570–1642)

Much of what we know about the fur trade and early colonization of Acadia comes from the writings of Marc Lescarbot. A lawyer from Paris, Lescarbot came to Port Royal in 1606 and remained there until de Monts' fur trade licence was cancelled. Upon his return to France, Lescarbot published some poetry and books about his experiences. Because Lescarbot wrote about the year he spent at the habitation at Port Royal, historians have an eyewitness account of daily life there.

Lescarbot involved himself in life in Acadia. He became the colony's main provider of entertainment. He created stories, poems, and plays to entertain the men. Because he often visited the local Micmaq, he was able to relate their way of life to the men in the habitation.

When Poutrincourt returned from France to Port Royal in 1606, he was welcomed by a dramatic presentation of *The Theatre of Neptune*, written and directed by Lescarbot.

Both Micmaq and French joined in the performance. The mythical god Neptune (played by Lescarbot himself) appeared in a bark canoe to welcome Poutrincourt. He was surrounded by men of Neptune's court who praised the leaders of the colony in French and then in Micmaq. Trumpets and cannon completed the welcome.

Membertou (d. 1611)

Membertou was chief and shaman of a band of Micmaq who lived in the area of Port Royal. Much of the settlers' success in this new land was due to the kindness, hospitality, and guidance offered by Membertou and the local Micmaq. He was greatly respected, and often joined the French in the habitation. Membertou was the first North American to be baptized in his own country. When Poutrincourt and the French abandoned Port Royal in 1607, Membertou cared for and protected the habitation for three years until the French returned.

Mathieu Da Costa (d. 1607)

Mathieu Da Costa was a Black explorer and settler. Sources vary about how he came to North America. Some thought he came to America on a Portuguese fishing vessel, or with de Monts. Da Costa's ability as an interpreter and his knowledge of the Micmaq lifestyle added much to knowledge in the colony. A large part of the friendly relations between the Micmaq and the French can also be credited to Da Costa's skills and his friendship.

Canada Revisited

Mathieu Da Costa Award Program

A yearly contest named after Mathieu Da Costa gives students aged 9 to 19 an opportunity to share ideas about famous Canadians. Each entry (a short story, essay, or artistic representation) must show the accomplishments of someone from Canadian history who helped to build our nation and who represents the cultural **diversity** of our country. The contest is run by the Canadian Teachers' Federation in partnership with the Department of Canadian Heritage. For more information visit the website http:/www.ctf-fce.ca/ and choose menu option "What We Do." Next, click on "Mathieu Da Costa Awards Program."

Think about sharing your ideas and knowledge about someone important from Canadian history. Revisit Canada's past!

Diversity—variety; differences

Champlain at Quebec

In 1608, Champlain convinced de Monts to let him try to establish a settlement in the St. Lawrence valley, where there was better access to the Native peoples and the fur trade. Champlain went to New France as the leader of the 1608 expedition and established a habitation at Quebec. The habitation was built like a miniature European fortress. Champlain formed alliances with the Huron (also known as Wendat) and the Algonquin in hopes of expanding the fur trade.

After 1608, the fur trade in New France grew rapidly in the hands of the trading companies. The population of New France, however, did not grow. The trading companies were interested in profits, not in settlement. Champlain realized that control of New France depended on expanding the French population. The English and Dutch were competing with the French for land and furs.* Champlain continued to seek political and financial support from France. Several company structures were tried over the years to encourage the settlement necessary to maintain control of New France and the fur trade.

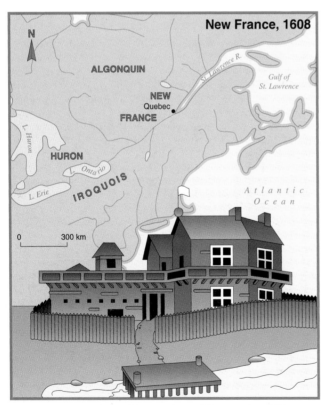

The habitation built by Champlain and his men in 1608 served as both living and working space.

---

*The English and French were not the only European powers active in the New World; the Dutch also were involved in mercantile and colonial activity here. See the map on page 30 which shows the extent of the Dutch territory before 1663.

Habitant—farmer in New France, and later in Quebec

Samuel de Champlain (1567–1635)

Samuel de Champlain was called the "Father of New France" because of the efforts he made to establish permanent settlements there. The settlements he helped to found included Ste. Croix Island, Port Royal, and Quebec City.

Champlain believed that it was part of his duty to bring Christianity to the First People. This caused him to act sometimes as a missionary for the Roman Catholic Church.

Champlain was a navigator and mapmaker by trade, and some of his maps are accurate even by today's standards.

Hélène Boullé (1598–1654)

Born and raised in Paris, Hélène Boullé married Samuel de Champlain when she was 12 and he was 40. She moved to New France with him in 1620, when she was 22, and stayed there until 1624. Then she returned to France and entered a convent, where she remained for the rest of her life.

Company of 100 Associates

In 1627 the French government granted the Company of 100 Associates a monopoly on the fur trade in New France. In return, the Company was supposed to bring 4000 French Catholics to settle in New France over the next 15 years. The Company allowed the settlers to trade for furs directly with the Native peoples if they sold the furs only to the Company. By 1663, due to the war in Europe between England and France, the Company of 100 Associates had gone out of business.

Company of Habitants

In 1645 the Company of 100 Associates allowed the Company of Habitants to take over the monopoly on the fur trade in New France. The Company asked the **habitants** to cover the costs of managing the colony and settlements. Control of the fur trade was left in the hands of officials appointed by France.

The Fur Trade and the Native Peoples

The settlement of New France was essential for control of the fur trade. The fur trade helped France remain wealthy and powerful. A fashion trend in Europe made furs very popular. Felt hats (made from beaver pelts) were considered a status symbol (see map on page 30). The tremendous demand for beaver meant that fur merchants could make large profits.

Numerous Native groups lived in the territory claimed by France. Algonquian peoples, including such Nations as the Algonquin, Micmaq, and Montagnais, lived in the eastern woodlands (see map, page 12). The Huron, a hunting and farming group, also lived in the eastern woodlands (see map, page 10).

Long before Europeans came to North America, the Huron had established an efficient trading network among the various Native peoples. Champlain, and later other French traders, established business alliances with the Huron and became part of this long-established trading system. Furs were exchanged for manufactured European goods, which were in turn traded for furs from Native peoples in the interior. Thus, furs from the interior finally reached the French through Huron go-betweens.

Alliances with the local Native peoples were essential for the Europeans. They supplied the Europeans with furs, food, and canoes, acted as guides and interpreters, and often saved their lives. Champlain formed alliances with the Algonquin and the Huron because they were a large group of established traders. The Huron and the other Iroquoian peoples had few disputes with each other before the arrival of Europeans and the fur trade. Competition for furs and alliances with different European powers strained relations between the groups and made them enemies.

The French needed the Huron to be their military allies to help fight the Iroquois, if the situation arose, as long as the English and French were enemies. The French and Huron took sides against the English, Dutch, and Iroquois.

The Fur Traders at Montreal. The Native peoples came to Montreal, then called Ville-Marie, each summer to trade their furs. The French and the Native peoples provided goods and services that were relatively equal in value to meet each other's needs.

The *Coureurs de bois*
("runners of the woods")

One of the reasons the Native peoples were essential to the fur trade was because they brought furs from the interior regions to the French trading posts of Quebec, Trois Rivières, and Montreal. The French could also obtain furs by going into the interior regions themselves. During times of hostilities, it was safer to have the Native allies bring furs to the French, but high profits could be made by those who were willing to venture into the interior rivers and lakes and bring back beaver pelts themselves. During peaceful times, more and more young men of New France were attracted to the high profits and adventure in the fur trade. These men were entrepreneurs, working for themselves rather than representing a company. These energetic and daring adventurers became expert canoeists and shrewd businessmen. They were known as *coureurs de bois* or "runners of the woods."

Trading between Native bands was customarily done through family contacts. To become part of this family trading system, some of the young French men stayed to live with a band during the winter. These young men adapted to the Native way of living, often marrying Native women and becoming part of their bands. Friendships and trust were thus established between the Native bands and the French traders.

These family ties were useful in trading sessions. Soon the French had trading alliances with numerous Algonquian and Huron groups. Later the French used these trading alliances to establish political alliances against the English.

The *coureurs de bois* expanded the fur trade and explored farther and farther into the interior of the country. They extended French influence over an increasingly large amount of inland territory.

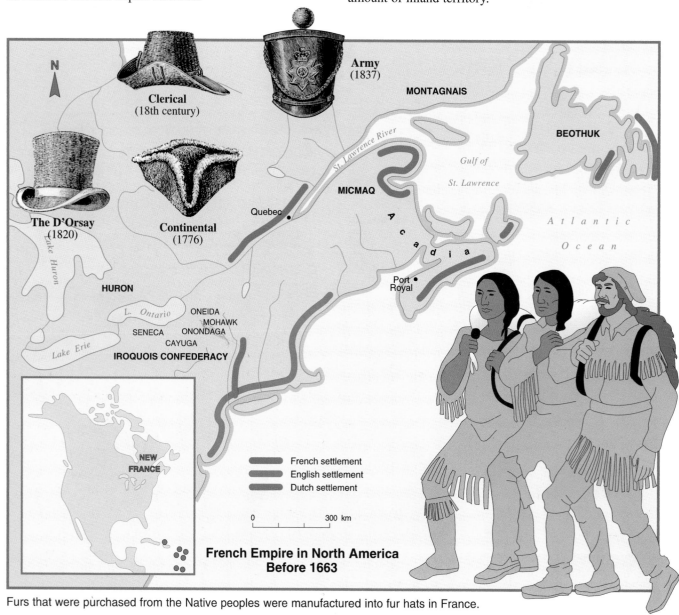

Clerical
(18th century)

Army
(1837)

MONTAGNAIS

BEOTHUK

St. Lawrence River

Gulf of
St. Lawrence

MICMAQ

Quebec

Atlantic

Ocean

The D'Orsay
(1820)

Continental
(1776)

Lake Huron

HURON

Port
Royal

L. Ontario   ONEIDA
            MOHAWK
SENECA   ONONDAGA
        CAYUGA
Lake Erie
IROQUOIS CONFEDERACY

NEW
FRANCE

French settlement
English settlement
Dutch settlement

0   300 km

**French Empire in North America
Before 1663**

Furs that were purchased from the Native peoples were manufactured into fur hats in France.

Read this imaginary conversation between a French man and an Iroquois man as a dialogue. Each is attempting to explain his culture. Read what the French man says.

Then read the Iroquois man's reply directly across the page, followed by the French man's reply. Try reading with different voices to create a better dialogue.

French man

Iroquois man

French man	Iroquois man
In France, our society is organized by a class system based on power and status. The class into which you are born determines your power and status. Many of us think it is very important to acquire power and wealth.	Our society is organized around a belief that all are born equal. Power and wealth mean different things to us than they do to you.
Our system of land ownership allows only certain classes to own land.	We believe that we are the Keepers of Mother Earth; the land is not ours to buy, sell, or claim.
Permanent buildings and cities are part of our way of life in France. The most powerful people have the largest and most expensive buildings.	Some of our people have permanent homes, but they are unlike yours. Many of us move with the seasons and animals, so our homes are portable.
We have a state and a government headed by a ruler. We call our ruler a king. Our ruler and advisors make all of the governmental decisions for all of the people.	We have non-state societies. This means that the power is not in the hands of one group or one person. As a result, we hold group meetings to discuss important topics and make decisions. Our leaders may try to persuade us, but they do not have the power to make the final decision. Decisions are based on the wishes of the people. Arriving at a consensus is important.
Business and industry are important in France. We have merchants who buy and sell goods. Through trade we accumulate wealth.	We produce enough to meet our needs and share with our kin. We also trade with other groups. Gift-giving is an important part of trading. Accumulating possessions is not important to us.
It is important for us to explore and conquer new lands to acquire raw materials and markets for our manufactured goods.	We believe that there is plenty of land for all. We do not need to take over new land to gain power and wealth.
Our laws are written down. We also have a legal system with courts, judges, and jails.	Our laws are not written down. We have no need for courts, jails, or judges because wrongs are dealt with by families or individuals.
Most of us are Christians. We build churches in which we worship our God.	Spirituality is central to our lives, but we do not have special buildings in which to worship. We believe in a Creator.

Étienne Brûlé (c. 1592–1633*)

Étienne Brûlé was an explorer and adventurer. When Brûlé was a teenager, Champlain encouraged him to live among the Huron people to learn their language and way of life. Brûlé became one of the first *coureurs de bois*, exploring west of Quebec for the French fur trade. His travels took him into present-day Ontario, where he was the first European to see Lakes Erie, Huron, Ontario, and Superior.

Champlain accused Brûlé of assisting the English Kirke brothers after they had captured Quebec in 1629. Brûlé returned to live among the Huron. He was probably killed there under the suspicion he had been dealing with enemies of the Huron.

Jean Nicollet (1598–1642)

Nicollet was a young *coureur de bois* and interpreter between the French and the Algonquian and Nipissing people. By living among them he was able to learn their language and customs and added to the knowledge the French had about the area. He encouraged the Native people to trade with the French at Trois Rivières (Three Rivers) rather than with the English on the Hudson Bay.

He carried with him a Chinese robe, which he planned to wear at the Chinese court, if he were to locate the much sought-after Northwest Passage. He never did get to wear it as he never reached China. Nicollet is also credited with being the first European to visit Lake Michigan and what is now the American Northwest.

Robert La Salle (1643–1687)

Robert La Salle was educated in France. He was an explorer, seigneur, and **entrepreneur**. He owned and operated several fur trading posts including Fort Frontenac near Kingston. In 1673, two French explorers, Louis Jolliet and Father Marquette, travelled south together on the Mississippi River to its junction with the Arkansas River. La Salle continued their explorations and claimed the areas he visited for France.

Most historians give La Salle credit for leading an expedition of French and Native interpreters and guides that explored the last 435 km of the lower Mississippi River and for naming the region Louisiana. Some historians question whether he travelled the Ohio River and Mississippi River at the dates he claimed.

---

*Dates for many of these historical figures may be approximate as sources vary and information may be incomplete (c. stands for *circa* and means approximately).
Entrepreneur—a business person who invests in a business, hoping for a profit, but risking a loss

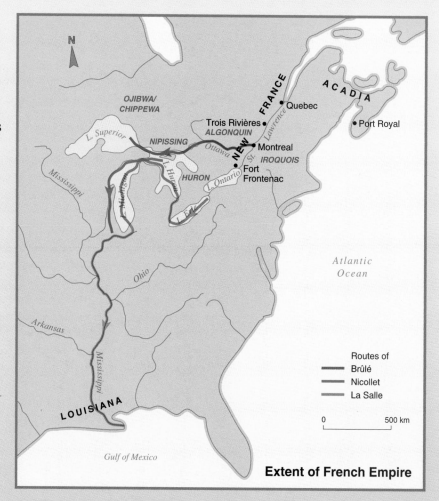

Extent of French Empire

Routes of
— Brûlé
— Nicollet
— La Salle

0   500 km

Adam Dollard (1635–1660)

In 1660, Adam Dollard des Ormeaux fought a legendary battle at the Long Sault (the rapids on the Ottawa River) during the wars when the French, the Huron, and their other allies were in bitter conflict with the Iroquois and their allies.

Dollard was an army commander at Montreal. He had set out with a small band of men to ambush Iroquois hunters as they returned home with their furs. But instead of finding a few hunters, they ran into a large army which was mustering to attack Montreal and Quebec. Dollard's band consisted of only 17 French men and 44 Huron and Algonquin allies. They were no match for the Iroquois, who brought in 500 reinforcements. Nevertheless, they took shelter in an abandoned fort and held out for about a week. All the French were killed and most of the Huron and Algonquin, but as a result of the battle, the Iroquois **dispersed** and went home.

Dispersed—went in various directions; scattered
Seigneur—a person granted land (a seigneury) by the French king to divide into lots and assign to habitants (farmers).

Louis Hébert (1575–1627)

Trained in France as a pharmacist, Louis Hébert first came to Ste. Croix Island and then to Port Royal with de Monts, Champlain, and Poutrincourt. Hébert's wife Marie and Poutrincourt's wife (whose name doesn't appear in the history books) were the first French women to come to New France.

In 1616, Champlain asked Hébert to become the fur trade company's doctor at Quebec. Hébert's house was the first one built in Quebec's Upper Town. In addition to his duties as doctor and pharmacist, he worked with his wife and children to cultivate and harvest the land that had been granted to him. The produce from the Hébert farm not only fed that family but was greatly appreciated by the fur traders and colonists in Quebec. Hébert is credited with being the first person to sow wheat in New France. He is remembered as Canada's first **seigneur**. He realized that while the fur trade was important to the young colony's survival, it was the products from its soil that would make the colony truly independent.

Marie Hébert (c. 1588–1649)

Marie Rollet was the first French woman to remain permanently in New France. She and her husband Louis Hébert are officially recognized as Canada's first non-Native farmers. Marie worked with her husband to clear the land of trees, build their house and barn, cultivate the soil (by hand, as they didn't have a plow), plant the seeds, and harvest the vegetables and grain crops. Her contributions to the food supply in the small colony were greatly valued by Champlain and others. Marie Hébert worked hard, doing many household and farming jobs, and raising children. She also helped her husband care for the sick and injured, and started classes for the children of the local Native people.

A monument to Louis and Marie Hébert is located in Quebec City.

Michel Sarrazin (1659–1734)

Sarrazin came to New France as Surgeon-Major with the French colonial troops. As the only European doctor in the colony, he cared for the soldiers, settlers, fur traders, and Native people for 50 years. In addition to caring for the sick, he spent a great deal of time working as a scientist. Most of the early scientific data on our country's plants, animals, and minerals were accumulated by Sarrazin. In addition to being Canada's first scientist, he also had his own seigneury and was a member of the Sovereign Council (see pages 61–63).

For Your Notebook

1. Why would Brûlé have been important to Champlain?

2. The Northwest Passage is mentioned on page 32. What is it and why was Nicollet trying to find it?

3. How do we know about the lives of those who leave no diaries or personal accounts?

4. Select individuals from Focus On pages who you feel could be called heroes (see pages 26–27, 32–33).

   a) What qualities do these individuals have?

   b) List some heroes of today. What qualities do these heroes have?

   c) Compare heroes of the past with heroes of today.

The Catholic Church

(Prior to 1663)

Champlain believed that it was partly his responsibility to spread the Roman Catholic religion in New France. As a result, he encouraged the Jesuits—a group of Catholic missionary priests—to come to North America to **convert** the Native peoples to Christianity. The French king and his ministers believed that New France would be a stronger colony if everyone were Roman Catholic. In 1627, Cardinal Richelieu, a powerful church and state leader, declared that only Catholics could **emigrate** from France to New France.

While the trading companies controlled New France, the main **institution** in the colony was the Roman Catholic Church. The Church concerned itself with the religious life of the colony as well as establishing schools and hospitals. The Jesuits played a leading role in these developments.

The Jesuits

The Jesuits, who first arrived in New France in 1625, were called the "Black Robes" by the Native peoples. They established a college for the sons of settlers at Quebec in 1635, and established hospitals and convents by bringing groups of nuns to New France.

The Jesuits built permanent mission churches and schools for the Huron in Huronia between 1639 and 1649. Huronia is the name of the entire area where the Huron people lived. The Jesuit headquarters were located in the mission of Sainte-Marie in Huronia. This mission contained a chapel, a hospital, a bakery, a carpentry shop, and a blacksmith shop. The Jesuits at this mission also planted crops and imported livestock from France. (Photographs on pages 35–37 show the reconstructed mission of Sainte-Marie in Huronia.)

The Jesuits had considerable political influence in New France. Beginning in 1647, the Superior of the Jesuits was one of the three main members of the Superior Council, which administered the colony. François de Laval, a Jesuit, arrived in Quebec in 1659. He was later appointed the first Bishop of New France in 1674.

The Jesuits left written records of early life in New France in the *Jesuit Relations*, annual reports that they sent home to Paris.

Convert—change someone's religious beliefs to one's own
Emigrate—leave one's own country or region to settle in another
Institution—organization or association established for some public or social purpose (e.g., the Church, the family, and the educational system)

Women Who Came to New France for God and Church

The Jesuit priests were not the only people who came to New France to spread the Roman Catholic faith. Other religious men and women also came to establish religious settlements. Many religious women, including the Ursuline Nuns, named after Saint Ursula, came to New France. These women made important contributions to the early settlement in New France:

- Marie Guyart, also known as Marie de l'Incarnation, came to Quebec in 1639 with other Ursuline Nuns. The nuns founded a convent and school for girls. Marie's letters home to France are important descriptions of life in New France.

- Jeanne Mance came to Montreal in 1642. She established a hospital there and spent more than 30 years nursing the sick and wounded.

- Marie de la Peltrie was a rich French woman who went to Quebec in 1639 and helped found the Ursuline convent and school. In 1642, she went to Montreal and helped Paul de Maisonneuve establish a Catholic settlement there.

Stamp reproduced courtesy of Canada Post Corporation/NAC

Marguerite Bourgeoys (1620–1700)

Marguerite Bourgeoys arrived in New France in 1653. She set up a school and cared for the poor and the sick. When young French women started to arrive in the colony, she gave them a home and helped them to find suitable husbands.

Huronia

Huronia was the name given to the entire area where the Huron people lived. Between 1639 and 1649, the Jesuits built permanent mission churches and schools in Huronia.

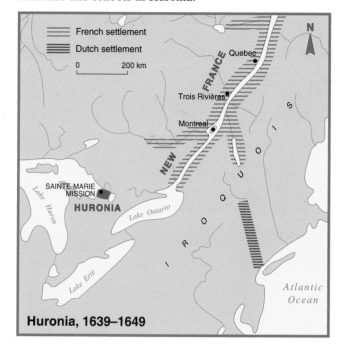

Huronia, 1639–1649

The Huron people were farmers and traders. Their alliance with the French had brought them new materials and tools, but it had also brought them into contact with many European diseases, especially smallpox and measles. From 1634 to 1640, more than 12 000 Huron—nearly half the population—died of these diseases.

The disease problem was compounded by hostilities between the Huron and the Iroquois. In the late 1640s, the Iroquois attacked the fur **brigades** of the French and the Huron. The Iroquois traded with the Dutch, who supplied them with guns. The French did not supply their allies, the Huron, with many guns because the laws in New France forbade it. The French supplied guns only to those Huron who had converted to Catholicism. Consequently, the Huron, who were already weakened by disease, were at a double disadvantage compared to the Iroquois.

In 1648 to 1649, the Iroquois began attacking and destroying Huron settlements. By 1649, only the mission at Sainte-Marie was left. The Jesuits and the remaining Huron decided to retreat and burned the mission themselves before the Iroquois arrived. Finally, in March 1649, 1000 Iroquois warriors attacked Huronia. The combination of disease, death, and war completely destroyed Huronia. The remaining Huron—numbering

---

Brigade—group of canoes, carts, or dogsleds carrying trade goods and supplies to and from inland posts

approximately 500—retreated. Some starved during the following winter; others were adopted into other Native groups.

The French were left without Native trading partners. They tried to find another Native group that would take over the role of the Huron. In the end, they had to venture out into the continent themselves to obtain furs. This move led to the expansion of the French fur trading empire.

After 1650, the Catholic Church turned more of its attention to the needs of the French people in the settlement rather than to missionary efforts.

Different Points of View

Historians debate the reasons behind the Iroquois attacks on Huronia. Some historians believe that the Iroquois attacked because they wanted to enlarge their fur trade area. Others say that the Iroquois were uninterested in the fur trade, since they did not step in as traders for the French. This group believes that the Iroquois wanted to destroy their enemies, the Huron.

Canada Revisited

The chapel has been reconstructed at Sainte-Marie among the Hurons.

This is a palisade around the reconstructed Huronia mission.

Focus On: Sainte-Marie among the Hurons (Canada Revisited)

The presence of the Roman Catholic Church was not limited to the area now called Quebec. The first European community in what is now Ontario was established in 1639 by French Jesuits at Sainte-Marie among the Hurons. (The Hurons are also known as Wendat.) It was 1200 km from Quebec.

The photographs on these two pages show the reconstructed Sainte-Marie among the Hurons. It stands on the original site, on the southeastern shore of Georgian Bay, near Midland, Ontario, in the heart of what was Huronia (Huron territory). The French built the mission to bring Christianity and European education to the Huron people. They built the settlement with a palisade for protection from attacks from unconverted Huron. Although some Huron accepted their teachings, others resisted strongly.

Within five years of its beginning, Sainte-Marie had grown into a community that included residences, a hospital, a church, gardens, livestock, a granary, a cookhouse, and blacksmith and carpenter shops.

From this location, Jesuit priests travelled to surrounding Huron villages to teach the people European ways and assist them with medical care.

The Huron taught the Jesuits cures and survival skills such as using a canoe and snowshoes. They also brought corn to the French priests. Huron people interested in learning more about Christianity would visit Sainte-Marie.

Right: Huronia is the area where the Huron people lived. Sainte-Marie quickly became an established community. By 1647, there were 42 French at the mission; by 1648, there were 66 French and Christian Huron residents.

Below: The Huron were a matrilineal society. Women farmed, wove, cared for the home and children, and made pottery.

Left: *Donnés* were men who offered their labour to assist the Jesuits with their work. Stone and timber available in the area were used to construct buildings.

Above and Below: Missionaries from surrounding villages would visit Sainte-Marie. In addition, in one year the Jesuits estimated they had 6000 Native visitors.

Above: Livestock, including cows and pigs, were transported from Quebec by canoe.

Paul de Maisonneuve (1612–1676)

Paul de Chomedey de Maisonneuve was the founder of Ville-Marie, a religious mission known today as Montreal. He governed the area from 1641 to 1665, when it became a **Royal Colony**.

At age 13, Maisonneuve trained as a soldier. As part of his education he studied with some of New France's greatest missionaries. They influenced his plans to establish a religious colony in New France.

Deeply religious, Maisonneuve's main goal was the conversion of the First People to the Roman Catholic faith. In the late spring of 1641, Maisonneuve set sail for New France with two ships. On board were several religious personnel (the most famous being Father de la Place and Jeanne Mance), soldiers, a doctor, and settlers (mostly men but a few women).

In spite of the many cautions Maisonneuve received from the settlers at Quebec regarding their enemies the Iroquois, Maisonneuve was determined to establish his mission. Maisonneuve is said to have replied:

Sir, what you are saying to me would be good if I had been sent to deliberate and choose a post; but having been instructed to go to Montreal by the Company that sends me, my honour is at stake, and you will agree that I must go up there to start a colony, even if all the trees on that island were to change into so many Iroquois.

Maisonneuve is said to have chopped down the mission's first tree. The following description of Ville-Marie was written during the summer of 1643:

The building consists of a fort for defence, a hospital for the sick, and a lodging already capable of housing 70 persons who live there.... with two Jesuit Fathers who are like pastors to them; there is a chapel there that serves as a parish, under the title of Notre Dame, to whom, with the island and the town which is designated by he name of Ville Marie, it is dedicated. The inhabitants live for the most part communally, as in a sort of inn; others live on their private means, but all live in Jesus Christ, with one heart and soul.

Iroquois attacks on the tiny settlement of Ville-Marie over the next 25 years constantly threatened the survival of the tiny mission settlement. It was difficult to build homes or plan and care for crops when enemies were often waiting in ambush. Finally, in 1653, one hundred French soldiers arrived in Ville-Marie—enough men to provide the residents with protection outside the fort and allow the settlers some opportunity to carry out their duties in their homes and fields.

In addition to attacking the settlers, the Iroquois constantly attacked the Native and French shipments of furs to Ville-Marie. By the 1660s, Ville-Marie had become the centre of the fur trade and a base for soldiers in New France.

Canada Revisited

A monument to (Paul de Chomedey) Maisonneuve, the first governor of Montreal, is found in the Place d'Armes in Montreal. A huge cross, visible for many kilometres at night, has been placed on the summit of Mont Royal. This modern-day cross stands at the location where Maisonneuve raised a cross in 1643 to fulfil a promise he made to God if the colony were saved during the flood of 1642.

Royal Colony—a colony governed directly by a king or queen in another country

Jean de Brébeuf (1593–1649)

The French and Iroquois had been enemies since 1609 when Champlain formed a military and trade alliance with the Huron. Especially vulnerable to Iroquois attacks were the Jesuit Missions in Huronia.

Father Brébeuf was one of the many Jesuit priests who lived in Huronia. Through Father Brébeuf's 15 years of reports in *Jesuit Relations*, historians have learned a great deal about the Huron people who lived there. In addition to his attempts to convert the Huron to Christianity he recorded their customs and culture. He learned their language so he could translate prayers and hymns into Huron. Brébeuf's description of the territory and people living between Quebec and Huronia was a valuable reference for missionaries, explorers, and fur traders for many years.

In 1648 to 1649, the Iroquois began attacking and destroying Huron settlements. In 1649, a number of Jesuits, including Gabriel Lalemant and Jean de Brébeuf, were taken prisoner, tortured and killed by the Iroquois at the Mission of Saint-Ignace.

Kateri Tekakwitha (1656-1680)

Kateri Tekakwitha was born Tagaskouita (or Tekakwitha), of a Christian Algonquian mother and a Mohawk father (who followed the Mohawk religion). She was sick with smallpox as a young child, and the disease left her face scarred and greatly weakened her eyes. She was baptized and renamed Kateri at the age of 19. The Mohawk in her village threatened her with death because of her conversion to Christianity. She fled to a mission at Caughnawaga (near Montreal). There she was known as a kind,

gentle woman and was given the name the Lily of the Mohawks.

She was a devout Christian. She died young—barely 24 years of age. People told of a miracle in which the smallpox scars on her face disappeared at her death, and she was thought by some to have saintly powers.

Kateri Tekakwitha was the first Aboriginal person to be honoured with beatification, the first step towards becoming a saint in the Roman Catholic Church.

For Your Notebook

1. Chapter 2 includes three sections focusing on contributions made by historical individuals in the 1600s. (See pages 26–27, 32–33, and 38–39).

   a) Make notes about the individuals and their contributions described in each set of pages. Use a note making method from Appendix pages 264–265.

   b) With a partner, brainstorm for ideas about what the biographies within each section have in common. Look for patterns and connections.

   c) Create a title and icon for each of the three sections called "Individuals."

2. The picture on this page was created in 1722. The picture on page 38 was created in 1965.

   a) Is one a more reliable source of information than the other about the time and people shown? Discuss as a class.

   b) Look at the paintings on pages 25 and 29. What information do these give about the fur trade and Native–European interaction?

   c) In the Tools of Learning section of your notebook, tell what you have learned about viewing.

Canada Revisited

Father Brébeuf is a patron saint of Canada. A shrine at Midland, Ontario, honours the eight Jesuit martyrs* of Huronia. Thousands of people from around the world today also make pilgrimages to the shrine to Kateri Tekakwitha at Saint-François-Xavier mission at Caughnawaga, where her relics are preserved and her life honoured.

*A martyr is a person who is made to suffer and often die for his/her beliefs.

Acadia

(1603–1663)
A Timeline of Acadian History

Early History

The fur trade was the main source of wealth for France. This wealth was obtained through trading monopolies granted by the French king. The individual (or investors in a company) who obtained the monopoly paid for the expedition's ships, supplies, protection, and cost of settlement. Profits from trade were returned to the investors and the French king.

Pages 25 to 27 described the earliest French settlement attempts in Acadia* in 1603 at Ste. Croix and Port Royal. In 1608 French traders moved to the richer fur areas along the St. Lawrence River and a habitation was built at Quebec. French settlement in Acadia continued around the Bay of Fundy.

The timeline at the bottom of pages 40 and 41 focuses on some of the people and events that contributed to the establishment of Acadia. The numbers in the text on these pages refer to the corresponding items on the timeline.

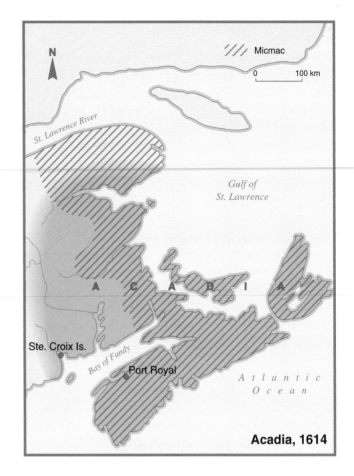

Acadia, 1614

1 De Monts, Poutrincourt, and Champlain established a French settlement on Ste. Croix Island and then in Port Royal between 1603 and 1607. The settlement was abandoned when the French king cancelled their monopoly.

2 Poutrincourt returned to Acadia in 1610, with Father Fléché, Claude de La Tour, and his son Charles. In their absence, Chief Membertou had protected the habitation. Father Fléché focused on converting the Micmaq to Christianity while the others concentrated on farming and fur trading.

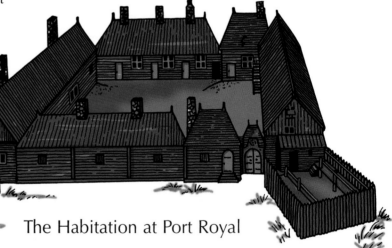

The Habitation at Port Royal

3 More colonists arrived at Port Royal in 1611, along with Father Biard and Father Massé.

*Acadia included present-day Nova Scotia, Prince Edward Island, and parts of New Brunswick and Quebec.

1603–1607	1610	1611	1613	1627	1628	1628–1632
De Monts (p. 26), Poutrincourt (p. 26), Champlain (p. 28)	Poutrincourt (p. 26), Father Fléché (p. 26), Charles de La Tour (p. 26), Membertou (p. 27), Micmaq	Father Biard, Father Massé (p. 26)	English claim Acadia, Charles de La Tour (p. 26)	Company of 100 Associates (p. 28) granted fur trade monopoly	William Alexander (p. 45)	English ships occupy St. Lawrence
①	②	③	④	⑤	⑥	⑦

Note: Timeline is not to scale

Struggle for Control

  Although Acadia was not important to the French as a major supplier of furs, its location made it crucial. Control of Acadia gave a nation power in North America. The French and the English, who were competing with each other for power in the New World, and for the rich fish and fur resources in Acadia and the St. Lawrence area, also fought for possession of the colony of Acadia.

4 While Poutrincourt was in France in 1613 to raise money for the Acadian colony of Port Royal, it was attacked and most of its buildings destroyed by a force from Jamestown, Virginia, led by English captain Samuel Argall. As a result, Acadia was claimed by the English. For the next 150 years the English and French fought each other over control of Acadia. In spite of the destruction, many of the French in the colony, including Charles de La Tour, refused to give up. They resorted to trading for furs, hiding from the English, and harassing them wherever possible.

5 The St. Lawrence area proved to be a very successful fur trading area; the fur trade grew and large profits were made. Over the years many monopolies were given to different fur trade companies. In 1627, the Company of 100 Associates (also called the Company of New France) was granted a monopoly on the fur trade in New France. Their monopoly extended from the North Pole to Florida.* Interested only in fur trading, the Company discouraged settlers from coming to New France. France and England were at war in Europe.

6 William Alexander attempted to establish a Scottish settlement at Port Royal in Acadia in 1628, calling it New Scotland (Nova Scotia).

7 English ships regularly attacked French ships between 1628 and 1632; the English occupied the St. Lawrence area.

---

*An interesting situation since the English and the Dutch had already laid claim to parts of the New World as well. The previous claims of the First People were ignored in all of these European land claims.

8 The Kirke brothers, fighting for England, attacked Quebec and forced Champlain to surrender in 1629.

9 Acadia was officially returned to the French in 1632 as part of a peace settlement at the end of a war fought in Europe between France and England. Scottish settlers returned to Scotland. Three hundred French settlers came to Acadia.

10 Port Royal became a popular area for settlement in 1633, as did Quebec.

11 Trois Rivières was founded the following year, 1634.

12 Ville-Marie (Montreal) was founded in 1642.

13 The Company of Habitants took over the monopoly of the fur trade in New France in 1645. Charles de La Tour's fort, Ft. Sainte Marie, was attacked by D'Aulnay and his men. The fort was defended by Marie de La Tour but eventually fell.

14 The English attacked Port Royal again in 1654 and captured all French settlements around the Bay of Fundy. The English retained control over the southern part of Acadia, while the French controlled northern Acadia.

15 The Treaty of Westminster (a peace treaty between England and France) returned French forts in Acadia to the French in 1655.

16 In 1663 the French government took over the control of New France and established royal government. (This topic will be covered in Chapter 3.)

For Your Notebook

1. Read the sections called Cause and Effect and Timeline on pages 257 and 269 of the Learning How to Learn Appendix. Add cause and effect and timeline to your WordBook using one of the methods for recording vocabulary found on page 269.

2. Select two events on the timeline on pages 40 and 41 that had an impact on the people of Acadia. Create two cause and effect charts showing these events.

3. How might the history of Acadia have changed if the events you chose in Question 2 had not taken place?

1629	1632, 1633	1634	1642	1645	1654	1655	1663
Kirke brothers, Champlain (p.45)	Acadia returned to French, French settlers immigrate to Port Royal, Quebec	Trois Rivières founded	Ville-Marie (Montreal) founded (p. 38)	Company of Habitants (p. 28), Charles de La Tour, Marie de La Tour (pp. 44, 45)	French control north Acadia, English control south	Treaty of Westminster	French control New France with Royal Government (see Chapter 3)
8	9 10	11	12	13	14	15	16

Note: Timeline is not to scale

Acadian Way of Life

Under French rule, New France remained a separate colony from Acadia. Both colonies were French, both spoke the French language, and followed the Roman Catholic religion and French laws. By the 1730s, the Acadians had developed a distinct culture; they weren't French and they weren't "Canadian." They were Acadian. Their lifestyle evolved around farming, hunting, and fishing.

Farming

Since the land was fertile, farming became the basis of the Acadian way of life. Trees provided lumber for the building of homes, furniture, barns, mills, and boats. Any surplus crops could be traded for manufactured goods such as woven fabrics, tools, and molasses.

Farming organization in Acadia was very different from the seigneurial system used in France and New France (see pages 70–72). The Acadians developed a unique method of reclaiming low lying, marshy lands from the sea. In the painting on page 43, *Repairing a Saltmarsh Dyke*, a group of men are working together to repair a sod dyke. Earth walls (B) covered with sod were built along the water (especially the Bay of Fundy) and various river banks (D) to keep the water from flooding low lying marshy areas (A). Gates in the dyke (C) swung open to allow water to flow out at low tide. The gates closed, preventing water from flowing back in at high tide. After several years the low lying lands dried out, leaving fertile soil (A) where wheat, hay, flax, and oats were planted. Although the dykes had to be constantly repaired, this was easier than clearing vast numbers of trees to create farm-land from forest, as they did along the St. Lawrence River.

Self-sufficiency

Barnyard animals supplemented the crops that Acadians grew and vegetable gardens and fruit trees provided food. Wild animals were also hunted.

Acadians made almost all of their own clothing, furniture, and tools.

Social Life

The people in Acadia had a healthy lifestyle. There was food in abundance. Epidemic diseases, so common in France, didn't strike Acadia. Nor did many people get killed in fighting, as the Acadians preferred not to take part in the fighting between the French and English.

The family and the Church were the main institutions in Acadia. While the French monarchy did grant some seigneuries in Acadia, the seigneurs did not influence the people's lives as they did in Quebec.

The Acadians maintained generally peaceful relations with the Micmaq. In some families, one of the partners was Micmaq or Malecite.

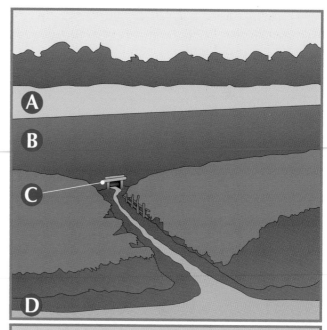

(A) low lying marshy land
(B) dyke (constructed of five or six rows of vertical logs driven into the ground; trees, earth, and grass were packed between the logs, and then covered with earth
(C) gate in the dyke (the door was opened to drain water from the field and closed to prevent sea and river tidewater from entering the field)
(D) water (sea or river)

When women and families settled in Acadia, large houses such as this began to be built.

Inside, the whitewashed walls provided a pleasing and warm atmosphere, as did the huge fireplace. Furniture was homemade, as was the clothing the people wore, Since families were large, usually with about nine children, there were always lots of helpers, both indoors and in the fields.

What the Acadians couldn't make they obtained through trade from the New England colonies (see page 46), especially from Boston. Even though the French and English were enemies, the Acadians tried not to get involved in their wars. In the painting *Trading*, you see the Acadians exchanging goods with the traders from the Thirteen Colonies—furs and wheat for metal goods, cloth, dishes, rum, and sugar.

Top Right: *Trading.* Very few French ships came to Acadia to trade, so the Acadians traded with people from the Thirteen Colonies—wheat and furs for manufactured goods.

Below: Micmac Indians, Anon. Canadian, #6663, National Gallery of Canada, Ottawa

Above: *Repairing a Saltmarsh Dyke.* The Acadians reclaimed low, marshy lands from the sea. Dykes were built of earth covered with sod. The dykes held back the water so the fields could be dried out and used for farming.

Right: *Acadians Cutting Saltmarsh Hay.* Each Acadian family had a vegetable garden, fruit orchards, fields of wheat, hay, and livestock. Hay was cut and dried to feed livestock during the winter.

Above: The Micmaq lived in Acadia long before the Acadians settled in this area. This painting, titled *Micmac Indians,* shows use of the local environment.

Charles de La Tour (1593–1666) and Marie de La Tour (1602–1645)

Charles de La Tour came to Port Royal with his parents at age 17 at the time that Poutrincourt (see page 26) returned in 1610, after several years of absence. Charles de La Tour's father was Claude de Saint-Étienne de La Tour. When the English pirate Samuel Argall attacked Port Royal in 1613, young Charles de La Tour, along with the others at the fort, escaped into the forests. Over the next few years, they lived with and received help from the Micmaq. La Tour was involved in the fur trade at this time.

To protect French power and fur trading rights in the area, he had a fort built on the southern tip of what is now Nova Scotia. In 1627, when France and England went to war, all of New France fell to the English except La Tour's fort. Over the years, Charles de La Tour took on a greater leadership role in Acadia.

In 1632, when Acadia was officially returned to France, a small number of French settlers moved into the area, with the largest number (300) coming in 1632. La Tour moved his fort, now called Fort Sainte Marie, to the mouth of the Saint John River. Both La Tour and Charles D'Aulnay claimed to have a monopoly on the fur trade in Acadia. In 1635, Charles D'Aulnay, whose fort was at Port Royal, was appointed governor of Acadia. By 1640, the dispute between La Tour and D'Aulnay had become violent.

When his first wife, who was Micmaq, died, La Tour arranged for an agent in France to find a French wife for him. In 1640, Marie married Charles de La Tour and moved from France to Fort Sainte Marie on the Saint John River.

Whenever her husband left the fort, leadership fell to Marie. In 1645, aware that the fort was poorly guarded, D'Aulnay attacked with over 200 men. Marie fought gallantly alongside her few dozen men, but they were greatly outnumbered. Marie was forced to surrender Fort Sainte Marie. She died three weeks later while in captivity.

With his wife, Marie, dead and Fort Sainte Marie in enemy hands, Charles de La Tour moved to Quebec. Charles D'Aulnay drowned in 1650, and Charles de La Tour later married D'Aulnay's widow, ending the old feud over Acadia. La Tour and his new wife Jeanne returned to Acadia, where Charles became governor.

Despite fierce resistance Marie de La Tour and Fort Sainte Marie's other defenders were defeated by D'Aulnay and his men.

In 1654, the English attacked Port Royal again and captured all the French settlements around the Bay of Fundy. La Tour was captured and sent to England as a prisoner. He returned to Acadia, but not as the governor. He spent the remainder of his years as a fur trader and farmer at Fort Sainte Marie with his wife Jeanne.

William Alexander (1602–1638)

Alexander is known as the founder of a Scottish colony at Port Royal in 1628. France and England were at war at this time. During wartime it was legal for private ship owners to attack enemy ships and keep for themselves what they captured. These people were often called privateers. In an act of war, English privateers captured 400 settlers and a fleet of 20 supply ships on their way to Champlain's Quebec. The ships belonged to the Company of New France (a new trading company). It is thought that the ships were captured by the English Kirke brothers and that Alexander later joined forces with them. The records show that during 1628/29 William Alexander obtained a trade monopoly for the New World with the Kirke brothers and several others.

In July of 1629, the Kirke brothers (fighting for England) forced Champlain to surrender Quebec to the English. The historical records are vague, but it seems that Alexander did not take part in this attack but went on to build forts in Cape Breton and then at Port Royal. Little is known of these forts or of the people that settled there. It appears that this early Scottish colony was abandoned in 1632.

For Your Notebook

1. Create a web to summarize French settlement in the 1600s. List details about the important people and events in Acadia, New France, and Huronia.

2. Summarize French settlement in the 1600s by creating a timeline of important individuals, places, and events.

3. In 1670, the population of Acadia numbered 400–500. In 1686, it was about 800; in 1711, about 2500; in 1750, more than 10 000.

   a) Create a line or bar graph to represent these figures.

   b) What reason(s) account for the increase over the years?

British Colonization

The American Colonies

In the early 1600s, England* began to establish colonies in the area now known as the northeastern United States. The English mercantile system differed from France's because the English merchants, not the state, directed the economy. English individuals or groups who applied to the king or queen for charters were interested in profit. The charters allowed them to create settlements in the hope of increasing their profits. The merchants became wealthy and the state became more powerful. This approach allowed the state to remain free of responsibility for the new settlements. It also provided the state with a new source of revenue from taxes, which could be placed on any of the colony's exports.

The first successful English colony was established at Jamestown in 1607. A trading company, the Virginia

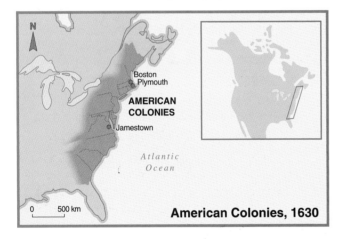

American Colonies, 1630

Below: This is a group of singing townfolk at the reconstructed Plymouth Colony.

This young man at the reconstructed colony of Plymouth is bringing in hay to provide food and bedding for his animals.

Company of London, sponsored the colony. The company had originally expected the settlers to find gold and silver to make themselves and the company rich like the Spanish had done. This did not happen and the settlers nearly starved to death. Only the development of tobacco as a **cash crop** saved the colony and made it a financial success.

Other English colonies were begun along the east coast of North America. Plymouth Colony was established in 1620 by a group of people who wished to find religious freedom in North America. This colony grew quickly and became prosperous. In 1630, the colony of Boston was established.

The English settlements quickly developed into 13 separate colonies that stretched southward down the Atlantic Coast of North America. These settlements became known as the Thirteen Colonies. They were settled by the English, Irish, Scottish, German, and Dutch. By 1770, the population of the Thirteen Colonies stood at approximately 2 100 000. Fishing, farming, and fur trading were the most profitable industries in the colonies.

*In 1707, with the Act of Union, England and Scotland officially took the name Great Britain.
Cash crop—a crop grown for sale rather than subsistence

The Hudson's Bay Company

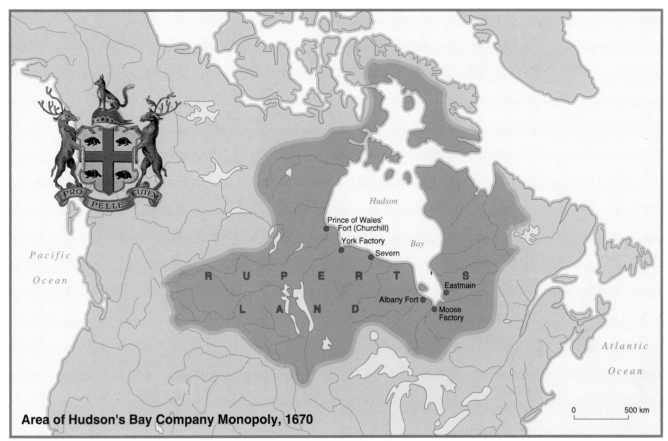

Area of Hudson's Bay Company Monopoly, 1670

Like the French, the English were very interested in gaining wealth from the fur trade in North America. The Hudson's Bay Company proved to be the most lasting of all of the fur trading institutions. Surprisingly enough, considering French and English rivalry and conflict, the Hudson's Bay Company was formed on the advice of two French fur traders, Pierre-Esprit Radisson and Médard Chouart des Groseilliers. These two had tried to persuade the French that the best way to develop the fur trade was to set up trading posts on Hudson Bay. This way, all of the Native peoples whose river systems fed into the Bay could bring in their furs by canoe. The French were not interested—in fact, the French governor fined Radisson and Groseilliers for illegal fur trading—so they presented their idea to the English. The English saw this as a way to increase their power and influence in North America, and to make profits from the fur trade.

The Hudson's Bay Company was formed by a group of English investors. These men persuaded King Charles II of England that huge profits could be made by developing the fur trade in the northern part of North America. They asked for a charter and exclusive trading rights on a large tract of land, which would be controlled by the Company.

The king agreed, and on May 2, 1670, he granted a charter to "The Governor and Company of Adventurers Trading Into Hudson's Bay." The charter was granted in the name of Prince Rupert, the king's cousin. As a result, the Hudson's Bay Company land became known as Rupert's Land. The charter gave the investors a monopoly over the trade in all the territory whose rivers drained into Hudson Bay.

Although the Europeans acted as if the land were uninhabited, there were many Native peoples who made their homes in Rupert's Land. The Company did not talk to them about taking over their lands, or consider how this might affect them.

The Hudson's Bay Company forts were erected at the mouths of the main rivers flowing into Hudson Bay. Native peoples acting as go-betweens brought furs by canoe to the forts for trading. These furs were exchanged for European goods and were in turn traded for more furs from the Native peoples. The Company was dependent on the Native peoples for their interior trade.

Through the fur trade both the Native peoples and Europeans got goods that they could not produce themselves.

Review

Cues to Learning

You will notice some icons on the review pages. These are your cue to refer to the Learning How to Learn Appendix on pages 256 to 271 for strategies on how to do these activities or to the Research Model on pages x and xi. See the inside front cover for directions on accessing our homepage.

 Complete a self-assessment for one assignment from this chapter. See page 267 for ideas.

Understanding Concepts

Making Predictions

1. At the beginning of Chapter 2 (page 23), you made some predictions based on the Overview, your preview of the chapter, and what you already knew. Use what you have learned from reading the chapter to fill in the third column of the Prediction Chart.

2. Discuss the "Questions to Talk About" on page 19 based on what you have learned about European exploration and colonization in North America.

Recording Vocabulary

3. Using one of the methods for recording vocabulary, add these words to the WordBook section of your notebook.

- alliance
- Acadia
- *coureur de bois*
- Jesuit
- institution
- prediction
- overview
- footnote

4. Here are some of the main ideas from the chapter.
   - colonization
   - fur trading companies
   - European/Native interaction
   - Iroquois and Huron alliances

   Do either a) or b).

   a) Create a concept poster of one of these ideas. Present your poster to the class.

   b) Use a web, mind map, outline, or chart to create a permanent set of notes about one of the above ideas. Explain your work to a classmate.

Working with Information

5. Go through the Overview for this chapter again. Identify each image on page 22 as mercantilism, exploration, and/or colonization.

6. Review all the different examples of power found in this chapter. Work with a partner to draw a mind map that organizes all of these examples on one sheet of paper.

7. What is the purpose of prediction for learning? Record your ideas in the Tools of Learning section of your notebook.

8. A timeline is a visual way of showing events in the order in which they occurred. After studying each chapter, create a timeline of events for that chapter. Record the most important dates and events. Record between five and ten items per chapter. Another approach is to work as a class to create one large timeline for display. You can also use pictures to illustrate the events and people.

Developing Research Skills

9. Continue your class project "Passport to the Past." Refer to page 20 for a list of people from Canadian history.

Applying Concepts

10. Why have you been studying
    - French and English colonization?
    - Iroquois and Huron alliances?
    - historical individuals in Acadia and New France?

11. Try to think of as many ideas as you can for each of the following. Record your answers in the History Journal section of your notebook.
    What if...
    - co-operation, rather than mercantilism, had been a major policy of both the French and the British?
    - the French had not established Sainte-Marie among the Hurons?

12. Create a commemorative stamp to honour one of the important people included in this chapter.

13. Complete each statement with a paragraph entry.

    a) History Journal: In this chapter I discovered...
    b) Tools of Learning: What I think I did best in this chapter was...

14. Think about the early development (in the 1600s) of what is now Canada.

    a) What do you think is meant by "development" in this case? Discuss this with a partner.
    b) Think about people of that time, such as are listed below. Discuss with a partner how each of the following people would feel about this type of development: a Huron woman, a French explorer, a Micmaq man, a Hudson's Bay Company trader, the king of France, an Ursuline nun
    c) Refer to the Glossary for a definition of exploitation. Compare it with your definition of development. Discuss this with your classmates. Record this in the WordBook section of your notebook.
    d) With your partner, take turns in the roles of the people listed above. Answer these questions as you think they might have answered them: Does development lead to positive or negative changes? Can development lead to exploitation? If so, when? How can this be avoided?

Challenge Plus

15. This chapter focused on the struggle for power that took place during the early development of Canada. Major aspects of the struggle include the desire for power, mercantilism, exploration, and colonization. As you review each of these topics, think about what each meant to the French, the English, and the Native peoples. Draw a chart to show relationships among the major aspects of the struggle for power.

16. Of what value is studying about New France and Acadia to us in today's world?

Canada Revisited

321 years later, Bay quits fur trade
The Canadian Press, Toronto (January 1991)

Hudson's Bay Co., the retail empire founded on the fur trade, has decided to stop selling furs.

The company which received its charter almost 321 years ago will start liquidating its inventory of furs in February, said Barry Agnew, vice-president of sales and promotion on Wednesday.

"It is ironic to a certain degree that the company is getting out of the business that made it a business," said Agnew.

The decision was denounced by the Fur Council of Canada as a betrayal of its "Canadian heritage."

Section III

Colonial Government 1663–1774

The Passport Tour group arrived in Quebec City to learn about New France and its royal government. Before touring the city they had an orientation session to discuss some concepts.

Ms. Ito turned to Ken. "The other day you talked about a hockey tournament in Ontario you had played in. Please tell the group the story you told me. There are some connections to the past we can make from it."

"I used to play hockey for Coach John Earnest," said Ken. "Notice that I said 'used to.' Coach Earnest had a reputation as a really good coach and I was thrilled when I finally made his team. What I didn't realize was that hockey with Earnest was hockey under a dictatorship.

"Let me give you an example. We were playing in a big tournament in Guelph last winter. We'd won our first game easily, but just squeaked through the second one. A third win was essential if we wanted to stay on the winning side of the draw.

"Coach Earnest stomped into the dressing room and barked at us, 'Team meeting in five minutes!'

"The game had been pretty rough, but we were pleased with the way we'd played. Most of the guys were planning to go out and celebrate the win. We were still talking about where to go and what to do as we dried our hair, then congregated around the coach.

"'You guys managed to squeak a win out of that game,' he said. 'But tomorrow night we may be playing against the home town team so it could be a tough one. I want to see you win by at least a three-goal margin. That means be in bed and asleep by 11:00 PM, breakfast at 6:15 sharp! At 7:00 AM we get together to

go over the video of tonight's game. Then we're going back to the arena to watch the Guelph–London game because we'll be playing one of those two teams. After lunch we've got ice time from 2:00 till 3:00 PM. Then you can grab an hour's rest and some supper before we play.'

"That was all he said, just started to walk away," said Ken to the other students.

"We offered an alternative— Dave, one of our best defencemen, told him we thought we'd like to go out for a while, catch a show or something, so an 11:00 curfew was too early. He suggested to Coach Earnest that we could order in pizza for lunch and watch the game video at noon rather than first thing in the morning—that way we would be more alert. Somebody else pointed out that we had seen Guelph and London play on Thursday, so maybe we could watch only part of the game.

"The coach didn't take it very

well," continued Ken. "He just glared at Dave and the rest of us and demanded to know just who we thought was coaching the team anyway. 'I know what the team needs,' he said. 'That's my job and I'm making the decisions here. Now, get back to your rooms, and forget about going out until we win this tournament.' And that was it—no discussion, no exceptions," Ken sighed.

Questions to Talk About

Discuss the following questions by referring to the story.

1. How does Ken's story relate to Canadian history?
2. How were the decisions made? From whom did the decision-maker take advice?
3. What role did ordinary people play in this system of decision-making?
4. a) From the decision-maker's point of view, what are the positives/negatives of this system?
   b) From the participants' points of view (in this case the players), what are the positives/negatives of this system?
5. How do the themes of power, co-operation, decision-making, and conflict apply?

Keep these questions in mind as you read Chapters 3 and 4. See if there are similarities between how the government of the colony of New France was organized and how the hockey team was organized.

Absolute Rule Decision-Making Model

An issue arises and a decision is required

The leader analyses* and considers alternatives by
• consulting with the group   **and/or**
• consulting with advisors or experts   **and/or**
• consulting resources (researching)
              OR
• consulting with no one/considering ideas on his/her own

The leader decides by selecting the "best" alternative
• using others' suggestions and advice   **and/or**
• using other information (research)
              OR
• using only his/her own ideas

The leader takes action on the decision by telling others what they must do and enforcing the plan

The leader's decision is carried out

For Your Notebook

1. Several alternatives (options) are available at each step of the Absolute Rule Decision-Making Model shown above. Which steps did the coach follow?
2. Draw an icon (visual representation) to represent the Absolute Rule Decision-Making Model.
3. a) How might you change the model the coach used if you were responsible for the team? Create your own model.
   b) What name would you give to the model of decision-making you have created? Draw an icon to represent your model.
   c) How might the model you created in b) be more/less effective than the one used by the coach?

*To separate a whole into parts and examine the parts

Chapter 3

New France: A Royal Government (1663–1760)

Overview

Use this Overview to predict the events of this chapter.

1663

Establishment of the Royal Colony. New France was then run completely by King Louis XIV of France and his appointed officials.

1665

Appointment of Jean Talon as intendant. New France was used as a source of raw materials and as a market for goods manufactured in France.

1672

Comte de Frontenac appointed as Governor General—recalled 1682 and reappointed in 1689.

1674

Laval made Bishop of Quebec.

Seigneurial System

A system whereby seigneurs divided up land for use among habitants. In New France the land was divided in long narrow strips to allow access to river transportation.

1701

Peace treaty concluded with the Iroquois. The extent of the French empire in North America is shown on the map. While this area was claimed by the French, most of it was not settled. Their degree of control was limited to their ability to defend the area.

Rupert's Land

Quebec

Thirteen Colonies

In addition to playing a part in the Royal Colony of New France, the Roman Catholic Church attempted to extend its influence to the First People.

King Louis XIV and his successors ruled New France through appointed officials. The people had little say in governmental policies.

Chapter 3 Focus

King Louis XIV claimed total power over the colony of New France in 1663 by declaring it a Royal Colony of France. The concepts of power, co-operation, decision-making, and conflict underlie the events of this chapter. The concepts of power and decision-making are the focus of Chapter 3.

Power

Co-operation

Decision-making

Conflict

Other Concepts and Main Topics

- absolute monarchy
- royal government
- seigneurial system
- life in New France
- the Church in New France

Chapter Project

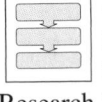 In this chapter you will carry out a major group project called the Governor's Banquet. Within the chapter you will follow the steps of the Research Model shown on pages x and xi. You will be involved in several activities, including a simulation. At the banquet, you will present the projects you have created based on your experiences studying this chapter. The banquet project is explained on pages 55 to 57.

 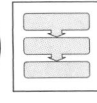 Continue your class project "Passport to the Past." Choose from the list of people on page 20.

Chapter Preview/Prediction

Examine the Overview on pages 52 and 53 and read the Chapter 3 Focus on this page. Think about what you already know about this chapter/topic. Create a Prediction Chart, like the one shown above, in your notebook. Look briefly through the chapter. Note headings, captions, and visuals and use this information to answer the questions. At the end of Chapter 3, you will complete the column "What I Found Out."

Prediction Chart—What Do You Think?		
Questions	My Predictions (fill out now)	What I Found Out (fill out at end of chapter)
1. What might be the major events?		
2. Who might be some of the important people or groups?		
3. Who might hold power?		
4. What conflicts might occur?		
5. How might the conflicts be resolved?		
6. How might decisions be made?		
7. What might be some examples of co-operation?		
8. Questions you have.		

Your guests at the Governor's Banquet (the chapter project) will enjoy revisiting the past even more if you include music, costumes, activities, refreshments, and props reflecting New France in the 1700s.

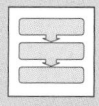

The Governor's Banquet

The Governor wishes to show visitors the many talents and accomplishments of the colonists of New France. During your study of New France, on a date yet to be announced, you will prepare and participate in a Governor's Banquet. As a class you may decide to invite another class, school staff, members of the community, or your parents to this special event. Your goals are to represent a variety of aspects of life in New France and to demonstrate how much you've learned.* Include as many of your projects on New France as you can. (You can find additional project ideas in Part 7 of the Simulation activity on page 69.) Dressing in the clothing styles of New France for the Banquet will make it more authentic and will add to the fun.

Steps for Planning

1.  As a class, brainstorm for ideas about what to include in the event. Decide together what types of displays and activities you will include.

2. Decide on the types of entertainment you may have at the banquet. Suggestions for a program are shown on the next page.

3. Decide how you might include projects you've made on New France at this banquet. See A Model for Carrying Out Research on pages x and xi and Presentations on page 267 of the Appendix.

4. You may wish to complete an Action Plan (see page 57) once you have looked at all parts of this assignment.

---

*Visit the Virtual Museum of New France (Canadian Museum of Civilization) at http://www.civilization.ca/vmnf/vmnfe.asp for more information about life in New France.

Use this sample program for a Governor's Banquet to help you plan and prepare throughout your study of Chapter 3.

Sample Program

1. Habitant families prepare food, arrange tables, and prepare entertainment.

2. Greeters at the door invite guests to view the various projects and artifacts which represent life in New France.

3. Escorts take guests to their tables where they find a copy of feature articles about New France. Allow them time to settle and read.

4. A drum roll signals the entry into the room of the master or mistress of Ceremonies (MC). The Governor is announced.

5. The Governor, his Sovereign Council, and the seigneurs and their families enter while other students play traditional French music. The Governor makes opening remarks about the colony's accomplishments.

6. Habitants serve beverages (while French music is played in the background). Habitants visit with guests and talk about their lives in New France.

7. A drum roll announces the arrival of habitant comedians and minstrels who tell jokes and stories based upon life in New France.

8. The MC announces a song presented by several *coureurs de bois*. (*En Roulant Ma Boule*, for example, is a well-known *voyageur* song.)

9. Drum roll. The MC announces refreshments (e.g., pea soup, *tourtière*) are to be served (see recipe on page 73).

10. Dancers (e.g., jig) or spoon players entertain guests during refreshments.

11. A play written by the class about colonists (e.g., habitants, *coureurs de bois*, Royal Government, king's daughters, Acadians) is presented.

12. Habitants, seigneurs, governor, intendant, bishop, and other colonists gather at the front. The audience is invited to ask questions about their lives. Students answer in role. Be sure someone has been assigned to co-ordinate this discussion.

13. Invite guests to join in a farewell dance.

14. Formal farewells and thanks.

Steps for Preparing

- Finalize the list of displays and presentations and prepare the program.

- Write a script for the master/mistress of ceremonies and for any other original portions of the program.

- Plan props, costumes, sets, supplies, and music. Who will organize, gather, and prepare the needed materials?

- Choose researchers who will gather additional information as needed (e.g., pea soup recipe, traditional French music).

- Decide what food and drinks you will serve. They should be as authentic as possible. Who will prepare the food? Where will you keep it until it is served? Who will serve it?

- Learn French–Canadian dances.

- Assign roles and responsibilities. Be sure to set deadlines and to meet as a group often to check your progress. Everyone should begin to practise their parts as soon as possible.

- Create invitations for those you wish to invite. Invite them as far in advance as possible and ask that they reply by a certain date, so you can plan properly.

- Rehearse as a group. Confirm what is left to be done.

- Arrange to meet as a class following the banquet to discuss your program's success.

Sample Invitation for Students' Guests

The honour of your presence and participation is requested at a banquet hosted by the Governor of New France on _____, 1752, at _____PM at the Governor's Palace, situated in Upper Town, Quebec City. The highlight will be presentations of _____, as well as exhibits created by our talented colonists. Entertainment and refreshments will also be provided. The Governor and his Sovereign Council eagerly await your arrival. Dress is formal: powdered wigs for Gentlemen and gowns for Ladies.
R.S.V.P.

Action Plan

1. Date of Presentation: ....

2. Today's Date: ....

3. List the assessment criteria for your project. Keep the criteria in mind as you complete your project.

   ....
   ....
   ....

4. Describe what you want your part of the presentation to look like and sound like.

   ....
   ....
   ....

5. Plan on paper what tasks have to be done. Assign a completion date for each task.

   e.g.,

Task	Completion Date	Done
1. _____	_____	_____
2. _____	_____	_____
3. _____	_____	_____

   (add to this list as needed)

Territorial Claims, 1663

By 1663, both the French and English had established colonies in North America. The English had settled along the east coast of what is now the United States. By 1670, they were trading for furs around Hudson Bay. The French settled along the St. Lawrence, where most of the people were involved in the fur trade, and in Acadia, where farming was the major occupation. As the map shows, the Spanish and Dutch had colonies farther south. In the rest of North America, First People lived as they had for thousands of years.

The French government had granted trading monopolies to individuals and companies in return for help in the colonization of New France and a share of the profits. By the mid-1600s, the small colony of New France was experiencing difficulty surviving. The Company of Habitants had received a trade monopoly but was deeply in debt and could not meet expenses. By 1658, Iroquois attacks threatened to destroy New France. The Iroquois succeeded in blocking the French fur trade and destroying their trading allies, the Huron. Neither the trading companies nor the Roman Catholic Church could solve the situation.

French colonies were about to fall to the English, the Iroquois, or both. In 1661, the leaders of New France sent an appeal to the king of France for **intervention**.

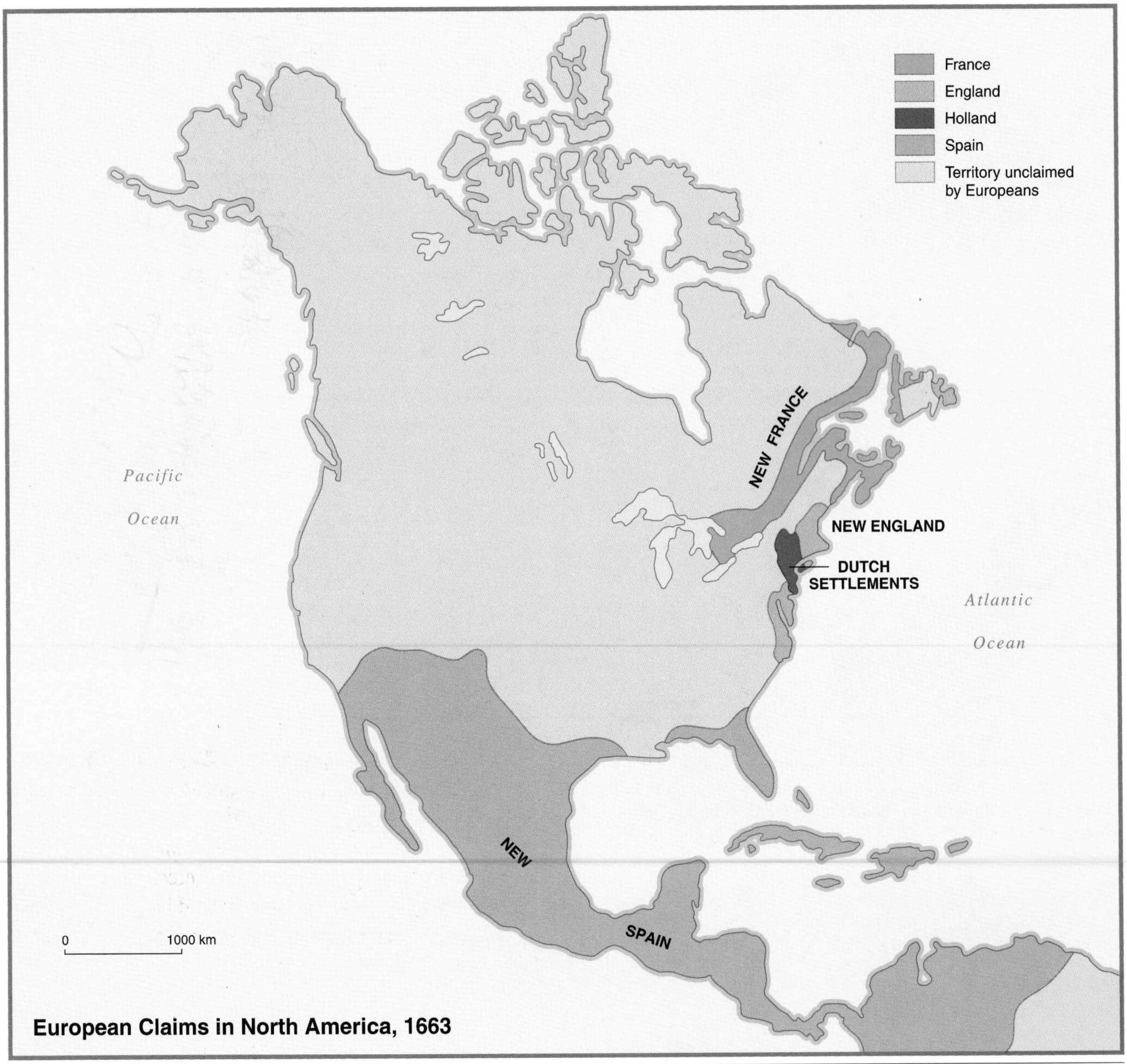

	France
	England
	Holland
	Spain
	Territory unclaimed by Europeans

Pacific Ocean

NEW FRANCE

NEW ENGLAND

DUTCH SETTLEMENTS

Atlantic Ocean

NEW SPAIN

0   1000 km

European Claims in North America, 1663

Intervention—involvement that is meant to assist or protect

58

A Royal Colony

King Louis XIV of France

 In 1663, in an attempt to solve New France's problems, Louis XIV of France established a Royal Colony in New France. New France's appeal came when Louis XIV was not at war in Europe and was eager to increase France's power and wealth by sponsoring wealthy colonies. In 1663, he took control of New France away from the trading companies. He assumed direct control over the colony, making it a Royal Colony. New France would be governed directly by the king, just as if it were another province in France. The trading companies would become businesses in the colony.

King Louis XIV of France made New France into a Royal Colony. Louis XIV was also known as the Sun King. He was an absolute monarch.

Absolute Monarchy

Absolute monarchs have unlimited power over their people and believe that the right to rule has been given to their ancestors and to them by God. The people have no role or influence in government affairs. Absolute monarchs usually appoint advisory councils that actually run the government. However, while these groups may give advice to the monarch, he or she may choose not to follow that advice.

King Louis was an absolute monarch. Many of the countries of Europe at this time, including Spain and Portugal, were also governed by absolute monarchs.

Absolute Monarchy

Leaders have unlimited power over their people. This power is not restricted by a set of rules (a constitution), or by **parliament**, or by groups (such as an aristocracy).

Colbert

King Louis XIV appointed Jean-Baptiste Colbert to be in charge of France's economy. Colbert's ideas were used to govern French colonies around the world. Colbert wanted to use France's colonies to help make France more powerful. He was very interested in mercantilism, and intended that the French colonies would become a source of inexpensive raw materials and a market for goods manufactured in France.

Parliament—the law-making body of government

Royal Government

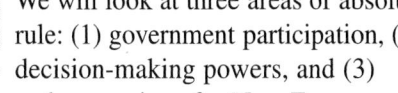

We will look at three areas of absolute rule: (1) government participation, (2) decision-making powers, and (3) majority rule. Examples are given for New France.

Characteristics of an Absolute Monarch

1. **In an absolute monarchy only the people selected by the ruler are allowed to participate in the government.**

   - In France and New France King Louis XIV was an absolute monarch.
   - Only those people selected by King Louis XIV were allowed to participate in government matters. These people are shown on the chart on page 61 as the king's advisors. They had some influence on the king but he did not have to listen to them.

2. **In an absolute monarchy one person, the ruler, has the power to make decisions.**

   - Absolute monarchs believe that their power is given to them by God, passed down through their ancestors.
   - Absolute monarchs believe they are responsible for the well-being of their subjects.
   - Absolute monarchs decide what is best for the people. They may or may not find out what the people want, or put the people's wishes into effect.
   - The power to make decisions about New France was held by King Louis XIV.

   - This does not mean that King Louis XIV of France made all the decisions. He appointed advisors, who made up the government of France, to make the decisions for him. If the king was unhappy with the decisions his council of advisors made, then he appointed new advisors who would make the kind of decisions he wanted.
   - The advisors in the French government passed on the king's decisions to the government in New France. The government in New France was made up of the governor, intendant, bishop, and Sovereign Council. If the government of New France did not follow the decisions made by the king's advisors (and the king), then they were recalled to France and were not allowed to keep their jobs.
   - In theory the people as a whole had no role or influence in the decision-making process.
   - In practice, because the distance from France to New France was so great, messages took up to a year to travel back and forth. This allowed the local officials of New France greater autonomy (greater freedom to make their own political decisions).

3. **Majority rule does not exist in an absolute monarchy. Minority rule and one-person rule exist in an absolute monarchy.**

   - The government of New France was made up of appointed officials in France and in New France. Minority rule existed in New France. The majority of the people did not have a say in the government.

Meeting of the Sovereign Council, by Charles Huot. Headed by the governor, intendant, and bishop, the Sovereign Council included officials in the government of New France who were appointed to carry out decisions made by the king and his advisors in France.

Photo: KEDL

Colonial Government in New France

 King Louis XIV of France was far too busy extending and protecting French interests in Europe to be able to devote all of his attention to New France. Under Colbert's guidance, the old system of rule by trading companies was replaced by a Royal Government appointed by the king. The king relied on officials or ministers to do most of the government's work.

He created a Sovereign Council of officials in New France. This council was to carry out orders from the king and his government in France. The people who settled in New France did not have any power over the king or the Sovereign Council. They could not change any decisions made by the ruler. Communication with New France was limited, however. Its distance from France and the fact that the St. Lawrence River was frozen for six or seven months of the year made it inaccessible. This meant that the local officials in New France often had far more power over the colony than the French government had intended. The senior members of the Sovereign Council were the governor, intendant, and bishop. When New France had a good governor and intendant (the king's representatives in the colony), the colony had good government. New France had a well-developed system of laws. However, members of the legal profession were barred from entering New France in its early days.

The people of New France had little official role in the government of the colony, but this did not make them any different from people in European countries. Women were completely excluded from the governing process in New France as well as in all European countries. Occasionally the intendant, who was in charge of justice, finance, and administration, called meetings of prominent local officials to discuss economic policies for the colony. These discussions did not, however, always result in the intendant taking the officials' advice.

The Royal Government in New France was both inexpensive and efficient. It remained intact until the British substituted their system of government in 1763.

For Your Notebook

1. Look closely at the historic painting on page 60. Which people in the scene appear to have the most power and authority? What visual clues are given to show this?

2. How can you decide if the information shown in historic pictures is accurate? What questions can you ask yourself when using pictures to gather information?

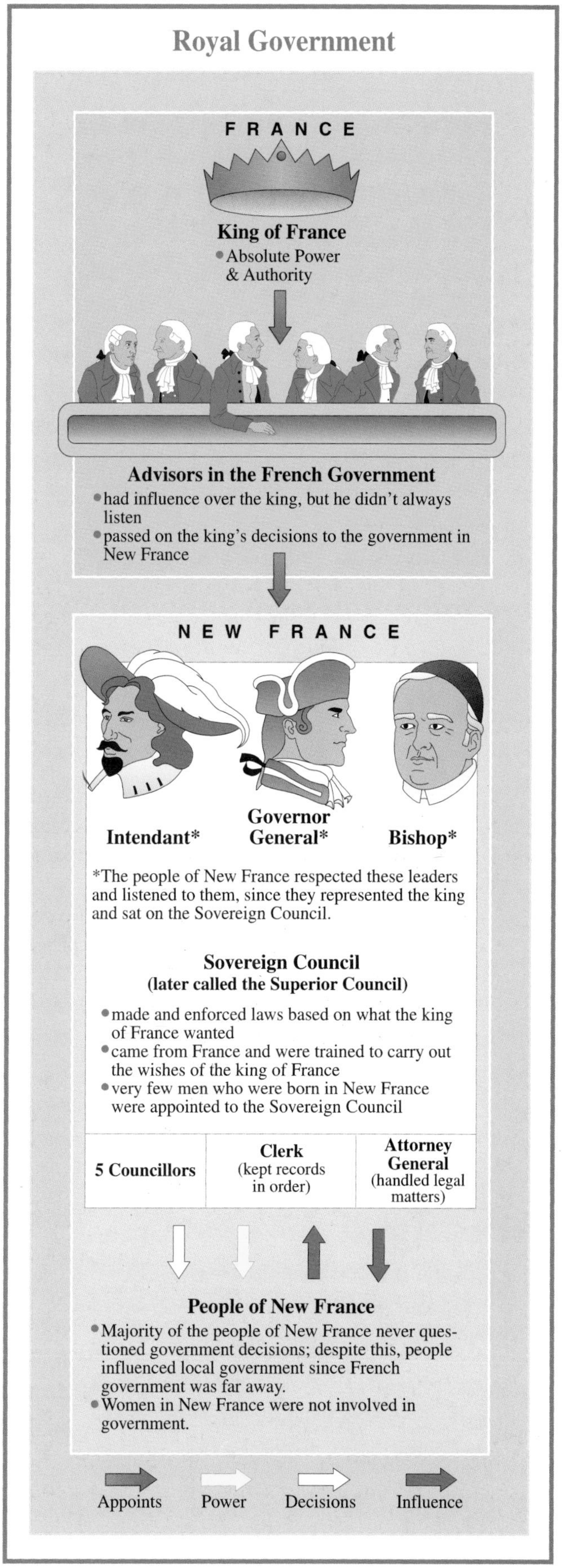

Royal Government

F R A N C E

King of France
- Absolute Power & Authority

Advisors in the French Government
- had influence over the king, but he didn't always listen
- passed on the king's decisions to the government in New France

N E W   F R A N C E

Intendant*   **Governor General***   **Bishop***

*The people of New France respected these leaders and listened to them, since they represented the king and sat on the Sovereign Council.

Sovereign Council
(later called the Superior Council)
- made and enforced laws based on what the king of France wanted
- came from France and were trained to carry out the wishes of the king of France
- very few men who were born in New France were appointed to the Sovereign Council

5 Councillors	Clerk (kept records in order)	Attorney General (handled legal matters)

People of New France
- Majority of the people of New France never questioned government decisions; despite this, people influenced local government since French government was far away.
- Women in New France were not involved in government.

Appoints	Power	Decisions	Influence

The government of New France is an example of absolute rule.

Important Officials in the Government of New France

The Governor General

- represented the king in New France
- served as a living symbol of the king's authority*
- was the highest ranking official in New France
- was appointed from the **nobility**
- was chosen from among military officers
- acted as master of New France in the king's name and thus was responsible for military planning, relations with the Native peoples, and ensuring that the other officials did their jobs

Comte de Frontenac (1622–1698)

Louis de Buade, Comte de Frontenac, was appointed governor of New France in 1672. He was a successful military governor, but because he quarrelled with the intendant and bishop he was recalled to France in 1682.

Frontenac returned to New France in 1689 to create peace by suppressing the Iroquois and to attack English settlements and finally expand France's fur trade. He remained there until his death in 1698.

Frontenac's major concern was the expansion of New France's fur trade.

The Bishop

- represented the Roman Catholic Church in New France
- ruled over **parish** priests and nuns of New France in the king's name
- was in charge of the missionaries, churches, hospitals, and schools
- was often a member of the French nobility appointed by the king
- reported to the king on colonial activities and ensured harmony among his parishes

François de Laval (1623–1708)

François de Laval, a Jesuit priest, arrived in Quebec in 1659. He was appointed the first Bishop of Quebec in 1674. Laval, who directed the spiritual life of New France for 29 years, was very active in attempting to convert the Native people to Christianity.

As a leading member of the Sovereign Council, Laval had strong political influence. He organized the parish system of New France. The **seminary** that Laval founded at Quebec became Laval University in 1852.

---

*In New France, the governor was officially a figurehead, but in actual fact he had a lot of power. A figurehead is a person who is the head of a country in name or title only but has no real power or responsibility.

Nobility—a person with special rank and authority by virtue of birth or title (e.g., duke, duchess, count, countess, *marquis*, and *marquise*)

Parish—district that is the responsibility of a particular church

Seminary—special school for the training of priests

The Intendant

- acted as chief **administrator** of New France in the king's name
- informed the king of colonial activities and ensured harmony among the people
- was appointed from the nobility
- supervised the day-to-day running of the colony, law and order, and matters relating to finance (money)

Jean Talon (1625–1694)

Jean Talon was the first intendant of New France. During his term, from 1665 to 1668, he conducted a **census** of the population.

Talon attempted to change the economic base of the colony from fur-trading to agriculture and industry, but found that this could not be accomplished without a larger population.

Talon arranged for settlers to come to New France, including over 1000 women known as the *filles du roi* ("king's girls" or "**king's daughters**"). He encouraged further population growth through marriage grants and baby bonuses (money given to a couple when they married and when they had children).

Talon tried to diversify (expand and vary) the economy by introducing new crops such as flax and hops*, by starting a shipyard and lumber industry, and encouraging mining.

Canada Revisited

A modern-day statue of Bishop Laval.

The Château Frontenac, built in 1892, overlooks the St. Lawrence River and occupies a central location in the old walled-in city of Quebec. This is a favourite spot for tourists, since many activities such as the Quebec Winter Carnival take place there.

Administrator—person in charge; official; manager
Census—an official count of the people of a country or district to find out the number of people living there
King's daughters—women who came at the king's expense to New France to marry and settle there
*Flax was grown to make a cloth known as linen. Hops are an essential ingredient in making beer.

Changes to New France

New France became a French province in 1663. The Sovereign Council was appointed to carry out orders from the king of France and his government in the colony of New France.

Talon studying plans at the shipyard at Quebec in 1672

Intendant Jean Talon tried to make New France less dependent on supplies from France by establishing industries such as shipbuilding, brewing, and shoemaking. Government financing was provided to assist farming, shipbuilding, brewing, fishing, and tanning, but the industries did not become profitable and were a drain on the finances of the French government.

Population growth in New France was encouraged. Many French settlers immigrated at the government's expense. Over 7000 French immigrants arrived in the colony between 1663 and 1760. This included many retiring soldiers. To further populate the colony, over 1000 young women came from France to New France to marry

Immigrants by Gender and Decade* 1608–1759			
Period	**Men**	**Women**	**Total**
Pre-1630	15	6	21
1630–39	88	51	139
1640–49	141	86	227
1650–59	403	239	642
1660–69	1075	623	1698
1670–79	429	369	798
1680–89	486	56	542
1690–99	490	32	522
1700–09	283	24	307
1710–19	293	18	311
1720–29	420	14	434
1730–39	483	16	499
1740–49	576	16	592
1750–59	1699	52	1751
Unknown	27	17	44
TOTAL	6908	1619	8527

the single men there. These women, many of whom were orphans, were called the *filles du roi* (the "king's daughters") because their passage (cost of voyage) and wedding **dowries** were provided by the government (see painting on page 65). The table above shows the increase in population due to immigration to New France.

Population growth was encouraged in other ways in New France. Government grants were given to families with over 10 children. Royal wedding dowries were awarded to couples who married early (under 20 for men, under 16 for women). Fathers were fined for having single children of marriageable age.

To strengthen New France's most important industry, the fur trade, Governor General Frontenac encouraged friendships with some Native peoples, exploration, and military activity. In the painting on page 65, the Comte de Frontenac is seen meeting with Iroquois chiefs at Cataraqui (Kingston) in 1673.

To protect the colony, **militia** companies were formed that involved all men aged between 16 and 60.

Dowry—money or property that a woman brings with her into marriage

Militia—citizens who were not regular soldiers but who underwent training for emergency duty or local defence

*Information in chart from *Historical Atlas of Canada: From Beginning to 1800* (Vol. I), ed. R. Cole Harris. Toronto: University of Toronto Press, 1987. Reprinted with permission.

English–French Conflict
Garakontié (d. 1677/78)

As a negotiator Garakontié spent his life attempting to bring about and maintain peace between his people, the Onondaga (one of the Iroquoian Five Nations) and the French. Through his negotiations he was able to protect the interests of both cultures (Iroquoian and French). As a chief he was known as an excellent speaker and politician. He became a Christian and he was baptized by Bishop Laval in the Cathedral in Quebec. A huge feast was held in his honour. On many occasions he was able to promote the teachings of the missionaries. He seemed to have followed the idea that the best future course for the Iroquois was to work with and learn from the French, rather than to oppose and fight them. For this, he was often greatly opposed by his own people. He was influential in the treaty negotiations held between Governor Frontenac and the Iroquois in 1673 at Cataraqui (now Kingston), shown in the painting to the right.

Exploring Further

1. You are an entrepreneur who recently arrived in New France. You wish to invest in a local business. Create a brief business plan that includes the type and location of your business, how you will let others know about your business, and three reasons why you believe you will be a success.

2. Pretend you are assisting the intendant in writing a census report to the king. Use the population chart on page 64 to describe the immigration trends to him. Give reasons for the increase in the 1660s. Explain the differences between the numbers of men and women immigrating.

3. In a diary entry, write about one of your adventures in the militia.

4. Why do you think Garakontié was a valuable member in Frontenac's negotiations with the Iroquois?

Life in New France

A Seigneury

In New France, the seigneurial system was the model by which land was allotted, cleared, and farmed by habitants. It was the basis upon which a year-round food supply became available and population expansion could occur. A seigneury was more than a farm—it was a community.

The following simulation will allow you to experience life on a seigneury in New France. You will need to conduct some research in order to prepare.* Once your research is completed, you will be involved in creating your own seigneury and characters. Projects and activities, including this one, that you complete during your study of New France will be important for your participation in the Governor's Banquet, introduced at the beginning of this chapter.

As a class, decide on criteria to evaluate the parts of your project. Think about how you can best fulfil the requirements.

*Visit the Virtual Museum of New France (Canadian Museum of Civilization) at http://www.civilization.ca/ vmnf/ vmnfe.asp for more information about life in New France.

Part 1: Gathering Information

a) Individually, begin a web similar to the one below.

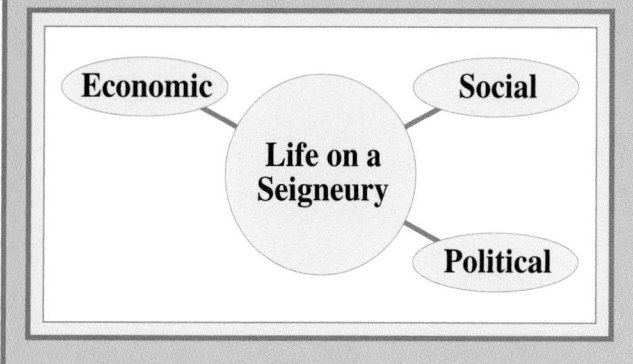

b) As you read this chapter add information about life on a seigneury in New France to your web. This will help you prepare for the activities to follow.

Part 2: Creating the People of the Seigneury

a) Your teacher will divide your class into three seigneury groups with approximately nine or ten students in each. Each seigneury group should appoint a seigneur to head the group. Seigneurs may be either male or female.

b) Characters will be assigned to each group member from the list on this page, "Suggested Families and Characters."

c) "Create" your character. Record the information about your character and your family on paper, using the format shown on the "Personal Record" card. Make the characters historically accurate, based on what you've learned about New France.

Suggested Families and Characters

Key: M=Male F=Female
Numbers refer to ages of children

Langois: seigneur; wife (3 grown children living in Ville-Marie)

Lefebvre: habitants—husband; wife; 4 children (M3, M7, M14, F15)

Boucher: habitants—widow; 2 children (M12, M17)

Father LeBlanc: (local priest) (Note: nuns did not live in seigneuries, just in towns.)

Beauport: habitants—husband; wife; 1 child (F1)

Tremblay: habitants—husband; wife; 7 children (F1, F4, M8, M11, M12, F13, F15)

Dupont: frequent visitor, *coureur de bois*

Lamoureux: habitants—single man (occupies 1/2 of parents' plot); elderly father; elderly mother

Simard: single man (recently arrived from France) age 26

Grenier: habitants—husband; wife; 5 children (M3, F5, F6, F8, M9)

Personal Record Card

Family Name (in role):..

Members:

.... Age:.............
.... Age:.............
(add to this as needed)

My Name:..

Most important possessions:
(buildings, equipment, supplies, livestock)
....
....

Activities: (e.g., What do you harvest, grow, trade, hunt, fish, make?)
....
....

My specific role(s) and duties:
....
....

Other: ....
....

Attach a portrait of yourself & family

continued on page 68

Part 3: Meeting the People of the Seigneury

a) Your seigneur will assign you a farm plot from the map shown below. Add the following information to your Personal Record:
   - Farm plot # _____
   - Advantages of this location:
   - Concerns about this location:

b) Your seigneur wants to conduct a census to report the colony's population to the intendant. He has requested that everyone in the seigneury come to this meeting. You will each briefly introduce yourself (your character) and your family using the information from your Personal Record.

c) Once the formal meeting is over, take some time to get to know your neighbours. Ask each other questions about your background (in role).

Part 4: Creating the Seigneury

a) Now that your plot has been assigned, you should each create a rough design of your farm. You will be using this design to create a more detailed version (3-D visual, diorama) of your seigneurial plot. Refer to the pictures in this chapter for ideas.

- Using shoe boxes (or shoe box lids), design and create the plot you were assigned.* The priest can create the church site, and the *coureur de bois* the shoreline and surrounding countryside. Be sure to plan ahead carefully with your group so that the individual parts (e.g., farm plots, church site, shoreline) can be joined together later to create a large model of a seigneury.

- You should refer to your Personal Record to be sure to fulfil all your duties correctly. This may require representing them in both visual and written forms.

b) As a group, assemble the various part of your seigneury.

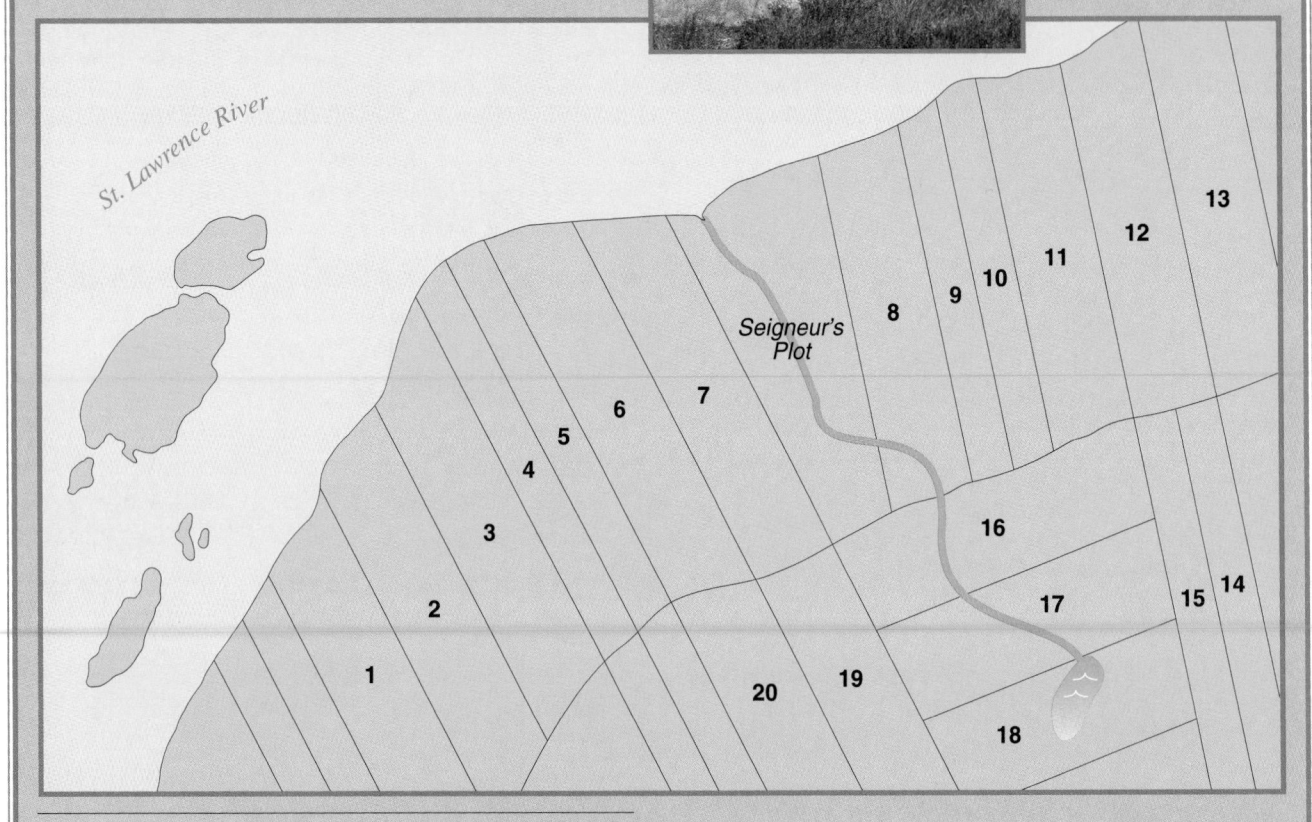

*An alternative to this activity could be the creation of seigneurial plots on poster paper.

68

Part 5: A Report to the King

Your seigneur wishes to find out how you are all doing as he has been asked by the intendant to send a report to the king of France. Discuss the questions which follow. The seigneur should assign someone to record on chart paper the information gathered during your discussion.

a) What activities are you involved in during winter, spring, summer, and fall?

b) What challenges do you face and how do you address these?

c) How do you rely upon each other while living on the seigneury?

d) Do you depend upon anyone outside your seigneury? How?

e) Who is attending school? Why doesn't every youngster attend school?

f) What **technology** are you most grateful for?

g) What technology would you like to see developed?

h) Has the government assisted you? How?

i) The 15-year-old daughter of Monsieur and Madame Lefebvre is to marry the 17-year-old son of Widow Boucher. What type of ceremony will they have? Where will they live?

j) What successes have you experienced?

k) What plans should you make for your future?

Part 6: Life in New France

Share and discuss your ideas in a meeting involving everyone from the three seigneuries.

Part 7: Using What You Know for Special Projects and the Governor's Banquet

Think about the projects and activities you have planned or are working on in history class. A few classes from now, you will be participating in the Governor's Banquet. Select from the project suggestions listed below. These will not only show what you have learned about life in New France, but they can also be included as features of the Governor's Banquet program.

a) Create a short story, poem, diary, or letter to a friend in France describing a year in your family's life. (If, like most habitants, you are not **literate**, have someone else scribe what you create.)

b) Rewrite a short story about New France into play format.

c) Interview another character (or several) from one of the other seigneuries. Most people at the time were unable to read and write and there were no newspapers. How would you communicate information about New France?

d) Select and learn a series of songs that are representative of French-Canadian culture. Describe their origin and significance to French-Canadian culture.

e) Find French-Canadian recipes to create a recipe book.

f) Create the "soundtrack" (using script and sound effects) of an important event on your seigneury (e.g., wedding, meeting, dance, Christmas).

g) Working with others, write and present a play featuring the characters from the seigneury role-play/simulation.

h) Prepare and present a New France fashion show with models or cutout dolls. Write the commentary that goes with each outfit. What makes the clothing suitable for life in New France?

  For more presentation and writing ideas, turn to the Appendix.

Technology—the knowledge and application of developments in science, manufacturing, business, and the arts
Literate—able to read and write

The Seigneurial System

Structure of the Seigneuries

New France grew along the banks of the St. Lawrence River. Since the river formed the main transportation route, every habitant wanted land along the rivers of New France. For this reason, seigneuries were divided into long narrow strips of land. Each had a section of river front and extended back into uncleared bush away from the river. As the land was passed through the generations, the strips were subdivided. Only when the land along the St. Lawrence was completely used did the colony start a new row of seigneuries behind the first ones. These long, narrow strips of land are still visible along the St. Lawrence River today.

Since the king owned all of the land in New France, he granted the use of the land to people who became seigneurs. The seigneurs then divided the land into smaller lots and brought in settlers called habitants to farm it. Both the seigneurs and the habitants had specific duties. Their land could be taken away if the duties were not performed.

Duties of the Seigneur

- Subdivide the seigneury into 32-hectare parcels and grant land to the habitants.
- Build a house and flour mill on the seigneury.
- Contribute to the construction of a church.
- Report to the intendant information about the population of the seigneury, the amount of land under cultivation, and the dues paid.

Duties of the Habitant

- Use the seigneur's mill and pay the miller.
- Pay annual dues to the seigneur (*cens et rentes*) in produce or cash.
- Build a house and farm the land.
- Perform unpaid labour for the seigneur a few days each year (*corvée*).

A view of the Château Richer, Cape Torment, Thomas Davies, #6275, National Gallery of Canada, Ottawa

A view of the Château Richer, painted by Thomas Davies in 1787, shows houses, barns, sheds, crops, eel traps, fields of wheat and peas, and livestock typical of New France.

Women and the Seigneuries

Unlike legal systems found in some European countries the French system of justice allowed women to hold seigneurial land. Women in New France were encouraged to marry by the age of 16. They often inherited land when their husbands died. Some women took charge of their inherited land; others kept it only until a son was old enough to farm it. Other women, such as Madeleine d'Allonne, held their own seigneuries.

> ### Madeleine d'Allonne (1646–1718)
> Madeleine d'Allonne was one of the first women in New France to take charge of a large seigneury. She cleared the land, built a house and barn, and raised her own crops. She also spoke out in support of the rights of settlers.

Compared to France

The French officials who governed New France attempted to fashion the new colony after the mother country. Many old French institutions became part of the way of life in New France. These institutions were adapted so that they suited life in the New World. Consequently, New France appeared to be structured by old-fashioned institutions, but in reality, often only the names were the same. Pages 70–79 examine two institutions in New France: the seigneurial system and the Church. You have already studied a third institution—government.

The seigneurial system was an example of how a traditional French institution changed radically in New France. In France, peasants obtained farmland through the seigneurial system. This was a modified version of a medieval European method of distributing land (called feudalism). Across Europe in the Middle Ages, peasants were granted land by their lords in return for military service, a portion of their produce, or the performance of other unpaid duties. This system was still in effect in France when New France became a Royal Colony.

The seigneurial system in France and New France had some differences. In France, the seigneurial system provided seigneurs with great profits and cheap labour. In New France, it benefited the habitant as well as the seigneur. The habitants had increased independence, land, and income. Being a seigneur in New France meant status, but not necessarily wealth.

The new seigneuries were not as wealthy as those in France; seigneurs were often little wealthier than successful habitants. Many of the seigneurs were more interested in enjoying the status of their position than in living on their

Every autumn the women of New France melted animal fat and beeswax to make candles for the long, dark winters. They dipped strings into this melted mixture over and over again, allowing each layer to harden.

seigneuries or fulfilling their obligations. The position of seigneur actually became that of a high-status land agent. The seigneur's traditional role as a military commander was taken over by a habitant called the captain of the militia.

The habitants gained increased independence and wealth under this new system. Land was plentiful, so habitants were frequently allowed to cultivate as much as their families could farm. The St. Lawrence River made roads a secondary form of transportation, so habitants did not lose their most valuable farming time performing *corvée*. In addition to these factors, the fur trade presented a few habitants with another source of income and freedom.

Exploring Further

1. Research land distribution in Quebec today. Are the long narrow strips of land still in existence or have new property lines been created?

2. Visit the Parks Canada website for a list of historic sites. The address is http://parkscanada.pch.gc.ca/ What historical sites exist showing life in New France in the 1600s?

Settlement in New France

The St. Lawrence River was the largest and most important river in New France. The three cities of New France—Quebec, Montreal, and Trois Rivières (Three Rivers)—were all on the St. Lawrence River. Settlement in New France was most often near lakes and rivers. People depended on rivers and lakes for transportation. In warm weather they travelled by canoe or larger boats or rafts with sails. In winter they travelled by horse and sleigh on the frozen rivers.

The French brought their customs and language to their new home. Soon the French culture (way of life) was found throughout New France. French families began to build farms along the St. Lawrence River. The long, narrow strips of farmland stretching back from the river are shown in the illustration and modern-day photograph below.

All of the land in New France legally belonged to the king of France. Each seigneur was in charge of several strips of land. A seigneur could build a large house for himself, but he also had to build a church and a mill so his habitants could grind their grain into flour. Habitants did not own their farms, but were granted use of them by the seigneur. Habitants were allowed to remain on the land as long as they paid their dues. It was a seigneur's job to make sure that the land was well looked after.

Canada Revisited

Left: The long narrow strips of land still can be seen in some parts of Quebec today.

Food

The people of New France had to produce as much of their own food as possible. Many sources of food and ways of preserving food were learned from the First People. The people of New France ate a lot of meat from farm animals such as cattle and pigs, and from the area's wildlife (birds, fish, moose, deer, rabbits, and porcupines). Eels were caught in baskets in the river and salted, smoked, or dried. In their gardens, habitants grew such vegetables as corn, beans, peas, asparagus, cabbage, and cucumbers. They also grew fruit and nut trees, and berry bushes. Most meals included milk and cheese. Two favourite dishes were *tourtière* (meat pie) and *sipaille* (wild game pie).

Habitants made whole-wheat bread from the wheat that they grew on their farms and ground at the mill. Most families had large outdoor ovens built of stones held together with clay. Once or twice a week these large ovens were heated with wood fires to bake bread.

The people of New France had to learn how to preserve food so they would have something to eat during the long cold winter months. Winter meat was left out in the cold until frozen, then kept in a small shed attached to the house, or it was salted, smoked, or dried. Vegetables, particularly peas, could be dried. Root vegetables were stored in underground cellars. Berries could be cooked with sugar to make jam.

The habitants got up early and put in about two hours of work before breakfast. At about eight o'clock, they would have a breakfast that might include bread, pancakes, and milk. They ate again at noon

and around four o'clock, but the biggest meal was after they finished the day's work, at about eight o'clock in the evening.

Tourtière

750 g ground lean pork
1 small onion (chopped very fine)
125 mL boiling water
1 garlic clove (chopped) or 5 mL garlic powder
1 mL celery salt or 1 small branch of celery leaves
1 mL pepper
7 mL salt
1 mL sage
pinch of cloves (ground)
3–4 medium-sized potatoes, boiled and mashed
pastry for a two-crust pie, 22 cm in diameter

1. Put the first nine ingredients in a large, heavy saucepan (about 3 litres in size). Cook over low heat, stirring, until the meat is no longer red and you have about half of the liquid left.

2. Cover and cook gently for a further 30–45 minutes.

3. Mix the mashed potatoes into the cooked meat mixture. Cool.

4. Preheat the oven to 230°C.

5. Roll out the pastry into two circles. Line the pan with one circle. Fill with cooled meat mixture. Place the other circle on top of mixture. Seal edges and slash top of crust to let steam escape.

6. Bake for 10 minutes, then reduce heat to 180°C and bake 30–40 minutes longer. Makes six servings.

Variations: Can be made with boiled chicken and pork mixture, or a mixture of ground meats; pork is usually part of the mixture.

Historical note: This recipe is called *tourtière* because it was originally made with *tourtes* or passenger pigeons. Since the disappearance of passenger pigeons, the recipe uses various meats. Traditionally, *tourtière* is served on Christmas Eve.

—Recipe courtesy of Linda McDowell

Clothing

In the early years of New France, clothing was made of animal hides or from woven linen or hemp. Linen and hemp came from plants grown in New France. Linen or hemp clothing was lined with leather or fur for warmth.

When the habitants began to raise sheep, the women spun the wool and wove cloth. Woollen underclothes kept people warm in winter and absorbed perspiration in summer. Women wore long dresses. They might wear several skirts for warmth. Over the dresses they sometimes wore aprons and shawls. They wore small white caps or bonnets on their heads. Men wore leather breeches, woven shirts, and leather jackets. They often wore woollen caps called tuques. Both men and women's shoes were leather moccasins or wooden clogs. Children wore the same styles of clothing as adults.

In Quebec, some wealthy people wore the fine silks and long wigs that were fashionable in France.

Homes

Most houses in New France had stone foundations. Walls of houses built in the 1600s were of square-cut timbers. Spaces between the timbers were filled with **mortar**. Houses built in the 1700s often had walls of stone. Sometimes the stone walls were covered with pine boards,

Mortar—a cement-like mixture used to hold bricks, stones, or timber together

which were whitewashed. Roofs were made of thatch or overlapping boards and were steeply sloped so snow would slide off. Windows were made of greased paper or parchment (made from skin of sheep). These windows let in a little light, but no one could see out of them. The houses of the habitants often had only one room, with an attic above for sleeping. The seigneur usually had a larger house.

Habitants made their own furniture, usually of birch or pine. This would include a table, chairs, benches with backs, cupboards, and cradles. They often painted their furniture with homemade paint. Red was a favourite colour.

The most important part of the house was the large stone fireplace, which gave heat and light. Wealthy people might have an iron stove as well. In the 1600s, beds sometimes had walls with doors, making them like tiny rooms. In the 1700s, beds sometimes had curtains. The floors were usually wood. There might also be homemade rugs that were woven, braided, or hooked from rags.

For Your Notebook

1. Refer to pages 73 and 74 to compare New France with the present day. How were/are needs of food, clothing, and shelter met?

The Habitant Work Calendar

December
butcher animals, smoke, freeze, or salt meat

November
plough, spread manure

October
harvest vegetables

August–September
harvest grain—oats, barley, rye, wheat

June–July
gather berries, make hay

May
plant seeds

March–April
make maple syrup, shear sheep

January–February
thresh grain

WINTER

SPRING

SUMMER

FALL

Choices to Make! New France—1672

by Nancy Sellars Marcotte

How odd it was to feel so safe when she was so far away from anything she had ever known! Geneviève had lived through so many uncertainties in her life. She had always been the one who didn't quite belong.

Geneviève was an orphan. She had been raised in the home of her aunt and uncle. They had treated her kindly, but they had six children of their own, all younger than Geneviève. It was difficult for a shoemaker to support six children, even in Paris, where the cobblestones wore shoes out so quickly.

Geneviève had always known that she would have to make her own way in life. Her uncle would not be able to provide any dowry at all. With no money or household goods to bring into a marriage, she was unlikely to find a husband. When she was 12, she was very glad to find a position in the kitchen of a nobleman's house on the outskirts of Paris. The cleaning and scrubbing that she had to do was very difficult, but she always had enough food.

But the nobleman and his wife were elderly, and the other servants sometimes whispered that perhaps soon they would not need so many servants. The women were particularly worried about where to go if they no longer had jobs in the nobleman's household.

It was another household servant, Françoise, who told Geneviève that the king wanted young women to go to New France. At first Geneviève had laughed. She knew, of course, that young men sometimes went to New France. Some of them went to trade for furs from the Native people. Others, she understood, were farmers, and some were soldiers. But Geneviève did not have a clear idea of where New France was, or how anyone went there.

Françoise's stories began to seem more and more unbelievable. Because the two girls were well-mannered, they could become King's Daughters. Geneviève had not believed this at all until Françoise had explained that they would not be invited to go and live at the palace. It was just that the king wanted many French families living in New France. There were many single men there. In fact, Françoise said, there were 15 French men for every French woman in New France. The king would provide dowries for young women who were willing to go and live in New France and marry these young men.

Geneviève had never travelled farther than the outskirts of Paris, but somehow, just a few months after her 14th birthday, she found herself beside Françoise in a wagon jolting toward the seacoast. Then she was aboard a wooden sailing ship and France was just a memory, far behind her.

After six long weeks they arrived at Quebec. From the ship Geneviève stared at the walled city on the low land near the river. High above on the cliffs was a magnificent stone château.

The month was June, and Geneviève did not think she had ever felt such heat. As the girls clambered from the ship into the rowboat that was to take them to shore, her attention was divided. The settlement of Quebec, the strange little insects that were nipping at her wrists and neck, and the jostling group of men who stood at the shore watching the girls all distracted her.

Geneviève was a little frightened. Since she had travelled so far, she wanted to be sure that she did not end up in a life that would cause her unhappiness. She soon learned that the nuns who looked after the King's Daughters were as much concerned with the girls' happiness as with providing brides for the young men of New France.

Françoise, always so sure of her decisions, was married within the month. Her husband was a widower, 11 years older than Françoise, whose wife had died of fever the winter before. He was a shipbuilder with a fine house in Quebec. Françoise came back often to see Geneviève, to tell her about the two stepchildren that she was helping her husband to raise. Already Françoise was enthusiastic about the seminary that Bishop Laval had started in Quebec. "If one of our sons chooses to become a priest, he can train right here at Quebec," she told Geneviève. "He can study Greek and Latin and French and mathematics. And do you remember when we thought that all the men of New France were fur traders or farmers or soldiers? Well, my sons can be

Jean Talon Visiting the Settlers. Jean Talon sometimes visited the habitants in their homes in order to see for himself what life was like for people living on the seigneuries.

apprentices and learn how to be shipbuilders or shoemakers or brewers as well!"

Geneviève was also eager to hear the stories told by King's Daughters who had passed through the convent a few years earlier. One of them, a lovely red-haired young woman named Anne, was just two years older than Geneviève, but already she and her husband had three young children. They lived on a seigneury a short distance west of Quebec.

"Our life is very good," she told Geneviève. "Our farm is long and narrow, and my husband built our house near the river. Every winter, when the farming is not busy, he builds a little more furniture. We have a fine bed with curtains around it. Our baby sleeps in a cradle beside the bed, and the two older children sleep in the loft above."

Anne told Geneviève about life on a habitant farm. "We spin our own wool from our sheep. Then we weave or knit clothes for our families. For families with over 10 children,

there is a special allowance, but we must pay a fine if we have daughters over 16 who are not married. And any men over 18 who are not married must pay a special tax, and they may lose their hunting and fishing licences."

Anne's proudest story was of the day that Intendant Jean Talon made a visit to her home. "He has already made a census of the population to see how many there are of us in New France. Occasionally he comes around to visit our homes. When he stopped at our house, he said that the bread I bake in the seigneur's oven is as fine as any he has tasted, either in France or New France."

As the summer passed, Geneviève met several young men. She knew that each of them was looking for a wife. Geneviève knew that the nuns hoped that she would choose one of the young men to marry, as nearly every other King's Daughter had done, but she did not feel ready to make that decision. The nuns allowed her to help with the

teaching of the young French and Huron girls who came to them to learn a little reading and writing and arithmetic, as well as skills that they would need when they had families to raise. As she helped the younger girls, Geneviève was an eager pupil herself. She knew that women of New France were fortunate to learn how to read and write. So many of the men did not because they worked in the fields from childhood.

She also spent time helping the nuns look after the sick and injured who came to their hospital. The first time that Geneviève had to cut one of her patients to let some of his blood out, she felt very sick. However, the nuns thought that this cured many infections and fevers, so she carefully learned the skill.

Summer turned to an autumn of vibrantly coloured trees. Then came winter, colder than Geneviève could have imagined. It was too cold for the pupils to come to school in the winter, but Geneviève was kept busier than ever helping the nuns tend to the sick. When spring came round again, Geneviève realized she was no longer a newcomer to New France. Soon she would be helping the next year's King's Daughters with advice about the ways of New France.

"I must decide soon whether I will marry one of these habitants and raise a family of my own, or whether I will remain with the nuns and help all the people of New France," she thought. "But that is why I came to New France—so I could make choices, and not just live the life that circumstances would thrust upon me."

Apprentice—a person who works with a skilled craftsperson in order to learn that craft

The Church in New France

Harvest Festival, William Bent Berczy, #16648, National Gallery of Canada, Ottawa

Harvest Festival. The success of crops was vital to the habitants of New France.

The Roman Catholic Church played a very important part in the Royal Colony of New France. Nearly all of the people in New France were Roman Catholic because Cardinal Richelieu and the king of France had passed a law that only Roman Catholics could settle in New France.

The role of the Church changed when New France became a Royal Colony. Under the trading companies, the Church had been chiefly concerned with missionary work among the Native peoples. After the campaign against the Iroquois, the number of settlers increased and more priests were needed for the people on the seigneuries and in the towns. Education, hospitals, and charity also became Church business. In today's world, few institutions would attempt to deal with so many different responsibilities. Bishop Laval met these needs by bringing in more French priests and starting a seminary at Quebec in 1663. The seminary trained boys born in New France for the priesthood.

The Church held an influential position in the government of the Royal Colony. The bishop was one of the three most important members of the Sovereign Council. This meant that Church opinions were considered whenever decisions about the colony were being made.

The Church's power in New France was limited by the growing independence of the population. When the Church tried to **tithe**, or tax, farm goods as heavily as it did in France, the seigneurs and habitants refused to pay more than one twenty-sixth of their yearly produce. This sharply limited the Church's income in New France.

Tithe—a tax of one-tenth of income or produce of land, paid to help support the work of the Church

78

Religious Role

One of the seigneur's duties was to provide his habitants with a church. These churches were usually small wooden or stone buildings. Each area, or parish, was also supposed to have its own priest. Often there were not enough priests, so one priest would have to travel from parish to parish. The priests performed many services for the people:

- spiritual service—celebrated mass, heard confessions, baptized babies, performed marriages and funerals

- legal service—recorded business transactions, drew up marriage contracts, drew up wills

- government service—registered births and deaths, acted as government officials, relayed government announcements

- personal service—provided the latest news and gossip from other parishes

For the habitants, the church was the centre of religious life and much of their social life. The priests provided community leadership and tried to see that the teachings and wishes of the Roman Catholic Church were followed.

The three main towns each had a church. The church in Quebec was a stone cathedral with an organ and bells. The bishop or another high-ranking priest conducted the mass.

One of the goals of the Roman Catholic Church was to convert the Native peoples to Christianity. Priests and nuns continued to do missionary work throughout the homeland of the First People and on the reserves in New France.

Role in Health Care

The Church was the only institution in New France outside of the family that cared for the sick, the elderly, orphans, and people with disabilities. This type of care usually became the work of the nuns. These women worked very hard in very difficult conditions to ease suffering and help the habitants. The Ursuline nuns established the colony's first hospital in Quebec in 1639. In 1659, they established a hospital in Montreal.

Educational Role

The Church was the only source of education in the Royal Colony. The priests and nuns taught children the Roman Catholic religion, reading and writing in Latin and French, and arithmetic. Many children, especially boys, did not get any schooling at all. In Quebec, Bishop Laval's seminary trained those boys who were planning to enter the priesthood. Boys who were not intending to become priests often remained **illiterate** because they were needed to work on the farms. The shortage of priests also made it

In 1640, most children in New France were taught by their parents. These Native children, being taught by the Ursuline nuns, probably had lessons in the Roman Catholic religion, French, and basic mathematics.

difficult to provide boys with schooling. Girls often received a better education than their brothers. The Ursuline nuns established schools for young Native and French girls at Quebec and Trois Rivières. In Montreal, a nun named Marguerite Bourgeoys started the same type of school for girls (see page 34). Some nuns travelled to the seigneuries to teach the children. In 1676, a boarding school was set up for the daughters of rich merchants and colonists.

In most European countries at this time, women were poorly educated, if they were educated at all. European visitors to New France were often surprised to find that many women of New France were more educated than their husbands.

Canada Revisited

Noël Levasseur (1680–1740)

Noël Levasseur, an artist born in Quebec, carved many of the statues and altars in Quebec's new churches and chapels. He also carved furniture, family coats of arms, and ornamentation for the houses and shops of New France. Handcarved wooden scrolls of the royal coat of arms of France, dating from 1727, are on display in the Quebec museum and in the National Archives of Canada.

Illiterate—able to read or write at a low level of skill or not at all

Madeleine de Verchères (1678–1747)

Madeleine de Verchères was fourth oldest in a family of 12 children. They lived with their parents on the south shore of the St. Lawrence River on a seigneury that had been granted to her father by Intendant Talon. On seeing young Madeleine, one might not have guessed that her decisive and courageous action would serve to fend off a terrifying attack on the seigneury.

Because of the potential of Iroquois attacks, a simple fort had been built on the seigneury. The palisade,* which was approximately 3.5 to 4.5 metres high, had a bastion** at each corner and a single gate. A crude shelter was built inside the fort.

Madeleine was 12 years old at the time of the Iroquois' first attack on the Verchères' seigneury. For two days the Iroquois attacked the fort. Inside, her mother took control. Along with the four men in the fort, she managed to stop the attackers.

Two years later (in 1692) the Iroquois attacked again. This time both Madeleine's parents were absent from the seigneury. Several versions of the events of the second attack have been written. The following primary source, written shortly after the event, describes the second attack.

On 22 Oct. 1692 then, at eight o'clock in the morning, with only one soldier on duty at the fort of Verchères, some Iroquois, who had been hidden in the thickets nearby, suddenly seized some 20 settlers working in the fields. Madeleine, who was 400 paces from the stockade, was pursued and quickly overtaken by an Iroquois who seized her by the kerchief she was wearing around her neck; she loosened it and rushed into the fort, closing the gate behind her. Calling to arms and without stopping to listen to the cries of some women who were distressed at seeing their husbands carried off, she wrote, "I went up on the bastion where the sentry was…. I then transformed myself, putting the soldier's hat on my head, and with some small gestures tried to make it seem that there were people, although there was only this soldier." She fired a round from the gun against the attackers, which "fortunately had all the success I could hope for in warning the neighbouring forts to be on their guard, lest the Iroquois do the same to them."

…the noise of the cannon… "struck [the Iroquois] with terror, upset all their calculations and at the same time signalled all the forts on the north and south shores of the river from Saint-Ours as far as Montreal to be on their guard. With each fort passing the word on up to the next after the first signal from Verchères, up to Montreal, a hundred men were sent to bring it help, which arrived shortly after the Iroquois had disappeared into the woods."

The Iroquois Attack of Fort Verchères. Notice that in this painting Madeleine is still wearing the kerchief around her neck—showing a different version of this historical event than told in this narrative.

*High fence built of pointed stakes
**Section of the fort that extends out to give a better view and aid defence

Right/Below: One of the best ways to see Quebec's historic Lower Town is to take a walking tour or ride in a *calèche** to sites like the Château Frontenac.

Below: Some of the walls of Old Quebec (Vieux-Québec) are still in existence today.

Right: French-Canadian carvings make wonderful souvenirs.

Below: Saint-Jean-Baptiste Day is celebrated on June 24.

*A small, horse-drawn carriage

Review

The icons are your cue to refer to the Learning How to Learn Appendix (pages 256–271) for ideas on how to complete these activities.

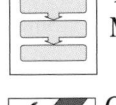 This icon is a reminder to turn to the Research Model (pages x–xi).

Complete a self-assessment for one assignment from this chapter.

Understanding Concepts

Checking Predictions

1. At the beginning of this chapter (see page 54), you made some predictions on what you thought this chapter would be about. Now use what you have learned from reading the chapter to fill in the third column of the Prediction Chart that you began earlier.

2. Refer to the "Questions to Talk About" on page 51. Discuss the questions based on what you have learned about colonial government in New France. Record the important ideas.

Recording Vocabulary

3. Using one of the methods for recording vocabulary, add these words to the WordBook section of your notebook.

- diversify
- sovereign council
- habitant
- king's daughter
- census
- parish
- biography
- analyse
- examine
- evaluate
- conceptualize
- decision-making

Conceptualizing

4. Here are some of the main ideas from the chapter.
   - absolute monarchy
   - colony of New France
   - Royal Government
   - seigneurial system
   - minority rule
   - role of the Church
   - role of women

   Do either a) or b).

   a) 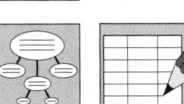 Create a concept poster about one of these ideas. Present your poster to the class.

   b)  Use a web, mind map, outline, or chart to create a permanent set of notes about one of the above ideas. Explain your work to a classmate.

Working with Information

5. 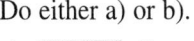 Refer back to the Chapter 3 Focus on page 54. Recall that power and decision-making have been the focus of this chapter. Review all the different examples of power and decision-making found in it. Work with a partner to draw a mind map that organizes all of these examples on one sheet of paper. Show how the desire for power and the methods of decision-making affected the Royal Colony of New France. Use simple line drawings and at least three colours. A sample mind map is shown on page 6 and in the Appendix on page 265. Share your mind map with others in the class.

6. Comparing involves seeing the similarities between two or more items or events.

   a) Refer to pages 50 and 51. Compare the decision-making model you created in For Your Notebook (Question 3 on page 51) with the one used by the coach in the Section III story and the one used by the government in New France. Create a chart by dividing your page into three headings as shown here.

	My Model	Coach's Model	New France Model
1.			
2.			
3.			

b) Using the chart you created, answer the Questions to Talk About on page 51 for each model. Use a coloured pen to mark any answers which are the same for all three models.

c) 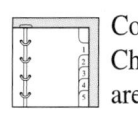 Work with a partner. In your notebook write out the steps one uses in comparing. Share your ideas with another group. As a class, write up the procedures involved in comparing. Add these notes to the Tools of Learning section of your notebook.

d) In chart form, compare the duties of a seigneur and habitant or compare the duties of the governor, bishop, and intendant. Use what you have learned about how to compare to write a comparison paragraph.

7. Add between five and ten entries to the timeline you started on page 48.

8. Compare your notebook to that of a partner. Check to see that items are not missing and are in the correct order. Organize your notes.

Developing Research Skills

9. Research means locating usable information on a topic by following an organized series of steps. A research project involves three main stages: Gathering Information, Examining and Organizing Information, and Presenting Information. As a class, create a list of the steps and activities that might be involved in each of these three stages. Refer to the Research Model shown on pages x–xi of this text. Add to your list. Record this in the Tools of Learning section of your notebook.

10. Decide which of the main topics, concepts, and projects covered in this chapter will require research. Locate some available reference materials and resources which would help your classmates with their projects. List suitable websites, publications, audio-visual resources, and local historic sites. Note that you are not actually completing the research project, but are helping to locate information.

11. Do research to find out more about how the arrival of Europeans in North America affected Native cultures or about how Native cultures affected Europeans.

Developing Communication Skills

Reading

12. Read "Sophie Quesnel" in *Ordinary People in Canada's Past*, Second Edition, by Nancy Sellars Marcotte or read the novel *The King's Daughter* by Suzanne Martel.

13. Ask your librarian to help you find information about the French Carignan-Salières regiment.

Writing

14. 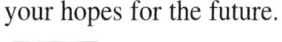 Write a story from the point of view of a "king's daughter" as she sails for New France. Tell about your hopes for the future.

15. In the History Journal section of your notebook, tell which person from this chapter you would like to have met. Why do you find that person interesting?

Listening and Speaking

16. In pairs, brainstorm for a list of effective listening strategies and the qualities of a good listener. Share your ideas. Place your notes in the Tools for Learning section of your notebook.

17. Locate and listen to some traditional French-Canadian music. Play samples of the music and explain its origins to your class.

18. Prepare the story on pages 76 and 77 for oral reading to your class.

19. You are King Louis XIV. Prepare and present a speech defending your right to rule.

20. 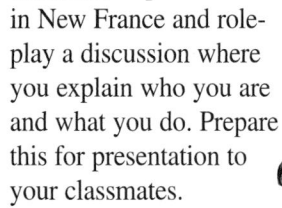 Dress up as one of the three most important officials in New France and role-play a discussion where you explain who you are and what you do. Prepare this for presentation to your classmates.

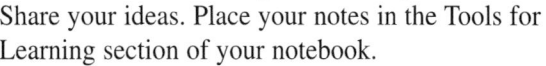

Viewing and Representing

21. In a small group, prepare a series of **tableaus** showing life in New France. Your tableau may represent a picture or a description of a scene found in a story or in your textbook.

22.  With several other people, create a collage that illustrates the decision-making process outlined in this chapter. Use bright illustrations, showing ideas from the Section III story and about New France, to make your work appealing and understandable.

23.  Design a brochure showing all the services provided by the Church in New France.

24. Prepare a game about New France and Royal Government. It may be a board game, card game, role-play game, or computer game.

Applying Concepts

25. You have now had the opportunity to complete various projects. An important step in learning is assessing your work. Complete the following steps alone or with other project participants.

   a) Select one of the projects you completed (e.g., for the Governor's Banquet).
   b) Review the project guidelines. What was the purpose of the project? What were the required parts? List these items on a piece of loose-leaf with the title, Chapter 3 Self-assessment.
   c) Rate your performance on each of the requirements according to how well each was done.

4 = excellent	1 = needs more work
3 = good	0 = not completed
2 = fair	

   d) Look at your highest scores. Think about why you gave yourself a high score for these items. Under the heading "Successes," list three things you would do again on a project.
   e) Look at your lower scores. Think about why you gave yourself a lower score for these items. Under the heading "Areas for Improvement," list three things you will do to improve your next project.
   f) Put this page in the Tools of Learning section of your notebook. Remember to read it again before your next project.

26. Refer to the Absolute Rule Decision-Making Model shown on page 51. Think of circumstances in your experience, or in our world today, in which this type of decision-making has happened or is taking place. When is this appropriate or inappropriate?

27. A French officer, Daumont de Saint-Lusson, reached Sault Ste. Marie on the eastern part of Lake Superior in 1671 and raised a cross, thereby proclaiming all land to the north, south, and west for France.
   a) In your opinion did Daumont de Saint-Lusson have the right to claim this land for France? Explain.
   b) If France had not claimed this land, what other European nation might have claimed it?
   c) How do nations get or claim new territory today?

28. 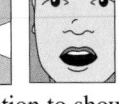 The King of France has just declared New France to be a Royal Colony. Create a visual or written presentation to show the points of view of the following:
   • Member of Company of 100 Associates
   • Iroquoian or Algonquian-speaking person
   • Official in the Roman Catholic Church
   • New settler/farmer

29. 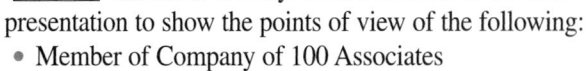 To find out how citizens feel about an issue today, a newspaper might do an opinion poll. An opinion poll was *not* done when fathers in New France were being fined if they had unmarried children of marriageable age.

Tableau—participants represent a scene by taking a position and not moving. This can be based on a picture, story, or idea.

a) Brainstorm for reasons why an opinion poll would *not* be done in New France.

b) What other ways do we learn about people's opinions on an issue in our society?

30. Why have you been studying
   • Royal Government in New France?
   • life on a seigneury?
   • the role of the Church in New France?

31. Try to think of as many ideas as you can for each of the following. Record your answers in the History Journal section of your notebook.
   What if...
   • seigneurs had demanded more dues (*cens et rentes*) and more unpaid labour (*corvée*) from the habitants?
   • the Roman Catholic Church had not played a role in the colony of New France?
   • the Royal Government had not offered incentives (rewards) and penalties (fines) to encourage population growth?

32. Complete each statement with a paragraph entry.

   a) History Journal: I used to think..., but now I think...

   b) Tools of Learning: What helped me understand the information in this chapter was/were...

Challenge Plus

33. Consider the technology available to people living in New France. What special technology did they borrow or develop to adapt to the challenges of their lives? Describe one technology we have today that you think they would have found most useful.

34. Design a website or history magazine for Section III: Colonial Government. Decide how to show important people, places, events, and ideas in an interesting way, to assist other students to understand and appreciate Canadian history. Some items you could create include: fact files, visuals (e.g., maps, illustrations, diagrams), samples of students' work, chapter summaries, study guides and practice quizzes, and games. You might also include an interactive part such as an opinion poll or survey, (and tables and graphs to show the results), a "write-in" question and answer column. Provide a list of related websites and resources.

Canada Revisited

Marguerite d'Youville (1701–1771)

Born at Varennes, Quebec, Marguerite d'Youville was the first person born in Canada to be named a saint by the Roman Catholic Church.

In 1737, d'Youville and four other women dedicated themselves to charity and the service of the poor. These women, known as the Sisters of Charity, or the Grey Nuns, were put in charge of the bankrupt Hospital General. They successfully reorganized the hospital into a home for the elderly, orphans, and homeless women. Today, over 13 000 women have become Grey Nuns. Marguerite d'Youville is the recognized founder of the order of Grey Nuns.

For over 100 years, attempts to have d'Youville canonized drew attention to her miraculous healing powers and prophetic gifts. In December 1990, Pope John Paul II proclaimed Marguerite d'Youville a saint.

Chapter 4
Struggle for Control
(1670–1774)

O v e r v i e w
Use this Overview to predict the events of this chapter.

1755
The French and British struggled to control the western fur territories.

1755
Deportation of the Acadians by the British soldiers.

The French and British fought to control the Atlantic and the colony of Quebec.

British General Wolfe

French General Montcalm

Quebec

Montreal

Louisbourg

1756
Seven Years' War formally declared.

1758 – capture of Louisbourg
1759 – capture of Quebec
1760 – capture of Montreal

Treaty of Paris

- ⊞ British
- ⊟ Spanish
- ⊟ Russian
- ■ French fishing rights
- ⊠ French

1763
British military rule ended French rule in Quebec. Treaty of Paris (a peace treaty) concluded the Seven Years' War.

1774
Britain decided on a policy of keeping Quebec both French and British.

1763
A British Royal Proclamation created original province of Quebec. Britain decided to assimilate the French into the British Empire.

Chapter 4 Focus

Chapters 2 and 3 dealt with New France's early history and the role of France as a colonial power. Chapter 4 is about events (up until 1774) in the conflict that occurred between France and Britain, as each tried to gain control of the area now known as Canada. **Biculturalism**, which developed in Canada as a result of French–English co-operation, will also be introduced. Decision-making and conflict are the focus of Chapter 4.

   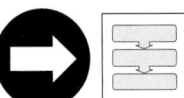

| Power | Co-operation | **Decision-making** | Conflict |

Other Concepts and Main Topics

- British–French rivalry and conflict
- British rule
- British alternatives for ruling the land and the Native and French people

Chapter Preview/Prediction

Examine the Overview found on the previous pages. Look through the chapter headings, pictures, and captions. Think about what you already know about the conflict between the French and the British. Read the Chapter Focus. Notice that decision-making and conflict are the focus of this chapter. List three possible causes of the French–British conflicts covered in this chapter. With a partner, list three decisions the French and British may have been required to make. Also list three questions you have about the topics to be covered. You will refer back to these notes at the end of the chapter.

Continue your class project "Passport to the Past." Choose from the list of people on page 20.

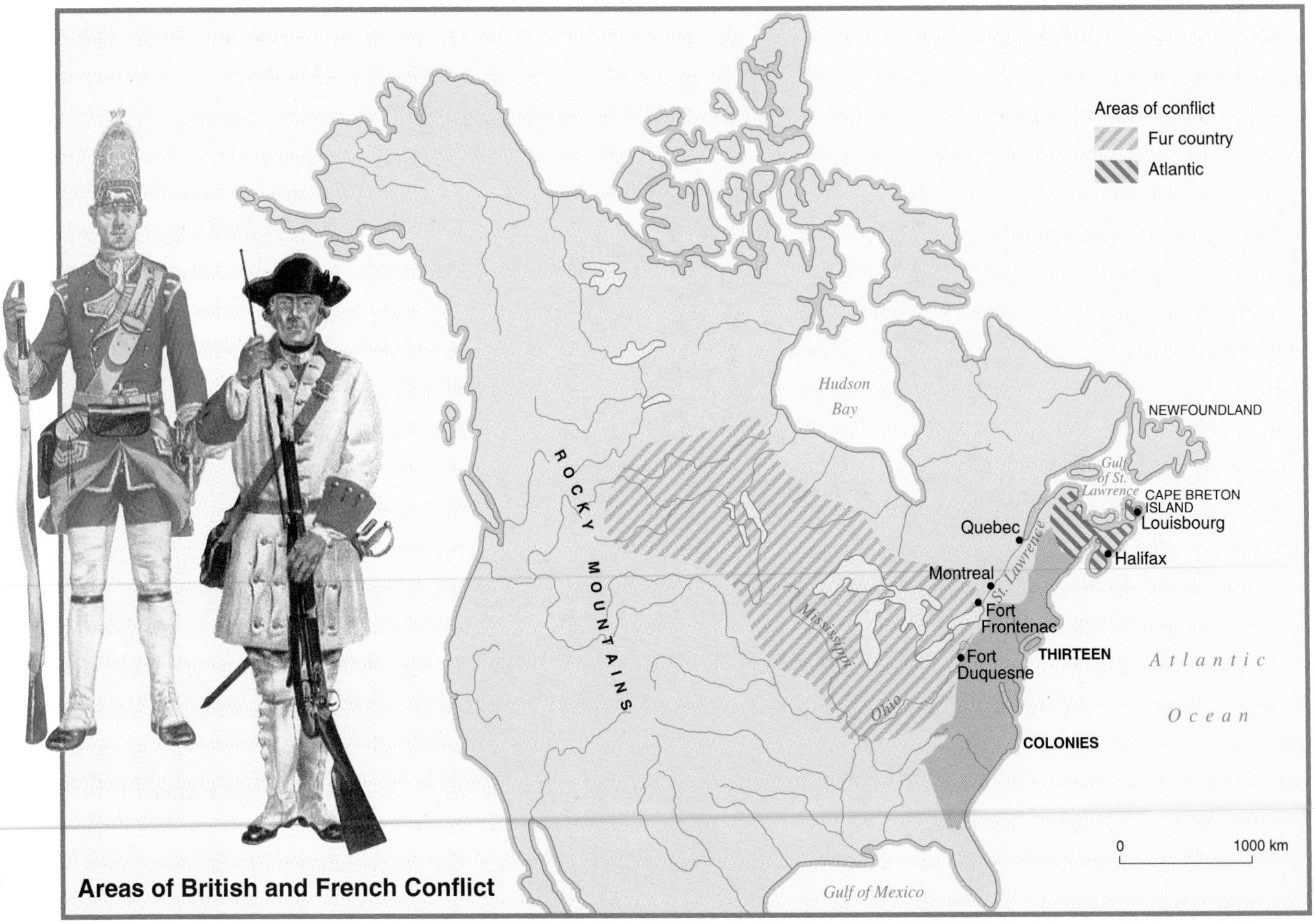

Areas of British and French Conflict

The British and French struggled to control two major areas: the fur country and the Atlantic Coast.

Biculturalism—two cultures existing side by side

Continuing Conflict Between Britain and France

Britain and France had long been at war with one another in Europe. These wars, over land, power, and wealth, eventually spread to North America. When treaties to end the European wars were struck, the effects were felt in North America. Land held by either the French or British changed hands as a result of the treaties. The first chart shows the results of the major wars between Britain and France and the resulting territory changes. The second chart outlines the organization of material in this chapter. Refer to it throughout the chapter to aid your learning.

The Wars between Britain and France

In Europe	In North America	Peace Treaty	Results in North America
War of the League of Augsburg (1688–97)	King William's War (1689–97)	Peace of Ryswick (1697)	• brief end to British–French hostilities
War of the Spanish Succession (1702–13)	Queen Anne's War (1701–13)	Treaty of Utrecht (1713)	• French surrendered forts in territories of Hudson's Bay Co. • French gave up claims to Newfoundland and Acadia • Iroquois declared British subjects • islands of the Gulf of St. Lawrence remained French
War of the Austrian Succession (1740–48)	King George's War (1744–48)	Treaty of Aix-la-Chapelle (1748)	• Louisbourg returned to French
Seven Years' War (1756–63)	French and Indian Wars (1754–63)	Treaty of Paris (1763)	• all French land possessions in North America except tiny islands of St. Pierre and Miquelon off coast of Newfoundland became British

British–French Conflict in North America

There were two main struggles in the attempts of Britain and France to control North America:

Area	Reason for Conflict
• the struggle to control the fur country (west to the Rocky Mountains and in the Ohio Valley) (See map page 88.)	• British desire to control the fur trade and to gain farmland • French desire to control the fur trade and to prevent British expansion into the western part of North America
• the struggle to control the Atlantic (Louisbourg, Halifax, and Acadia) (See map page 88.)	• rich fishing areas and strategic location

The Struggle to Control the Fur Country

Differences between French and British Fur Trade

With the establishment of the Hudson's Bay Company in 1670, the British developed a fur trading system that competed with the French for the wealth of the fur trade. Although both the British and French depended on the Native peoples to supply the furs, the British fur trade was different from the French in two major ways. While the French, under the direction of their Native guides, were exploring farther and farther inland searching for new fur territory, the British waited for the Native people to bring furs to their forts around Hudson Bay.

The second major difference between the British and French fur trade was that the Hudson's Bay Company was formed by a group of merchants who put their money together to share the risks and the profits. They were only interested in profits from the fur trade and had little interest in colonization. The French fur trade was controlled by the government, and colonization was important to France. This was why they developed the seigneuries and sent colonists to New France, and protected the fur trade whenever possible.

Cultural Exchange

Only a small percentage of the Native peoples ever had any direct contact with the Europeans. In spite of this, European products, such as metal weapons, pots, and pans, were available in areas where no Europeans had ever been. In just a few generations the lifestyle of the Native peoples began to change. Many Native peoples lost skills that were required to make their own weapons and utensils. They began to rely on the trade goods of the Europeans. Many hunting bands gave up their nomadic lifestyles of moving from place to place hunting large game and formed new, small family groups, hunting in a smaller region and tanning animal skins for pelts. These pelts were then traded to other Native peoples acting as go-betweens, or to Europeans for European goods, such as guns, ammunition, food, clothing, and metal pots and pans. The lifestyles of the farming and hunting peoples, like the Iroquois, were also affected by contact with Europeans.

The key to French and British success in North America lay in the help they received from Native men and women.*

---

*For more information on Native and European interaction, see page 29.

Animal pelts obtained by the Native peoples were traded for European trade goods, such as guns, metal goods, and clothing.

France Protects the Fur Trade

The French did two things to try to protect the fur trade that was so important to their control in North America. They took military action against the British and they expanded inland.

Military Action Against the British

Armed clashes occurred between the two sides from 1679 to 1713, but neither the British nor the French were able to take complete control of the Hudson Bay area. In 1713, the Treaty of Utrecht ended the European war between the French and British and made all of the Hudson Bay posts British property. The French were no longer allowed to enter the fur territory through Hudson Bay. They had to travel overland from Montreal via the St. Lawrence River and the Great Lakes.

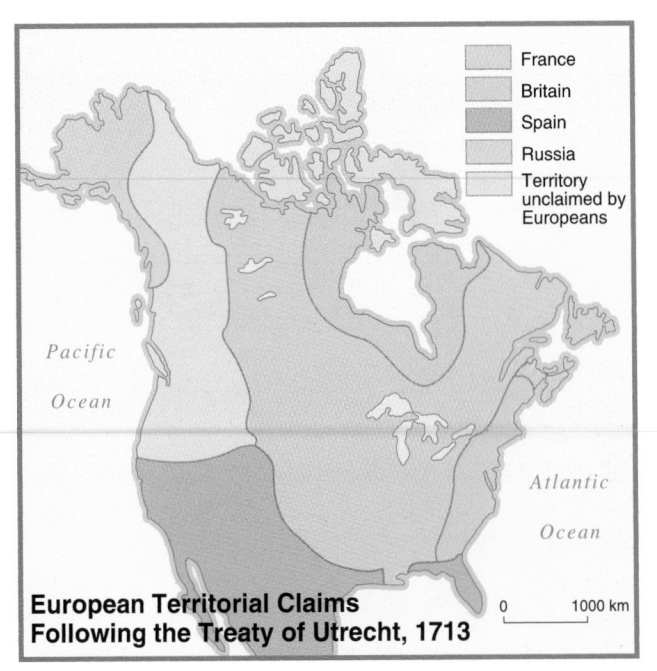

France
Britain
Spain
Russia
Territory unclaimed by Europeans

Pacific Ocean

Atlantic Ocean

European Territorial Claims Following the Treaty of Utrecht, 1713

0   1000 km

Expansion Inland

In the late 1600s, under the direction of Governor Frontenac, New France had expanded south into the Ohio and Mississippi valleys so that it stretched over a vast area from the Gulf of St. Lawrence down to the Gulf of Mexico.

Hoping to stop the Native people from taking their furs to the British trading forts near Hudson Bay, the French sent Pierre La Vérendrye to establish French trading forts inland, closer to the Native people. During the 1730s and early 1740s, La Vérendrye established many French fur trading posts and expanded French control north and west. The Native people began taking their fur pelts to the inland French forts rather than travelling the long distance to Hudson Bay. The British fur trade began to suffer.

Years earlier, the Hudson's Bay Company had sent an explorer, Henry Kelsey, to the interior. Kelsey's journey, which lasted from 1690 to 1692, took him to present-day Saskatchewan and possibly to Alberta. However, Kelsey had not been successful in persuading the Native people to bring their furs to the posts on Hudson Bay.

In 1754 the Hudson's Bay Company sent another trader, Anthony Henday, to the interior. Henday spent the winter of 1754–55 with the Blackfoot in present-day Alberta. However, he also failed to persuade the Plains

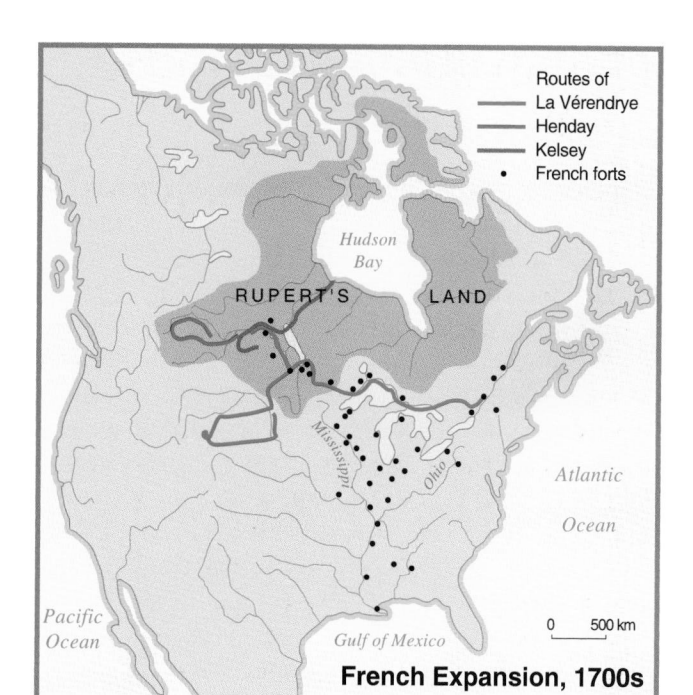

French Expansion, 1700s

Routes of
La Vérendrye
Henday
Kelsey
• French forts

people to travel to the Hudson's Bay Company forts on Hudson Bay. Henday recommended that the Hudson's Bay Company build trading forts inland, but this did not occur until 1774.

Kelsey hunting buffalo with the Assiniboine. Kelsey was the first European to see large herds of buffalo grazing on the Prairies.

The Struggle to Control the Atlantic

In addition to their attempts to control the fur trade, Britain and France also struggled to control the Atlantic coast of North America.

Louisbourg

The struggle to control the Atlantic coast was concentrated on the French colonies of Île Royale (Cape Breton Island) and Acadia. Île Royale was important because Louisbourg, the centre of French power, was located there.

When France and Britain signed the Treaty of Utrecht in 1713, France lost Acadia and the colony of Newfoundland. (See map page 90.) Newfoundland had been an extremely important fishery as it was located close to the Grand Banks, an excellent fishing area. The French were left with Île St. Jean (Prince Edward Island), St. Pierre and Miquelon, and Île Royale. The French moved their Newfoundland fishing operations to these islands for a time, but since fishing was such a profitable business, they needed a much larger fishing base in the New World. A location on Cape Breton Island (Île Royale) was selected and construction began on Louisbourg in 1720.

Louisbourg was much more than a fishing station. The French needed a military and naval base from which they could control the Gulf of St. Lawrence and guard the approaches to New France. The fortress, which was built on a natural harbour, was not only impressive, but also thought to be impossible to break into. Besides a fortress, Louisbourg was also an important royal capital, a French naval base, and a thriving centre of commerce.

The British saw Louisbourg as a threat to their control in North America, despite its flaws. (Although reputed to be strong, Louisbourg was poorly constructed and it was surrounded by hills from which an enemy could attack.) The colonists in New England (see map page 58) demanded protection from the French and the Native peoples, so the British constructed the fortress of Halifax in 1749 (see page 95).

Louisbourg remained an important French fortress from 1719 until 1760. Twice within this time—1745 and 1758—it was captured by the British. In the attack of 1745, William Pepperell led 4000 New Englanders from Boston. They approached Louisbourg from land and were able to capture the fortress in 46 days. Although the fortress was returned to the French in 1748 through the Treaty of Aix-la-Chapelle, the British had learned that Louisbourg could be conquered.

Above: The *fleur-de-lis* marked the buildings of King Louis XIV and King Louis XV.

Louisbourg was one of the major military fortresses in the New World. The military citadel dominated the town from the top of the largest hill. This citadel housed a garrison of several hundred soldiers, a prison, and a chapel.

Focus On: Louisbourg (Canada Revisited)

The photographs on pages 92 and 93 show the reconstructed Louisbourg. Louisbourg was one of the busiest seaports in the New World. Ships from the French navy and merchant ships (private trading vessels) from France made frequent trips to and from Louisbourg. Merchant ships from Quebec, New England, the West Indies, and England arrived at Louisbourg on a yearly basis to unload their cargoes of building materials, hardware, fishing supplies, clothing, food, and passengers. These same ships then picked up cargoes of dried and salted fish for delivery to the markets of Europe. In the harbour area there were many inns, taverns, and shops.

Above: Louisbourg had a number of wealthy residents, such as the governor and other high-ranking officials. There was a growing middle class of innkeepers and merchants. Many poorer people worked as servants and labourers.

Left: The majority of the population in the town consisted of young, single men. They worked in the fishing industry or were soldiers from the garrison.

Above: An occasional Micmaq could be seen in the town visiting from the interior of the island on which Louisbourg was built.

Right: Fishing was a major industry at Louisbourg as it was located close to the Grand Banks. These waters were visited by hundreds of European fishing ships each year. The fish were dried on wooden racks.

Note: Visit the Parks Canada website for a list of various historic sites, including the Fortress of Louisbourg. The address is http://parkscanada.pch.gc.ca/

93

An Exercise in Problem Solving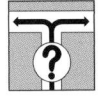

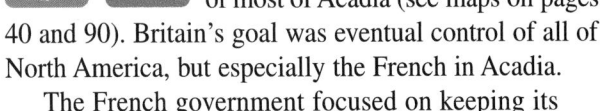 As a result of the Treaty of Utrecht (1713), Great Britain gained control of most of Acadia (see maps on pages 40 and 90). Britain's goal was eventual control of all of North America, but especially the French in Acadia.

The French government focused on keeping its remaining territory in New France (Île St. Jean, St. Pierre and Miquelon, and Île Royale where Louisbourg had been built).*

The French missionary Jean-Louis Le Loutre was especially influential in keeping Acadia French. Trained as a priest in France, Le Loutre (1709–1772) came to Louisbourg in 1737 to do missionary work among the Micmaq. But it was his efforts to keep the Acadians both Roman Catholic and loyal to the French that had the greatest influence. Le Loutre believed almost any tactic was permissible to make sure the Acadians retained their Catholic faith. For almost 18 years, he was influential in controlling the Micmaq and directing their hostility against the British. During this time he managed to escape being caught by the British, even though they offered a reward for his capture.

1. Look at the picture of Louisbourg above. Imagine you are Le Loutre and have just arrived in Louisbourg. The year is 1737. You see many Acadians in town. They are trading food for goods they can't grow or make themselves. You will be leaving soon to establish a mission among the Micmaq. You are curious about how the Acadians and Micmaq live.

Work as a triad to carry out the following exercise.

a) One of you takes the role of Le Loutre: write up a series of questions you wish to ask the Acadians and the Micmaq. The other two take the roles of an Acadian and a Micmaq. Anticipate what Le Loutre will ask you and carry out research by reading pages 96 and 97 on the Acadians and pages 12 and 13 on the Algonquian Nations, which included the Micmaq.

b) Le Loutre should write up a list of ways to meet the goals of French policy. The Micmaq and the Acadians should each present support for or concerns about Le Loutre's plans.

---

*In addition to the remaining lands in North America, the French still controlled colonies in the Caribbean. They planned to carry out trade between New France and the Caribbean colonies and focused on making as much money as possible from their colonies.

The British Build Halifax

Just as the British and French took action to counteract the other's control of the fur trade, each took action to control the Atlantic region. The French built Louisbourg in 1720 and the British began building the fortress of Halifax in 1749. The fortress, built on a harbour, was designed to provide protection for the British colonists in New England from Native and French raids. Halifax became a powerful British base.

Halifax was built differently from Louisbourg. It was a townsite surrounded by five stockades rather than a fortified stone city like Louisbourg. A stockade is a fort or a camp defended by a wall of strong upright posts. Halifax did not need to be a stone fort because it was located at the end of a narrow sea passage that could be easily defended.

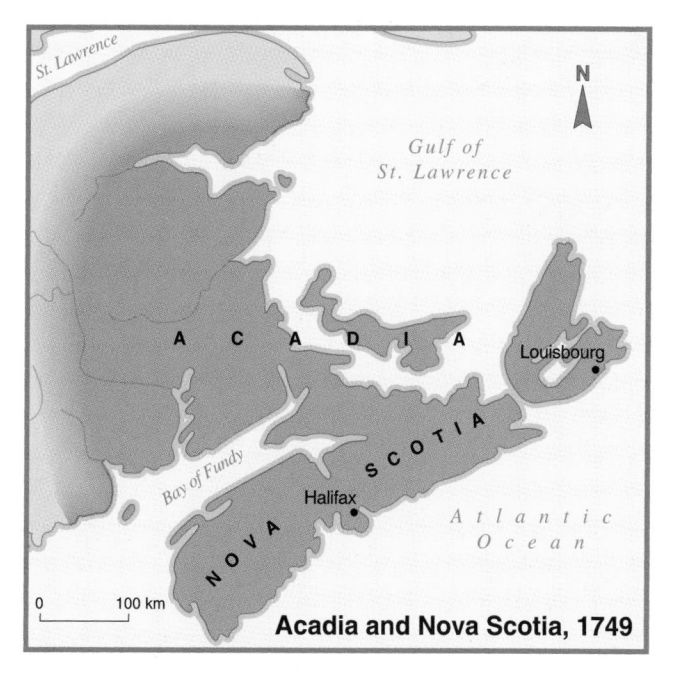

Acadia and Nova Scotia, 1749

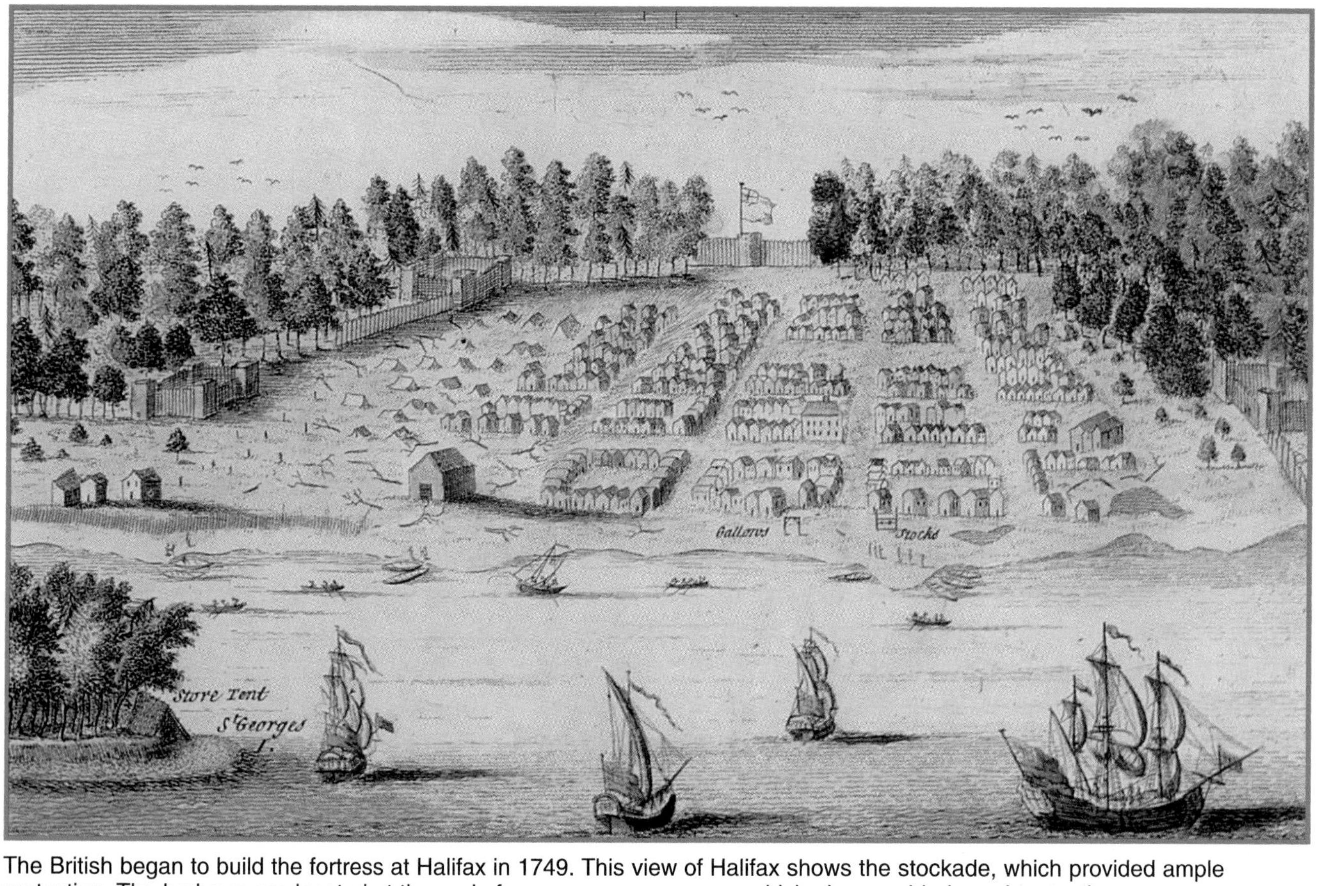

The British began to build the fortress at Halifax in 1749. This view of Halifax shows the stockade, which provided ample protection. The harbour was located at the end of a narrow sea passage, which also provided good protection.

Acadia

 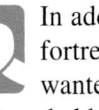

In addition to wanting to control the fortress of Louisbourg, the British wanted to take over and control the remaining territory held by the French in Acadia. Paul Mascarene played an important part in helping the British carry out their goals.

Paul Mascarene (1684–1760)

Born and raised as a Protestant in France, Paul Mascarene moved to England when he was in his early twenties. He joined the English army, where his ability to speak French made him a great asset. Mascarene was assigned to an administrative position at Annapolis Royal (formerly Port Royal) in 1739, primarily due to his ability to speak French.

It was his responsibility to hear and settle disputes among the French-speaking Acadian population. His knowledge of the French language and culture was an asset. Mascarene sympathized with the Acadians. He treated them fairly, but to the Acadians he remained a symbol of their enemy—the British. He believed in the British way of life but he was unable to convince the Acadians of its value, or persuade them to switch their loyalty to Britain. However, with a small group of British troops, he did manage to control and govern the Acadians.

British–French Conflict Continues

When the Roman Catholic priest Father Le Loutre (see page 94) arrived in Louisbourg in 1737, hostilities between France and Great Britain had been brought to an end by the Treaty of Utrecht. The British controlled the area except for Louisbourg. Le Loutre remained on friendly terms with the British at first. King George's War broke out in 1744 (see page 89) and tensions between the Acadians and the British became high once again. Mascarene and his English troops managed to defend Annapolis Royal against two attacks by the French. Most of the Acadians remained neutral. After Louisbourg was captured by the British in 1745, the French were without official government leadership in Acadia. During this time most of the French-speaking Acadians continued to remain neutral. Encouraged by Le Loutre, the Micmaq fought for France against the British.

With the signing of the Aix-la-Chapelle peace treaty in 1748, Louisbourg was returned to the French (see page 89). As a response, the British expanded their military presence in the area. Halifax was built in 1749 (see page 95). Treaties were signed between the British and the Micmaq. When Le Loutre heard about these treaties he tried to persuade the Micmaq to break the peace. In the years that followed, Le Loutre continued to encourage Acadian resistance against the British.

In this painting by Lewis Parker, we see Le Loutre in 1754 with two Micmaq at Fort Beausejour, a French fort in Acadia.

Le Loutre is said to have told the Acadians that the British would force them to give up their Catholic religion. He said that if the Acadian men didn't fight the British their priests, wives, and children would be sent elsewhere, and he would abandon them. He urged them to move to French-occupied areas. Most Acadians did not follow Le Loutre's advice, even when he told them he would have the Micmaq destroy their farms and homes.

Many historians believe that Le Loutre truly thought the Acadians were ready to fight the British. He thought they would give up their land and move elsewhere rather than sign an unconditional **oath of allegiance** to the British and lose their religion. He continued to encourage the Micmaq to carry out attacks against British settlers or soldiers.

Oath of Allegiance

After the Treaty of Utrecht the French Acadians had a year to leave the area. During the years of British control in the Atlantic, hostilities continued between British and French forces in Europe and North America. There were many attempts by British administrators to get the Acadian population to submit to British authority, but most of the Acadian population remained neutral. The governor of Nova Scotia tried to get them to sign an oath, but the Acadians insisted on remaining neutral. They were afraid that if they signed the oath, they would have to fight for the British against the French and the Micmaq. In 1730, when Governor Phillipps assured them they would not be expected to fight for Britain, over 500 Acadian men (only a small fraction of the population) agreed to sign the following oath.

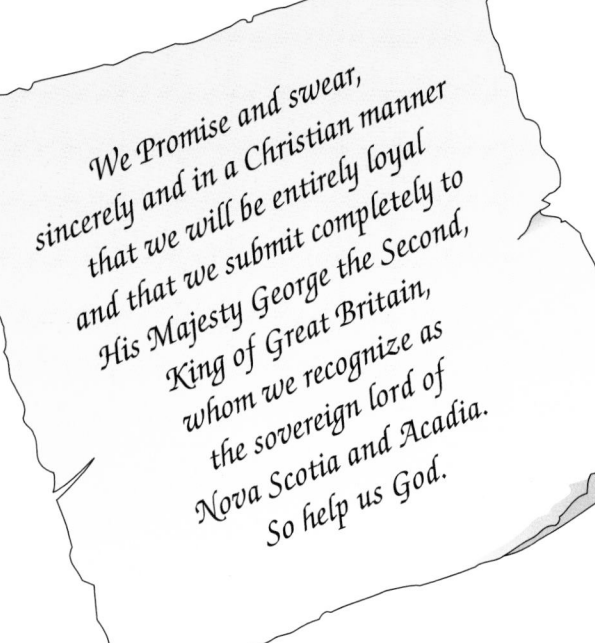

We Promise and swear, sincerely and in a Christian manner that we will be entirely loyal and that we submit completely to His Majesty George the Second, King of Great Britain, whom we recognize as the sovereign lord of Nova Scotia and Acadia. So help us God.

Oath of allegiance—a promise of loyalty to a country and/or ruler

An Exercise in Decision-Making

By the 1750s it seemed that there would be another war between France and Britain in Europe. Governor Lawrence decided that the Acadians must again be asked to pledge their loyalty to Britain. They refused. Governor Lawrence had to make a decision. What was to be done with the Acadians? What would you do? Read the imaginary comments below.

Acadian

We've lived here peacefully for over 40 years and have proven we are not a threat to the British. Besides, this wouldn't be the first time we refused to sign such an unconditional oath.

British Governor Lawrence

France and Britain will soon be at war in Europe. That will mean more French–British conflict in the North American colonies. You Acadians must take an oath of allegiance to Britain so we can be sure you will fight for us and not help the French. If you don't take the oath, you must suffer the consequences.

Making the Decision

In small groups, decide what Governor Lawrence should do. Use the steps shown in the Decision-making model on page 262 of the Appendix. Be prepared to defend your choice.

Find out more about Acadians at this website:
http://www.schoolnet.ca/
Choose Digital Collections and then Social Studies to find "The Acadian Odyssey."

The Deportation of the Acadians

The British were concerned about the number of French settlers in Acadia compared to the number of British settlers there. The Acadians were asked again to take an oath of allegiance to the British or they would be **deported**. They refused to take the oath, and in 1755 the British began to deport them from their lands and put them aboard British ships. They were taken to the Thirteen Colonies and to Louisiana. Their homes were burnt and all of their property was **confiscated** by the British. Some people were sent back to France and some escaped to Cape Breton Island. Many died in the deportation. Many families were separated and never saw each other again. Some of the Acadians did return many years later. The major deportation of the Acadians happened in 1755, but it continued until 1762. It is estimated that as many as 11 000 Acadians were deported during this time.

The Deportation of the Acadians from the Isle of St. Jean, by Lewis Parker, shows the Acadians being forced from their homes.

For Your Notebook

1. Were Governor Lawrence's orders to deport the Acadians too harsh? Why do you think he made the decisions he did?

2. Read the poem "Evangeline" by Longfellow. You may need to ask your librarian for help to locate the poem. As you read, imagine how Evangeline and her family and friends must have felt as they were separated from their homes and loved ones.

3. The Acadians were not prepared for the consequences of their refusal to take an oath of allegiance to the British. Do you think they would still have refused if they had known that Governor Lawrence planned deportation? Discuss in a group.

4. Today there is a large Acadian population in New Brunswick and in Louisiana (the Cajuns). (See map on page 32.) How do you think this came about?

Deport—to remove or move away; to force people away from their homes or a country by government order

Confiscated—property taken away by someone in authority, usually by a government

Acadian Resistance

Charles de Boishébert (1727–1797) first went to Acadia from Quebec as a young soldier of 19. In following years, he fought many battles to protect French settlements from the British. In 1754, he took command of Fort La Tour on the Saint John River. When the British captured the fort, Boishébert escaped, disguised as a settler.

In 1755, the British forced thousands of Acadians to leave their lands. Boishébert took to the woods and led the settlers in resistance. Here is his story, as one of his followers might have told it.

"Our people are farmers, not fighters. Most of us come from farms that our families have owned for more than 100 years. All we wanted was to be left alone to work our land in peace.

"Then the British came. They wanted us to swear loyalty to their king, perhaps even to fight other Frenchmen. Our priests told us to refuse, and we obeyed.

"My village is called Petitcodiac. In September 1755, we heard the British were on their way to attack us. They planned to destroy our village and burn our farms. Then they would herd us like cattle onto ships and send us far from our homes.

"By September 3, the British were almost upon us. Like a miracle, help arrived. Charles de Boishébert came out of the woods to save us. He led a rough band of Micmac warriors and ragged Acadian farmboys.

"Boishébert was outnumbered, but he fought like a demon. The battle raged for three long hours. At last the British fled, leaving many dead behind them. Boishébert had lost only one man.

"Boishébert asked the young men of our village to join his band of fighters. I agreed at once, and so did others. Then he gathered up some of the poorest families from our district to lead us back to the Saint John River, where other farmers had gathered for protection.

"For the next two years, we harassed the British until they did not dare to leave their forts. I learned to move silently in the woods like a Micmac warrior. I learned to strike without warning and take my enemy by surprise.

"As time passed, food became more scarce. Many farms had been burned, and crops were poor from those that remained. Boishébert had many hungry families to feed. He set up a refugee centre on the Miramichi and tried to build more farms there. But I suppose, deep in our hearts, we knew we were doomed to failure."

—from *Great Canadian Lives: Portraits in Heroism to 1867* by Karen Ford
Reprinted with permission of ITP Nelson

Exploring Further

Primary source excerpts and historical stories often reflect only the point of view of one person involved in an event.

1. According to the character in this story, why did the Acadians refuse to swear loyalty to the British king?

2. What reasons might other Acadians have given?

3. Was the character in this story initially a British supporter, French supporter, or neutral? How did this change?

4. Write a story with a new character showing how his or her point of view differs from that in this story.

Focus On: Allegiance (Canada Revisited)

Today in Canada, people may voluntarily pledge an oath of loyalty to the Queen and to Canada for a variety of reasons, such as taking an elected position in government or joining the military. A person from another country who wishes to become a Canadian citizen must apply to Citizenship and Immigration Canada. If the applicant meets all of the requirements, he or she will be asked to swear the Oath of Citizenship shown below.

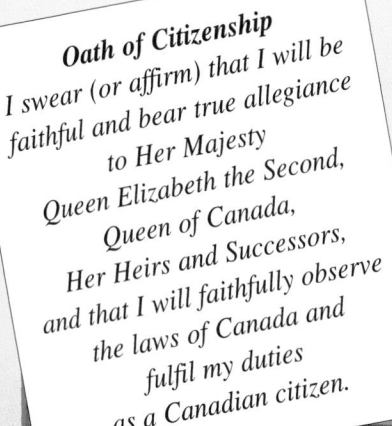

Oath of Citizenship

I swear (or affirm) that I will be faithful and bear true allegiance to Her Majesty Queen Elizabeth the Second, Queen of Canada, Her Heirs and Successors, and that I will faithfully observe the laws of Canada and fulfil my duties as a Canadian citizen.

Exploring Further

1. What does it mean to be a Canadian citizen? What rights are involved? What duties and responsibilities are involved?

2. When taking an Oath of Citizenship in Canada, a person swears "true allegiance" to the Queen and to Canada.

   a) What does allegiance mean in this case?

   b) In what ways are people asked to show their allegiance to Canada? How do you show your allegiance to Canada?

   c) Think of times or situations when people are asked to pledge allegiance, other than to their ruler or country. Compare the expectations of this type of allegiance to allegiance to a country.

   d) Is allegiance a feeling or behaviour?

3. Create a concept poster to represent one of the following:

   - your ideas and beliefs about citizenship

   - your ideas and beliefs about allegiance

   - ideas and examples about allegiance related to your study of Canadian history (for example, the Acadians)

Below:
Before receiving their certificate of Canadian citizenship, people are asked to swear the oath of citizenship at a special ceremony.

Final Struggle for Control of North America

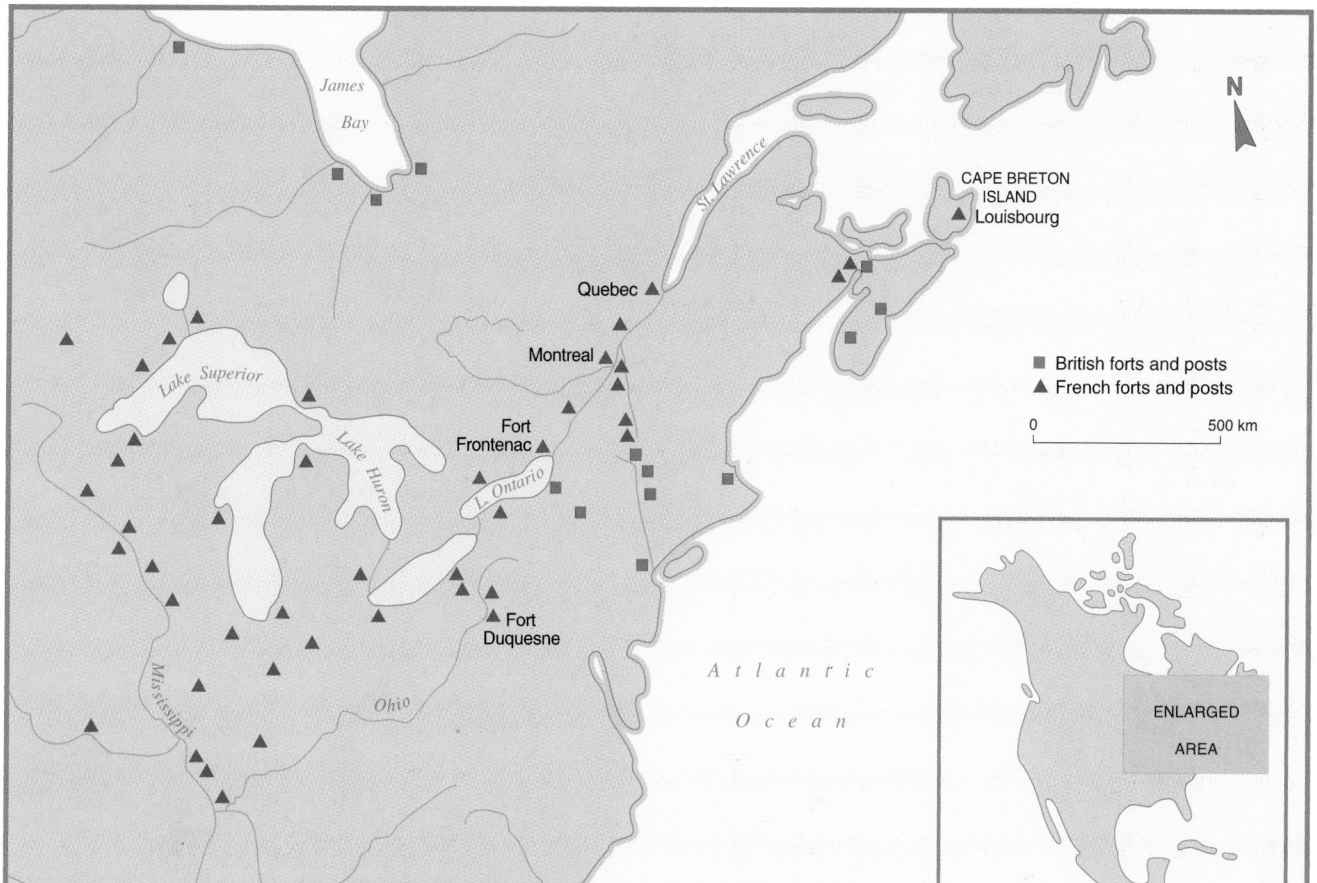

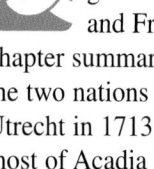

British and French Forts in North America Before the Seven Years' War

We have seen that there was a continuing struggle for control in the New World between Britain and France. The chart at the beginning of the chapter summarizes this conflict. These struggles caused the two nations to go to war in Europe. The Treaty of Utrecht in 1713 gave Newfoundland, Hudson Bay, and most of Acadia to the British. The French reacted by building the fortress of Louisbourg on Cape Breton Island and the Acadians refused to take an oath of allegiance to Britain. When the deportation of the Acadians occurred in 1755, it was clear that France and Britain would soon be at war again in Europe and that conflict between the two empires would increase in North America. One year later, in 1756, the Seven Years' War broke out in Europe between France and Britain. This war had an enormous effect on the history of North America.

The French and the English used different strategies in their struggle to control North America. The French kept most of their soldiers in Europe. Their plan was to use a small number of soldiers to fight the many British in North America. They believed that if fewer French soldiers in North America could keep a large number of British occupied, then the larger French forces in Europe could defeat the British there.

The British were determined to defeat the French in North America. They sent seven or eight times more men than the French did to North America. They planned to attack the French on three fronts: Louisbourg, the Ohio Valley, and Quebec. (See above map.) The British knew that it was important to control the St. Lawrence River because this was the route that French supply ships used to reach Quebec and Montreal. Control of the St. Lawrence depended on the control of Louisbourg.

For Your Notebook

1. Use the map above to decide what effect the British strategy would have on the French colonies of Louisbourg, Acadia, and Quebec.

War in North America: A Three-Pronged Attack

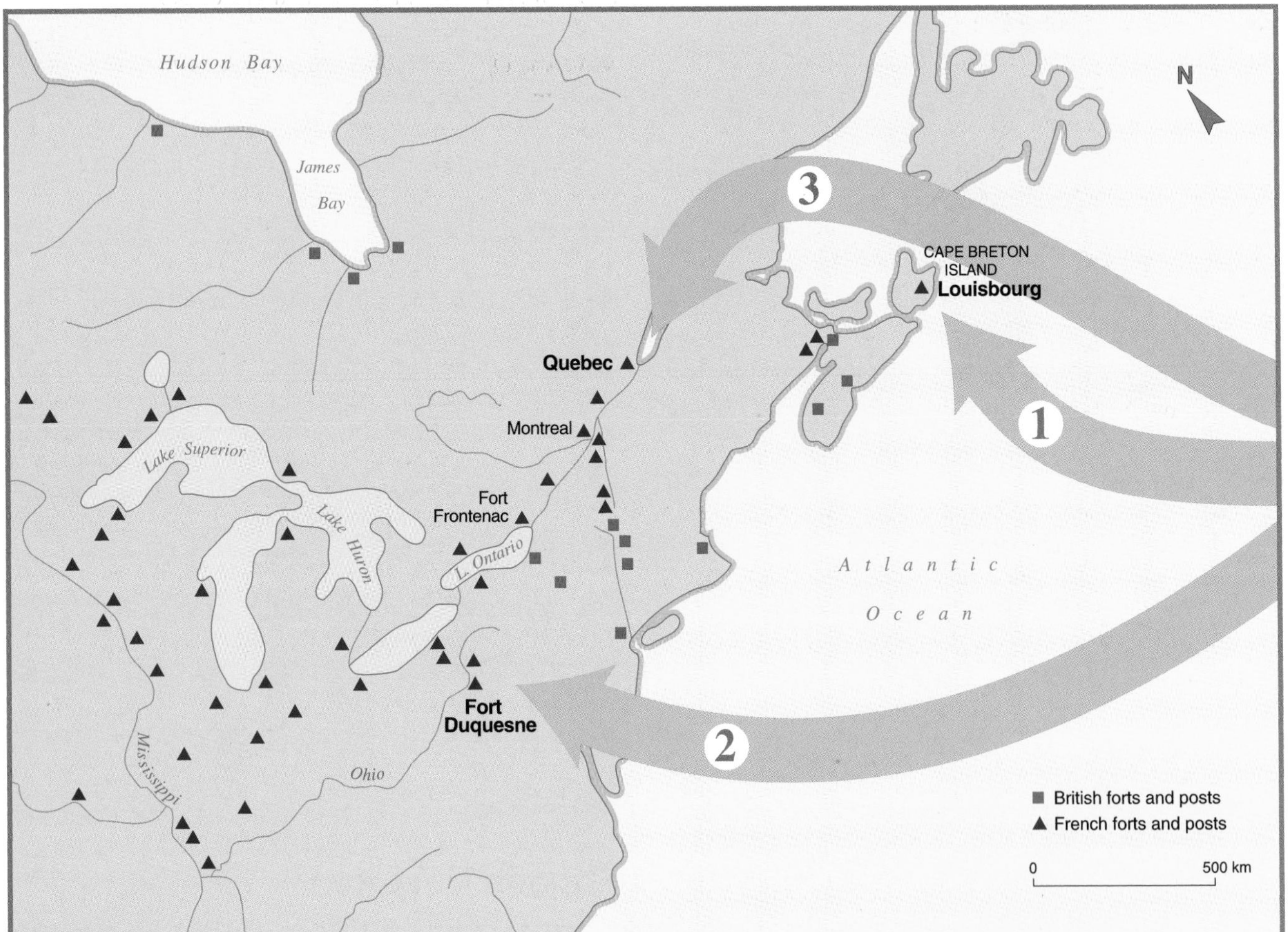

British Attacks on the French During the Seven Years' War

During the Seven Years' War, the British attacked the French in three areas: Louisbourg (1758), the Ohio Valley (1758), and Quebec (1759).

1. The Capture of Louisbourg

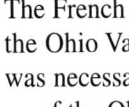

The British needed to capture Louisbourg in order to gain control of the entrance to the St. Lawrence River. If successful, they could sail down the river to attack Quebec.

In June of 1758, the British attacked Louisbourg. Imagine the surprise of the French inside the fortress when they saw 200 British ships in the harbour outside their fortification. The battles did not last very long. After fighting for almost 60 days, the British landed on the high ground overlooking Louisbourg and bombarded the fortress. By the time the French surrendered, Louisbourg had been almost completely destroyed by the British.

2. The Capture of the Ohio Valley

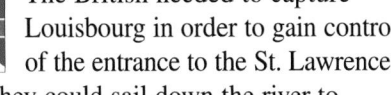

The French had many fur forts in the Ohio Valley. British control was necessary to reduce French influence in the large area of the Ohio Valley.

Prior to the fall of Louisbourg, the French had been successful in defending the Ohio Valley. This situation changed quickly with the fall of Louisbourg in July of 1758. In August, Fort Frontenac, a French fort near Lake Ontario, was captured by the British, followed in November by Fort Duquesne in the Ohio Valley. With the French driven back toward Quebec by the British and with Louisbourg captured, the British now were free to travel down the St. Lawrence to the heart of New France—Quebec.

3. The Capture of Quebec

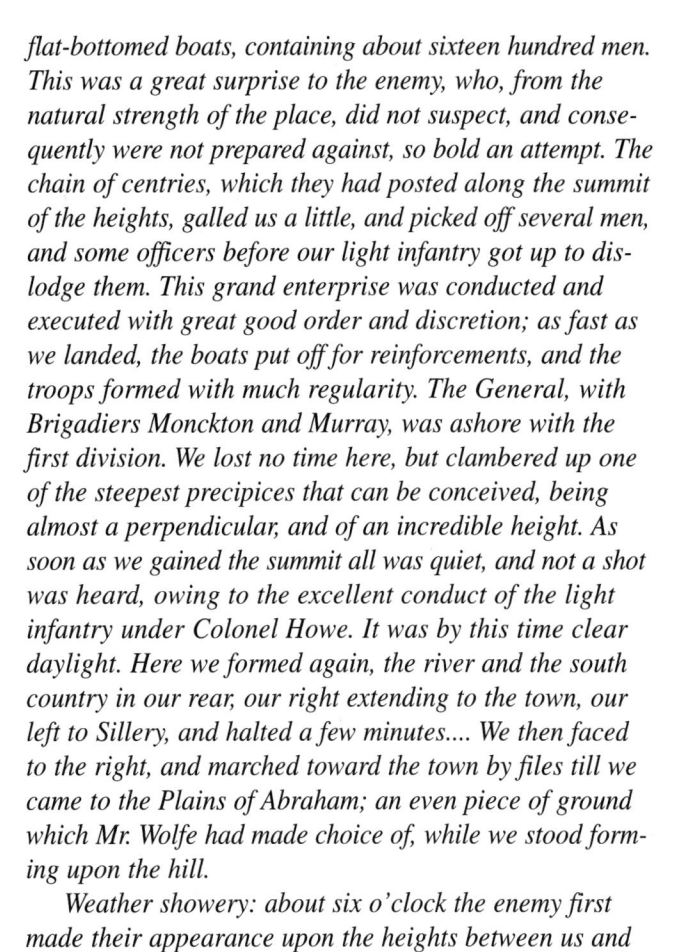

Quebec was the centre of French power in North America. British capture of the colony of Quebec would mean the end of French control in North America. The British, under the command of General James Wolfe, waited until the spring of 1759 to attack Quebec. Over the summer the British fleet sailed up the St. Lawrence and bombarded the city of Quebec from the water, while the British troops tried to land on the Beauport shore. Wolfe tried for almost three months to capture Quebec without much success. He finally decided to attack from upriver to cut off the source of Quebec's supplies.

The British Attack

British Captain John Knox described the first part of the attack on Quebec City in his journal as follows.

Eyewitness Account

Thursday, September 13, 1759.

Before daybreak this morning, we made a descent upon the north shore, about half a quarter of a mile to the eastward of Sillery; and the light troops were fortunately, by the rapidity of the current, carried lower down, between us and Cape Diamond. We had in this debarkation thirty flat-bottomed boats, containing about sixteen hundred men. This was a great surprise to the enemy, who, from the natural strength of the place, did not suspect, and consequently were not prepared against, so bold an attempt. The chain of centries, which they had posted along the summit of the heights, galled us a little, and picked off several men, and some officers before our light infantry got up to dislodge them. This grand enterprise was conducted and executed with great good order and discretion; as fast as we landed, the boats put off for reinforcements, and the troops formed with much regularity. The General, with Brigadiers Monckton and Murray, was ashore with the first division. We lost no time here, but clambered up one of the steepest precipices that can be conceived, being almost a perpendicular, and of an incredible height. As soon as we gained the summit all was quiet, and not a shot was heard, owing to the excellent conduct of the light infantry under Colonel Howe. It was by this time clear daylight. Here we formed again, the river and the south country in our rear, our right extending to the town, our left to Sillery, and halted a few minutes.... We then faced to the right, and marched toward the town by files till we came to the Plains of Abraham; an even piece of ground which Mr. Wolfe had made choice of, while we stood forming upon the hill.

Weather showery: about six o'clock the enemy first made their appearance upon the heights between us and the town; whereupon we halted and wheeled to the right, thereby forming the line of battle....

Canada Revisited

Today there is a park on the Plains of Abraham, the site of the 1759 battle between the French and the British.

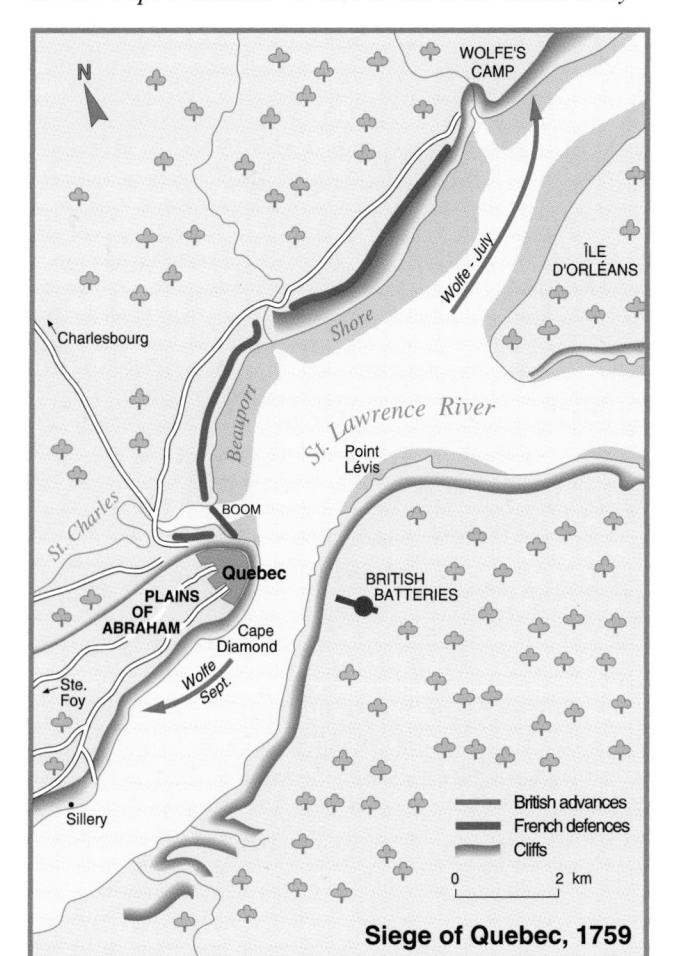

Siege of Quebec, 1759

The French React

In the early morning of September 13, 1759, Montcalm, the leader of the French forces in Quebec, received word that the British army, by a surprise plan, had landed its troops over a poorly defended cliff upstream from Quebec City at Anse aux Foulons. Wolfe's soldiers were waiting on the Plains of Abraham, three kilometres from Quebec City.

The French forces under the command of the Marquis de Montcalm were not all gathered in one place. A portion of the army was 16 kilometres away on the Beauport shore, where it was expected that the British would attack. Montcalm had to decide:

- Should he keep his army in the fortified town of Quebec and wait for the British to attack?

- Should he send word to the rest of his army to attack the British from behind?

- Should he attack immediately, with the men he had, on the Plains of Abraham?

The Battle on the Plains of Abraham

Montcalm took his men and went to meet the British on the open fields of the Plains of Abraham. The French troops were at a disadvantage because they were used to fighting in the forest, not open fields. They made a disorganized charge on the British, who waited until they were near and then fired on them, causing the French ranks to break and retreat in disorder. In less than an hour the battle was over. Both Wolfe and Montcalm died from wounds received in the fighting. Quebec had been taken by the British.

British Captain Knox's Eyewitness Account of the Battle Continues:

The enemy had now likewise formed the line of battle, and got some cannon to play on us, with round and canister shot; but what galled us most was a body of Indians and other marksmen they had concealed in the corn opposite to the front of our right wing, and a coppice that stood opposite to our centre, inclining toward our left. But Colonel Hale, by Brigadier Monckton's orders, advanced some platoons alternately, from the forty-seventh regiment, which after a few rounds obliged these skulkers to retire. We were now ordered to lie down, and remained some time in this position. About eight o'clock we had two pieces of short brass six-pounders playing on the enemy, which threw them into some confusion, and obliged them to alter their disposition; and Montcalm formed them into three large columns. About nine the two armies moved a little nearer each other. The light cavalry made a faint attempt upon our parties at the battery of Sillery, but were soon beat off; and Monsieur de Bougainville, with his troops from Cape Rouge, came

down to attack the flank of our second line, hoping to penetrate there. But by a masterly disposition of Brigadier Townshend, they were forced to desist; and the third battalion of Royal Americans was then detached to the first ground we had formed on after we gained the heights, to preserve the communication with the beach and our boats. About ten o'clock the enemy began to advance briskly in three columns, with loud shouts and recovered arms, two of them inclining to the left of our army, and the third towards our right, firing obliquely at the two extremities of our line, from the distance of one hundred and thirty,—until they came within forty yards; which our troops withstood with the greatest intrepidity and firmness, still reserving their fire and paying the strictest obedience to their officers. This uncommon steadiness, together with the havoc which the grape-shot from our field-pieces made among them, threw them into some disorder, and was most critically maintained by a well-timed, regular, and heavy discharge of our small arms, such as they could no longer oppose. Hereupon they gave way, and fled with precipitation, so that, by the time the cloud of smoke was vanished our men were again loaded and, profiting by the advantage we had over them, pursued them almost to the gates of the town and the bridge over the little river, redoubling our fire with great eagerness, making many Officers and men prisoners....

Our joy at this success is inexpressibly damped by the loss we sustained of one of the greatest heroes which this or any other age can boast of—GENERAL JAMES WOLFE, who received his mortal wound, as he was exerting himself at the head of the grenadiers....

The Officers who are prisoners say, that Quebec will surrender in a few days: some deserters, who came out to us in the evening, agree in that opinion, and inform us, that the Sieur de Montcalm is dying, in great agony, of a wound he received today in their retreat....

An Exercise in Decision-Making

1. Why do you think Montcalm made the decision he did?

2. What decision would you have made if you were Montcalm? Use one of the decision-making models from this textbook, or design one of your own, to help you arrive at a decision.

A View of the Taking of Quebec, September 13, 1759—Quebec falls to the British. This painting shows a view of the day's events as though they were all happening at once, but really the events took place from late at night until the following morning.

Montreal

After the British took Quebec, the French army and officials retreated to Montreal. The British occupied Quebec over the winter. The French made an attempt to drive the British from Quebec in the spring of 1760. They marched from Montreal to Quebec and were able to force the British to retreat behind the town's walls. The outcome of the struggle for Quebec now depended on whether the first ship through the St. Lawrence that spring brought British or French reinforcements. The first ship to come was British and the French retreated to Montreal again.

In September 1760 the British troops marched to Montreal, burning crops along the St. Lawrence River as they advanced. The French governor, Vaudreuil, realizing future resistance attempts were futile, agreed to peace and surrendered to the British troops. Chevalier de Lévis, the commander of the French army, rather than surrendering the French flags to the enemy, ordered that they be burned. British control in North America was finally achieved.

Surrender of Montreal. On September 8, 1760, Governor General Pierre de Rigaud de Vaudreuil de Cavagnial surrendered Montreal to the British commander, Jeffrey Amherst.

Louis-Joseph, Marquis de Montcalm (1712–1759)

Louis-Joseph de Montcalm was born in France near Nimes. He joined the French army at the age of nine and was a captain at age 17. He won distinction in the War of the Austrian Succession.

By 1756 Montcalm had retired and was living with his wife and children in the south of France when he was asked to go and lead the French forces in Quebec. He did not want to go, but went because he thought it was his duty.

Montcalm quarrelled with Vaudreuil, the governor general of Quebec. Montcalm thought Vaudreuil could not be a good military leader because he was born in New France and had no experience of European warfare. Actually Montcalm was not experienced in the **guerrilla warfare** that was successful in New France. Montcalm's strategy of withdrawing troops from the interior to defend Quebec was not successful.

On September 13, 1759, Montcalm was surprised to find the British soldiers lined up on the Plains of Abraham. He could have avoided the battle—the British would have had to withdraw soon because winter was coming. Both the British and the French had 4500 soldiers, but the British had forced the French into fighting in the well-organized European style of warfare, so the British won.

Montcalm was **fatally** wounded at the Battle of the Plains of Abraham. There is a highly romanticized historical painting that shows him dying on the battlefield. Actually he died the next morning in Quebec.

by George Townshend, M245, McCord Museum of Canadian History, Montreal

(detail) (*Major General James Wolfe*), 1759

General James Wolfe (1727–1759)

James Wolfe was born in the County of Kent in England. He was not a strong child, but he was determined to be a soldier like his father. He chose a lifetime career in the British army, joining at age 13. He served in Europe and Scotland.

Wolfe came to North America during the Seven Years' War. He served under Lord Amherst in the assault on Louisbourg. He led front line troops who helped the British capture that fort in 1758. After the capture of Louisbourg, Wolfe returned to England, but was selected to command the expedition against Quebec.

In 1759, Wolfe and his men spent an uncomfortable summer camped beside the St. Lawrence River near Quebec, looking for a way to take the city. Wolfe often quarrelled with his officers. He allowed his men to burn farms in the area around the city. The British soldiers were not used to the hot Canadian summer, and many of them became very ill. However, Wolfe's men won the Battle of the Plains of Abraham because they were well disciplined fighters who were able to fight on an open field rather than in the guerrilla style preferred by French militia (see pages 103–104).

Wolfe was very unpopular. There is a highly romanticized painting of his death. Some officers who were there refused to be in the painting.

Guerrilla warfare—fighting in small bands, making sudden attacks and ambushes on the enemy
Fatally—to death

An Exercise in Critical Thinking

Points of View

What was to happen to the people of New France and Acadia? Although the French had been defeated by the British in North America, until the European war between the two countries was settled, the future of New France was undecided.

In this part of the chapter you will be asked to do some critical thinking and to look at issues from several points of view. Critical thinkers realize that there is always more than one position to take on an issue.

This activity should take approximately three class periods. To help you understand the various points of view that existed in New France after the British gained control over the French territory, you will be asked to engage in a group role play activity that ends with a brief writing assignment.

Period One

Your teacher will divide your class into five groups. Use the following as a guide: Native people—five students; Seigneurs—five students; French Clergy—five students; Habitants—eight students; British Merchants— three students. Role play cards follow. Imagine you are one of the people described on the cards. Carry out the instructions on your role play card.

1. Native People

You have gathered together to decide on your future now that the British have defeated the French. You live in the lands to the west of the Thirteen Colonies. Every week more and more British colonists are moving across the Appalachian Mountains onto the lands where you farm and hunt. Try to reach a consensus. Decide what you wish to tell the British governor about this situation.

2. Seigneurs

You are members of the seigneurial class in Quebec. Several of your group are part of the government's Sovereign Council. You have gathered together to discuss recent events in the colony. You are very concerned about what will happen to you now that the British have won the war. Will you be deported from your lands by the British, just as the Acadians were? What will happen to your government? There are approximately 60 000 French ruled by fewer than 1000 British. What problems will result from this? You have heard that the British will not allow any Roman Catholics to participate in government affairs! Some of your habitants have had problems because British laws and customs are different from French laws and customs. Discuss the situation with your fellow seigneurs and make plans as to what you should do. What alternatives are open to you and your habitants? Discuss the consequences of each alternative. When you have arrived at a decision, outline your plans in a letter to the bishop of Quebec. Ask him if the clergy wishes to join you in your plans.

3. French Clergy

As members of the Roman Catholic clergy, you have gathered together to discuss the future of the French in Quebec now that the British have won the war. The habitants are very concerned and you have instructed the local priests to tell them during Church services that they should obey their new masters. You are concerned with *La Survivance* (cultural survival) and that the British will not allow your people to keep their Roman Catholic religion and French language. You have heard that the British will not support your efforts to collect one twenty-sixth of the grain the habitants grow. You need this tax to help you look after the sick and needy, to educate the children, and to continue your work in Christianizing the Native people. Discuss these issues and make plans as to what you should do. What alternatives are open to you and your people? Discuss the consequence of each alternative. When you have arrived at a decision, outline your plans in a letter to the bishop of Quebec.

4. Habitants

You have gathered together along with some of your fellow habitants to discuss your future. You are very concerned about what will happen to you now that the British have won the war. Will you be deported from your lands by the British, just as the Acadians were? There are approximately 60 000 French to be ruled by fewer than 1000 British. The local priest has encouraged you to obey your new masters, as have your local seigneurs, but you have many concerns. You have heard that the British system of landholding surveys lots in squares rather than in long narrow strips like the seigneurial system you are used to. You fear you will lose your land and your homes. You have heard that you will have to pay more dues, more taxes, and will not be able to use the local wheat mill. Rumours are everywhere! Discuss the situation with your group and make plans as to what you should do. What alternatives are open to you? Discuss the consequences of each alternative. When you have arrived at a decision, outline your plans in a letter to your local priest.

La Survivance—refers to the French concern for preserving their distinct culture, including the Roman Catholic religion, French language, and French civil law

5. British Merchants

You are part of a small group of British merchants who moved into Quebec in 1761 from the Thirteen Colonies (after the British captured Quebec). Customs and traditions certainly are different here. The 60 000 people all speak French, and all are Roman Catholics living under a different system of government and laws than you are used to. Even their system of landholding is strange to you. You had anticipated that large numbers of British merchants would move north to Quebec from the Thirteen Colonies but this has not happened. There are only about 1000 of you here, but you realize that with the help of the British government you hold a dominant and influential position. Perhaps if you **petition** the British government it will be possible to have an elected **assembly** in the Quebec government, just as you did in the Thirteen Colonies. You could dominate this assembly, and in turn the colony, especially if you are able to exclude all Roman Catholics from participating. As far as you are concerned the British won the war and should use their victory to good advantage. Discuss the situation and make plans as to what you should do. What alternatives are open to you? Discuss the consequences of each alternative. When you have arrived at a decision, outline your plans in a letter to the British government.

Periods Two and Three

1. Each group is to read the letter they have written out loud to the class. The Native group is to explain what they wish to do. After each group has finished, answer the following questions:

   a) What is the speaker saying? **Paraphrase** the main points in your notebook or use a web or mind map to record the main ideas.

   b) Record emotionally charged words that tell how the speaker feels.

   c) What position is the speaker taking?

   d) What values do you think are important to each speaker?

2. Critical thinkers realize there is more than one point of view on every issue. As a class, list as many alternatives as you can think of that the British had in dealing with the French and the Native peoples. List these alternatives on large chart paper for reference as you study the rest of

this chapter. Which alternative do you think the British will turn to first?

Alternatives Open to the British	
1	
2	
3	SAMPLE
4	

Petition—a formal request to a government or authority by a group of people, asking for a specific action

Assembly—at this time, an elected group that proposed bills. The Assembly had little power, as the governor or his council could reject its decisions.

Paraphrase—to express the meaning of a book, a passage, or a set of words in different words

British Military Rule

British Military Rule is established in Quebec.

In North America, the war between Britain and France ended when the British captured Montreal in September 1760. However, the Seven Years' War continued in Europe and other parts of the world until 1763. Until the war was over and a peace treaty signed, the **Canadiens** continued to hope that New France would be returned to France.

Between 1760 and 1763, the British army in New France set up a temporary government. This is known as the period of British Military Rule. British military governors were appointed at Quebec, Montreal, and Trois Rivières. Supreme authority was in the hands of the British commander-in-chief, General Amherst, in New York. Some of the French officials returned to France, but most of the colonists stayed. British Military Rule was not a harsh **occupation**. The British military rulers did not wish to cause any further disruption in the colony of New France and did not make any great changes to life in the colony during this three-year period.

Canadiens—French-speaking people born in New France (Quebec). The name shows that the Canadiens were distinct from the French in Europe.
Occupation—the control of an area by a foreign military force

Life of the Canadiens

This period of British Military Rule—from 1760 to 1763—was a time of uncertainty for the Canadiens. Until a peace treaty was signed, it was unknown how daily life and government in New France might become different under British rule.

The Canadien soldiers in the militia were allowed to return to their homes, and they were promised that their property would not be taken away. However, many found that their property had been destroyed. Many farms along the St. Lawrence River east of Quebec had been burned by British soldiers during the summer of 1759. Much of the Lower Town of Quebec that the British had been able to reach with cannon shots all through the summer of 1759, including many homes and businesses, had been destroyed.

The Canadiens were uneasy, remembering the deportation of the French Acadians during British occupation in 1755. They had questions about whether or not they would be asked to swear an oath of loyalty (allegiance) to Britain or face deportation. They also had questions about maintaining their French language and culture, and Roman Catholic religion.

The Jesuits were forced to return to France. Since they had run the schools, the educational system of the Canadiens was seriously weakened. However, because the orders of nuns were allowed to stay, the hospitals that they ran continued to operate. In fact, there are stories about the French nuns knitting stockings to help keep the British soldiers warm during the winter of 1759–60.

Many of the business people of New France were actually from France. When they returned to France, their place in business was often taken over by British merchants, many of these coming from the Thirteen Colonies.

Some aspects of life in New France changed very little under British Military Rule. The French language and Roman Catholic religion were maintained. The role of the Catholic priests in meeting the needs of the people also continued. French **civil law** and the French language were used in the courts. The seigneurial system continued.

The British wanted to co-operate with the French during this time of uncertainty, so daily life in New France changed little between 1760 and 1763. However, during the time of British Military Rule New France lost its main political, business, and religious leaders, who returned to France.

The Treaty of Paris (1763)

In 1763, the war in Europe between Britain and France ended and the Treaty of Paris was signed. By the terms of this peace treaty, France surrendered all of its possessions in New France and Acadia to Britain. The French kept two tiny islands, St. Pierre and Miquelon, off the coast of Newfoundland.

Effects of the Treaty of Paris

- Economic stability was restored, as the British troops paid for goods with coin money.*

- The military courts used French civil law.

- The French were assured they would not be deported.

- The Roman Catholic religion was retained.

- The seigneurial system was retained.

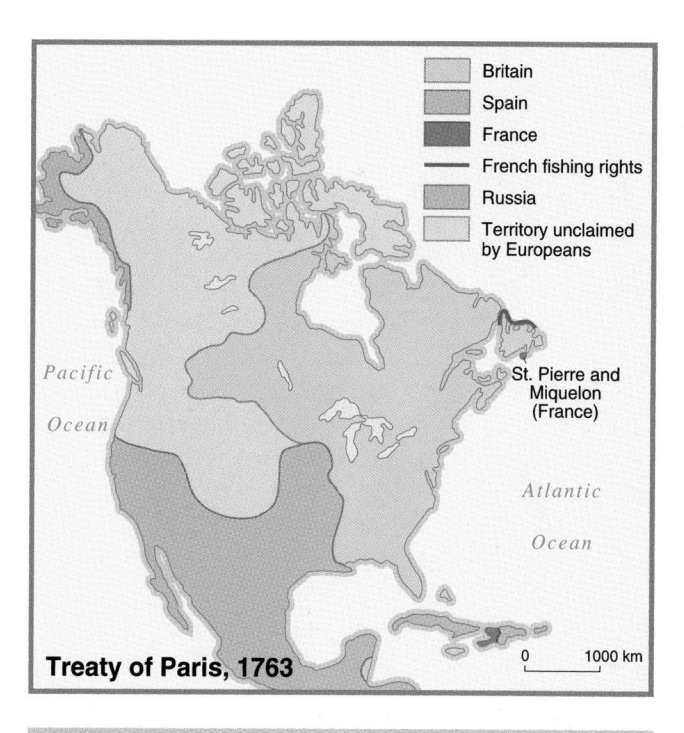

Treaty of Paris, 1763

Legend:
- Britain
- Spain
- France
- French fishing rights
- Russia
- Territory unclaimed by Europeans

Pacific Ocean

St. Pierre and Miquelon (France)

Atlantic Ocean

0   1000 km

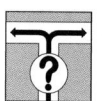

An Exercise in Problem Solving

1. Return to the five groups used in the role-play activity on pages 107 to 109 (Native people, seigneurs, French clergy, habitants, and British merchants).

2. Analyse the facts presented in the Treaty of Paris. How do they affect your role-play group?

3. List these facts on large notepaper (wall chart).

4. Reorder or regroup the facts you listed, placing those items that are similar together. Record them on a graphic organizer or chart.

5. Analyse the facts again.

6. Hypothesize what you think may happen to your particular group as a result of the Treaty of Paris.

7. Share your hypothesis with the rest of the class.

Civil law—having to do with private rights of citizens, especially property disputes

*There was considerable economic chaos in New France as a result of the Seven Years' War. The British introduced a number of economic changes that added to the economic uncertainty.

Alternatives Open to the British

The British colonial policy was ethnocentric, which means many British believed that their culture was superior to the French and the Native peoples' cultures. These beliefs were central to the British policies regarding both the French and the Native peoples. Another feature of British policy was their belief in claiming and ruling conquered lands.* When the French signed the Treaty of Paris in 1763 they had to surrender to Britain all claims over French lands in North America except the islands of St. Pierre and Miquelon.

Britain felt that the Canadiens were still too much of a threat to North America. Approximately one-third of the continent of North America still had French people living there, with French militia and Native allies. Britain still considered the French a threat to their colonies to the south—the Thirteen Colonies. The British also had to consider the large number of Native peoples living in the territory they now claimed.

After the Seven Years' War was over and the Treaty of Paris was signed, the British had to make some major decisions as to what they should do with the French and Native peoples living on the lands that were now part of the British Empire. The British had five alternatives: deportation or expulsion, maintaining the status quo, isolation, assimilation, or biculturalism. These are described in the right column of this page.

For Your Notebook

1. Use a mind map, web, paragraph, or outline notes to summarize each of the alternatives.

2. Apply one or more of the textbook icons (power, co-operation, decision-making, or conflict) to each of the alternatives. Be prepared to defend your choice.

Exploring Further

1. Divide your class into five groups. One of the five alternatives will be assigned for you to work on.

   a) Consider what Canada would have been like today if that alternative had been followed exclusively.

   b) Design a mobile to illustrate that alternative. Add illustrated examples to your mobile as you progress through this textbook.

---

*Claim over conquered lands was not unique to Britain. It was standard European policy to claim and rule conquered lands.

Legend: 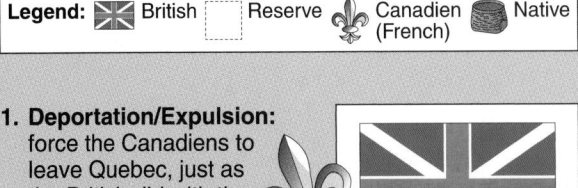 British   Reserve   Canadien (French)   Native

1. Deportation/Expulsion: force the Canadiens to leave Quebec, just as the British did with the Acadians from 1755 to 1762.

2. Maintain the status quo: allow the Canadiens to keep their system of doing things—their laws, customs, language, and religion; keep existing reserves for the Native people.

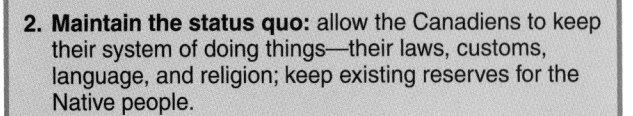

3. Isolation: create separate territories, one for the British, one for the Canadiens, and one for the Native peoples. Each territory would have its own system of government, language, and religion. People living in these territories would be protected by the government.

4. Assimilation (when a culture is absorbed into another): enforce British laws and require acceptance of British customs, language, and religion by the Canadiens and/or the Native peoples; encourage British immigration to create a majority. This alternative is also called Anglicization.

5. Biculturalism (having two cultures): support or encourage both British and Canadien ways of doing things. The term biculturalism is a modern one. The British did not seriously consider biculturalism in 1763.

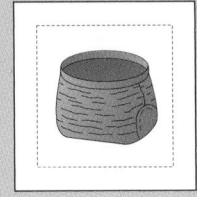

An Exercise in Decision-Making

Divide your class into two groups with one half of the class working on each exercise.

Exercise 1: There were over 60 000 French-speaking, Roman Catholic people living in Quebec who were used to French laws and customs. What was to be done with the French people and with the colony of Quebec? What kind of government should there be? The government in Britain had to make a decision.*

Earlier in this chapter you looked at the British occupation of Quebec mainly from the point of view of the people who lived there. In this exercise you are asked to take an alternative point of view—that of the British government. As advisors to the British government, discuss in pairs the alternatives and consequences, then decide what you would do if you were the British government. Refer to the information on page 112, "Alternatives Open to the British," to help you in your decision-making. You may wish to use the chart below in making your decision. Be ready to defend your choice.

With a partner, prepare an official report to the British government outlining your points of view.

Exercise 2: In the past, most Europeans disregarded the fact that the lands they were moving onto had been occupied by Native peoples for thousands of years. They believed that the lands were theirs because they had planted their country's flag, established control, and set up homes. Britain did not have a formal policy towards Native peoples. By the mid-eighteenth century, the British Parliament began to think about and write down policies on how it should formally address issues of the Native peoples of the New World.

a) Pretend that you are advisors to the British government. Discuss in pairs the alternatives and consequences, then decide what policy you would take towards the Native peoples. Refer to page 112, "Alternatives Open to the British," to help you in making a decision.

b) With your partner, prepare an official report for the British government outlining your point of view and making recommendations regarding British policy about Native peoples.

A few tips:

- 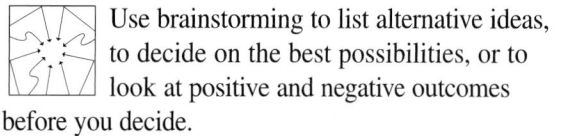 Use brainstorming to list alternative ideas, to decide on the best possibilities, or to look at positive and negative outcomes before you decide.

- Create your own decision-making model or use the one on this page or from the Appendix page 262.

An Exercise in Critical Thinking

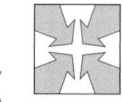

Each group is to read aloud in class its reports written for the exercise above. After listening to the reports, discuss the following questions:

1. Find words in the reports that tell how the writers feel about the issue.

2. Define "point of view."

3. What points of view do the writers take?

4. Do you feel the writers have enough information about the issue to arrive at a good decision? Why or why not?

5. Compare your ideas and your classmates' ideas (decisions) with the solution chosen by the British, which is outlined on the next page.

Decision-Making Chart

Issue to Be Solved			Decision

SAMPLE

---

*Britain had strict anti-Catholic laws (e.g., Roman Catholics could not hold public office or vote).

The Proclamation of 1763*

Introduction

In 1763, the British government issued a royal proclamation outlining what was to be done in Quebec. This is known as the Proclamation of 1763.

Aims: to make Quebec British (Assimilation)

- to ensure that British institutions and laws, customs, language, and religion were enforced in Quebec

- to attract British settlers to Quebec

- to limit the size of Quebec, cutting the Montreal fur traders out of the western fur trade

- to reassure the Native peoples that their interests in the fur trade and their hunting grounds in the Ohio Valley would be protected

Part of the population in Quebec consisted of long-time British subjects, mostly merchants, who were still loyal to Britain. Britain believed they should give these people what they wanted, over the next decade or so, to create a strong, loyal base. They believed that in time the French could be assimilated or absorbed into the British way of doing things.

The British government realized that the Native peoples were unhappy because many people from the Thirteen Colonies were moving west across the Appalachian Mountains into their territory.** If the boundaries of Quebec and the Thirteen Colonies were limited, the Native peoples would be happy, since traders, trappers, and settlers were forbidden to enter their territory unless they had a special government licence.

Key Terms

Settlement Patterns: Settlement in the Ohio and Mississippi Valleys was forbidden. Trappers, traders, and settlers had to have special government licences to enter lands set aside for the Native peoples.

Language: Use of the French language was allowed to continue.

Religion: The Roman Catholic religion was allowed to continue but the Church had no official status; the Protestant religion was to be introduced and promoted.

Government: Quebec was to be ruled by an appointed British governor and an appointed Executive Council (to be drawn from the English-speaking military and merchant **elites**) and an elected Legislative Assembly (as soon as the English population was large enough to warrant it).

- British laws and court system were created to replace French laws (except for French civil laws, which were allowed to continue for settling property disputes).

- Roman Catholics were to be barred from legal positions and could not be elected to the Legislative Assembly.

Exploring Further

1. In your role-play groups established on pages 107–109, predict how your "characters" (seigneurs, French clergy, Native people, habitants, and British merchants) would have felt about the Proclamation of 1763. Record your predictions on large chart paper and display on the wall.

---

*The Proclamation of 1763 is sometimes referred to as the Royal Proclamation of 1763.
**Also the Native peoples had lost their traditional trading partners, the French.
Elites—special groups, usually more educated or richer than others

Colony of Quebec, 1763

The Proclamation of 1763 reduced the size of Quebec.

After the Proclamation of 1763

As a result of the Proclamation of 1763, civil rule replaced military rule in Quebec. The British found that the Proclamation did not result in assimilation (absorbing one culture into another) of the French the way they had hoped.

The Anglo-Americans from the Thirteen Colonies did not come north to live in Quebec (instead they moved westward). The French greatly outnumbered the British in Quebec. For every 100 Europeans in Quebec, 97 were French and three were British. Thus there was no strong British culture into which the French could be assimilated. The priests and the seigneurs tried hard to maintain the French culture.

The Native peoples had been promised a western reserve where colonists from the Thirteen Colonies could not go. Even though the Proclamation of 1763 forbade settlement in the Ohio and Mississippi Valleys, colonists were moving west into Native lands.

British Governors in Quebec

Governor James Murray

The first British governor general appointed to Quebec was James Murray. He had been one of General Wolfe's officers and was the military governor of Quebec during the period of British Military Rule (from 1760 to 1763). It was Governor Murray's job to enforce the conditions of the Proclamation of 1763. The British wanted the Proclamation of 1763 enforced so that they could have political power and make profits from the fur trade. However, Britain and the creators of the Proclamation were a long distance away from the colony. Thus the officials in Quebec had a certain amount of freedom in interpreting and enforcing the Proclamation of 1763.

The conditions of the Proclamation of 1763 were difficult for Governor Murray to enforce. The British merchants wanted to control the colony through an elected assembly so they could vote on and pass whatever laws benefited them the most. The British merchants revived

the fur trade but their attitudes and opinions contrasted sharply with those of the habitants of New France.

Murray grew to like and respect the Canadiens—especially the clergy and the seigneurs. He made many **concessions** towards the French, which provoked hostility from the British merchants.

Governor Murray interpreted the Proclamation in favour of the Canadiens and allowed French to be spoken in the smaller courts. Some of Murray's other concessions were quite important:

- In an effort to maintain harmony with some 60 000 Canadiens, Murray did not call the assembly, although the Proclamation of 1763 made provision for this.*

- He believed that co-operation with the Catholic Church could strengthen the loyalty of the population. When the Roman Catholic Church in Quebec chose Briand as bishop, Governor Murray confirmed him as Superintendent of the Roman Catholic Church in New France.

The British merchants wanted the Proclamation of 1763 enforced. Through their many influential contacts in the British Parliament and their many letters of complaint, they pressured the British government to recall Murray to Britain. Sir Guy Carleton was sent out to be the colony's new governor.

Governor Guy Carleton

Sir Guy Carleton became the governor of Quebec in 1768. He saw that British control of Quebec was dependent on the support of the large population of Canadiens. Loyalty and support were important because at this time, the people in the Thirteen Colonies to the south were starting to have disagreements with the officials in Britain. He wanted to make sure that the Canadiens would be loyal to Britain. To ensure this support, Carleton made friends with the leaders of the Canadiens, the seigneurs and the clergy. He thought that if the leaders accepted British rule, the rest would also agree. Carleton encouraged the British government to allow the French people to keep their system of laws and their Catholic religion. Carleton rejected the policy of assimilation and encouraged acceptance of allowing the two cultures to exist side by side.

Although they did not use the term biculturalism, this policy of allowing two cultures—French and British—to exist side-by-side is a forerunner of the biculturalism we have in Canada today. These ideas were officially recognized and supported by the British government when they passed the Quebec Act of 1774.

Concession—giving in
*Had Murray done so, he would have given the British minority political control over a huge French majority

The Quebec Act, 1774

Introduction

The Quebec Act was passed by the British government in an attempt to keep the loyalty of the Canadiens.

Aim: to preserve and strengthen the British Empire by allowing both the French and British ways of doing things

The British hoped the Quebec Act would combine both the French and British ways of doing things while maintaining the French character of the colony.

This was an example of biculturalism—where two cultures (British and French) exist side by side in the same country. The British government decided that the best way to gain the loyalty of the Canadiens was to allow them to maintain the French character of Quebec and preserve the French culture. Quebec was to become both British and French.

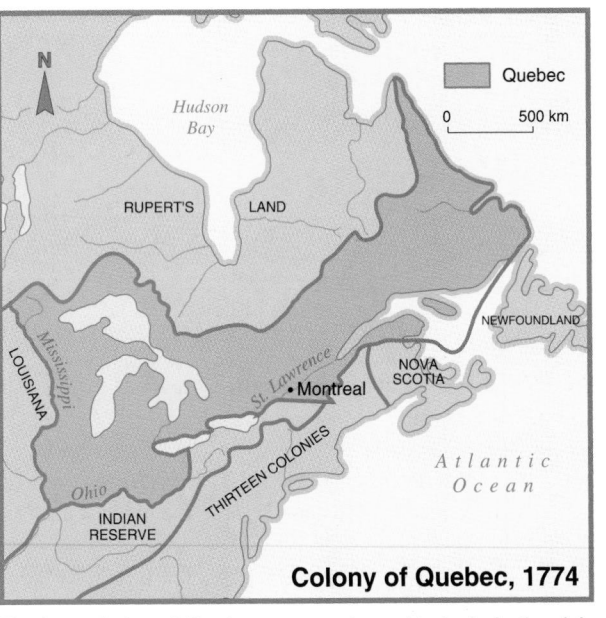

Colony of Quebec, 1774

The boundaries of Quebec were enlarged to include the rich fur trading areas between the Ohio and Mississippi rivers.

Key Terms of the Act

Language: Use of the French language was allowed to continue.

Religion: The Roman Catholic Church was allowed to continue and to collect tithes (church taxes).

Landholding System: The seigneurial system was allowed to remain. The governor could also grant land according to the British freehold system.

Government:

- Quebec was to be ruled by an appointed British governor and an appointed council.

- An elected assembly (although promised earlier) was not introduced at this time.

- Roman Catholics could hold government positions.

- French civil law was to continue along with English criminal law.

British Government
- made the important decisions
- appointed the governor

Council (appointed)
- advised the governor on policy and law-making

Appoints

Governor
- tried to carry out wishes of the British government
- was very powerful
- had the power to reject suggestions

An Exercise in Critical Thinking

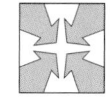

Reactions to the Quebec Act

Who	Reaction	Why
Who?	anger	• westward expansion cut off (French had control of Ohio Valley) • fear of tighter British control • called the Quebec Act intolerable
Who?	delight anger	• boundary extended into very large area would increase fur trade business • less political power as a result of no assembly
Who?	pleasure	• kept religious influence and ability to tithe (tax)
Who?	pleasure	• kept land and privileges • kept French civil law • French language expected to remain
Who?	indifference	• kept Canadien way of life but under control of Church and seigneurs
Who?	upset	• north of the Ohio River not much change • south of the Ohio River great numbers of settlers moving west from the Thirteen Colonies

1. Use this list to decide who held each point of view described in the above chart. Select from: British merchants in Quebec, British in the Thirteen Colonies, Native people, French seigneurs, French habitants, French Catholic Church officials.

2. Form into your role-play groups established on pages 107–109 (seigneurs, French clergy, and others). Compare the predictions you recorded on the wall chart (see Exploring Further on page 114) with the way the various groups reacted to the Quebec Act (above). Share your results with your classmates.

3. In your role-play groups decide what new problems your group thinks the Quebec Act would create. Present these hypotheses to the class as a bulletin board display, mural, collage, poster, story, play, or mobile.

4. Why is it important to look at an issue from different points of view?

Review

The icons are your cue to refer to the Learning How to Learn Appendix (pages 256–271) for ideas on how to complete these activities.

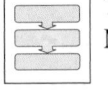  This icon is a reminder to turn to the Research Model on pages x and xi.

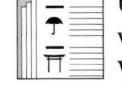 Complete a self-assessment for one assignment from this chapter.

Understanding Concepts

Checking Predictions

1. At the beginning of this chapter (page 88) you made some predictions and wrote down three questions about the chapter. Use what you have learned from reading the chapter to confirm or correct your predictions and to answer the three questions you listed.

2. Refer to "Questions to Talk About" on page 51. Discuss the questions based on the type of government in Quebec that resulted from the Quebec Act. How did the system of government change from Royal Government (as you studied in Chapter 3) to the government established by the British in the Quebec Act?

Recording Vocabulary

3. 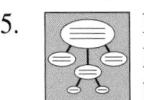 Using one of the methods for recording vocabulary, add these words to the WordBook section of your notebook.

- point of view
- paraphrase
- petition
- military rule
- assembly
- civil law
- proclamation
- critical thinking

Conceptualizing

4. Here are some main ideas from the chapter:
- territorial expansion and claims
- British and French rivalry and conflict in North America
- War in North America: a three-pronged attack
- deportation or expulsion
- treaty
- assimilation
- status quo
- biculturalism
- isolation
- the Proclamation of 1763
- the Quebec Act, 1774

Do either a) or b).

a)  Create a concept poster about one of the ideas. Present your poster to the class.

b) 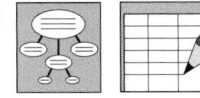 Use a web, mind map, outline, or chart to create a permanent set of notes about one of the ideas.

Working with Information

5. 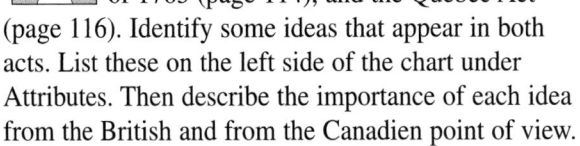 Refer to the Chapter 4 Focus on page 88. Notice that Decision-making and Conflict have been the focus of this chapter. Create two webs, one to represent various examples of decision-making and one to represent various examples of conflict found in this chapter.

6. 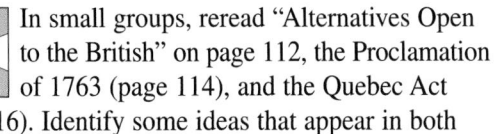 In small groups, reread "Alternatives Open to the British" on page 112, the Proclamation of 1763 (page 114), and the Quebec Act (page 116). Identify some ideas that appear in both acts. List these on the left side of the chart under Attributes. Then describe the importance of each idea from the British and from the Canadien point of view.

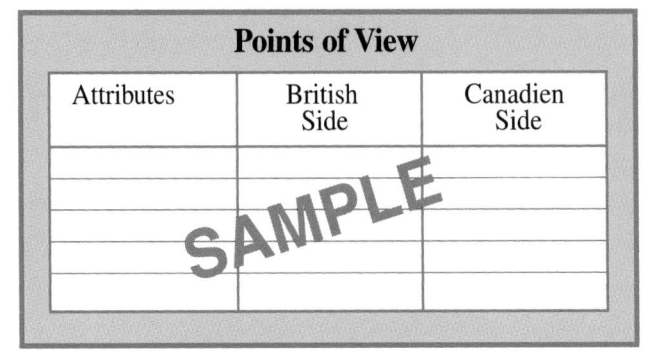

Points of View

Attributes	British Side	Canadien Side

SAMPLE

7. In the Proclamation of 1763, the British government aimed to limit the size of Quebec. Why?

8. Why was the aim of assimilation of the French into British culture not successful?

9. Why did the British want Murray to call an elected assembly? Why did he choose not to do so?

10. 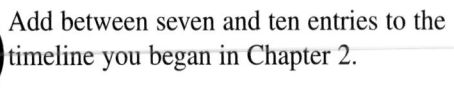 Add between seven and ten entries to the timeline you began in Chapter 2.

11. 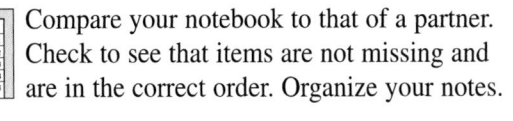 Compare your notebook to that of a partner. Check to see that items are not missing and are in the correct order. Organize your notes.

Developing Research Skills

Decision-making and Critical Thinking

12. Recall the Research Project Model introduced on pages x and xi. While this chapter did not involve a specific research project, you did look at several decision-making and critical thinking models and exercises. These are valuable skills when you are doing research. Record the following terms and their definitions in the Tools of Learning section of your notebook. You will see them throughout the textbook.

Decision-making:
- alternatives
- interpret
- evaluate
- consequences

Critical Thinking:
- issue
- point of view
- analyse
- priorities

Brainstorming

13. In the following activities you are not required to actually carry out the research projects suggested, but you are being asked to come up with ideas about how you might carry out your research.
   a) Gathering Information: Imagine that you were asked to research the adventures of Henry Kelsey, the explorer. Brainstorm for a list of possible questions you could use to guide your research.
   b) Organizing Information: Imagine you have been asked to research the life of a twelve-year-old in New France and you are gathering information on this topic. Brainstorm for a list of ways to organize this information.

Eyewitness Accounts and Primary Sources

14. Textbooks contain information drawn from a variety of sources. Some information has been taken from primary sources. Examples include diaries, maps, paintings, and legal documents in which information was recorded by someone who lived at the time the historic events took place. In this textbook you will find many examples of this type of information in pictures or quotations. (Refer to "Sources" on page 269 in the Appendix for more information.)
   a) Find examples of an eyewitness account and an historic painting in Chapters 3 and 4. How can you tell that these are from primary sources?
   b) What are the advantages of using primary sources when doing research? What are the disadvantages?
   c) Why may bias be a concern when using primary sources? (See "Bias" on page 256 in the Appendix.)

   d) How do you give the writer, speaker, or artist credit for their words, work, or art?

Paraphrasing

15. With a partner, read the statements on Alternatives Open to the British on page 112. Take turns at paraphrasing each of the five statements without looking back at the original statements.

Research Topics

16. Do research to find out more about the western expansion of the Thirteen Colonies into Native lands or do research on the Cherokee and "The Long March" into Oklahoma. Present your findings in a written report.

Developing Communication Skills

Reading

17. Read the story "Antoine Boulanger" by Marie Moser in *Ordinary People in Canada's Past,* Second Edition, by Nancy Marcotte. Record your reaction to Antoine's experiences in your History Journal.

Writing

18. Read Question #14 and think about your answers. Look back at page 80. Re-read the primary source excerpt written in *italics* about the events on the Verchères seigneury.
   a) From whose point of view is this written?
   b) Does the painting support that point of view? How?
   c) Write about and illustrate the event from the point of view of an Iroquoian person who was there.

19. 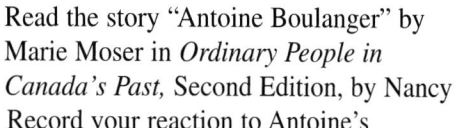 Work in groups to develop a newspaper that covers one of these events: the capture of Quebec in 1759, the Proclamation of 1763, or the Quebec Act of 1774. Include the political, social, and economic changes that result from these events.

20. 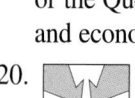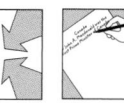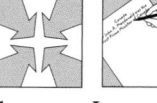 Select a partner. One of you writes a journal entry as a recently deported Acadian and the other as Governor Lawrence. Share your entries with each other.

21. Which person from this chapter would you like to have met? Write a paragraph to explain why you find that person interesting.

22. In your History Journal, discuss the three most surprising things you learned in this chapter.

23. Write and present a dialogue between Governor Murray and a concerned British merchant.

Listening and Speaking

24. This is a listening game. Form into groups of four or five and have each person say one fact or idea he or she learned while studying this chapter. The person who goes next must add a new fact or idea, but must first repeat those mentioned by everyone else, in the order they were already mentioned.

25. Do a radio interview with one or several of the important people from this chapter. Choose people from your class to play these roles. Then, during the call-in segment, have classmates ask the guests questions.

26. Think about a topic covered in this chapter that you would like to know more about. Make up a list of suitable questions and call a local library to find out about the resources they have. Ask about their archives. Take notes so that you can share with your classmates what you have found out about locating resources and reference materials.

27. You are a guide at one of the following:
    * Louisbourg (between 1719–1760)
    * Halifax (1749)
    * Acadia (just prior to the deportation in 1755)
    * Quebec (before or after the capture by the British)

    Guide one or several classmates around your chosen place. Be prepared to answer questions.

28. Write and present the official announcement that Governor Lawrence may have prepared to tell the Acadians of their choices and the possible consequences.

Viewing and Representing

29. Select five pictures in this chapter and tell a partner about them as though you are a person in the scene.

30. In a group of three, create a large map showing New France from 1670 to 1774. Visually represent three important events that took place in New France during this time period.

31. Using the eyewitness accounts and the map and pictures on pages 103 to 105, make a visual representation of the battle on the Plains of Abraham.

32. Develop a diorama to show the concept of cultural exchange between Native people and Europeans (see page 90).

33. Create a visual showing the differences between the French and British fur trade discussed on page 90.

Applying Concepts

34. Turn to page 112 to read about ethnocentrism.
    a) Add this word to the WordBook section of your notes.
    b) As a class, discuss what Eurocentrism might mean and come up with some examples.
    c) Compare ethnocentrism and Eurocentrism.
    d) Eurocentric points of view are present in some primary source records and art. Why is an awareness of this needed when studying history?

35. Select an issue from your school, or find a news clipping about an important issue. Describe the issue from several points of view. Why is it important to look at an issue from several points of view? (See page 262 for more information on issues.

36. List five different issues that have forced you to make decisions within the last year. Simply outline what the question/problems were. Do not give any hint of your decisions. Now exchange your list with someone else in the class.
    a) Read the list you receive carefully, and choose one issue. Use your own decision-making model or one covered in this text to help you analyse the issue.

After you have weighed all the alternatives and consequences, come to a decision.

b) With your classmate, discuss the conclusion you have drawn. Does your decision match the decision that was made by your classmate? Why? Why not? Which decision do you think is better?

37. Why have you been studying
   • French–British conflict?
   • the Proclamation of 1763?
   • the Quebec Act, 1774?

38. 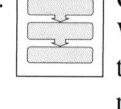 Try to think of as many ideas as you can for each of the following. Record your responses in the History Journal section of your notebook.

What if...
a) the French had defeated the British in the battle on the Plains of Abraham?
b) British aims to assimilate the French (Proclamation of 1763) had been successful?
c) the Europeans had adopted the Native political, economic, and social structure.

39.  Complete each statement with a paragraph entry.

a) The most important thing I learned in this chapter was . . .
b) In completing Chapter 4 activities, I learned . . . about my thinking.

Challenge Plus

40. Refer back to Question 4. Create a large mind map or web combining all of the topics listed. Use large chart paper so this can be displayed.

41. Complete a research project on this topic: Why is the Proclamation of 1763 considered the basis for Native land claims (Aboriginal rights) today?

42. Develop a multimedia presentation about the most important economic, social, and political change(s) you learned about in this chapter.

43. 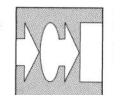 Select an issue introduced in this chapter. Investigate related Canadian current events. How do the issues that arose between 1670 and 1774 relate to present-day issues? Issues for investigation might include: Aboriginal rights; economic, political, and social rights of women; French **sovereignty**.

44. 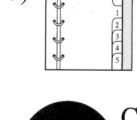 Show the various causes leading up to the battle on the Plains of Abraham.

45. Research newspaper items with deportation as a part of the story.
a) What is the viewpoint of the deported person?
b) What is the viewpoint of the government?
c) Conduct a survey of ten people to find out the viewpoint of some Canadian citizens.
d) Record your thoughts about deportation in your History Journal.

46. Complete your website or magazine assignment for Section III.

Canada Revisited

Quebec City was protected by a fortified wall. This picture shows one of the two gates in the wall.

Sovereignty—independence; being free from control by another authority (or government)

121

Section IV

British North America 1774–1815

"The British government sure had a lot of different people to try to rule!" said Roberto.

"French, Native, and British people—all with different values," added Ken. "It'd be like Brenda and me trying to tell the rest of you what to do!"

"I'd sure want a say in how things were run!" declared Erin.

Ms. Ito began handing out pages. "Speaking of governing, I had transcripts* of some Students' Council sessions faxed here. Let's read them and make more connections..."

Fairmont School Students'
Council Transcript
Meeting Notes: Nov. 4
Topic: Guests at School Dances
John: Some of the kids want to bring friends from other schools to our dances.
Farrah: I don't think it should be

---

* In this case transcripts are word-for-word records of the Students' Council meetings (probably tape recorded and then typed).

---

allowed. Our dances are crowded enough as it is!
Tammy: Yes, but I know how they feel. My boyfriend goes to Marpole School and I'd like to bring him to our dances.
Saul: Yes, and we can go to the dances at some other schools, so they should be able to come to ours.
John: Maybe we should ask the Fairmont students to vote on this issue.
Sam: What's the point of that? They elected us as Students' Council so we could make decisions on their behalf. I think we should vote.
John: Okay, how many in favour? Eight against six. Okay, we've voted in favour of letting students from other schools come to our dances.

Meeting Notes: Nov. 10
Special Meeting at the request of the principal, Mrs. Cherniak.
Topic: Guests at School Dances
Mrs. Cherniak: I'm afraid that I can't allow you to have students from other schools at your dances. There is a school policy that prohibits it. There is a safety issue involved when outsiders are on school property.
Farrah: But we voted on this issue as the Students' Council on behalf of all the other students at Fairmont!
Mrs. Cherniak: I'm sorry. It doesn't matter. This involves a school rule. As the Students' Council you have been elected to represent other students in our school by making decisions that affect them. That is a type of representative government. But you are still students who are under the school's authority and care. The school rules are for your safety and well-being. In this case, your decision can not be allowed.

Discussion after Mrs. Cherniak left.

Tammy: I still think the school rule not allowing other students to attend our dances is unfair.

John: Maybe we should write a letter giving our point of view.

Farrah: We could ask Mrs. Cherniak to read it at the next staff meeting.

Tammy: I know that the final decisions are made by the principal and teachers, but I think that they should at least know that we don't agree with them.

Saul: And I also think we need to find out what decisions we *can* make.

*Council members all agreed. Meeting adjourned.**

Questions to Talk About

Refer to the section story and discuss the following questions. At the end of Chapters 5 and 6 you will review them in light of the information you will gain about **representative government**.

1. In a governing body such as the Students' Council, do the people or elected representatives make the decisions?

2. Who makes the final decisions? Who has the power? How does this make the student council's situation unlike that of a representative government?

3. What are your alternatives when you do not agree with the decisions made by the person or people who have the power?

4. Which alternative was chosen by the students you read about?

---

*Stopped at the end of a session.
Representative government—citizens elect people who represent them in their legislative assembly

Chapter 5 Focus

The two chapters in Section IV answer the question: What factors contributed to British North America's expansion? Both chapters also trace the development of representative government. The concepts of power, co-operation, decision-making, and conflict underlie the events in Chapter 5. The concept of conflict will be the focus of the chapter.

Power

Co-operation

Decision-Making

Conflict

Other Concepts and Main Topics

- Thirteen Colonies
- participatory democracy
- representative government
- protest
- taxation without representation
- American Revolution

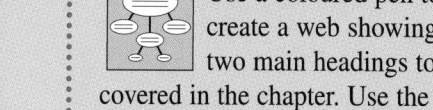

- reactions in Quebec and Nova Scotia to the revolution
- soldiers of the Thirteen Colonies invade Quebec
- loyalty to Britain in British North America

Chapter Preview/Prediction

Read the Chapter 5 Focus found on this page. Examine the Overview found on the next page, and look at the headings and pictures found in Chapter 5. You can identify the major headings because they are the largest. In this chapter, major headings are in red.

Use a coloured pen to create a web showing the two main headings to be covered in the chapter. Use the information you gathered by looking through the chapter to add as many supporting details to the two branches of your web as you can, using the same colour. Finally, record two questions about this chapter to which you hope to learn the answers by the end of Chapter 5. Once you have completed your study of Chapter 5, you will work with your web again.

Continue your class project "Passport to the Past." Choose from the list of people on page 20.

Chapter 5

The American Revolution
(1775–1783)

1774

The Thirteen Colonies, along the east coast of North America, had a population of about 2.5 million people. The colonists elected representatives and decided how the colonies were to be governed. The First Continental Congress of the Thirteen Colonies met. Grievances were discussed.

1775

The Thirteen Colonies protested British taxes. The first battle of the American Revolution was fought at Lexington and Concord.

1775

Soldiers of the Thirteen Colonies invaded Quebec.

1776

The Declaration of Independence stated that the Thirteen Colonies were free and independent of British control. The United States of America came into existence in 1783 after many long years of fighting.

The Thirteen Colonies

By 1763, Britain had defeated France in the Seven Years' War in Europe. New France became a British colony at that time. The Thirteen Colonies to the south of New France, along the coast of the Atlantic Ocean, had been British colonies. Colonists had been sent to the Thirteen Colonies to settle and produce raw materials that would add to the wealth of Great Britain. Others went to gain religious or political freedom.

As in New France, settlers had begun to come to the Thirteen Colonies in the early 1600s. But by 1775, the population of New France was only about 70 000. The Thirteen Colonies had a European population of about 2.5 million people at this time.

Each of the Thirteen Colonies was different, but they can be divided into three groups based on their location.

Location

New England

Most of the New England settlers came from England and Scotland. These colonies were first settled by religious groups whose beliefs were not accepted in England. The economy was based on wheat farming and trade with the islands in the Caribbean Sea to the south. The seaport towns were prospering. Boston had a population of 15 000. Many people in the seaport towns made their living from the sea, or as craftspeople and merchants.

The Middle Colonies

The middle colonies had many different religions and nationalities compared to the other colonies. They were settled by Dutch, Swedes, English, Germans, Scots, and Irish, as well as others. These colonies were known as the "breadbasket" of the New World because most people were farmers. Ships loaded with crops from the Middle Colonies left from the harbours of New York and Philadelphia. These crops were sold in Britain and the West Indies.

The Southern Colonies

Many of the southern colonists were from England. Others were Scots, French, and Germans. The main industry was agriculture. Many workers were needed for the huge tobacco, sugar, and rice farms, which were called **plantations**. These plantations were owned by a small, powerful group of people. Few settlers were willing to work for wages on the plantations when they could have small farms of their own, so the plantation owners used slaves from Africa as workers. At that time **slavery** was still legal in much of Europe, North America, and elsewhere. It was not entirely **abolished** in the states, colonies, and territories of North America until 1865 (see page 241).

The only large cities in the southern colonies were Charleston, with a population of 10 000, and Baltimore with 5000.

Thirteen Colonies, 1775

Legend:
- New England
- Middle Colonies
- Southern Colonies

0 — 500 km

Plantations—large farms where crops were grown
Slavery—a system whereby a person was owned and controlled by another. Slaves had no civil rights. They could be bought and sold as property, families were often separated, and children of slaves were born into slavery.
Abolish—to legally end
*Maine became a state in 1820. Prior to that, it was under the jurisdiction of Massachusetts and referred to as "District of Maine."

Government

The colonists had two levels of government: one to handle local affairs, the other to deal with colonial issues.

Community Government

Communities in the New England colonies had a form of local government to look after day-to-day problems. This form of local government came to be called the town meeting. All free adult males were encouraged to take part in the decision-making process. This is an example of participatory democracy. Citizens would gather together to decide on how much they should be taxed, to discuss town problems, and to elect town officers. The elected town officers did not make the laws, they just administered and enforced them.

Representative Government
Citizens elect people who represent them in their Legislative Assembly (decision-making body). Every voter has a voice in government, but only a small group actually makes the decisions.

Veto—the right or power to forbid or reject
*The colony of Nova Scotia also had representative government. It was granted an assembly by Britain in 1758.

Colonial Government

Each of the Thirteen Colonies had a form of representative government. The first representative assembly in North America was called the House of Burgesses. It was in Williamsburg, Virginia, one of the Thirteen Colonies. The governor invited each community in the colony to send two representatives to the Legislative Assembly. This assembly could pass laws for the colony, as long as the laws did not go against the laws of Britain. But the colonial laws could be **vetoed** by the governor.

This photograph was taken at the reconstructed Williamsburg. It shows the interior of the House of Burgesses, the first representative assembly in North America.

Each of the other colonies established a system of government similar to that of Virginia.* In most cases, the government consisted of a governor (as a representative of the British government), a council of men who helped the governor, and a representative assembly, which made the laws. The governor and his council were appointed by the king and the members of the representative assembly were elected. The colonies of Rhode Island and Connecticut were exceptions to this. In these colonies the voters elected the governor and the council, as well as the representative assembly.

The number of people who could vote was much more limited than it is today. Only the free adult males of the colonies and the small number of women who owned property could vote for their representatives. Slaves and most women could not vote; neither could men who did not own property of a certain size or could not prove that they had an income and paid taxes of a certain amount. Also, many people who could vote did not because they did not have the time to make the journey from their isolated pioneer farms. Thus the representatives were elected by a very small proportion of the population.

Even though the laws passed by the assemblies could be vetoed by the governor, the assemblies had a surprising amount of power. That is because they controlled how the money was spent. This means that they could decide whether or not the governor could have the money to carry out the things he wanted to do.

The colonists were used to having a form of representative government, even though many decisions were still made in Britain by the British government and they were still subject to the laws of Britain.

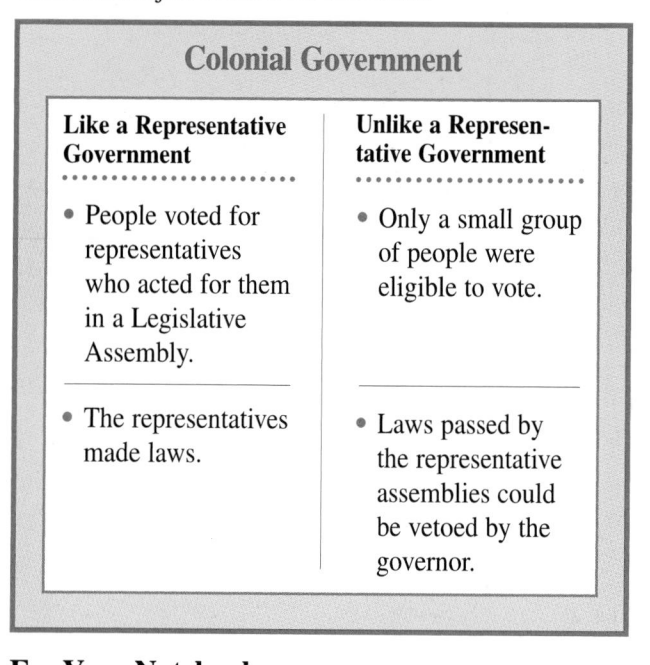

Colonial Government	
Like a Representative Government	**Unlike a Representative Government**
• People voted for representatives who acted for them in a Legislative Assembly.	• Only a small group of people were eligible to vote.
• The representatives made laws.	• Laws passed by the representative assemblies could be vetoed by the governor.

For Your Notebook

1. In some ways the representative assemblies in the Thirteen Colonies were like a representative government and in other ways they were not. Your Students' Council is also a form of representative government. Design a chart like the one above comparing your Students' Council to a representative government.

The Thirteen Colonies Protest

Due to Britain's victory over France in the Seven Years' War, New France now belonged to Britain. However, Britain's troubles were far from over after the Seven Years' War. The war had been expensive and had resulted in a high national debt. It was also expensive to maintain an army in the Thirteen Colonies. Britain decided to impose certain taxes on the people of the Thirteen Colonies to help pay these costs.

Many of the colonists did not see the need for a British army in the colonies since they no longer needed protection from French forces at Quebec or Louisbourg. To them, the army was a waste of tax money.

The people of the Thirteen Colonies protested vigorously against taxation without representation. Because they had no elected representation in the British Parliament, the colonists objected to British taxes. Some of their protests are shown on page 129. They felt it was unfair that their taxes were being used to help run the British government when they were not allowed to elect representatives to speak for them in the British Parliament.

Taxation without Representation
Being taxed without benefit of elected representatives to speak on your behalf.

The people of the Thirteen Colonies and the British government had different points of view for many years. Between 1660 and 1774 the British government passed a series of laws or acts that many of the colonists did not like. They felt that the British government had no business interfering in their lives in this way. The British government felt that its laws were fair and just. Here are the opposing points of view of the people of the Thirteen Colonies and the British government on the Navigation Acts of 1660 and 1668, on the Proclamation of 1763 (see page 114), and on taxation without representation. Below are two imaginary points of view based on actual historical accounts. Read the colonists' point of view first and then read across the page to the point of view of Great Britain.

The Navigation Acts: 1660 and 1668

Colonists

These Acts will not allow us to use our own ships to carry goods to and from Britain. This prevents us from making money on the transport of these goods. Furthermore, goods from other countries in Europe are very expensive in the colonies because they have to go to Britain, where you tax them, before they come here. We also think it is unfair that we have to sell most of our goods to you. We should be able to sell them to whom we please.

Great Britain

Do not forget that our trade laws also do not allow British merchants to buy tobacco that isn't grown in one of our colonies. These laws help you. Besides, the American colonies belong to us. Therefore you should be helping us, not some other country. Furthermore the mother country needs to be strong in order to protect you from enemies.

The Proclamation of 1763

Colonists

You have ordered the settlers who live west of the Appalachian Mountains to move back into the Thirteen Colonies. These people have made their homes there. You are forcing them to start all over again. This is very unfair. This land is already ours anyway, since some of our colonies were given it in their charters. Also, you aren't allowing any fur traders to cross the mountains without your permission. You are destroying the livelihood of these men.

Great Britain

We are trying to prevent another war between the Native people and the settlers. There is still lots of room for settlement in the Thirteen Colonies. More land is not needed yet. Also, if we allow the land west of the Appalachians to become settled, the fur-bearing animals will be driven away. The fur trade is almost the only way we can make any money from our North American colonies.

Taxation without Representation

Colonists

Why should we pay so many taxes to Great Britain? This makes us very angry. We should have elected representatives in the British Parliament who will stand up for our rights.

Great Britain

We have stationed an army of 10 000 men in the colonies to enforce law and order and to protect you from further Native attacks. This army is very expensive to support. Why should the people of Britain have to pay for this army? The members of the British Parliament keep your interests in mind and represent you just as well as they represent the people of Britain.

Events Leading Up to the American Revolution

This chart shows some of the events leading up to the American Revolution. They involve taxes imposed by the British and describe the colonists' protests against the taxes. You will see that some of these protests were peaceful and some were violent. The British actions are marked with red. The colonists' reactions are marked with purple.

1764 Sugar Act
- Taxes were put on imported goods such as sugar and molasses.
- Some colonists **boycotted** sugar.

1765 Stamp Act
- All legal documents and newspapers had to be stamped, at a cost ranging from one cent to several dollars.
- Angry speeches were made in colonial assemblies.
- Merchants boycotted British goods.
- Tax collectors were terrorized.
- The house of Governor Hutchinson of Massachusetts was wrecked by a mob.
- In 1766 the Stamp Act was withdrawn.

1767 Townshend Acts
- Taxes were placed on glass, tea, silk, paper, paint, and lead.
- The sale of British goods fell by almost two-thirds.
- In 1770 taxes were dropped on everything but tea.

1773 Tea Act
- The East India Company was given the sole right to sell tea in North America.
- East India Company ships were refused admittance to the harbours of New York and Philadelphia.
- At the Boston Tea Party, about 40 or 50 people from Boston, disguised as Native people, dumped three boatloads of tea from British ships into the harbour.

1774 Intolerable Acts
- Boston was closed to all shipping until all the destroyed tea was paid for. Public meetings were forbidden, and 4000 British troops were stationed in the area (one soldier for every four Bostonians).
- The Quebec Act gave Quebec, with its relatively tiny French-speaking population, control of the largest piece of land in British North America— the Ohio Territory. It was considered to be an Intolerable Act. It seemed to be an attempt to prevent the colonists from expanding westward.
- The people of the Thirteen Colonies boycotted British goods.
- Many colonists secretly began to collect arms and ammunition.
- The colonists began to raise an army of 122 000 men, two-thirds of whom were **Minutemen.**
- In September 1774, the first Continental Congress was held (see page 144).

Boycott—refusal to trade with a country or company or to buy its products
Minutemen—armed men ready to fight at a moment's notice

The American Revolution

In 1775 the protests broke into the armed conflict known as the American Revolution, or the War of Independence. This resulted in the formation of the new United States of America, independent of Great Britain.

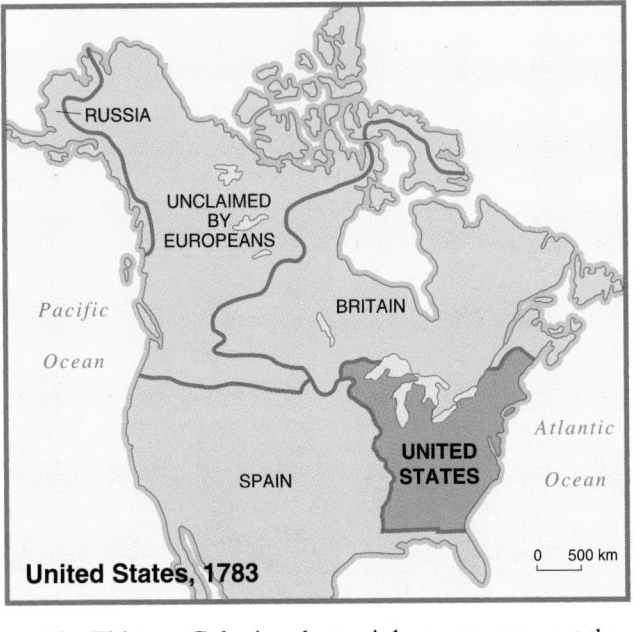

United States, 1783

The Thirteen Colonies chose violent protest to get the changes they wanted. The people in the two other major British colonies of Quebec and Nova Scotia did not choose violent protest at this time, although they had many of the same complaints as the Thirteen Colonies.

The people of Quebec and Nova Scotia were different from the American colonies. They chose to remain part of the British Empire rather than join with the Thirteen Colonies in their fight for independence from Britain.

The People of British North America Remain Loyal to Britain

It occurred to the American revolutionaries that the people of the colonies of Nova Scotia and Quebec must also have many complaints against the British. The Stamp Act of 1765, for instance, caused them some hardship. The *Quebec Gazette* printed the following notice:

This is to inform the public that the printers of this gazette find themselves obliged to stop publication as of this day, given the small number of subscribers they now have, caused by the Act for the imposition of a stamp tax!

In Halifax, the owner of the *Halifax Gazette* lost his contract as official printer for the Nova Scotia government because he refused to put the required stamp on his newspaper. In fact, on the day that the Stamp Act came into effect, he used a skull and crossbones in place of the official stamp.

The Thirteen Colonies thought that the Canadiens in Quebec, having been so recently defeated by the British, would be ready to rebel against them. Also, Quebec and the Thirteen Colonies were neighbours since they shared a long border. Nova Scotia was farther away, but three-quarters of its population was from the Thirteen Colonies.

Quebec

Conflicting Messages

George Washington

In 1775, two messages were delivered to the people of Quebec. General Washington, who was later to be the first president of the United States, tried to convince them that they should join the revolution.

Come, then, my brethren, unite with us ... let us run together to the same goal. We have taken up arms in defence of our liberty, our property, our wives, and our children; we are determined to preserve them or die. We look forward with pleasure to that day ... when the inhabitants of America shall have one sentiment, and the full enjoyment of the blessings of a free Government ... the grand American Congress have sent an Army into your Province... not to plunder, but to protect you. ...

Bishop Briand of Quebec reminded the people of Quebec of their duty to the British king:

The remarkable goodness and gentleness with which we have been governed by his very gracious Majesty, King George the Third . . . the recent favours with which he had loaded us, in restoring to us the use of our laws and the free exercise of our religion . . . would no doubt [cause you to support] the interests of the British Crown.

The Soldiers of the Thirteen Colonies Invade Quebec

The American revolutionaries decided to send a two-pronged attack into the colony of Quebec. One army, under General Richard Montgomery, took the well-travelled route up the Richelieu River to Montreal. He was able to capture Montreal easily. Guy Carleton, the governor of the colony, escaped disguised as a French trapper, or he probably would have been captured.* Montgomery then continued on to Quebec City.

General Benedict Arnold and his troops had a much more difficult time. They took the overland route from Maine to Quebec, finding their way through dense forests and foul swamps. They ran out of food and were forced to eat candles and roasted moccasins. As a result of starvation, disease, and desertion, Arnold had only half of the 1200 men he had started with when he finally joined Montgomery at Quebec City. By the time the two armies camped outside the walled fortress at Quebec, they were facing both the hardship of a cold winter and the ravages of smallpox. In spite of Montgomery's boast that he would eat Christmas dinner in Quebec City, the armies were not able to attack until New Year's Eve, in the middle of a driving snowstorm. Two hundred Americans, including General Montgomery, were killed. The British defenders lost only six men. The American revolutionaries were left with little choice but to call off the attack. They remained camped outside the city for the rest of the winter. In May of 1776, the British navy arrived with reinforcements and the Americans were forced to return home. The American invasion of the colony of Quebec had failed.

If Montgomery and Arnold had been successful in their invasion attempt on the colony of Quebec, there was a slight possibility that British North America might have taken part in the American Revolution. The French subjects, however, were deeply distrustful of their English-speaking American neighbours. The British newcomers to Quebec still felt a strong loyalty to Britain.

Soldiers from the Thirteen Colonies attacked Quebec City on New Year's Eve, 1775. They expected that the Canadiens would welcome them as liberators, but instead they were seen as invaders.

---

*Other sources report that Carleton retreated with his troops. What reasons might there be for different versions of the same event? What is similar, and likely true, from both accounts?

Nova Scotia

The Americans did not attempt to invade the colony of Nova Scotia, as they had done with Quebec. Nova Scotia was quite isolated from New England and did not participate in pre-revolutionary activity. Nova Scotians' attention at that time was taken up with a Christian religious revival called the Great Awakening.

It might seem surprising that most people of Nova Scotia did not decide to join the American rebellion against British rule. Many Nova Scotians actually were Americans. Either they or their parents had been born in the Thirteen Colonies. The people of Nova Scotia were sometimes called "Neutral Yankees." (Yankees is a term for Americans.) In 1767, the total population of Halifax was 2822 people. Of these, 1351 people called themselves Americans. Although many had strong ties to American colonists, most Nova Scotians would not join the Americans in rebelling against British rule.

Focus On: British North American Feelings about the American Revolution

Colonists in British North America held a wide variety of points of view on the American Revolution. Fourteen points of view follow.*

The People of Nova Scotia's Responses

We should join the Americans! We too are taxed unfairly by the British!

I agree that the British are taxing us unfairly. But if we decide to fight against the British, we will get no help from the Americans. They have no extra ammunition to send us.

We have fathers, brothers, and sons fighting in New England. We should not side with the British against our loved ones.

Yes, but we are becoming rich from providing for the needs of the British troops. Why should we side with the Americans? Besides, General Washington was asked to invade Nova Scotia and he refused.

I also think we should join the Americans in fighting against the British. But with our small communities, which are scattered everywhere, it is impossible to get people to unite for a common cause.

I am a Halifax merchant. Don't forget that we depend on Britain for trade. We would be poor without Britain. Besides, the British navy controls the ocean. The navy would destroy any American ships bringing troops here.

I used to be on the American side. But I don't know how they can expect us to be on their side when their privateers attack our coastal settlements.

The People of Quebec's Responses

The British have treated us fairly. The Quebec Act protects our Roman Catholic religion. The Americans might force us to give it up.

I don't care what the governor and the Church tell us to do, I'm not going to join the militia to fight the Americans!

I wish the Americans would just go away and leave us alone! What would we gain by joining them?

What have I to gain by helping the Americans? They have never helped me. They compete with me for trade with Britain.

We must defend our homeland against the Americans. The British have protected our seigneurial system of land ownership. The Americans would take it away.

But there are so many Americans! Some of them are our cousins! And Quebec is so much closer to the Thirteen Colonies than to Britain!

I'm for loyalty to the British. They've been good to me. I say take up arms against the Americans!

For Your Notebook

1. Make a chart showing the positions of the colonists in Nova Scotia and Quebec.

2. Summarize the reasons why the people in Nova Scotia and Quebec either supported or opposed the American cause.

3. Imagine that you are a 15-year-old Nova Scotian living in or near Halifax. Your father came to Nova Scotia from Boston, and your mother came from Britain. Write a passage of dialogue for a family discussion of whether Nova Scotians should join the Americans. You can include other people, such as a neighbour who used to live in Quebec.

*These are imaginary points of view based on actual historical information.

Review

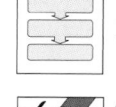

The icons are your cue to refer to the Learning How to Learn Appendix (pages 256–271) for ideas on how to complete these activities.

This icon is a reminder to turn to the Research Model (pages x–xi).

Complete a self-assessment for one assignment from this chapter.

Understanding Concepts

Checking Predictions

1. When you created your web at the beginning of the chapter you made predictions about the content based upon what you already knew and your first look at the chapter. Use a different coloured pen to add details to your web about what you have learned. Underline supporting details you correctly predicted. Use what you learned from reading the chapter to answer your questions on the bottom of your prediction page.

2. Discuss the "Questions to Talk About" on page 123 based on what you have learned about government in the Thirteen Colonies.

Recording Vocabulary

3. Using one of the methods in the Appendix for recording vocabulary, add these to the WordBook section of your notes:

   - congress
   - Thirteen Colonies
   - veto
   - boycott
   - bias
   - fact and opinion

Conceptualizing

4. Here are some main ideas from the chapter:
   - participatory democracy
   - representative government
   - taxation without representation
   - protest (violent and non-violent)
   - the American Revolution
   - reactions in Quebec and Nova Scotia to the revolution

   Do either a) or b)
   a) Create a concept poster about one of the ideas. Present your poster to the class.

   b) Use a web, mind map, outline, or chart to create a permanent set of notes about one of the ideas. Explain your work to a classmate.

Working with Information

5. Create a Cause and Effect chart which shows the various causes of conflict in the Thirteen Colonies. Show how this leads to other events and more conflict. Was the conflict resolved? How?

6. a) Define absolute rule and representative government.

   b) Compare the concept of representative government found in this chapter and absolute rule in Chapter 3. Include at least five criteria for comparison. Use a comparison chart like this one.

A. Absolute Rule	Criteria	B. Representative Government
	1.	

7. Refer to page 132. Decide if each statement is an example of fact or opinion. Is it possible to have both facts and opinions in the same paragraph? If so, label that paragraph both Fact (F) and Opinion (O). Discuss your answers as a class. Make a list of ways to distinguish facts and opinions. Add the list to the Tools of Learning section of your notes.

8.  Add at least five entries to your timeline for this chapter.

9. Compare your notebook to that of a partner. Check to see that items are not missing and are in the correct order. Organize your notes.

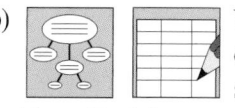

Developing Research Skills

10. Investigate the life of General George Washington. What does he mean to Americans?

11. Locate information about Bishop Briand. What were his accomplishments? How did his life impact ours?

12. Do research to find out the details of the journey taken by General Benedict Arnold and his troops on their way to Quebec. Trace their route on a map.

13. Decide which of the main topics, concepts, and projects covered in this chapter will require research information. Create a list of reference materials and resources to help your classmates with their projects. Include suitable websites, publications, audio/visual resources, and local historic sites on your list. You are helping to identify sources of research but you do not have to complete the research project.

Developing Communication Skills

Reading

14. Ask your librarian to recommend novels for you to read which are set during the time of the American Revolution.

15. Read about the American Declaration of Independence. What is its significance?

Writing

16. In your History Journal, tell of one person, place, idea, or event that you learned about which you had never heard of before. Why do you think you have not learned of this until now? How can you relate this to your life now?

17. Imagine you are an American colonist. Write a letter to the editor of a local newspaper describing your reaction to one of the Acts introduced by the British government.

18. What might have happened if Montgomery and Arnold had been successful in their invasion attempt of Quebec? Write the story.

19. Look at the picture on page 131 showing the attack on Quebec City. Write a poem to describe the event. Whose point of view does your poem represent?

Listening and Speaking

20. Work with another student to stage an interview between a newspaper reporter for the *Boston Gazette* and an American colonist. In response to the reporter's questions, the colonist gives his/her reasons for engaging in violent protest. After the interview, discuss whether or not you agree with the colonist's reasons.

21. One way to express protest today is to write and record songs which make a statement of protest. Find examples of protest songs. Play them for the class and discuss the protest message of each. Does the message of the song include a bias? Fact? Opinion? (See Bias on page 256.)

22. Imagine you are in the Thirteen Colonies. Randomly choose teams for a debate. One team should represent the "yes" (affirmative) side and one team should represent the "no" (negative) side. Use the following issue for debate: All forms of protest being expressed by the colonists should stop.

Viewing and Representing

23. Find an example of a movie or television show in which the characters are involved in non-violent protest. Summarize this and lead a class discussion. Was the protest effective? Why or why not? What forms of protest would have been effective?

24. Using recyclable materials, create a sculpture to represent one of the main ideas or concepts covered in this chapter. See if your classmates can guess the meaning you intend it to have.

Applying Concepts

25. Survey several adults. Make a list of questions to find out more about the taxes they pay. Examples follow: What kinds of taxes do adults pay? How is the amount owed in taxes decided? Where does the money go? Is it a fair system? How might it be changed? What would happen if there were no taxes?

26. Based on what you know so far about participatory democracy and representative government, do you

think everyone who qualifies should vote in elections? List reasons. Are there any exceptions? What will the legal right to vote mean to you?

27. Why have you been studying
    - the American Revolution?
    - protest?
    - representative government?

28. 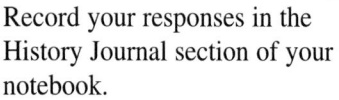 Try to think of as many ideas as you can for each of the following. Record your responses in the History Journal section of your notebook.
    What if...
    a) representative government had never been introduced to the colonists in the Thirteen Colonies?
    b) the people of the Thirteen Colonies had never protested against taxation without representation?
    c) General George Washington had successfully convinced the people of Quebec to join the revolution?

29. How do you think the Native people who were loyal to the British reacted to the American Revolution? Hypothesize about what they did.

30. Another way to communicate ideas (and sometimes to show protest) is to use political or editorial cartoons.
    a) What purpose do political cartoons serve? How are they effective? In what ways are they created?
    b) Collect a series of political cartoons from the newspapers over several days. You may also gather more information from articles or the news about the issues shown in the cartoons. Create a scrapbook. Under each cartoon, identify the main message intended by the cartoonist. Explain the visual and written clues that are used in the message.
    c) Select an ongoing news story or several different news stories. Create political cartoons to represent the news events.
    d) Select a topic (event, person, or idea) covered in this chapter. Create a political cartoon representing that topic. Share your cartoon with your classmates.

31. Complete each statement with a paragraph entry.

a) History Journal: I wanted to read more about . . . because . . .
b) Tools of Learning: What I'd like to learn to do better is . . .

Challenge Plus

32. 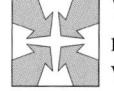 Working with a partner, reread the arguments made by Bishop Briand and George Washington on page 130. Evaluate the arguments by asking the following:
    a) What reasons are given to support the arguments?
    b) Were there any contradictions in the points made?
    c) Were irrelevant facts cited?
    d) Which argument is the strongest? Why?
    e) Discuss what is meant by "arguments" in the question above. What strategies does one use when evaluating arguments?
    Make a list. Create a handout or set of notes and share them with your classmates for them to include in the Tools of Learning section of their notebook.

33. Locate Canadian, British, and American books about Benedict Arnold. Do the three books reflect the same or differing points of view about him? If there is a difference, why do you think that is the case?

34. Read about democracy. How is this applied in our world? What are the exceptions? Create a special report on video about "The State of Democracy in the World." Consider the economic, social, and political effects of a democratic system. Play the video for the class. Ask for their reaction to help you assess what you have done.

35. Design a website or history magazine for Section IV: British North America. Decide how to show important people, places, events, and ideas in an interesting way, to assist other students to understand and appreciate Canadian history. Some items you could create include: fact files, visuals (e.g., maps, illustrations, diagrams), samples of students' work, chapter summaries, study guides and practice quizzes, and games. You might also include an interactive part such as an opinion poll or survey (and tables and graphs to show the results), a "write-in" question and answer column. Provide a list of related websites and resources.

Chapter 6
The Loyalists
(1776–1815)

O v e r v i e w
Use this Overview to predict the events of this chapter.

1783
Loyalist migration to British North America after the American Revolution.

After the American Revolution, Thayendanegea, a Loyalist and leader of the Iroquois Six Nations Confederacy, led his people to settle on a reserve in British North America.

The Loyalists started new lives in British North America.

Cape Breton Island

Nova Scotia

1784
New Brunswick created. Cape Breton Island established as a colony separate from Nova Scotia (reunited in 1820).

1791
Passage of the Constitutional Act. Quebec divided into Upper and Lower Canada, each with its own laws and system of government. Representative government established.

Upper Canada

Lower Canada

War of 1812–1815
War between British North America and the United States of America.

Chapter 6 Focus

Chapter 5 dealt with the American Revolution and its effects on British North America. Chapter 6 covers approximately the same period, but provides details about how the areas that were to become Canada and the United States began to distinguish themselves as separate countries. Chapter 6 also examines how representative government was established in British North America. The concepts of power, co-operation, decision-making, and conflict underlie the events of this chapter. The concept of decision-making is the focus of Chapter 6.

 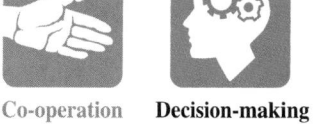 

| Power | Co-operation | **Decision-making** | Conflict |

Other Concepts and Main Topics

- Loyalists
- Constitutional Act, 1791 (representative government)
- communities
- War of 1812
- westward expansion of fur trade

Chapter Preview/Prediction

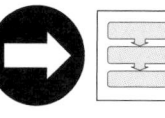 This chapter focuses on three topics in particular. The visuals to the right illustrate these topics. An illustrated overview of the first topic, the Loyalists, is provided to the left on page 136. Read the Overview, examine the visuals to the right, and look through the chapter. Use Cause–Effect charts like those below to make predictions. As you study the chapter, add details to your chart.

Causes → ① Loyalists come to British North America → Effect(s)

Causes → ② The War of 1812 → Effect(s)

Causes → ③ Fur Traders expand westward → Effect(s)

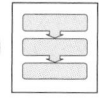 Continue your class project "Passport to the Past." Choose from the list of people on page 20.

1. Loyalists come to British North America

2. The War of 1812

3. Fur traders expand westward

The Loyalists

Beginning in 1776 and continuing for a decade, a steady stream of political **refugees**, called Tories, came to the British colonies of Quebec and Nova Scotia from the 13 American colonies. After the Treaty of Paris in 1783, these people came to be known as Loyalists.

The Tories fled from the Patriots because they did not agree with the Patriots' belief that British rule should be overthrown. Some Tories were killed by the Patriots. Others endured a punishment called being "tarred and feathered." Tories left the Thirteen Colonies in order to get to safer British territory. Since the colonies to the north had remained British and were close by, they settled there.

Patriots (Rebels) were loyal to the Thirteen Colonies. They wanted to separate from Britain to form the United States of America.*

Tories (Loyalists) were loyal to Britain. They did not want to separate from Britain. Most Loyalists moved to the remaining British North American colonies of Quebec and Nova Scotia.*

Photograph Courtesy of the Delaware Art Museum

Tory Refugees on Their Way to Canada. During and after the American Revolution, thousands of Loyalists travelled north by land and sea to settle in British North America.

Many of these Tories had been physically mistreated by the Patriots, their businesses destroyed, and their homes taken away from them. In the Treaty of Paris of 1783,** which ended the American Revolution, the Americans promised to repay the people whose homes or other property had been destroyed. This promise was never kept.

The coming of the Loyalists changed British North America greatly. Their arrival resulted in the creation of two new colonies. The new colony of New Brunswick was formed from a part of the colony of Nova Scotia. Also, the colony of Quebec was split into Lower Canada (now the province of Quebec) and Upper Canada (now the province of Ontario).

Refugee—person who leaves home or country to seek safety elsewhere
*Both the Patriots and the Tories had several different colours and styles of uniforms.

**There are two treaties called the Treaty of Paris. The treaty of 1763 ended the Seven Years' War; the treaty of 1783 ended the American Revolution.

There Were Many Kinds of Loyalists

The Patriots described a Loyalist as "someone whose head is in England, whose body is in America, and whose neck should be stretched." This saying meant they thought the Loyalists should be hanged for their loyalty to Britain and the British government. But did all of the Loyalists leave the Thirteen Colonies because they were loyal to Britain? The examples below explain some of the other reasons why people left the Thirteen Colonies.

Some people in the Thirteen Colonies were neutral and did not want to choose a side in the American Revolution. However, they were sometimes harassed by Americans for failing to show support for the American cause. Eventually, the tormenting led some of the colonists who had formerly been neutral to choose the British side.

A commonly held opinion has been that the Loyalists were mainly of British descent. However, their nationalities varied. As well as the English, the Irish, and the Scots, there were Loyalists of German, Dutch, French, Iroquoian, and African ancestry. These people hoped that Britain would protect their special customs and traditions.

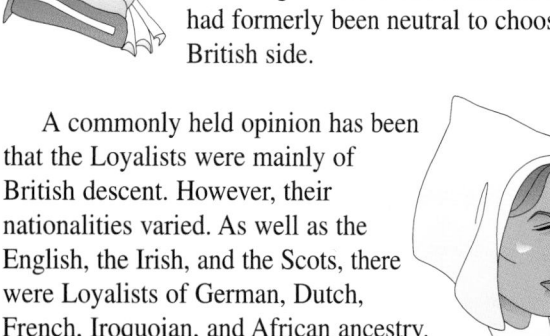

The Loyalists were loyal to the British monarchy. They feared the democratic ideas of the Americans. They knew that if they stayed in the United States their children would be forced to accept democratic ideas. They moved north to British territory where they felt their way of life would be protected.

Some Black people came to British North America as slaves and went where their "owners" went. Many Black people came as free people, like the other Loyalists, and others became Loyalists to gain their freedom. The British offered Black slaves their freedom if they helped the British cause.

Most of the Iroquois, like Thayendanegea (Joseph Brant), were Loyalists (see page 153). They had fought alongside the British regiments. Many of the Iroquois believed that they had more to fear from American farmers, who wanted to move onto lands where the Iroquois lived, than from the British.

The Loyalists were people of many different religions. There were Presbyterians, Anglicans, Methodists, Lutherans, Roman Catholics, Quakers, and Mennonites. Some of these religious groups were afraid that their religion would be lost. They wanted Britain's protection.

Most Loyalists came from colonies controlled by the British army. Loyalists who held British government jobs had no choice but to leave.

Some people became Loyalists on the basis of which recruiter, British or American, offered the best deal to settlers. Loyalists were offered free land in British North America. This greatly influenced their decision to go there.

Some Loyalists may have thought that it would not be long before their new home would be part of the United States anyway. Therefore, they thought they were not leaving their own country forever.

Some people became Loyalists because they expected Britain to win the war. They wanted to be on the winning side. However, Britain did not win. If their support of the Loyalist cause was known, they had to flee. Those who had not voiced their opinions as openly quickly became Patriots.

139

Where the Loyalists Went

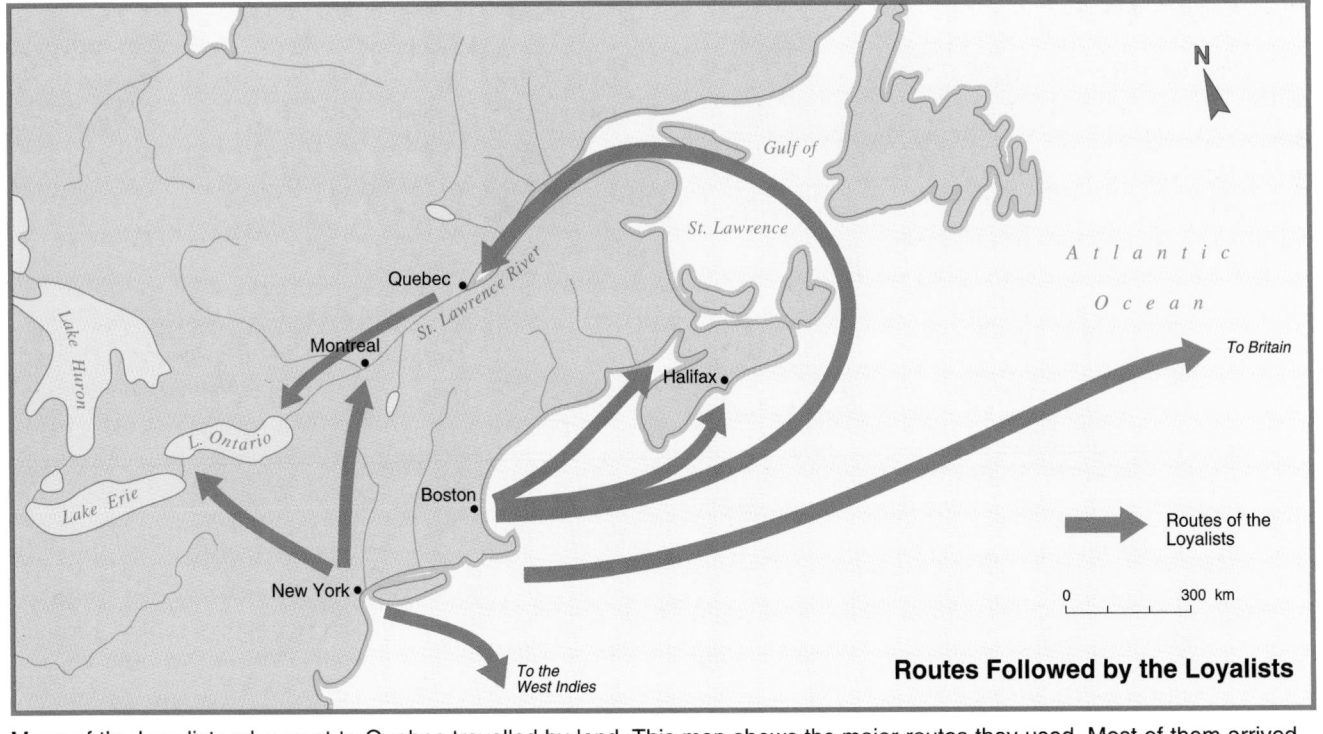

Many of the Loyalists who went to Quebec travelled by land. This map shows the major routes they used. Most of them arrived between 1776 and 1785. The Loyalists who went to Nova Scotia travelled by sea.

Loyalists had been leaving the Thirteen Colonies since 1776. In the Treaty of Paris of 1783, which ended the American Revolution, the American Congress agreed to ask the American states to pay the Loyalists back for any of their property that had been taken away or destroyed during the revolution. The American states refused to do this. After the revolution was over, there was still a great deal of anger against the Loyalists who remained in the United States. Farms and businesses were burned; Loyalists were beaten. The practice of tarring and feathering continued.

By 1785, two years after the end of the revolution, as many as 100 000 Loyalists may have left the United States. The Loyalists did not have many choices of places to go. Some went to Britain, others to the West Indies. Between 40 000 and 45 000 went to British North America.*

The Treaty of Paris of 1763, which ended the Seven Years' War between France and Britain, had given the colonies of Newfoundland, Nova Scotia, Quebec, and Prince Edward Island to Britain. Newfoundland and Prince Edward Island had very small populations of settlers. Nova Scotia had a settler population of about 20 000. A large percentage had moved there from the Thirteen Colonies. Most were of British or German descent.

The province of Quebec had been given to Britain under the Treaty of Paris of 1763, but it was definitely not British. Most of the people—about 98 000 of a population of 113 000—spoke French and had French traditions.

Because of their loyalty to Britain, the Loyalists would be protected by the British government in British North America. Also, the government would give each Loyalist family or individual a piece of land and some supplies to help them start a new life. About 34 000 Loyalists went to Nova Scotia, and about 7000 to Quebec.*

During the American Revolution, Loyalists brought about 2000 slaves with them to British North America.** Over 3000 Black people who had gained their freedom by fighting for the British settled in what is now New Brunswick and Nova Scotia. During the War of 1812 (see pages 166–171), slaves in the United States were promised freedom and land grants in British North America in exchange for their loyalty to the British. As many as 2000 Black people arrived, although some did not stay. Plots of land granted to them were typically small, of poor quality, and in separate communities on the edges of towns. Many did not receive land grants as promised. Black immigrants were not always welcomed and often faced discrimination.

---

*Figures for the number of Loyalists who settled in present-day Canada are not exact. Some did not apply for aid and therefore were not in the official records. Some who came did not stay. Some returned to the United States or moved on to other places.

**Slavery had existed since the 1600s in New France. Slavery was abolished in the British Empire in 1833. From the end of the American Revolution to 1816, approximately 5500 Africans came from the United States to British North America, particularly to Nova Scotia and New Brunswick. By the 1850s there were at least 30 000 Black people in what is now Ontario.

The British Colony of Nova Scotia

At the end of the American Revolution, in 1783, the only major port in the American colonies that the defeated British still held was New York. Many Loyalists went there so that the British could protect them from the victorious American Patriots. At New York the Loyalists waited for British ships to take them to Nova Scotia.

The Loyalists who went to New York included those who had fought in Loyalist regiments for the British army during the revolution. At the end of the revolution the British government gave them a choice between being sent back to their homes with three months' pay or being transported to Nova Scotia. Because the Loyalists were in danger of being persecuted if they returned home, they had no real choice. Many of the former soldiers decided that they would be much better off to take their families to Nova Scotia, where they could start a new life.

Here is part of a letter written by the wife of a Loyalist soldier, on June 6, 1783:

Kind husband,

I am sorry to acquant you that our farme is sold...they said if I did not quitt posesion that they had aright to take anythink on the farme or in the house to pay the cost of a law sute and imprisen me—I have suffered most every thing but death it self in your long absens pray grant me spedy releaf or God only knows what will become of me and me frendles children.... They say my posesion was nothing youre husband has forfeted his estate by joining the British Enemy with a free and vollentary will and thereby was forfeted to the Stat and sold. All at present from you cind and loveing wife.

Phoebe Ward

For families like the Wards, Nova Scotia seemed like a good place to go. It was a British colony, but very few people lived there. The low population ensured that there would be plenty of land available for the Loyalists.

Some of the Loyalists were so thankful to arrive on British soil that they knelt and kissed the ground. One Loyalist, the Reverend Jonathan Beecher, wrote:

As soon as we had set up a kind of tent, we knelt down, my wife and I and my two boys, and kissed the dear ground and thanked God that the flag of England floated there. We resolved that we would work with the rest to become again prosperous and happy.

The Coming of the Loyalists, 1783. Many Loyalists faced great hardships when they had to start new farms or businesses in British North America.

Unfortunately, some Loyalists were soon disappointed in their new home. They called it "Nova Scarcity." The winters were harsh and food was scarce. In many areas the land was unproductive. They complained bitterly at how poorly the British government had rewarded them for their loyalty to Britain during the revolution.

By 1785, about 34 000 Loyalists had made the journey to Nova Scotia. This was over one and one-half times as many people as the 20 000 already there. The Loyalists settled in three main areas—Halifax, Shelburne, and the St. John River Valley.

Areas Where the Loyalists Settled

Halifax

Halifax had been founded in 1749. By the time the Loyalists began to arrive in 1783, Halifax was a well-established community, with schools, churches, and stores. It was the British military centre and capital of Nova Scotia. The British-appointed governor and many soldiers lived there, as well as families. In Halifax, the Loyalists were expected to fit into the community, rather than make their own new life, as they did in Shelburne and the St. John River Valley. Only a small number of Loyalists settled in Halifax.

The Church of St. Paul and the Parade at Halifax in Nova Scotia.

Shelburne

About 10 000 Loyalists went to settle at Port Roseway. They renamed it Shelburne and made it, for a short time, one of the largest cities in all of North America. The Loyalists had high hopes for the new lives they would have in Shelburne. There was an excellent harbour and few people, which meant that they would be able to live their own lives and not have to fit into an established community, as the Loyalists who settled in Halifax had to do.

A thriving town quickly developed, with stores, taverns, churches, three newspapers, and a shipbuilding industry. Benjamin Marston, a resident of Shelburne, describes how early in 1784 some 50 citizens of the city "danced, drank tea, and played cards in a house where six months ago there was an almost impenetrable swamp."

Unfortunately, though, the land around Shelburne was unsuitable for farming. When the British government's food rations began to run out, people began to leave. In a short time, it went from a boom town of 10 000 people to a few hundred people. Many of the new houses were either taken apart and shipped to Halifax, where they were set up again, or they were destroyed for firewood. Soon much of the city looked like a grassy ghost town with stone fireplaces scattered about.

The St. John River Valley

About 15 000 Loyalists settled in the St. John River Valley, in an area that would later become the colony of New Brunswick. This group of settlers had problems with their new situation.

They began to ask for a separate colony almost immediately. They did not want to be part of the colony of Nova Scotia. They felt that Halifax, the capital, where most of the government officials were located, was too far away.

The government was not well prepared for the arrival of the Loyalists. The first night after landing, the Loyalists had to hack away bushes and trees in order to find room to set up their tents. Some were so dismayed by this situation that they simply sat down and cried.

The government did not provide enough tools and building materials to help the Loyalists build their new homes. As a result, some of the women and children died from cold weather or starvation during the first winter.

The distribution of land to the Loyalists was another major problem. The land had not been divided into lots when the first Loyalists arrived. Therefore, they could not be sure that they actually owned the land upon which they were building their homes. In fact, Loyalists had already built 1500 frame houses and 400 log huts near the harbour, when the government informed them that the area was needed as a refugee settlement area for new arrivals.

Later arrivals were unhappy because the lots that they were given were much smaller than the lots given to Loyalists who had arrived earlier. In fact, in Parrtown (later renamed St. John) the last town lots were one-sixteenth the size of the first lots.

Favouritism was also a problem. Loyalists who had held important positions in the Thirteen Colonies received more land than Loyalists who were not considered as important.

Thomas Peters (1738–1792)

Thomas Peters was a former slave. He served with the Black Pioneers, an all-Black British regiment, during the American Revolution. In 1783, Peters and other veterans of the Black Pioneers were transported to Nova Scotia, where they had been promised town lots in Shelburne, in addition to land outside the city.

Instead, the British government gave them only poor land outside of Shelburne. When they built on this land, their homes were burned down by people from Shelburne. They finally settled in an all-Black community outside Shelburne called Birchtown.

Peters travelled among the Black communities in Nova Scotia and New Brunswick gathering support. Then, in 1790, he travelled to Britain. There he met members of Britain's anti-slavery movement. These people had started a new colony in Africa, called Sierra Leone. They offered to transport free Black people from Nova Scotia to Sierra Leone. On January 15, 1792, about 1200 Black people, including Thomas Peters, sailed from Nova Scotia to Sierra Leone. There was to be equality among people of all races in this new colony.

Unfortunately, the colony only lasted a year. There were many difficulties from the beginning. Many colonists died on the voyage to Africa. Droughts, tornadoes, fever, and feuds among the colonists made the first year a disaster. However, even though the colony collapsed, there are still descendants of the Nova Scotia colonists in Sierra Leone today.*

The British Colony of New Brunswick

In 1784, Nova Scotia was divided and the British colony of New Brunswick was founded. (See map on page 145.)

A New Colony Is Formed

The Loyalists Want a New Colony

The Loyalists in the St. John River Valley had many reasons for wanting a new colony. They felt that they were too far from the government capital in Halifax. They felt that the distant government treated them unfairly. The Loyalists also believed that they were unlike the people who were already settled in the colony of Nova Scotia. Many of these people were formerly from the New England

colonies and had remained neutral, favouring neither side during the revolution. The people in Nova Scotia had not been forced to leave their homes like the Loyalists had. The Loyalists felt that what they had suffered during and after the revolution made it difficult for them to live with people who had not suffered or taken part in the revolution. They thought a separate Loyalist colony where they could live with people like themselves would be better.

This idea was expressed by Edward Winslow, one of the Loyalist leaders:

A large proportion of the old inhabitants of this country are natives of New England, or descendants from New Englanders. They never experienced the violence of political bad feelings. They remained quiet during all the persecutions. They kept an affection for their former country. On our side are people who served in the military. They are angry from a series of misfortunes and are jealous to an extreme. Either of these kinds of people may form useful societies among themselves, but they can't be mixed.

A final reason had to do with the possibilities of the area. The St. John River was easy to navigate. The soil was fertile. Fish and timber were plentiful and the coastline had many good harbours. It looked like a place where new settlers could become prosperous.

 ### The British Government Agrees

The British government recognized certain advantages in the formation of a Loyalist colony separate from the colony of Nova Scotia.

- If the colony of Nova Scotia were split, it would be less difficult to control because there would be a governor in each of the two colonies. The governor in Halifax would no longer have to worry about governing a place so far away.

- A new colony government would provide administrative positions for wealthy and well-educated Loyalists who were demanding them.

- A strong Loyalist colony on the American border would provide protection against the influence of the American idea that colonists should rebel and govern themselves. The British government did not want the people in its remaining North American colonies to be influenced by this idea.

New Brunswick developed representative government soon after its formation as a colony. The first Legislature met in 1786, just two years after the colony of New Brunswick separated. Representative government means that the people of New Brunswick could "rule" by choosing others to act for, or represent, them in government.

---

*There are also thousands of descendants of Black Loyalists living in Nova Scotia today.

The British Colony of Prince Edward Island

Île St. Jean (as Prince Edward Island was called then) had become British property in 1763, by the Treaty of Paris. The British renamed it St. John Island. It was called St. John Island until 1799, when it took the name of Prince Edward Island.

In 1767, the British had divided the island into 67 townships of approximately 8000 hectares. The townships had been given to British noblemen or officers. These people owned the land but did not choose to live on it. These absentee landlords chose to live in Britain instead of the colonies.

The landholding system on St. John Island when Loyalists came there in 1784 was like an English version of New France's seigneurial system. All the land was owned by a favoured group of people. The difference between the landholding system on St. John Island and that in New France was that the St. John Island landholders did not bring in settlers as they had promised, and many of them did not even pay their taxes.

When the Thirteen Colonies held their First Continental Congress (a meeting to discuss their complaints about Britain) in 1774, the people of St. John Island, as well as the people of Quebec and Nova Scotia, had been invited to attend. They had not been interested in gaining independence from Britain, but did want to gain some rights as colonies. However, they had decided not to send any representatives to the meeting.

By 1784, there were still only about 1000 people living on St. John Island. Approximately 600 Loyalists decided to try to settle there. They found that they had to pay high rents and could not buy their land, since it was already owned by the absentee landlords.

Eventually some of the Loyalist farmers decided that if the British landlords did not have to pay taxes, then they should not have to pay the high rents. The story is told that the first person in a neighbourhood to see a rent collector coming would blow on a large seashell to sound an alarm. Then the farmers would drive away the collector with clubs and pitchforks.

Some of the farmers were so discouraged by the fact that they could not own the land they worked, that they left St. John Island. Others stayed on in the hope that one day the land would be theirs.

The British Colony of Cape Breton Island

Like New Brunswick, Cape Breton was made a separate colony from Nova Scotia in 1784. Up to this time the British government had not allowed people to settle there. There was coal on the island but the British government did not allow factories to be built because they would compete with the factories in Britain. However, in 1784 Cape Breton Island was opened to the Loyalists. About 3000 settled there. Most did not stay long. They did not like the fact that they could only rent, not buy, their land. As on St. John Island, most of the land on Cape Breton Island was owned by absentee landlords who lived in Britain. In 1820, Cape Breton was **re-annexed** to Nova Scotia.

Cape Breton Council, by Charles Walter Simpson. The Cape Breton council had to deal with the large numbers of Loyalist refugees moving into the area.

The British Colony of Newfoundland

In 1784, the British still showed no interest in having Newfoundland grow in population. All of the attention of the British government was still directed toward the fishing industry there. As a result, settlement was not encouraged. The government did not transport any Loyalists to Newfoundland.

Re-annex—to unite with a province or country again

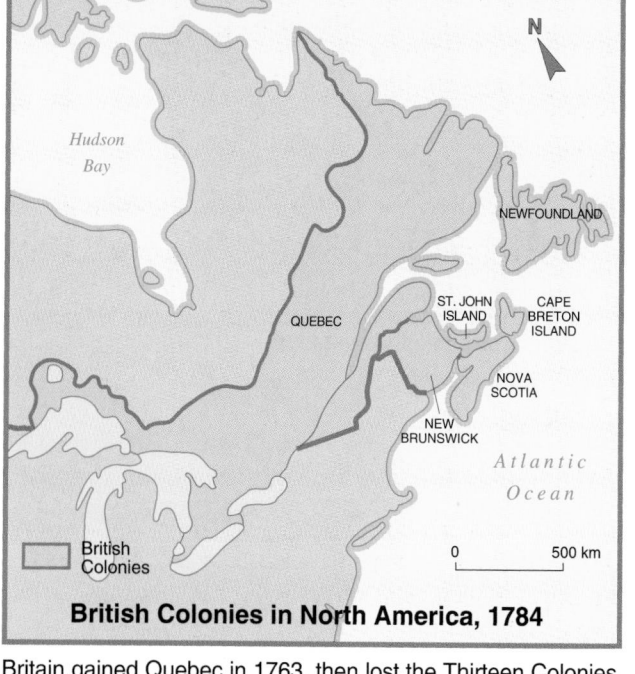

By the 1760s, semi-permanent fishing stations had been established in many of Newfoundland's harbours.

British Colonies in North America, 1784

Hudson
Bay

NEWFOUNDLAND

QUEBEC

ST. JOHN
ISLAND

CAPE
BRETON
ISLAND

NOVA
SCOTIA

NEW
BRUNSWICK

Atlantic

Ocean

N

British
Colonies

0   500 km

Britain gained Quebec in 1763, then lost the Thirteen Colonies during the American Revolution. The result by 1784 was a very different British North America.

Opportunist—a person who takes advantage of a situation for his or her own benefit

For Your Notebook

1. In which three areas did the Loyalists settle in Nova Scotia? Briefly summarize the Loyalist experience in each of these places.

2. Why did the Loyalists in the St. John River Valley want the British government to create a new colony for them?

3. Why did the British government agree that a new colony should be created in the St. John River Valley?

4. Explain the landholding system on St. John Island (later called Prince Edward Island) at the time of the arrival of the Loyalists.

Exploring Further

1. Benedict Arnold is an interesting person from these times. He began as a Patriot, married a Loyalist, and then offered to spy for the British. He escaped from the Patriots on a British ship, but left his British contact behind to be hanged as a spy. After the war he was hated by both Patriots and Loyalists (for abandoning his contact). Read more details about Benedict Arnold. Decide whether you think he was a Patriot, a Loyalist, or an **opportunist**. Justify your answer.

145

The British Colony of Quebec

Loyalists started coming to Quebec in 1776, and 7000 had arrived by 1783. Six thousand were crowded into temporary refugee camps on the seigneury of Sorel, waiting for the government to decide what to do with them.

The British government urged Governor Haldimand to encourage the Loyalists to go back home. The British government thought they complained too much and cost too much money. However, Governor Haldimand realized that it was highly unlikely that they would return to the United States. There was too much hatred against them there. Also, their farms, homes, businesses, and any other possessions left behind had all been taken over by the Patriots. They really had no good reasons to return. The Loyalists had given up everything and expected the British government to make up for their losses.

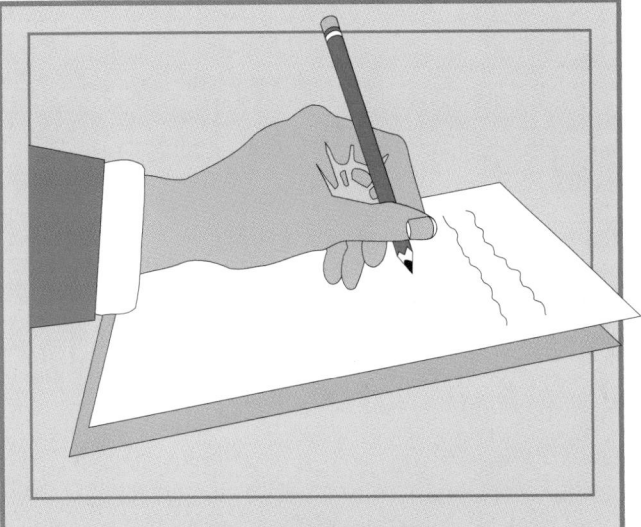

A Petition

A petition is a document containing a request directed to the government. It contains statements describing what the petitioners want changed and has space for the petitioners to sign their names. People might sign a petition requesting anything from the construction of a road to the lowering of taxes. People who want others to sign their petitions often go door-to-door or stand in markets or other places where many people will see them.

An Exercise in Problem Solving

1. Divide into groups of four. Imagine you are a member of a Loyalist family consisting of two parents and four children leaving one of the Thirteen Colonies for Quebec. Your father's life is in danger and you have only a few hours to prepare for your journey. You have two horses and a small cart. List the possessions you would take with you.

2. Imagine that your family is travelling toward the colony of Quebec. You decide to write a petition to Governor Haldimand, to be delivered when you arrive.

   In the petition you describe the following:

   • what you will need (land, food, clothing, seed, farm and household tools)

   • the hardships you expect in your new home

   • the help you expect Governor Haldimand to give you

A Loyalist Petition

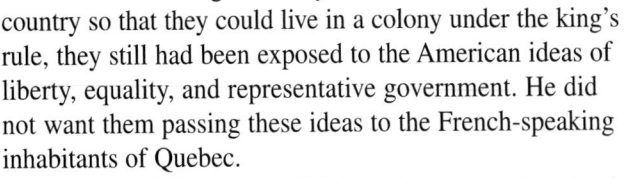

Governor Haldimand did not want the Loyalists mixing with the French-speaking population. Even though the Loyalists had left their own country so that they could live in a colony under the king's rule, they still had been exposed to the American ideas of liberty, equality, and representative government. He did not want them passing these ideas to the French-speaking inhabitants of Quebec.

Governor Haldimand decided to give the Loyalists land on the frontier to the west, as far away from the French as possible. Another reason for putting them there was so that they could serve as a first defence in the case of an American attack.

The Loyalists knew that they would need many things if they were going to be pioneers in a new land. They listed the items they wanted in a petition to Governor Haldimand.

146

The Loyalists

Part 1
by Brenda Bellingham

James Jones slipped past the open door of the dining room. Father, Mother, Will, Charlotte, and Lizzie were sitting around the long oak table waiting for him. James's eye felt watery and painful, and he kept his head down to hide it. His shirt was torn and bloodstained. If only he could change into clean clothes before his father saw him. He started to creep up the stairs.

"Well, James, I see you have been scrapping again." Father stood in the hallway and spoke sternly. "Clean up quickly and come to the table."

After James had joined the others, Father asked, "And what was your reason for fighting this time?"

Will glanced across the table at James and winked. Will was sixteen, too old to go to school. He helped Father work the farm.

James took courage. "Please, sir, I couldn't help it. I had to fight. John Harvey called me a Tory."

Six-year-old Lizzie tossed back her braids. "I thought John Harvey was your best friend."

James felt miserable. Until today John, who lived on the next farm, had been his best friend.

"You did well to fight, young James," Will's hearty voice pointed out. "He's no friend to call you a Tory."

"Exactly what is a Tory, Father?" James asked.

"Nothing but a name, James. A name given by the rebels to those of us who are still loyal to His Majesty King George III of England."

"Father, is John a rebel then?" Charlotte asked.

"It would seem so." Father exchanged worried glances with Mother. "James," he said, "I want you to stay away from John Harvey in future. D'you hear?"

Before James could answer, loud voices, the sound of splintering wood, and a scream from the kitchen sent Father for one of the muskets hanging beside the fireplace. Before he could reach it, the door burst open.

"Hold!" Amos Harvey stood in the doorway, his musket pointed at Father. Behind him stood half a dozen other men, all with muskets.

Father straightened his back. "What's this, Amos?" he asked.

Father's voice was calm. James's own heart pounded in his throat. Will darted towards the firearms, but one of Amos's companions pointed a musket and ordered him to stay where he was.

"The Continental Congress has ordered that all Tories hand over their arms," Amos Harvey answered Father. "My committee and I are here to see the order is obeyed."

Two of his companions strode to the wall and removed the muskets.

"Neighbours," Father said, "I have a family to feed and defend. Won't you leave us one musket? Surely you cannot believe I'm a danger to you. I am just as much

against the new taxes the British collect from us as you are. I too believe we colonists should have the right to tax ourselves. But I do not believe it is wise to break all our ties with the mother country."

Amos Harvey narrowed his eyes. "If you are really for us, Thomas Jones," he said, "break your oath of allegiance to the British crown and swear loyalty to the State of New York."

"You know I cannot do that, Amos," Father answered quietly. "When I became a **magistrate**, I swore an oath of allegiance to His Majesty King George III. A man of honour does not lightly take or break such an oath."

"Arrest him!" Amos ordered. Two men seized Father and bound his hands behind his back.

"No!" Mother cried. "My husband speaks the truth. He is loyal to this colony, and to the king."

The men ignored Mother and marched Father away. "Be brave, Hannah," he called over his shoulder. "Will, take care of your mother and the children."

Mother's face was pale but she stood proudly as the men went out the door. Will went to her. Charlotte held Lizzie as the little girl cried quietly. James's legs were shaking and he sank onto his chair.

He had heard stories about Loyalists in other, larger towns who had been tarred and feathered, but he had never expected their own neighbours in their own little town

Magistrate—judge of a local court

to turn against his family. Would they tar and feather his father? People had died from such treatment. Suddenly James felt ill. He ran outside to be sick.

Three days passed and the family heard nothing from Father. In the evening they gathered together in the parlour—even baby Sarah in her wooden cradle. Mother sat in her rocking chair reading aloud from *Gulliver's Travels* by the light of one candle.

Will stood beside the window keeping watch through a gap in the curtains. Outside, the wind blew in the dark night. Rain pattered against the windowpane like someone urgently tapping to come in.

"Hush!" Will urged. "Someone's here." He was across the room in two strides.

James tried to follow him out, but Will pushed him back into the room. James glanced at the empty gun hooks beside the fireplace. Oh, for a musket!

When Will came back he had Lawyer Cook with him.

Mother jumped up. "What news, Mr. Cook?"

Lawyer Cook put his finger to his lips. "Your husband sends word that you are to leave your home, Ma'am," he said in a low voice. "You are to take the children and go to your brother in Quebec."

"But not without my husband!"

"Hush! Yes, without him. The rebels have sentenced him to jail."

"For what crime?" Will asked.

"For **treason**," Mr. Cook answered. "The rebels call it treason to be loyal to the king. Ma'am, do not hesitate. Take your children and go, while there is still time."

Treason—betrayal of a country or ruler

Charlotte showed Mr. Cook out and came back followed by the two slaves, Mary and Pete.* James could not remember a time when they had not been part of the household.

"Beg pardon, Missus," Mary said, "but we heard you talking with Lawyer Cook. Please take us with you. Don't leave us behind."

"You understand the dangers, Mary?" Mother asked. "We might all be set upon by rebels and killed. Or the rebels could take you from us. As far as they are concerned, we are outlaws and can be dealt with as they see fit."

"We understand," Pete said. "We'd rather take our chances with you and the little ones. We're scared to stay. Scared we'll be sold to different families—never see each other again."

"We will be glad to have your help on the journey," said Will. He looked around at them all and managed a grin. "Cheer up, everyone. Let us obey Father and trust in God to bring us safely to Quebec. Then, as soon as I have seen you settled with Uncle, I shall join the king's army and fight to rescue Father and bring us all back home to live in freedom."

Refugees

Moving quietly, like shadows, everyone set swiftly to work. Only baby Sarah slept, unaware of the danger. They each made a small bundle of clothing. Mary helped Mother bundle up the bedding. Pete and Will packed small tools in a wooden keg. Charlotte and Lizzie

---

*At this time in British North America and the Thirteen Colonies, it was legal to have slaves. See pages 125, 240, and 241 for more information about the practice of slavery and its eventual abolition.

took sacks of flour, salt, bacon, lard, and preserves—anything they could carry from the pantry. James helped carry everything to the barn, silently, with no lantern to light the way. The rain had stopped, but heavy clouds darkened the night. There was no moonlight to give them away.

"You may bring one thing with you," Will said.

James felt a bit ashamed of his choice. It was a little wooden horse and wagon, not a plaything for a ten-year-old boy. His father had carved it for him when he was four years old.

It was one o'clock in the morning when they made their way out to the barn for the last time. Pete was helping Will hitch up the horses. Mary handed Sarah up to Mother, who sat in the wagon. When all were ready, Will took the reins. James, Lizzie, and Charlotte were sitting on the bundles. Pete closed the huge barn doors behind them. As they left the yard, Mother kept her eyes straight ahead. Charlotte sat with her arm around Lizzie.

James looked back. The frame house stood solid and safe against the sky, as if it would last a hundred years. He thought of the comfortable furniture still in the rooms and the pretty china his mother had treasured. Then he looked at the wagon loaded with lumpy bundles and wooden boxes. James did not look back again.

For days the family travelled. Once they had to hide all day in the woods because there were rebels nearby. A couple of times they were given shelter by friendly Loyalists. One night they slept in the burned-out ruins of what had been a fine farm.

James wondered about their own farm. Mostly he wondered about his father. Was he still in jail? Was he still alive? Each night, under the quilt, he held onto the little wooden horse and wagon his father had made for him.

It was almost four weeks before they reached the Quebec border. They had to wait while the border guards asked a lot of questions and examined their luggage. At last they were told they could pass through and carry on to Fort Île aux Noix on Lake Champlain.

Other families, with their goods piled up on wagons like the Jones family, already waited there. Some people had come on horseback with few belongings. Some had walked from home, bringing only as much as they could carry. James thought himself lucky when he saw their worn-out shoes and weary faces.

"What are we all waiting for?" he asked his mother.

"My brother is coming by boat to collect us and take us to Sorel." She gazed anxiously up the Richelieu River.

After two days the boat came. It held not Uncle Solomon, but James's father.

"Oh, Tom!" cried Mother, "I wondered if we would ever see you again. I've been so frightened for the children."

James stared at his father. Father was much thinner than he had been the last time James had seen him in New York. "Father, how did you get here ahead of us?" he asked.

Will added, "Did you have to fight your way out of jail?"

Father grinned. "My cellmate and I captured our jailer when he brought us our miserable supper. Then we headed for the woods. We were men with a price on our heads. We were fortunate to meet a group of Mohawks who guided us to safety. Once in Quebec, we signed on with Colonel Butler's Rangers and got a uniform each in place of our own tattered clothes. We have yet to see action, but we're ready to serve. In the meantime, I can see you settled at Sorel, where you'll be safe until the war's end."

Pete moved restlessly. Father

looked at him and said, "Pete, I know you would like to join the fighting. But since you have come this far, I hope you will be so good as to remain with my wife and children until I can return. I know you had hoped to be granted freedom by the government for fighting in the war. I promise that you and Mary will eventually be free."

Pete nodded and looked at Mary. "Thank you, sir. We will stay."

Sorel. What kind of place would that be? At any rate it would be safe and they would not have to look over their shoulders all the time. And

Father would be near. For the first time in weeks, James felt cheerful.

Friends

The family, with Pete and Mary, finally reached Sorel. Charlotte sat beside James in the wagon as it lurched along the muddy roadway. She looked at the untidy mixture of tents and ramshackle wooden huts.

Father glanced back from the driving seat. "Most of these people are like us. They've had to leave their homes and belongings behind. Some of them got away with little more than the clothes on their backs. We'll have to make do with what the governor can provide. Let's hope the war will soon be over and we can all go home."

At first, James found tent life fun. His mother couldn't scold him for getting dirty. In all that mud it was impossible to keep clean. And there was only one water pump to share with dozens of others. But soon he grew tired of being crammed into such a small space.

Fall came and the nights were cold. Sometimes he felt as if he had lain awake, shivering, all night. He was glad when his father came to take them to a house in a French village.

"Thank goodness," Charlotte said. "Now we can grow our own food. I'm so tired of salt pork and peas. I don't think the governor knows of any other kind of food."

Father shook his head. "I'm afraid we'll have no farm, Charlotte. We'll still have to live on salt pork and peas."

The house in the village was built of stone. Father said they were lucky to find it, as all the towns and villages close to Sorel were crowded with Loyalists. James thought they were lucky too, until he went up the village street to explore. Two boys came from behind a house. The boys shouted angrily at James in a language he could not understand.

As James stood, too surprised to move, a boy with hair as yellow as a corn cob came up behind him.

The boy said, "They're villagers and they don't like us."

James recognized the boy. He had caught glimpses of him dodging amongst the tents at Sorel. "What were they saying?" he asked.

"They were telling us to go back where we came from."

"I wish I could," James said. "Nobody wants us, not the people we left, not the ones we've come to. I wish I had a proper home."

"You'll get one when the war's over," the yellow-haired boy said. He had lively blue eyes and his wide grin made James feel better.

"My name's James Jones," he said. "What's yours?"

"Adam Davey. I reckon we should be friends," Adam said.

"Friends," said James as he shook Adam's hand. It felt good to have a friend again.

Father returned to his duties with Butler's Rangers at Niagara. Sometimes Butler's men, along with Iroquois allies, made swift raids into enemy territory. At other times, they went behind enemy lines to rescue Loyalist families.

One day Father and Will came home looking weary and sad. "The war is over," Father said. "The rebels have won."

Charlotte broke the silence. "When are we going home again? I'm so tired of salt pork and peas."

"We can't go home, Charlotte," Father said. "The rebels took our farm and sold it to one of their so-called Patriots. We no longer have a home, but the king has promised each Loyalist a free grant of land." The governor will let us know where our land is next spring."

Up the River

One spring day Will came home waving a copy of the *Quebec Gazette*. "It says here we're to pack and be ready to leave. From Sorel, we will go to the village of Newark,* on the Niagara River."

Five weeks after leaving Sorel, the group they were travelling with arrived at Newark. What a relief! The men had pulled slips of paper from a hat to see where their property was. James's family travelled to their land with Adam's family. Some former slaves went to the towns to work for wages, but Pete and Mary decided to stay with the Jones family until they could find employment together in a town.

Farmers Again

The men got together and worked on each family's house in turn. First they chopped down a few trees. Then, they cut notches in the logs and piled them one on top of another to build the walls. The cabins measured only 6 metres long by 4.5 metres wide by 2 metres high.

"Gather up all the wood chips and mix them with mud," Adam's father told the younger boys. "Stuff the whole mess between the logs. It'll keep out the wind."

"Careful how you handle those panes of glass for the windows, boys," Mother warned. "There's

---

*Newark is now known as Niagara-on-the-Lake.

only one window for a family." Mother hung a blanket over the door opening. For now the family had to make do with a dirt floor.

The fireplace was the most important part of the house. The men dragged boulders to build the fireplace walls. They made the chimney from logs, plastering them well with mud so they would not catch fire.

"When are we going to put in the crops?" James asked.

"It'll be too late to plant crops this year, James," Father said.

"We can clear more land over winter," Will added. "Then we'll be ready to work the soil and plant come next spring."

Lizzie looked anxious. "What do we eat while we wait?"

Charlotte pulled a face. "Salt pork and peas." James groaned.

Mother shushed him. "We've been given some flour and a little salt, and we're supposed to get butter next time we go to the depot for our rations. King George isn't treating us too badly, I suppose."

By the end of the winter the men had cleared a small field. After the snow melted, the whole family spent days picking rocks. Soon it was time to plant their first crop.

Over the next two winters they cleared more land so that each spring they could plant more wheat and corn. It became easier to feed the family without depending on King George's salt pork and peas. They planted apple, peach, and cherry trees and looked forward to future years when the trees would produce fruit.

Father smiled. "I think we can begin to call ourselves farmers again."

Government Help

Provisions and Tools

The Loyalists in Quebec were not given all of the items they had requested in their petition. However, they were given enough supplies to last for three years. Each family was given one tent. One musket was given to every five men (with 1 kg of powder and 2 kg of lead balls). Governor Haldimand thought that the men would spend their time clearing the land and planting crops if they could not spend it hunting. Each man was given an axe, a spade, and a hoe for this purpose. Small groups of families were given an ox, a plough, and building tools to share. Clothes were provided for three years' wear. Flour, beef, pork, salt, and butter were given to each family.

The following seed supply was given to the members of the community: 2 kg of onion seed, 5 kg of Norfolk turnip, 4 kg early Dutch turnip, 5 kg large Dutch cabbage, 6 kg celery seed, 8 kg orange carrot, 2 kg short top radish, 1 kg parsley seed, 36 dm³ of marrowfat peas.

It is interesting to note that the wheat seed had to be purchased from Americans in Vermont and the Mohawk Valley. Some of the wheat must have come from farms once owned by Loyalists who had left those areas.

Land Grants

It was decided that the distribution of land would be determined by the rank in the Loyalist army of the male head of houshold and the number of people in their families. Army officers could draw more land than others, but they were not allowed to choose the land they liked best.

The land was divided into lots of about 80 hectares. Each lot was given a number. The numbers were written on pieces of paper and placed in a hat. Each man picked one of the lot numbers out of the hat and then hurried off to inspect his land. (See image #1 on page 137.) Because there were no roads, the most valuable land was located along the waterways. Land that proved to be too poor for farming could be left and another lot, farther inland, could be drawn.

Loyalists from the Thirteen Colonies were used to the British freehold system, where individuals held the title to their land. They did not like the seigneurial system, which was a type of leasehold* system. Although the British freehold system was not officially established in Upper Canada until the colony was created in 1791, Loyalists were permitted to purchase and sell the land grants to the others.

*Under the seigneurial system people who farmed the land did not own it. They were entitled to the products from their work and profit from surplus production. They paid some dues of work and products, but this was not rent in the usual sense. They had more security than renters, but less than owners. They had the right to leave use of the land to their heirs if they died.

An Example of a Loyalist Petition

To His Excellency General Haldimand, Governor General and Commander-in-Chief:

The Loyalists, going to form a settlement at Cataraqui, ask:

- That boards, nails, and shingles be given to each Loyalist family so that they may build houses and other buildings; that eight squares of window glass also be given each family.

- That arms, ammunition, and one axe be given to each male, aged fourteen or more.

- That the following things be given to each family:
  - one ploughshare and coulter**
  - leather for horse collars
  - two spades
  - three iron wedges
  - fifteen iron harrow teeth
  - three hoes
  - 2.5 cm and 1.25 cm auger
  - three chisels
  - one gouge
  - three gimlets***
  - one hand saw and files
  - one nail hammer
  - one drawing knife
  - one froe for splitting shingles
  - two scythes and one sickle
  - one broad axe

- That one grindstone be given for every three families.

- That one year's clothing be given to each family.

- That two years' provisions be given to each family, enough according to their number and age.

- That two horses, two cows, and six sheep be delivered at Cataraqui for each family.

- That seeds of different kinds such as wheat, Indian corn, peas, oats, potatoes, and flax be given to each family.

- That one blacksmith be established in each township.

—Adapted from the Loyalist Petition to Governor Haldimand, written at Sorel.

**A ploughshare is the part of a plow that turns the soil; the coulter is a sharp blade to cut the sod ahead of the ploughshare.
***A gimlet is a small hand tool used for boring holes in wood.

Building a New Life

The Loyalists had many hardships to endure. Although some merchants and **artisans** were able to continue their occupations, many people with no farming experience were forced to become farmers.

They lived in tents at first until a small shanty or hut could be built in preparation for winter. Then they began to clear the land to plant crops. Trees were cut down using handaxes. Trees that were too big for the pioneers' small handaxes were circled with a cut 1.5 metres above the ground. This would kill the tree by the next year. The stumps were often left to rot in the ground. When oxen became available they were used to pull the stumps out.

The Loyalists were so busy building houses, clearing land, and planting crops, that they had little time to worry about other things.

An Eyewitness Account

James Dittrick, a boy from a Loyalist family, described one hardship that he experienced:

We none of us had any shoes or stockings, winter or summer, as those we brought with us were soon worn out. At length my father tanned some leather, and I recollect the first pair of shoes he made which fell to my lot, greased and putting them too near the fire, on returning to my grief found that my shoes were all shrivelled up, so that I could never wear them. I[t] was twelve months before I obtained another pair, so many daily occurrences of life having to be attended to.

The Hungry Year

The year 1788 has become known as the "Hungry Year." The winter of 1787–88 was extremely cold. It was followed by a summer drought. The lack of rain caused the crops to wither and die. To make matters worse, this was the year when the British government ended its assistance to the Loyalists. The government thought that they could now manage on their own.

James Dittrick describes the Hungry Year:

The most trying period of our lives, was the year 1788 called the year of scarcity....

All the crops failed...for several days we were without food, except that the various roots we procured and boiled down to nourish us. We noticed what roots the pigs eat; and by that means avoided anything that had any poisonous qualities...

...Our poor dog was killed to allay the pangs of hunger, the very idea brought sickness to some, but others [ate it to avoid starvation.]

A few of the settlers starved to death. Most survived until 1789, when emergency supplies arrived. It has been estimated that half of the Loyalist population would have died if these supplies had not arrived when they did.

Fortunately, the harvest of 1789 was an excellent one. The Loyalists continued to live in their new homes. Many eventually became very prosperous farmers, but they never forgot the Hungry Year.

Sir Guy Carleton (1724–1808)

Sir Guy Carleton, later named Lord Dorchester, was commander-in-chief of the British forces at the end of the American Revolution. He worked long and hard on behalf of the Loyalists. He was responsible for the evacuation of the Loyalists from New York. All of the Loyalists were supposed to have gone by September 3, 1783, but Carleton stalled until November. By stalling for time, he allowed all the Loyalists who wished to escape New York time to reach safety.

Carleton had been governor of Quebec before Haldimand. He had been responsible for convincing the British government to proclaim the Quebec Act of 1774. (See page 116.) He became governor of Quebec again in 1786. In 1791, when the Constitutional Act divided Quebec into Upper and Lower Canada, Carleton became the first governor general of Canada. (See page 159 and 160 for more information about the Constitutional Act.)

Artisan—worker very skilled in his or her craft

Native People

During the American Revolution most of the Iroquoian peoples living in the Thirteen Colonies were loyal to the British and fought on their side.

When the revolution was over, Britain invited the Iroquoian people to move to British North America. Many of them did. Thayendanegea (Joseph Brant), a war leader of the Iroquois Six Nations Confederacy (formerly the Five Nations) during the American Revolution, led his people to the Grand River area (now called the Six Nations Reserve). In the years that followed, several other Native groups moved to British North America as well.

After the American Revolution, American settlers moved westward by the thousands into the lands set aside for Native peoples by the Proclamation of 1763.

Exploring Further

1. Find instances today of Native land claims. What are the issues involved? How are they the same as or different from those faced by Thayendanegea?

2. Find information about Molly (or Mary) Brant, Joseph Brant's sister. Prepare a report about this important Native leader.

An Exercise in Problem Solving

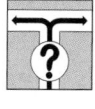

a) Describe and/or make a chart illustrating the type of government in existence in Quebec when the Loyalists arrived (see pages 112 and 116).

b) Read the stories on pages 147–150, and 154–155. Under the headings Language, Religion, and Land Ownership, describe what the Loyalists would have preferred to find in Quebec. In groups, draw a diagram on chart paper to show the way that the Loyalists would have liked to have seen the government organized. Present your government diagram to the rest of the class.

c) Describe in a letter from a Loyalist to Lord Dorchester how you think Quebec should be changed. A brief biography of Lord Dorchester (formerly called Sir Guy Carleton) is found on page 152. Read the biography of Thayendanegea (Joseph Brant) to consider a Native person's point of view.

Thayendanegea (1742–1807)

Thayendanegea, meaning "Two Sticks of Wood Bound Together for Strength," became a man of two worlds—the world of the Mohawks and the world of the Europeans. He attended school and could read and write English, Latin, and Greek. While at school he became a devout Christian and received his Christian name—Joseph Brant.

Thayendanegea became war leader of the Iroquois Six Nations Confederacy during the American Revolution. Under his leadership most of the Six Nations remained loyal to the British government. He and his men fought many battles against the Patriots.

After the war Thayendanegea led his people to British North America. Most settled on a reserve extending 10 kilometres on either side of the Grand River in what is now southwestern Ontario.

He spent many years fighting for the right of his people to treat the land around the Grand River as their own. In 1784 Governor Haldimand of Quebec signed a formal deed on behalf of King George III of Britain that gave the land to the Mohawks with the words "which they and their posterity are to enjoy forever." As agent for the Mohawks, Thayendanegea sold some land to settlers. He felt it was the right of the Native people to do with the land as they wished. In 1793 Lieutenant-Governor Simcoe of Upper Canada issued a new deed that stated that the land belonged to the Native people only so long as they remained on it. If they left it, the ownership would go back to the British government. They could not sell or transfer it. When the British government was appealed to, they agreed with Simcoe. This issue was not resolved in Thayendanegea's lifetime.

Thayendanegea was an exceptional leader during difficult times. He was a strong Loyalist during the American Revolution. However, after the revolution he was not afraid to stand up for his people against what he saw as injustices of the British government. He served as a bridge for his people between the old ways and the new, while at the same time working to maintain their distinct culture.

The Loyalists

Part 2
by Penney Clark

A great deal had changed for the Jones family since they had left New York during the American Revolution (see story on pages 147–150). Despite hard work and hardships, they, and many other Loyalists, were starting to think of Quebec as home. Pete and Mary had recently left the family to take up employment in another area of Quebec.

As the Loyalist communities became more established, people were also becoming concerned about their rights in the colony. Many wanted the representative form of government they had been used to in the Thirteen Colonies.

The coming of the Loyalists had greatly changed the lives of the people already living in the colony of Quebec. The French had concerns too and wanted to ensure that their way of life would continue. (Some French points of view are explored in the story "On a Seigneury" on pages 156–157.)

James burst through the door in his usual energetic way, shouting, "Is dinner ready yet?"

A peaceful scene greeted him. Sarah sat near the fire, singing a lullaby as she rocked her cornhusk doll to sleep.

His mother smiled as she turned from the fire, where she had been stirring stew in a large black pot. She pushed her hair off her brow and said, "Just go call your father and your brother. They're in the barn. Come back and wash up. Then we'll eat."

A few minutes later, the Jones family members sat down to their dinner of stew made from a deer shot by Father and vegetables grown by Mother, Charlotte and Lizzie. The roaring fire made the small cabin warm and snug in spite of the chill of the October evening. It would not be long before the winter winds would blow.

"We must all be grateful for this comfortable place," said Mother. "Not long ago we were sleeping in a tent at Sorel and eating government rations of salt pork and peas."

"It has only been a short time since the Hungry Year," Father quietly added.

"Do you think we will ever have another Hungry Year, Father?" Charlotte looked at her father, her eyes anxious in the flickering candlelight.

"No, silly," interrupted James, who often felt it his duty to explain the ways of the world to his younger sisters. "It will never be as bad as that. Even if we do have poor crops again, we will always have something saved from the year before. In the Hungry Year there was nothing to fall back on because there was nothing left over. We had been too busy building the house and clearing the fields to plant a large crop. We ate everything we grew as well as our government rations. Then, in the Hungry Year, the government rations stopped and we had poor crops. People almost starved. We never want to see times like that again!"

"Yes, we are very fortunate," Mother commented as she looked proudly around the table at her family. "The harvest this year has been bountiful. There will be plenty of food to last the winter, even with so many mouths to feed. Our home is warm and snug, thanks to the way in which Lizzie and James worked to mud the logs again so that the wind wouldn't get in."

"Even though he was arrested, we are also fortunate that Father wasn't tarred and feathered by the Patriots in the Thirteen Colonies," added Charlotte, who adored her father. "My friend Jenny's father has scars from the hot tar. It is a good thing that we left our former home in New York in the middle of the night like we did."

As the family continued to sit contentedly around the table, there was a loud rap on the door. Mother rose to open it. What a surprise! There stood their nearest neighbours, Mr. and Mrs. Davey.

"I hope we're not interrupting your dinner," began Mr. Davey, as he and his wife came through the door, "but we were on our way home from the grist mill and decided to stop for a few minutes. The harvest has been so good this year that there has been little time for visiting."

"You are right about that, my friend," replied Father, as he and his family rose and joined the Daveys around the crackling fire. Mother went to dip into her carefully hoarded supply of coffee to make a pot to offer the visitors.

"It's good to sit in front of a warm fire and enjoy a cup of hot coffee," began Mr. Davey. "There was a time not so long ago when luxuries like coffee were unheard of. Quebec is beginning to seem like home. Our lives are getting much better. During the long evenings this winter I intend to spend my time making some decent furniture for our home. I would like to replace those blocks of wood we call chairs."

"It would be good to replace some of the things we had to leave behind," agreed Mrs. Davey. "I am sure that all of our old things were either destroyed long ago or are sitting in the homes of whichever Patriots could get to them first. I still wish I had my beautiful china set," she sighed.

"What about payment for the prosperous farms we had to leave behind!" responded Mr. Davey.

Mother, who was always practical, interrupted firmly. "I have given up worrying about ever getting paid for the property we left behind in the new United States. It will never happen. We must put all that behind us and continue making a new life here in Quebec."

Here she paused while she tackled a difficult part of the sweater she was knitting. "Speaking of a new life," she continued after a moment, "I am certainly not pleased with the present type of government under the Quebec Act. I can understand why the civil laws were based on the system in France, since most of the people here were French-speaking. But, now that so many Loyalists have arrived here we feel there

should be some changes. We Loyalists have proven our loyalty to Britain by taking Britain's side in the American Revolution. We have paid for our loyalty by having to leave our homes and possessions behind and moving here to start a new life. But we certainly didn't come here to live under French law. We expect our own British law."

"Not only that, my dear," added Father. "We need to have an elected **Legislative Assembly**. We don't want a governor, even a British one, and an appointed council, to tell us

what to do. We had elected assemblies in the Thirteen Colonies; the people who live in Britain have an elected assembly, and we must have the same here!" he finished emphatically.

"If Governor Dorchester is wise, he will make sure that we have a Legislative Assembly so that we can have a say in how we are governed," agreed Mr. Davey. "The British government was very wrong to impose taxation without representation on the people of the Thirteen Colonies. Even so, the means of protest should have been

Legislative Assembly—the group of representatives elected to the Legislature to represent the people of a colony or province; a law-making body

peaceful, not the violence chosen by the Patriots."

"And what about protection for the Protestant churches?" asked Mrs. Davey. "The Roman Catholic church is protected by the Quebec Act, but many of the newcomers like us are not Catholics. We need protection too."

"It is not just the churches," added Mother. "We want to own our land under the same system of law we had in the Thirteen Colonies. We don't want to have to follow the seigneurial system."

"Oh, well," laughed Mr. Davey, as he rose from his chair. "We will not solve all of Quebec's problems during one evening's discussion. I am sure that the British government will be fair to those of us who have sacrificed so much for our loyalty."

"I hope so," replied Father. "But sometimes people do have to stand up for their rights," he added, "although certainly not with the violent means used by the Patriots in the Thirteen Colonies."

"Well, good evening, friends," said Mrs. Davey. "Tomorrow is another day, with more grain to be taken to the grist mill—and glad we are that we have it to take."

"Yes," agreed Mother. "We may have problems in our new home, but life is getting easier. We are no longer in danger of starving, and the British government will soon give us the Legislative Assembly we are asking for," she concluded confidently.

On a Seigneury

Spring was in the air that day in 1790 as 14-year-old Henri de Coursière walked with his family to the May Day celebration at the home of the seigneur. They made a pleasant-looking group as they walked down the village street. Monsieur Jean de Coursière carried little Jean-Pierre on his shoulders. Madame de Coursière walked along beside them. Strung out across the road were Henri and his five younger brothers and sisters, all dressed in their Sunday best, their faces still shiny from the scrubbing they had received with their mother's lye soap. Madame de Coursière and the girls wore little white bonnets on their heads and their good dresses, the ones they saved for church. Madame de Coursière, who was often chilly, had thrown a soft gray homespun shawl over her shoulders. Monsieur de Coursière and his sons wore leather breeches, wool shirts, leather jackets, and leather moccasins on their feet.

As the family walked along they greeted their friends and neighbours, most of whom were also on their way to the celebration. This was the day when all the *censitaires*, or

This is a detail from the painting called *Circular Dance of the Canadians,* by George Heriot.

seigneurial tenants, paid their *cens*, which was a token payment to their seigneur for living on his land.

There was another payment to be made, but not until November 11, which was the day dues were paid to the seigneur and tithes to the priest.

Both May Day and November 11 were days that the *censitaires* eagerly awaited. May Day was a welcome break from spring planting, and November 11 a pause before the long winter set in. Most of all they were holidays and a chance to meet with friends and neighbours for some merrymaking. Henri secretly hoped that he would be able to talk to Suzanne Grenier during the day. If he was really fortunate, perhaps he would even be able to sit beside her at the feast provided by the seigneur. It was too much to hope that he might hold her hand during the round dances that would follow the feast. She was beautiful and there would be others hoping for the same chance.

Henri sighed as he remembered that she was 15 and would probably be married before the next May Day celebrations, and likely to someone much richer than himself. He might inherit at least part of his father's river front farm one day. In the meantime he would have to try to get a small piece of land farther inland, since all the river front property on the seigneury already had tenants.

As Henri was daydreaming, his father's friend Jacques Rivard and his family came into view. Monsieur Rivard called out to them, "Hello, friends. Your seigneur has invited me and my family to the May Day celebrations on his seigneury."

"That is good news, Jacques," replied Henri's father. Henri knew that his father had not expected his friend to be at the celebrations since he was not a tenant on the seigneury, but earned his living as a **notary**. His father would enjoy the day even more now. Henri was glad for him. His life was not easy with seven children to support.

Monsieur Rivard joined Henri's father as Madame Rivard began to chat with Henri's mother and the Rivard children paired up with Henri's brothers and sisters. Since Monsieur and Madame Rivard had no children his age, Henri continued to amble along on one side of his father.

Monsieur Rivard walked on the other side. At first Henri continued with his daydream, but Monsieur Rivard's raised voice drew his attention to the conversation between the two men.

"I am growing impatient with Lord Dorchester," Monsieur Rivard was saying. "He doesn't do anything. When he was here as governor before and was known as Guy Carleton, he ran the government well. Since he changed his name to Lord Dorchester he has become like a new person. He can't make a decision anymore. The Quebec Act must be reformed. If we had a system of representative government we French-speaking people, who are in the majority, would have a greater say than the English-speaking people in the way the government is run. Why should the Loyalists, who have been here only a short time, have more influence than we Canadiens whose fathers and grandfathers were born and died here?"

"You are right, my friend," Henri's father calmly replied. "The Quebec Act must be reformed, but it is not necessary to take things as far as you suggest. We do not need to have an elected Assembly, but we do need to demand that Canadiens take a greater part in governing the colony. We have to make sure that Canadiens are on the appointed Councils. We have to protect our ways of doing things, such as our laws and our system of land ownership, from the influence of all these English-speaking people who keep arriving."

"Speaking of our system of land ownership," exclaimed Monsieur Rivard, "I wouldn't mind if we did change to the English system! I think people should be able to own their own land. I know you and the seigneurs disagree with me, Jean," he said. "You habitants seem content to live as you always have, as tenants of a seigneur; but I would like to see people have the opportunity to own their own land."

"The thing I am most concerned about is our religion," said Henri's father. "We Canadiens are Roman Catholics. Most of the newcomers to Quebec are Protestants. They are demanding rights for their religion. We must make sure our Roman Catholic Church continues to be protected."

"Our language must also be protected," added Monsieur Rivard. "The newcomers speak English. We must be able to speak French in our new Legislative Assembly, our laws must be written in French, and court cases must be tried in French."

Henri was just starting to get interested in the conversation. He wanted to ask whether or not either man thought that Lord Dorchester would soon reform the Quebec Act, but they had arrived at the Maypole. The conversation stopped as everyone gathered round to watch the seigneur wet the pole with brandy and fire a blank from his musket to blacken the pole. Then the other men raised their flintlocks and also fired blanks at the pole, blackening it from top to bottom. This was the first event of the May Day celebrations and Henri forgot the Quebec Act as his thoughts returned to Suzanne Grenier and his eyes began to search for her in the crowd.

Notary—someone trained in the law but who could not plead cases in court

An Exercise in Decision-Making

What Should the British Government Do?

After the arrival of the Loyalists the British government was faced with the problem of governing two groups of people with very different views and background, both living in Quebec.

British: (imaginary quotations)

- We fought for Britain during the American Revolution. We risked our lives and lost our homes for Britain. We deserve to have British laws and government now. We want an elected Legislative Assembly to make laws for us.

- We do not like the French seigneurial system of land-holding. We want to own our own land. We know the British officials have allowed us to sell and purchase the land grants, but we want to have legal title to the land.

- We want land set aside for our Protestant churches and schools.

- Since we are English-speaking, we want English as the official language. It will certainly be the language spoken in our Legislative Assembly since we will be electing English-speaking people like ourselves.

- We expect to be rewarded for our loyalty to Great Britain. If these changes are not made, we will feel like strangers in our new home.

French: (imaginary quotations)

- We were in Quebec first. Why should we have to change our laws and system of government because of these new people?

- There are more French-speaking people. We want to keep our seigneurial system. It has worked well for many years and will continue to work well.

- We want protection for our Roman Catholic religion. We do not want our children to attend Protestant schools.

- There are four times as many of us French-speaking people as there are English speakers. French must stay as the official language here in Quebec.

- Why should we have to change our ways for these new people?

- The Quebec Act of 1774 guaranteed us certain cultural rights, especially to our language and religion.

A decision had to be made. How could the British government best meet the needs of both the 30 000 English-speaking and 140 000 French-speaking people in Quebec?

1. Refer to the section on page 112 entitled "Alternatives Open to the British." As advisors to the British government, discuss each alternative and decide what you would do if you were the British government. Use the stories on pages 147–150, 154–155, and 156–157 and the information on this page as reference material. Record your information on a decision-making chart. Write a letter to the British government outlining your point of view.

The Constitutional Act, 1791

Introduction

The Constitutional Act of 1791 gave the people of Upper and Lower Canada their own Legislative Assemblies, thereby giving them representative government. Because the British government did not repeal the Quebec Act, its terms continued in existence.

Aims: to acknowledge the problem of a bicultural Quebec by dividing it into two colonies: Upper Canada and Lower Canada

- to provide governments, laws, and landholding systems satisfying both British and French
- to give the people elected Legislative Assemblies, but limit the assemblies' power.

By giving the people elected assemblies with limited power, the British government attempted to ensure that the situation in the Thirteen Colonies, did not happen in British North America. There, they believed, the legislative assemblies had had too much power and it led to revolution.

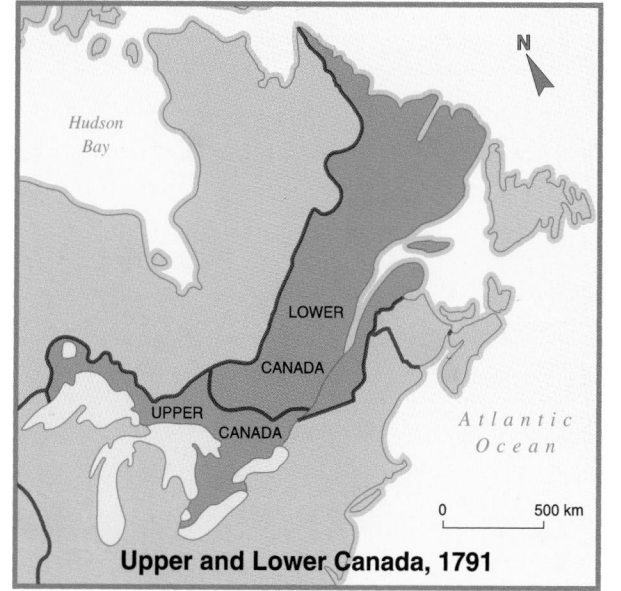

Upper and Lower Canada, 1791

Quebec was divided into two colonies: Upper Canada ("up" the St. Lawrence River), which is part of the present-day province of Ontario, and Lower Canada ("down" the St. Lawrence River), which is part of the present-day province of Quebec.

Bill—a proposed law to be debated and voted on. When it becomes law it is called an Act.

*Women with property could vote in Lower Canada until the 1830s, and in Upper Canada until 1849, but few did.

Key Term

Religion: one-seventh of all public lands in Upper Canada to be set aside for Protestant schools and churches (later called "Clergy Reserves"). In Lower Canada the system established under the Quebec Act was to be continued (protection for the Roman Catholic Church).

Government—Who Makes and Enforces the Laws

- governor general for Lower Canada would control affairs in both colonies; Upper Canada to have its own lieutenant-governor
- each colony to have an Executive Council (appointed) to advise the governor, and a Legislative Council (appointed) to propose **bills** and approve those bills passed by the Assembly
- each colony to have representative government, with an (elected) Legislative Assembly, and power to impose taxes, propose bills, and serve local needs. Voting was largely restricted to male property owners.*
- power of Legislative Assembly very limited; Executive and Legislative Councils and governor could block bills
- Upper Canada to have English civil law and criminal law; Lower Canada same system as Quebec Act (English criminal and Canadien civil law)

Landholding System

The British freehold system was established in Upper Canada. People could now hold the deed to their land. In Lower Canada the seigneurial system continued.

Refer to the government diagram on page 160.

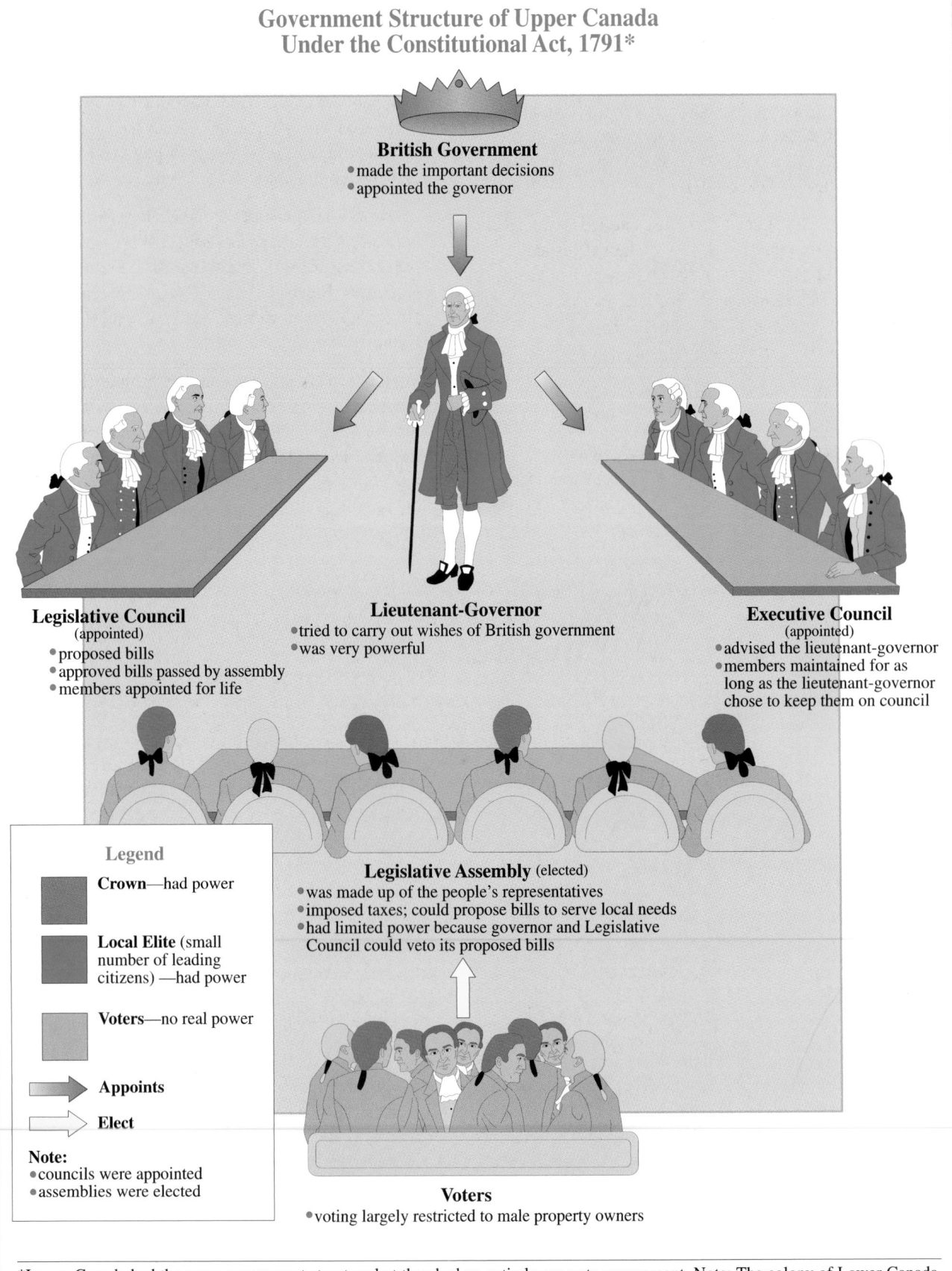

Government Structure of Upper Canada Under the Constitutional Act, 1791*

British Government
- made the important decisions
- appointed the governor

Legislative Council
(appointed)
- proposed bills
- approved bills passed by assembly
- members appointed for life

Lieutenant-Governor
- tried to carry out wishes of British government
- was very powerful

Executive Council
(appointed)
- advised the lieutenant-governor
- members maintained for as long as the lieutenant-governor chose to keep them on council

Legislative Assembly (elected)
- was made up of the people's representatives
- imposed taxes; could propose bills to serve local needs
- had limited power because governor and Legislative Council could veto its proposed bills

Legend

Crown—had power

Local Elite (small number of leading citizens) —had power

Voters—no real power

Appoints

Elect

Note:
- councils were appointed
- assemblies were elected

Voters
- voting largely restricted to male property owners

*Lower Canada had the same government structure but they had an entirely separate government. Note: The colony of Lower Canada had a representative government after the passage of the Constitutional Act in 1791.

An Exercise in Decision-Making

1. Turn back to page 116 and read the description of the Quebec Act of 1774. List the ways that Quebec stayed the same and ways that it changed with the Constitutional Act of 1791.

2. Return to the chart on page 112 entitled "Alternatives Open to the British." Five alternatives are listed. The British government chose one of these with the Proclamation of 1763 and another with the Quebec Act of 1774. Which alternative is represented by the Constitutional Act of 1791?

3. The power of the assemblies was intentionally limited in the Constitutional Act. Why was this done?

4. Throughout this book we have looked at three major ideas: Who participates in the government? Who has the power to make the decisions? Does majority rule exist? Answer these three questions for Upper Canada and Lower Canada now that representative government has been established.

5. Compare the government diagrams that you drew in the exercise on page 153, "An Exercise in Problem Solving," to the diagram on page 160. Discuss reasons for similarities and differences.

6. In the left-hand column of the chart below, decide who would fit in each of the six "Who" spaces. Select your answers from Loyalists, French seigneurs, French habitants, British government, British merchants in Lower Canada, and Roman Catholic Church.

7. Divide into six groups—one for each of the perspectives represented in the chart. As a group, write a letter to the lieutenant-governor of your new colony explaining how you feel about the Constitutional Act and why. Read your letter to the rest of the class.

Reactions to the Constitutional Act

Who	Reaction	Why
1. Who?	pleased	• could not be accused of taxation without representation • satisfied wishes of people for Legislative Assembly while keeping the real power in the hands of the British government
2. Who?	angry	• cut off from rest of English-speaking Protestant population • worried about power of Canadien Legislative Assembly
3. Who?	pleased	• kept religious influence and ability to tithe
4. Who?	pleased	• kept seigneurial system
5. Who?	indifferent	• kept Canadien way of life but still under control of Church and seigneurs • no influence in the government
6. Who?	pleased/displeased	• established English-speaking colony with own Legislative Assembly, but only male property owners could vote

Communities

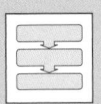

Honouring Your Community History

Part 1

Each of you will complete a different project designed to honour your community history. Then, during a special "Community Day" event in class, you can share your project with others. You may wish to plan your projects and event as a class, so that you can share them with another class, parents, or community members. You might also consider creating a special display or presentation in your school library, in a local shopping mall, public library, school board, or local government office.

Follow the Research Model found on pages x and xi to complete your project.

 Choose one of the projects listed here, one of your own, or a variation/combination.

- Write a special chapter for this book featuring your community.

- Locate or write community songs to reflect the development of your community.

- Write a "Trivia Challenge" for others to play. Include a variety of questions about your community's history.

- Develop a video documentary about the history of your area.

- Create a newspaper representing the early days in your area.

- Research or create recipes which reflect favourite foods historically enjoyed in your community.

- Visit a seniors' centre to ask about the past. Prepare a chart to compare several aspects of your life now with their lives at your age (e.g., favourite pastimes).

- Research to find out how your community got its name and write about it in legend form. Read the legend to the class.

- Create a "directory" of people and businesses that existed in the early years. What services would people and businesses require?

- Look at old buildings in your area and choose your favourite. Write a story from the point of view of this building at some point in history; create a poster to help others understand its importance.

- Create a museum display. Feature an important historical person or event in your community.*

- Create a series of signs which were (or might have been) posted on the shops and buildings of a main street in the early days. Indicate the actual size of large display signs and describe where they appeared.

- Describe what life was like during each of the four seasons for early settlers in your community.

- Research to find out how a main street (route) has changed over time. Represent this transformation with a series of visuals.

- Create a visual and written timeline for one of the following to show how it has changed in your community over the years: clothing, transportation, school, police force.

- Look at one or more of your community's historic buildings. Notice features like building materials, shape, signs, staircases, columns, porches, doors, and windows. How did buildings compare to present-day architecture?

- Put together a picture essay by photographing or drawing a series of "items from the past." This might include old houses, trolley tracks, sign posts, dates on buildings, and other historic items that are still in existence in your community.

- Create an historical newspaper feature about important entrepreneurs. How did they help to shape your community's history?

---

*Visit the Canadian Museum of Civilization at http://www.cmcc.muse.digital.ca/ to gather information and ideas.

- Imagine that you lived in your community when it was first being developed. Plan, then create a time capsule you would have prepared at that time. Remember, time capsules are put together to represent a time and place in history and are intended to be opened by future generations.

- Develop a puzzle about businesses, streets, buildings, schools, organizations, rivers, and recreation facilities in your community that have been named after a person. When? Why?

- Design a "Community Walking Tour." Plan a reasonable route and prepare a commentary (e.g., bank, school, post office, church, rail or bus depot, grain elevator, memorial, park, buildings, businesses, hotel, museum).

- Choose two time periods from the past (e.g., 50 years ago and 100 years ago). Write two "day in the life of..." stories featuring characters who might have lived at that time.

- Create posters showing various symbols of the cultures that helped to form your community.

- Present a series of tableaus representing life in your community throughout history.

- Plan a lesson or activity that might have happened in a school of long ago.

- Recreate your community in its early years in the form of a 3-D model or diorama.

- Create a thank-you card or letter for your community. What do you value about your community? Address your card to the community or to a specific person from the past.

- Select an important person from your community's history. Create a "biography box" to represent that person. On the outside of a shoe box, attach pictures and items that represent the events of that person's life. On the inside, place and attach items that represent his or her personality, memories, and point of view. Explain your biography box to the class.

- Design and create a magazine layout highlighting important historic sites around your community.

- Design and create the "roadway" of development on poster paper. Position road signs and billboards along a chronological route to create a timeline about your community.

- Develop several historical postcards representing your community at different times. Write a message on the back that reflects those times.

Part 2

After you have shared your projects, discuss these questions with your classmates.

- Why and how did your community form?

- What individuals and groups have come to your community throughout your history? When? From where? What attracted them to the area? Where in the area did they settle?

- How has the lifestyle changed over time for community members?

- Who made important contributions to the community? What were these people like?

- What important events have occurred throughout history? How did they affect your community?

- How has the appearance and environment of the community changed over time? Items to consider: shelter, food sources, technology, occupations, clothing, transportation, gender roles, customs and traditions, education, health care, communication, land distribution, ownership, laws, recreation.

- How can you best honour your community?

- In what ways can you best show the many special qualities and history of your community?

Add other questions you may have.

Culminating Activity
Design a crest/coat of arms for your community today. Explain each symbol used.

Emergence of Towns
York
Building the Colony's New Capital

British Governor General Dorchester meets with Mississauga chiefs to purchase land in the Toronto area.

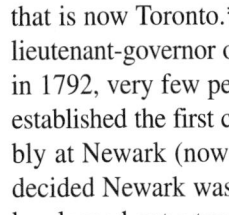 The above painting shows Lord Dorchester, the governor general, meeting with Mississauga chiefs in 1788 to buy land from them in the area that is now Toronto.* When John Graves Simcoe, the first lieutenant-governor of Upper Canada, arrived in the colony in 1792, very few people were living in towns. Simcoe established the first capital and the first Legislative Assembly at Newark (now Niagara-on-the-Lake). He soon decided Newark was too near American territory. In 1793 he planned out a town on the shore of Lake Ontario. Local Native people called the place Toronto. This location seemed well-suited for defence and transportation. In 1796, the settlement, renamed York, became the colony's new capital.**

Simcoe ordered wooden parliament buildings to be constructed immediately in the new town and roads to be cut out of the wilderness. The construction of Yonge Street and Dundas Street, still in use today, was begun. Yonge Street was built from York to Lake Simcoe and Dundas Street joined York to Niagara. These military roads would allow soldiers to move quickly to protect the colony in the event of an American invasion. It was not easy to travel on these unpaved roads, and travellers had to go around all of the tree stumps. The roads were impassable in times of spring run-off and heavy rains.

Lieutenant-Governor Simcoe opens the first Legislative Assembly in Newark in 1792.

At first, most of York's inhabitants were soldiers and government officials. Soon industries began to develop and attract skilled and unskilled workers. At the start of the War of 1812 (see page 166), York had about 700 residents. There were breweries, brickyards, a shipbuilding yard, a pottery factory, tanneries, and potash factories, which used wood ashes to make potash (also called "pearl ash").

York was described in 1813 in a book about Upper Canada:

....the ground on which it stands is not suitable for building. This at present is the seat of government, and the residence of a number of English gentlemen. It contains some fine buildings, ...among which are a court-house, council-house, a large brick building in which the king's store for the place is kept, and a meeting-house for Episcopalians;*** 1 printing, and other offices.... The fort in this place is not strong, but the British began to build a very strong one in the year 1811.

—from *A Geographical View of the Province of Upper Canada* by M. Smith

In 1804, eight years after it became the capital, York consisted of a few buildings along the shore of Lake Ontario.

---

*The Native headdress shown in this picture is actually typical of Plains people, rather than Natives from the Toronto area.
** In 1834, York reclaimed its original name and became the City of Toronto.
***Members of the Church of England (Anglicans).

Bytown

First Settlers in the Ottawa Valley

Settlement began in the Ottawa valley in 1800 when Philemon Wright brought his family and several other American settlers to present-day Hull at Chaudière Falls. At this site, across the Ottawa River from the future site of Ottawa, Wright intended to develop an agricultural settlement. However, it was the timber industry that developed. Wright managed to successfully send rafts of lumber all the way to Montreal and Quebec for export, in spite of falls and rapids, proving that it was possible. Lumbering remained the chief industry for many years. (The timber trade is explored further in Chapter 7. See page 190.)

In 1826, Colonel By chose a site on the south side of the Ottawa River for a new settlement. By this time, Wrightsville (shown above) was a well-established community.

Beginnings of Bytown

At the start of the War of 1812 (see page 166), when York was already a thriving community, the site of Canada's future capital city Ottawa was still a wilderness. Very few people lived on the south shore of the Ottawa River. Colonel John By, an officer in the Royal Engineers, was appointed by Great Britain to organize the building of a canal from the Ottawa River to Kingston. It was felt that a canal was needed in case the Americans decided to **blockade** the St. Lawrence River. If they did so, the supply route to Fort Henry at Kingston would be cut off. Fort Henry was one of the most important British forts in Canada. (Canals are explored in more detail in Chapter 8. See page 234.)

By the time Colonel By arrived on September 21, 1826, Wrightsville (named after Philemon Wright) was a well-established community. It had a busy lumber industry, a hotel, an **armoury**, three churches, and schools. Colonel By chose a location on the south side of the river for the new community, about a mile from Chaudière Falls. He divided the site into lots for the many workers who would arrive to build the canal or provide services for canal workers. He named the group of lots on the steep bank Upper Town. The other group of lots was called Lower Town. One hundred and fifty houses were built in the first two years. Two British army companies arrived, the Royal Sappers and Miners, with 80 soldiers per company. They were housed in barracks on the bluff, known as Barracks Hill.

The people who arrived during Bytown's early years included Americans and French-speaking Canadians, as well as Scottish, Irish, and English people. Conditions were not easy at first. Often people lived at close quarters, in poor conditions. They were exhausted from long working hours. Wages were generally low.

Bytown's population increased as more lumber mills and factories were built. By the time the Rideau Canal was completed in 1832, 1500 people lived in Bytown.

In 1855, when the population had reached 8000, people decided that it was time for a new name—one that did not include the word "town." It was named Ottawa after the Native people who lived in the area.

In 1858, following much indecision about where Canada's capital would be located, it was announced that Ottawa should become the capital of Canada.

Bytown as it looked in 1835 from the top of what is now Parliament Hill.

Blockade—close off; usually done to a harbour or port in wartime to prevent supplies from reaching their destination
Armoury—a place where weapons are kept

The War of 1812

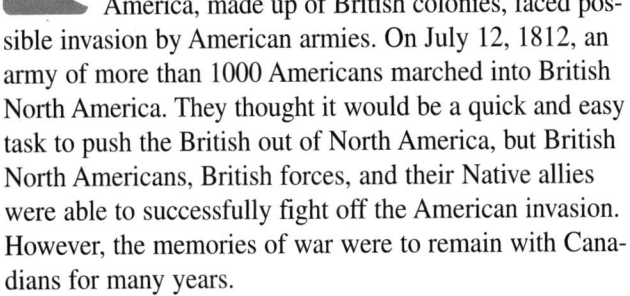

On June 1, 1812, United States President Madison declared war against Great Britain. British North America, made up of British colonies, faced possible invasion by American armies. On July 12, 1812, an army of more than 1000 Americans marched into British North America. They thought it would be a quick and easy task to push the British out of North America, but British North Americans, British forces, and their Native allies were able to successfully fight off the American invasion. However, the memories of war were to remain with Canadians for many years.

Causes of the War

By 1812, Britain and France had been at war in Europe for almost 20 years. As a result, European ports were blockaded. This angered Americans, who were neutral, because they could not deliver cargo to the ports because of the blockade.

Another source of friction was British interference with American vessels. Deserters from the British navy found work aboard American ships, where the pay was higher and the working conditions better. The British (both in peacetime and during the conflict) began to stop American merchant ships at sea and search them for deserters. Suspected deserters were removed and taken back into the British navy. A number of Americans who were not British deserters were also taken in this way.

A group of influential men in the United States called **War Hawks** were pushing for war against the British North American colonies for various reasons. Most of the good farmland in the United States was very expensive, but in British North America, plenty of inexpensive, good farmland was available. Also, some Native peoples were resisting the westward movement of American colonists. Americans saw the British North American colonists as possible allies for the Native cause. Tecumseh, a Native leader, had already gone to British North America to see if he could enlist help there. The Americans felt that if they could take over British North America, there would be less resistance from the Native peoples.

Modern-day historians tend to place national honour as the major cause for the War of 1812. By 1812, the British still had not accepted the Americans as political equals. They looked upon the United States as a colony,

War Hawks—group of young men in Congress who wanted war. They believed that the Americans could easily win a war if they invaded the colonies of British North America.
Sovereign nation—a country that is independent of the control of other governments
Congress—elected members of the Senate and House of Representatives of the United States of America

and not as a full **sovereign nation**. The Americans reasoned that if they were equals, the British would not take sailors off American ships. They felt that one nation should not treat another nation in such a manner.

An Exercise in Critical Thinking

"War Hawk." There is some evidence that Britain has been supplying guns, and perhaps money, to the Natives. If true, it is just another example of Britain interfering in our affairs. I say we declare war on Britain and invade the colonies of British North America!

Other Member of Congress. Britain does not have the right to stop American ships, take our sailors away and force them to serve in the British Navy. We fought and won in '76. It is time to stand up for our rights again and fight.

New England Ship Owner. The blockade is hurting me more than British shipowners. I have had to put my sailors out of work. My business is going to be ruined if this is not changed soon, but I don't want to go to war over this. Can't we settle this peacefully?

Southern Planter. I have been selling tobacco and cotton to Britain and now I can't do that because Congress has decided that our ships cannot sail for foreign ports. Has anyone thought about those of us who make our living selling goods to foreign countries?

1. The above statements might have been made by Americans prior to the War.
   a) What four causes of the war were mentioned?
   b) Match each of the imaginary statements with one of the four causes of the war given on this page. Create a quotation for the cause that is *not* covered above.
   c) Which of these people would be in favour of going to war? Which would not?
2. Write four comments that might have been made by someone British or by a supporter of the British.

166

Major Events of the War

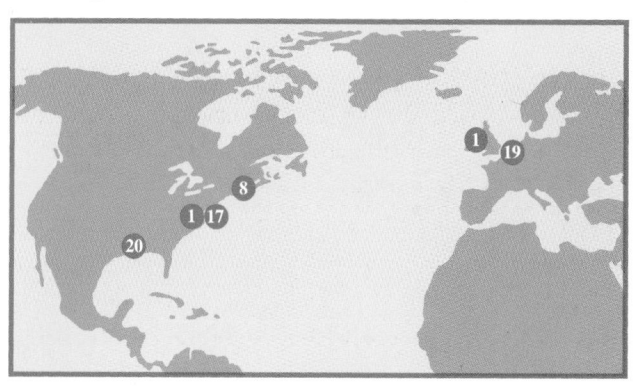

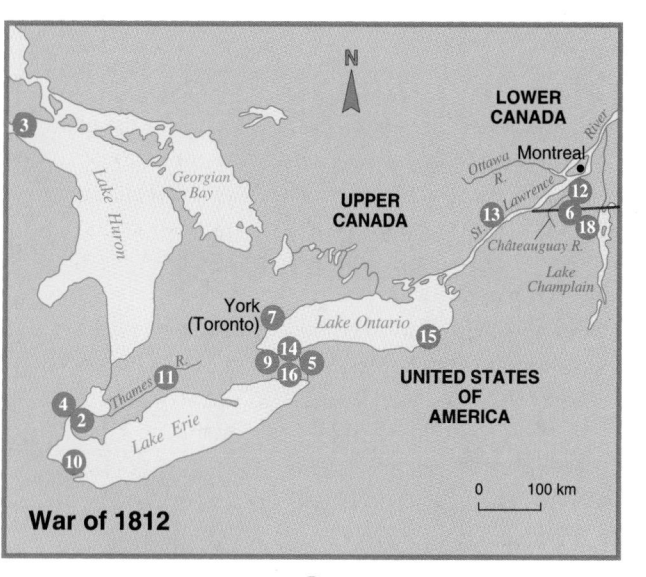

War of 1812

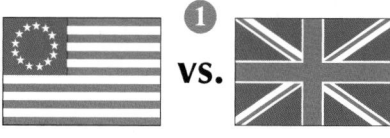

VS.

Key events in the War of 1812 are summarized on pages 167 to 169. Read about the events and then find the corresponding number(s) on the map above. Most events have additional visual material and this information is identified with the same number as the event. Not all events have visuals.

As you will see from the map and timeline, both sides had victories. There was no winner. By the end of the war, Britain had possession of some American territory but they returned it in the Treaty of Ghent. The War of 1812 has been called "the war that nobody won."

① **June 1812**—U.S. declared war on Great Britain.

② **July 1812**—American army, led by General Hull, crossed Detroit River and entered Upper Canada. Hull said, "I come to find enemies, not to make them; I come to protect, not to injure you." However, few people in Upper Canada were interested in joining the Americans.

The Bold Canadian
A Ballad of the War of 1812*

Come all ye bold Canadians,
I'd have you lend an ear
Unto a short ditty
Which will your spirits cheer,
Concerning an engagement
We had at Detroit town,
The pride of those Yankee boys
So bravely we took down.
* * *
"Our town, it is at your command,
Our garrison likewise."
They brought their arms and grounded them
Right down before our eyes.
Now prisoners we made them,
On board a ship they went,
And from the town of Sandwich
Unto Quebec were sent.

Come all ye bold Canadians,
Enlisted in the cause,
To defend your country,
And to maintain your laws;
Being all united,
This is the song we'll sing:
Success unto Great Britain,
And God save the King.

③ **July 1812**—A small number of British soldiers, fur traders, and Native allies captured Fort Michilimackinac on Mackinac Island in the channel joining Lake Huron and Lake Michigan. This, combined with news that British reinforcements were on their way, resulted in Hull's decision to return to Detroit.

④ **August 1812**—British commander General Brock and Native chief Tecumseh were victorious at Detroit. American General Hull believed Brock had gathered 5000 Native fighters (he only had 600) so Hull surrendered Detroit. Hull passed his sword to Brock to show the surrender of the American army. Not only did Hull's surrender prevent the Americans from invading through the western end of Upper Canada, it allowed Brock to gain 35 cannons, 2500 muskets, 500 rifles, ammunition, and provisions.

---

*This ballad is believed to have been written by Private Flumerfelt, one of the participants in the battle at Detroit.

5 **October 1812**—Battle of Queenston Heights; Brock killed; Queenston Heights taken from Americans.

The artist who painted the above picture showed the action as if it happened at once, rather than over 12 hours. On the left side of the picture, the American boats are shown crossing the Niagara River to reach the village of Queenston and American troops are waiting to board the boats. Above the American troops, on Lewiston Heights, we can see the smoke from two cannons which are directing their fire across the river at Queenston Heights. American troops who have reached the Canadian side can also be seen, scaling Queenston Heights. In the foreground an American boat is capsizing. In fact, three boats were caught by the current and ended up on the shore downstream from the other boats. These boats are shown in the bottom right corner of the picture.

On the hillside just outside the village, officers surround the body of General Brock. Brock was killed leading an uphill charge at the battle of Queenston Heights. His position in front of his men and his red coat made him an Leasy target. At the top of the painting, coming along the crest of Queenston Heights, is General Sheaffe's frontal attack on the American position, which ended the battle.

6 **November 20, 1812**— Salaberry's militia and 300 Native allies turned back Major-General Dearborn and his 6000 men from their invasion of Lower Canada.

7 **April 1813**—Americans captured York (later called Toronto), the capital of Upper Canada. Parliament buildings burned. This 1813 medal issued in Upper Canada shows an American eagle looking across the border at a British lion and a Canadian beaver.

For Your Notebook

1. A painting which records an historical event is a primary source document. Explain why caution is needed when a painting is your sole source of knowledge of an historical event.

8 **June 1813**—Naval battle. The painting shows the British boarding the American ship, the *Chesapeake*, at Boston Harbor.

9 **June 1813**—British at Stoney Creek stopped American advance into Niagara Peninsula. Battle at Beaver Dams.

10 **September 1813**—Americans destroyed British naval power on Lake Erie. Britain's naval domination of the upper Great Lakes ended.

11 **October 1813**—American victory at Battle of Thames River near Moraviantown. Chief Tecumseh killed.

12 **October 1813**—At the Battle of Châteauguay, American forces retreated from the British and Canadien force. (See Salaberry on page 170.)

13 **November 1813**—Battle of Crysler's Farm. A combined force of 800 British soldiers, Canadien militiamen, and First Nations allies defeated an American army of 7000 soldiers.

14 **December 1813**—Americans set fire to the town of Newark.

15 **May 1814**—British naval fleet captured American Fort Oswego.

16 **July 1814**—Battle of Lundy's Lane. Neither side could claim a victory, but Americans retreated to Fort Erie.

17 **August 1814**—Washington occupied for one day by British. President's mansion scorched by fire. Repainted white. Called "White House" ever since.

18 **September 1814**—Sir George Prevost led British south; defeated at Plattsburg on Lake Champlain.

19 **December 1814**—Treaty of Ghent (peace treaty).

20 **January 1815**—Battle of New Orleans. Andrew Jackson won a victory for the Americans. He did not know that the peace treaty had already been signed.

Heroes

In addition to the five people highlighted here, there were thousands of other heroes (e.g., sailors and soldiers) whose names have not been recorded in history books.

Sir Isaac Brock (1769–1812)

Isaac Brock was a British army officer who had served in the West Indies and in Holland before coming to British North America. Chief Tecumseh and General Brock greatly respected one another. They defeated the Americans at Detroit together.

Brock showed that, with determination and planning, it was possible to defeat the Americans. He lost his life as he led the charge at the Battle of

Laura Secord (1775–1868)

Laura Secord and her husband lived in Queenston in the Niagara region. James Secord was injured in the Battle of Queenston Heights in October 1812. While he was at home recovering from his wounds, Laura overheard some American soldiers discussing a surprise attack on the British. Laura decided to warn the British commander, Fitzgibbon. She became a hero when she fearlessly risked her life to help the British. Because the American troops guarded the roads, she walked 23 kilometres across fields and through forests. The attack occurred as planned, but the Americans ended up surrendering to Fitzgibbon.

Tecumseh (1768–1813)

Chief Tecumseh of the Shawnee was a well-respected Native leader. He wanted to protect Native lands from the Americans who were pressing westward, and he hoped that the British would help him.

He was a powerful ally of the British forces during the War of 1812. He and his men helped General Brock capture Detroit in 1812. By October of 1813, the Americans had advanced well into Upper Canada, while the British retreated. Tecumseh persuaded the British commander to take a stand at the Thames River, not far from present-day London, Ontario. Forty-eight of the British were killed and the rest surrendered. The courageous Tecumseh was also killed. With him died the Native peoples' hope for their own separate territory.

General Brock said of Tecumseh: *he who attracted most my attention was a Shawnee chief, Tecumseh... a more sagacious or a more gallant warrior does not I believe exist. He was the admiration of everyone who conversed with him.*

Charles de Salaberry (1778–1829)

French-speaking people were as anxious to defend their land against the Americans as were English-speaking people. Charles de Salaberry, who was born in Quebec, was an experienced officer in the British army when the War of 1812 began. He formed a militia corps called the Voltigeurs, which was composed almost entirely of men from Lower Canada.

In October 1813, Salaberry and his 1600 men, including the Voltigeurs, ambushed the Americans as they advanced along the Châteauguay River, which led to Montreal. His troops made so much noise that the Americans, believing they were confronted by a much larger army, turned around and went home. The Voltigeurs' success in defeating 4000 Americans at the Battle of Châteauguay prevented the Americans from attacking Montreal. It also prevented them from gaining control of the St. Lawrence River, which would have allowed them to cut off supplies to Upper Canada. The regiment saw a good deal of action during the war and was disbanded in 1815.

Catherine Lundy

The Battle of Lundy's Lane took place on July 25th, 1814, at the Lundy family property near Niagara Falls. Catherine, the wife of Thomas Lundy, was a young woman in her teens. Rather than fleeing, she stayed and gave drinking water to thirsty soldiers who had walked 14 miles to reach the site on that hot July day. During the battle she tended the wounded. Following the battle, Catherine was honoured by a visit from a British officer, who presented her with his sword.

Results of the War

Even though the War of 1812 had no winner, there were some long-term effects:

- American immigrants were discouraged from coming to British North America. British immigrants were encouraged, as it was felt they would be willing to defend the country if the Americans decided to invade again.

- The border between the United States and British North America was set at the 49th parallel, from the Lake of the Woods west to the Rocky Mountains. It was agreed the fur country of Oregon Territory would be jointly occupied.*

- The Rush–Bagot Agreement of 1817 freed the Great Lakes from military control. Each side was allowed to keep one armed ship on Lake Champlain and Lake Ontario and two on the other Great Lakes in order to prevent smuggling.

- Great Britain began to recognize the United States as a separate nation, although there was still distrust. The British built Fort Henry at Kingston for protection from possible American invasion. The Americans turned their attention southward and westward for expansion.

- People in Upper and Lower Canada had to co-operate with one another during the war. Their success brought feelings of pride and the beginnings of a sense of unity.

- Native allies were no longer needed for military purposes. The British government decided the Native peoples should now be assimilated (see page 112).

- The war increased trade along the St. Lawrence–Great Lakes route. Trade continued to grow after the war. However, it was expensive for Upper Canada to export its food, lumber, and furs along this route. The Lachine and Welland Canals, both of which opened in the 1820s, were built as cheaper alternative routes.

*This arrangement lasted until 1846 when the 49th parallel was chosen for that boundary as well.

- The Rideau Canal was first proposed near the end of the War of 1812 as an alternative route between Montreal and the Great Lakes (in case the Americans ever seized control of the St. Lawrence). It was completed in 1832.

- The Atlantic colonies enjoyed a period of prosperity during the war. They were able to continue their trade with the neighbouring New England states. As well, Halifax was Britain's main naval base in North America. The war created a demand for many products that local merchants supplied.

Canada Revisited

Above: Brock's Monument. A tall column marks the grave of Major-General Sir Isaac Brock at Queenston.

Right: The tunic worn by Major-General Brock the day he was killed is on display in the Canadian War Museum. The sash was a gift from his ally Chief Tecumseh.

Fur Traders

The previous pages discuss many of the important events and changes that occurred between the American Revolution and the War of 1812. One activity that continued throughout and beyond this time period, despite other changes, was the fur trade.

A Fur Trade Timeline

The numbers in the circles in the text refer to locations on the map on page 173 and on the timeline which runs along the bottom of pages 172 to 176. The timeline organizes events chronologically. Page numbers in brackets refer to information on the topics elsewhere in this textbook.

French Control

  When French explorers and traders came to North America, they wanted two main products: fish and furs.

1 In 1534, Jacques Cartier saw Aboriginal people wearing animal skins. Knowing these furs would bring high prices in France, the French built the first fur trade posts in North America.

2 Trading companies controlled and managed the French fur trade in North America. Between 1603 and 1645, the French state granted trading monopolies to individuals and companies who were expected to help in colonization by encouraging French settlers to come to North America.

In 1603, Pierre Du Gua de Monts was granted a monopoly on the fur trade in North America. In 1604, de Monts and Samuel de Champlain established the Ste. Croix Island settlement in Acadia. This settlement was moved to Port Royal in 1605.

3 From 1603–1663, the French Company of 100 Associates and several other companies had monopolies on the fur trade in New France. Because of the monopolies, people needed licences to go into the woods to trade with the Native people for furs. To be successful, the fur trade required the co-operation of Native and non-Native people. Therefore, the French set up trading alliances with various Algonquian peoples and groups of Huron.

The Huron, acting as go-betweens, bartered European goods for the furs that the Assiniboine and Cree people brought from the Canadian Shield. *Coureurs de bois*, acting on behalf of merchants in Montreal, Trois Rivières, and Quebec, encouraged the Huron traders to travel to the French posts on the St. Lawrence River.

When a French trader married a Native woman, he became a part of the Native trading system. The children of European fur traders and Native women became known as **Metis**. The Metis people were central to the history of the fur trade.

4 In 1608, Samuel de Champlain established a settlement at Quebec. Hoping to expand the fur trade with their help, Champlain formed an alliance with the Huron against the Iroquois. After 1608, the fur trade in New France grew under the direction of the fur trading companies. Settlement, however, did not increase.

Metis—people of mixed Native and European ancestry

1534	1603–1605	1603–1663	1608
Cartier (p. 15)	De Monts (p. 26), Champlain (p. 25)	Fur monopolies (p. 28), *Coureurs de bois* (p. 30)	Champlain (p. 28), Huron alliance (p. 29)
1	**2**	**3**	**4**

Note: Timeline is not to scale

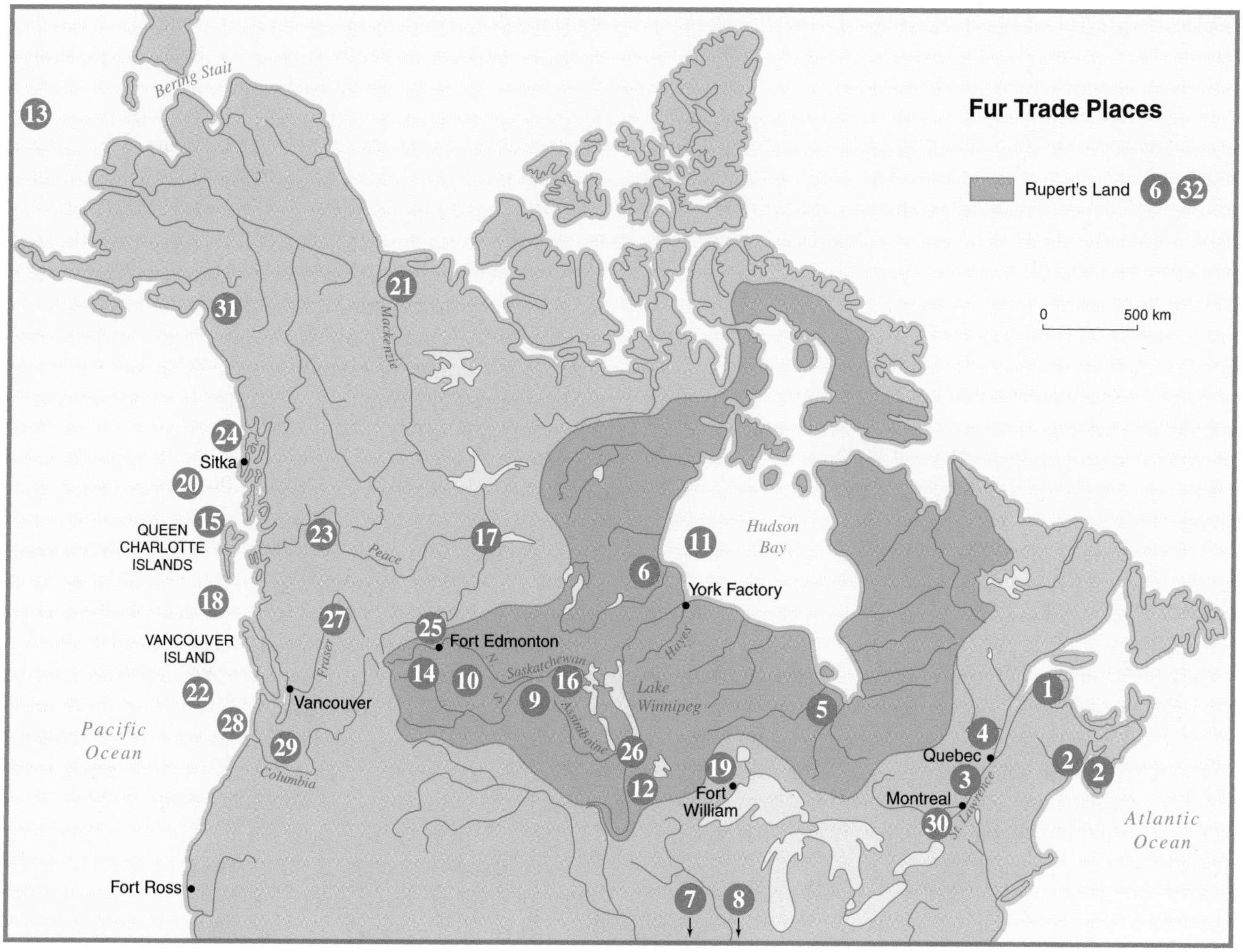

Fur Trade Places

Rupert's Land **6** **32**

0 ——— 500 km

Bering Strait

13

21

31

24
Sitka

20

15
QUEEN
CHARLOTTE
ISLANDS

23

Peace

17

11

Hudson
Bay

6

York Factory

18

27

25

Fort Edmonton

VANCOUVER
ISLAND

Fraser

14 10

Saskatchewan

16

9

Lake
Winnipeg

Assiniboine

Hayes

5

1

22

Vancouver

28

Pacific
Ocean

29

Columbia

26

12

19

Fort
William

4

Quebec

3

Montreal

30

2 2

Atlantic
Ocean

7 8

Fort Ross

English Enter

5 In 1661, independent French traders, Pierre Radisson and Médard Chouart des Groseilliers, explored the area north of Lake Superior. They were unable to obtain a monopoly from the French, so they approached the English, who were anxious to become part of the fur trade in North America.

6 In 1670, the Hudson's Bay Company (HBC) was formed. King Charles of England gave the HBC a monopoly on the fur trade in Rupert's Land, the land drained by rivers flowing into Hudson Bay. Rupert's Land is shown on the map.

The Native people living in Rupert's Land were not consulted by the HBC in this transaction. Fur trading forts were erected at the mouths of the main rivers flowing into Hudson Bay. Native people, acting as go-betweens, traded furs obtained from various Native groups in the interior for English trade goods (e.g., metal objects, guns, alcohol, and clothing). While the French, under the direction of their Native guides, were exploring farther and farther inland searching for new fur territory, the British (HBC) waited for the Native people to bring furs to their forts around Hudson Bay.

1661
Radisson &
Groseilliers (p. 47)

1670
Hudson's
Bay Company
(p. 47, 90)

1673
Jolliet &
Marquette (p. 32)

1682
La Salle (p. 32)

1690
Kelsey (p. 91)

5   6   7   8   9

Note: Timeline is not to scale

173

French Expansion

7 French explorers, fur traders, and missionaries were moving farther and farther inland from the area of the St. Lawrence River and the Great Lakes. In 1673, Louis Jolliet and Father Jacques Marquette travelled south on the Mississippi River to its junction with the Arkansas River.

8 In 1682, Sieur de la Salle explored the Mississippi River to its mouth in the Gulf of Mexico. Wherever the French explored, they built trading posts, flew the French flag (the *fleur-de-lis*), and claimed the land in the name of the king of France.

The French found that in the southern part of North America there was a scarcity of good quality furs, so they turned their attention back to the country north and west of Lake Superior, and south and west of Hudson Bay.

Native Contributions

The contributions of First People and Metis were essential to European exploration and the fur trade in North America. Native people (including the Metis) shared their skills and knowledge. They acted as guides and interpreters, involved the Europeans in inter-tribal trade, showed them how to trap and hunt, and provided food, shelter, clothing, and transportation.

9 In 1690, HBC trader Henry Kelsey was sent to the plains to encourage the Native people to bring their furs to the HBC posts on Hudson Bay.

10 Many Cree, Assiniboine, and Chipewyan people became go-betweens, carrying furs from the western peoples to the HBC posts on Hudson Bay. One example is Thanadelthur, a Chipewyan woman who acted as a go-between for Hudson's Bay Company traders. She is credited with promoting peace between the Cree and Chipewyan.

Competition

11 France and Great Britain were at war from 1679–1713. The French attempted to expand their fur-trading empire by military action. Several sea battles were fought between the French and the British in Hudson Bay. In 1713, the Treaty of Utrecht awarded all of the fur posts on Hudson Bay to Great Britain, therefore to the HBC. The French could no longer legally enter the northern and western fur territory through Hudson Bay. They had to enter the fur territory the long way—via the St. Lawrence River and the Great Lakes.

12 From 1731–1743, the La Vérendrye family explored Lake of the Woods and rivers farther west. They built fur trade posts in these areas to encourage the Native people to trade with the independent traders from Quebec, instead of going to HBC forts on Hudson Bay.

13 Beginning in 1741, Russian fur traders built posts on the West Coast. The Bering–Chirikov Scientific Expedition brought back to Russia reports of the abundance of sea otter and fur seals on the western coast of North America.

14 In 1754 and 1755, HBC explorer, Anthony Henday, travelled with Cree and Assiniboine guides up the Saskatchewan River. His job was to persuade the Blackfoot to trade with HBC, instead of with the French.

In 1763, as a result of the Seven Years' War between the French and the British, the French lost all their lands on mainland North America to the British.

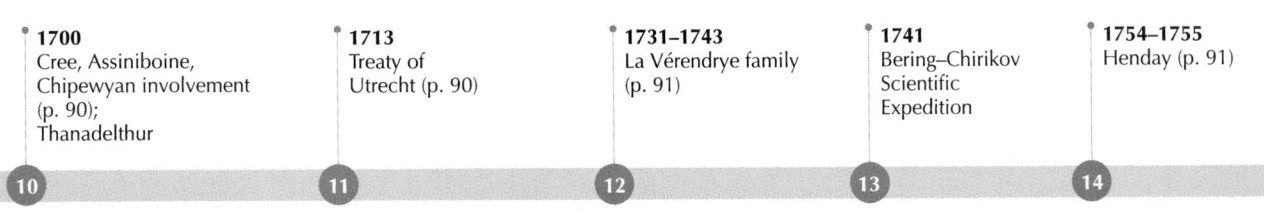

1700	1713	1731–1743	1741	1754–1755
Cree, Assiniboine, Chipewyan involvement (p. 90); Thanadelthur	Treaty of Utrecht (p. 90)	La Vérendrye family (p. 91)	Bering–Chirikov Scientific Expedition	Henday (p. 91)
10	11	12	13	14

Note: Timeline is not to scale

Rivalry: HBC vs NWC

To meet the English competition from the HBC the French and Scottish fur traders, with Montreal as their headquarters, organized **independent** trading groups. These men were known as Pedlars because they peddled or traded goods for furs. Well-known Pedlars included Peter Pond, James Finlay, and the Frobisher brothers. Other lesser-known Pedlars were Peter Pangman, Booty Graves, Charles Patterson, and a man known as France-ways.

The independent traders from Montreal that later formed the North West Company found themselves competing with the Hudson's Bay Company. (The beaver skin that the men are pulling on in the picture below represents the fur trade.) These entrepreneurs also competed among them-selves in a sometimes bloody and violent manner.

15 In the 1700s, the Spanish explored and traded as far north as the Queen Charlotte Islands. In 1774, Juan Perez sailed up the coast as far as Vancouver Island. Other notable Spanish traders and explorers were Esteban Martínez, Bruno de Hezeta, Juan Bodega y Quadra, and Acala Galiano.

16 In 1774, HBC trader Samuel Hearne built Cumberland House, the first HBC fort in the interior. Hearne was trying to trade for furs with the Native peoples before the independent traders could.

17 In 1778, independent trader Peter Pond built Fort Chipewyan northwest of Cumberland House, to try to get furs from the Native peoples before they reached HBC's Cumberland House.

18 Captain James Cook of the British Royal Navy visited Nootka Sound, Vancouver Island, in 1778. He was looking for the western entrance of the Northwest Passage (a route for ships leading from eastern North America to the Pacific Ocean.)

19 By 1783, independent traders from Quebec were joining together to try to be as strong as the HBC. They formed the North West Company (NWC) and, later, the XY Company. The men of the NWC came to be called Nor'Westers. Partners of these companies spent the winter in the North-West trading with the Native peoples, then brought the furs to Fort William (see page 177). There they met the Montreal traders, who took the furs to Montreal for shipment to Europe.

Many Metis men served in the fur trade as *voyageurs*, interpreters, and buffalo hunters. Metis women made **pemmican**, and the food the fur traders carried with them.

20 After 1788, American independent traders started coming to the Pacific Northwest to obtain sea otter and seal skins.

HBC

INDEPENDENT TRADERS

HBC

NWC

Independent—acting without help or influence of others
Voyageur—a boatman or canoeman, usually French-speaking, who travelled inland for the early fur-trading companies
Pemmican—a food made from buffalo meat, buffalo fat, and berries

1774 Perez, Martínez, de Hezeta, Bodega y Quadra, Galiano	1774 Hearne	1778 Pond	1778 Cook	1783 NWC (p. 191), XY Co.	1788 American Traders	1789 Mackenzie	1792 Vancouver	1792–1793 Mackenzie
15	16	17	18	19	20	21	22	23

Note: Timeline is not to scale

21 In 1789, Nor'Wester Alexander Mackenzie tried to reach the Pacific but followed the Mackenzie River to the Arctic Ocean instead.

22 In 1792, Captain George Vancouver, Royal Navy, explored the Pacific Coast of North America. Under the terms of the Nootka Convention, Spain gave up exclusive control of the West Coast, and the West Coast fur trade. Many fur traders continued looking for the Northwest Passage.

23 In 1792–1793, Mackenzie travelled west along the Peace, Fraser, and Bella Coola Rivers. He had finally found a route to the Pacific Ocean, but it was too rough to be a good trade route. Alternates using pack horses had to be found.

24 In 1799, the Russian American Company was formed and a settlement was built at New Archangel (Sitka).

25 In 1804, the NWC took over the XY Company and rivalry between the HBC and the NWC for the fur trade increased. This rivalry was particularly intense further west, in the Athabasca country. After 1812 this rivalry led to violence when the HBC allowed the Selkirk Settlers to begin a farming settlement at Red River. The NWC and Metis were afraid that the HBC would use the settlers to interfere with their fur trade routes and food supplies.

26 In 1807, Marie-Anne Lagimodière became one of the first non-Native women to settle in the west.

27 In 1808, Nor'Wester Simon Fraser followed the Fraser River to the Strait of Georgia.

28 An American, John Astor, founded the Pacific Fur Company in 1810, and in 1811 he established Astoria at the mouth of the Columbia River.

29 In 1811, a Metis woman, Charlotte Small, and her husband, Nor'Wester David Thompson, followed the

Columbia River to the Pacific Ocean. The Americans already had a fur trade fort at Astoria, at the mouth of the Columbia River. The Russians had one at Fort Ross in northern California. Thompson and his family returned to Montreal, and Thompson completed his remarkable map of Western Canada.

The Pacific coast of Canada was explored by Europeans looking for furs and a Northwest Passage.

End of the Fur Trade Era

30 The rivalry between the HBC and NWC ended in 1821 when the companies united under the name of the Hudson's Bay Company. In 1821, George Simpson, the "Little Emperor," was made governor of the HBC. He lived at Lachine, and used his business and trade skills to strengthen the HBC even more.

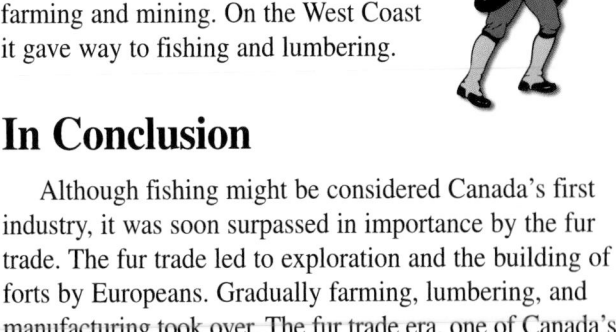

31 In 1867, Russia sold its North American colonies, including Alaska, to the United States of America.

32 In 1870, Rupert's Land was transferred to the Dominion of Canada. On the prairies the fur trade gave way to farming and mining. On the West Coast it gave way to fishing and lumbering.

In Conclusion

Although fishing might be considered Canada's first industry, it was soon surpassed in importance by the fur trade. The fur trade led to exploration and the building of forts by Europeans. Gradually farming, lumbering, and manufacturing took over. The fur trade era, one of Canada's most important and colourful, faded into the past.

1799 Russian American Company	1804 NWC–XY Company merge	1807 Lagimodière	1808 Fraser	1810 Astor, Pacific Fur Company	1811 Small & Thompson	1821 Hudson's Bay Company & North West Company unite (p. 191), Simpson	1867 Russia sells Alaska to USA	1870 Rupert's Land transferred to Canada
24	25	26	27	28	29	30	31	32

Note: Timeline is not to scale

Below: The reconstructed Fort William. Here, at the western end of Lake Superior, the wintering partners brought their furs, picked up more trade goods, and had exuberant celebrations before returning to the woods.

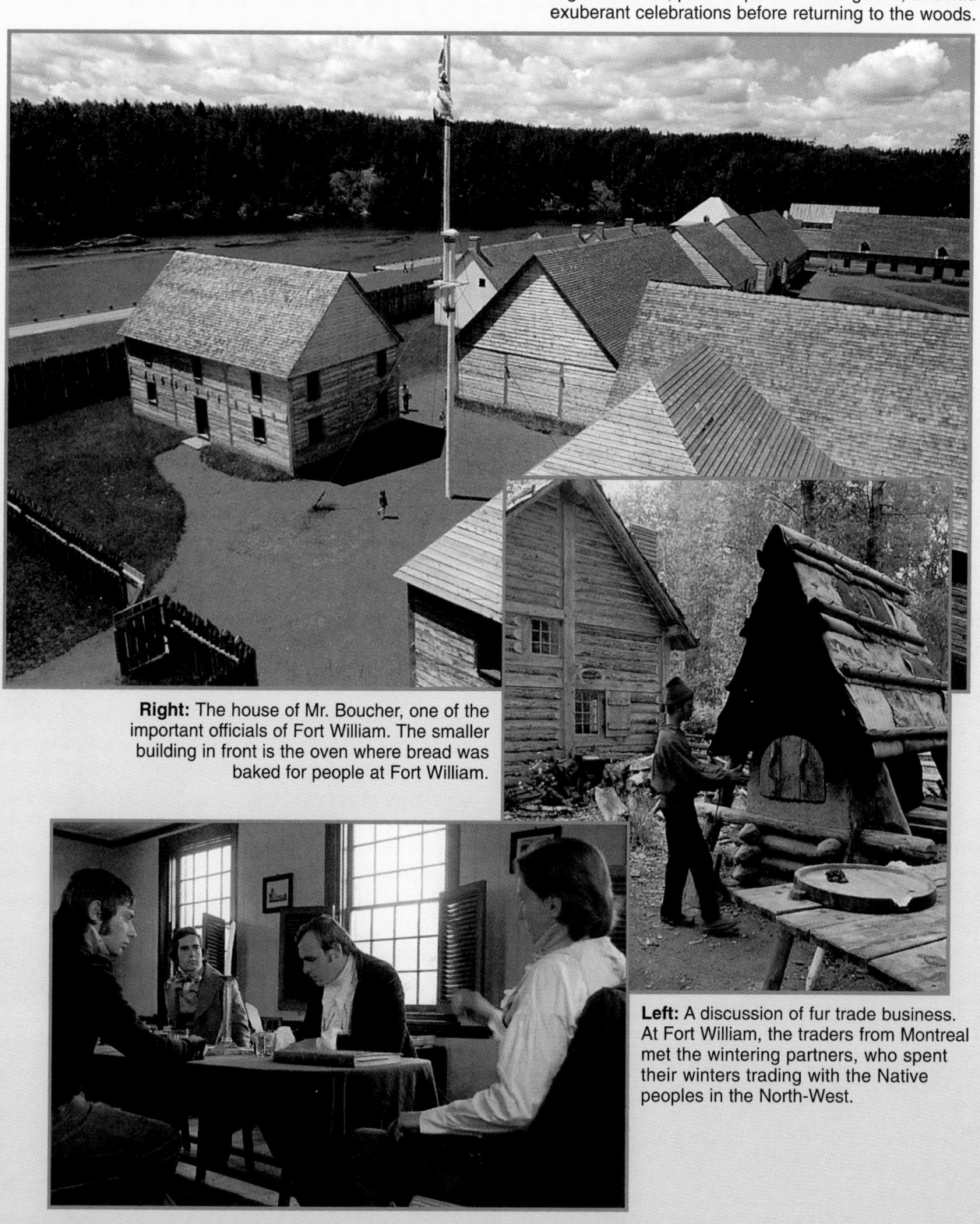

Right: The house of Mr. Boucher, one of the important officials of Fort William. The smaller building in front is the oven where bread was baked for people at Fort William.

Left: A discussion of fur trade business. At Fort William, the traders from Montreal met the wintering partners, who spent their winters trading with the Native peoples in the North-West.

177

Review

The icons are your cue to refer to the Learning How to Learn Appendix (pages 256–271) for ideas on how to complete these activities.

 This icon is a reminder to turn to the Research Model (pages x–xi).

 Complete a self-assessment for one assignment from this chapter.

Understanding Concepts

Checking Predictions

1. Review your Cause–Effect chart from the beginning of this chapter, for each of the three main topics for this chapter. Underline causes and effects you predicted. Compare your chart with a partner's. Add details you have learned.

2. Refer to the "Questions to Talk About" on page 123. Discuss the questions based upon what you learned about government in British North America.

Recording Vocabulary

3.  Use one of the methods found in the Appendix for recording the following vocabulary in the WordBook section of your notes:

- Patriots
- Tories
- re-annex
- petition
- legislative council
- legislative assembly
- executive council
- refugee
- problem solving
- hypothesis

Conceptualizing

4. Here are some of the main ideas from this chapter.
- flood of Loyalists to British North America
- formation of new colonies
- political change (representative government)
- Constitutional Act, 1791
- emergence of towns
- war between Britain and the United States
- competition between Hudson's Bay Company and North West Company
- part played by fur trade in exploring the West

Do either a) or b).

a)  Create a concept poster of one of these ideas. Present your poster to the class.

b) 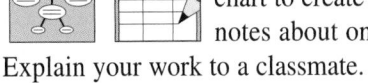 Use a web, mind map, outline or chart to create a permanent set of notes about one of the ideas.
Explain your work to a classmate.

Working with Information

5. 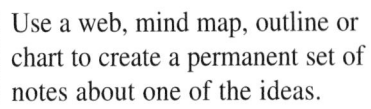 Review all of the different examples of decision-making found in this chapter. Work with a partner to draw a mind map that organizes all of these examples on one sheet of paper. Show how these examples helped bring about representative government. Use simple line drawings and at least three different colours.

6. Use the diagram of the 1791 Constitutional Act on page 160 to write a paragraph explaining how representative government works.

7. Reread the story at the beginning of Section IV (pages 122 and 123) and review the definition of representative government on page 126. In what ways do the students of Fairmont School have a representative government?

8. Think back to the Section III story and the Absolute Rule Decision-Making Model on page 51. Recall Royal Government in New France.

a)  With a partner, compare the Absolute Rule Decision-Making Model and representative government. How are decisions made? Who makes the decisions? Who does the decision-maker take advice from? What role do ordinary citizens play in decision-making? Share your ideas with the class.

b) Compare the decision-making model you developed for Chapter 3. How is your model the same or different from the idea of representative government? Use the questions in a) as a guide.

9. 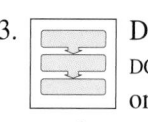 Add between seven and ten entries for this chapter to your timeline.

10. Create a visual timeline of the fur trade.

11. 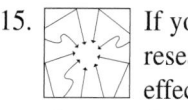 Compare your notebook to that of a partner. Check to see that items are in the proper order and no items are missing. Organize your notes.

Developing Research Skills

12. 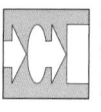 Carry out research to find out what parts/roles the Native and Metis peoples played in the fur trade. Present your findings to the class.

13. During the War of 1812–1814, Washington, DC (the American capital), was occupied for one day by the British. The President's mansion was scorched by fire, and later was painted white. It has been called the "White House" ever since. Do research to find out more about this story.

14. With your class, investigate in depth the various groups of people who were a part of the Loyalists' migration to Canada. Participate in a "Cultural Fair" in which you share their stories and traditions.

15. If you were going to research the causes and effects of the War of 1812, what questions would you use to guide your research? With a partner, brainstorm a list of questions. You are not expected to carry out this research project. Share your list of questions with the class.

16. Show the various causes and the effects of the War of 1812 in a chart.

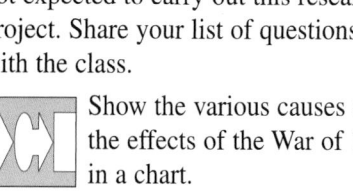

Developing Communication Skills

Reading

17. 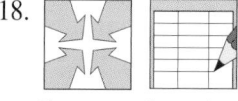 Read the story "The Loyalists." Parts 1 and 2 are found on pages 147–150 and 154–155. Create a comparison chart with three columns. Compare the economic, social, and political environment of the family at three different times in their life: in the Thirteen Colonies, during the Hungry Year, and at a time after Part 2 takes place (predict).

18. 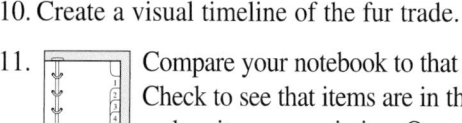 Read Parts 1 and 2 of "The Loyalists" and "On a Seigneury" (pages 147–150, 154–155, and 156–157). Compare the points of view of the French and the Loyalists living in Quebec using the following criteria: the Quebec Act, laws/court system, language, participation in government, taxation, religion, land ownership and distribution.

Writing

19. Imagine that you accompanied Alexander Mackenzie, Simon Fraser, or David Thompson on one of their explorations. Write a series of diary entries describing your experiences. Illustrate your diary entries with pictures and maps.

20. Lady Tennyson (wife of the famous British poet Alfred Lord Tennyson) once said: *You Canadians should be proud of the founders of your country. The United Empire Loyalists were a grand type of loyal, law-abiding, god-fearing men. No country ever had such founders, no country in the world.* Do you agree with Lady Tennyson? Explain your answer in the History Journal section of your notebook.

Listening and Speaking

21. Acting as a game show host, ask your classmates questions about the main topics covered in this chapter.

22. As a class, present an oral timeline of one of the main topics covered in this chapter. Take turns as you present the details in chronological order.

23. In pairs, write a script for a conversation that might have taken place between an American Patriot and his best friend, who he has just discovered is a Loyalist. Present the conversation dramatically (in play form) to your class.

24.  Write and present a tribute (speech honouring someone) about Tecumseh.

25. Plan an awards ceremony to recognize the accomplishments of several important people you learned about in this chapter. Choose classmates to play the parts of the award winners. Ask them to prepare a brief speech as a suitable response to the award.

Viewing and Representing

26. Design a poster showing the changes in British North America resulting from the arrival of the Loyalists.

27. Design a political cartoon that presents a viewpoint about the Constitutional Act.

28. Design and create a manual for settlers arriving in British North America. Provide information and strategies to assist them in facing the challenges of their new home.

29. Notice the feature called "Canada Revisited" on page 181. Create your own "Canada Revisited" by investigating the historical significance of several sites in your community. Or, create your "Canada Revisited" by using an historical site related to the content covered in this chapter.

Applying Concepts

30. The chapter Overview on page 136 focuses on the Loyalists. Create a chapter Overview page about the War of 1812 or the westward expansion of the fur trade.

31. 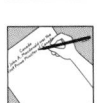 Fur traders were entrepreneurs. Prepare a presentation to show various aspects of the fur trade business. Include these topics: market, supply, demand, competition, advertising, partnerships, monopoly, profits, trade, and future prospects. (These terms are defined in the Glossary.)

32. 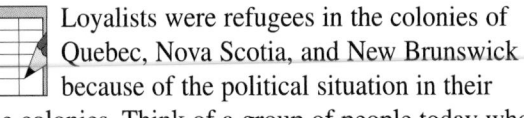 Loyalists were refugees in the colonies of Quebec, Nova Scotia, and New Brunswick because of the political situation in their home colonies. Think of a group of people today who have become refugees for political reasons. Compare the Loyalists and this group of people.

33. 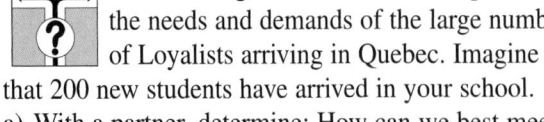 The British government had to respond to the needs and demands of the large number of Loyalists arriving in Quebec. Imagine that 200 new students have arrived in your school.
   a) With a partner, determine: How can we best meet the needs of all of our students? Think about space, resources, activities, co-operation, resolving conflicts, and the future.
   b) In the Tools of Learning section of your notebook, summarize and react to the problem solving steps you just followed.

34. Ask your parents or other adults if they have ever signed a petition. What did it request? Did the petition get results?

35. You have had the opportunity to read several quotations and eyewitness accounts.
   a) What role do these personal accounts play in our understanding of Canada's history?
   b) In what different ways do cultural groups pass their history on to the next generation?

36. Why have you been studying
   • the arrival of Loyalists to British North America?
   • fur trade competition?
   • the Constitutional Act, 1791?

37. 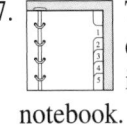 Try to think of as many ideas as you can for each of the following. Record your answers in the History Journal section of your notebook.

   What if...
   a) the Loyalists had never arrived in British North America?
   b) Upper and Lower Canada were never granted representative government?
   c) the War of 1812 had been won by the United States? By Great Britain?

38. Complete each statement with a paragraph entry.

   a) History Journal: What I liked reading the most was... because...
   b) Tools of Learning: One new learning strategy I used was...

Challenge Plus

39. Create a mobile to represent the effect of the War of 1812 on the development of Canada. Consider location of settlements, building of transportation routes, the locations of forts and capital cities, and our relationship with the Americans.

40. Choose students to participate in a debate on the effectiveness of the Constitutional Act as a way of responding to the demands of the people of Quebec. Listen to the debate and then write a paper, taking and defending your personal position for or against the Constitutional Act.

41. During the War of 1812, many English and French in Upper and Lower Canada fought against the Americans and considered them to be their enemies. Examine our social, political, and economic relationship with the United States. What is our relationship with the United States now? What has changed? Why?

42. You have learned about settlement patterns in British North America.

   a) Investigate how population distribution and settlement in this area have changed over the years. Obtain recent statistics* so that you can create graphs and/or charts to illustrate the present day.

   b) Conduct research to show how settlement, growth, and development over time have affected the natural environment.

   c) What do you predict for the future?

43. Read the ballad "The Bold Canadian" (page 167).
   a) From whose point of view is the ballad written?
   b) According to this ballad, who was responsible for defeating the Americans at Detroit? Choose from Upper Canada militia, the British army, and Native allies.
   c) Read again items 3 and 4 on page 167. Has your answer to b) changed? Why or why not?
   d) Research the battle at Detroit. Has your answer to b) changed? Why or why not?
   e) What have you discovered about using various sources (primary and secondary) when researching historical events? Why is it important to consider the point of view of the writer? Record your ideas in the Tools of Learning section of your notebook.

44. Complete your website or magazine assignment for Section IV.

Canada Revisited

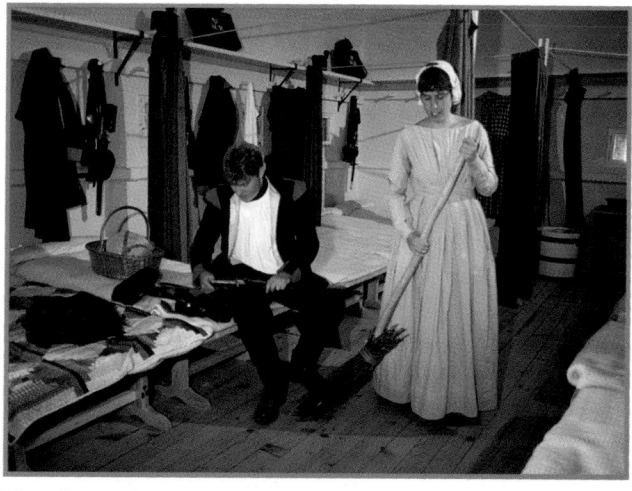

The above photograph shows a barracks in Fort Wellington. The British fort was built during the War of 1812 to guard the transportation route along the St. Lawrence River and prevent American invasion. This national historic site in Prescott, Ontario, is open to visitors.

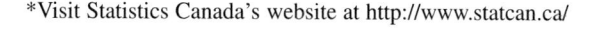

*Visit Statistics Canada's website at http://www.statcan.ca/

181

Conflict and Change
1815–1855

The Passport Tour students were reviewing what they had learned. "After the Constitutional Act of 1791, Upper and Lower Canada had elected representatives. So, does that mean they had a government like our government today?" Dakota asked.

"Being represented should mean the people had more power," said Brenda, " as long as the representatives were listened to."

"Wait a second," said Erin. "Think back to the Students' Council transcripts we talked about. Students' Council members are elected representatives of the students in the school and make decisions for them..."

"But when they voted in favour of letting friends come to school dances, the decision was overruled by the principal," Ken finished.

"Right," replied Ms. Ito. "The Students' Council has a higher authority, the school administration, that can overrule any decisions made by the elected representatives."

"Even with elected representatives, neither the students nor the people in Upper and Lower Canada were necessarily having their wishes met," Brenda concluded.

"Maybe if you tell us more about what the Students' Council at Fairmont School did, that'll help us to make connections to what was about to happen in Upper and Lower Canada," Ken suggested, so Ms. Ito related the rest of the story.

"All was not well on the Students' Council at Fairmont High. Mrs. Cherniak often was unable to meet with the whole Students' Council directly. She picked Kyle and three other Students' Council members to meet with her about the decisions Students' Council was making. Students around the school were beginning to voice their concerns. Some felt she had chosen Kyle and his crowd because they always agreed with her. Some felt Mrs. Cherniak's Special Council always tried to talk the rest of the Students' Council members into voting their way. Students were making comments like 'How come a few Students' Council members are making all the decisions for the rest?' and 'I want my representative's votes to count too!'

"Just when things were really starting to heat up, Mrs. Cherniak called a special meeting with the whole Students' Council. She told them she had discussed the Students' Council's letter of protest with the teachers. They had decided that the Students' Council and student body were mature enough to be responsible for their own choices on certain issues. From then on, there would be certain areas where the Students' Council could make decisions and the principal would not overrule those decisions. This would *not* include decisions where safety was an issue or that were against school policy or the law. They would include decisions where students could be expected to be responsible for their choices and actions."

"Now we're talking!" said Brenda, nodding her approval.

"But how would it change anything, really?" wondered Erin. "Kyle and his group would probably still try to influence the way the rest of the Students' Council members voted."

"Actually, the Students' Council came up with a good idea about that," Mrs. Ito replied. "They decided that the Students' Council should *elect* students to Mrs. Cherniak's Special Council, and should be able to vote them out of power if they didn't like the job they were doing—if they were not responsible to the students."

"Yeah, but the new council could be just as disappointing," Ken pointed out.

"If the Students' Council members elected the representatives, they should have been able to remove them if they weren't responsible to the decisions of the Students' Council," said Roberto.

"That's exactly what they proposed," Ms. Ito replied.

"Did it work?" asked Erin. "Did they get that much decision-making power?"

"Good question. Their power was tested. Some students made a suggestion to Students' Council that Honour Roll students should be able to miss classes to listen to a guest speaker on Friday afternoons," said Ms. Ito.

"Like they'd be allowed to decide that!" Ken laughed.

"Actually, Students' Council agreed to take the idea to Mrs. Cherniak. She told them that she'd thought very carefully about the decision to allow Honour Roll students to miss Friday afternoon classes, but..." Ms. Ito paused, "she did not agree with it."

Roberto scowled. "Well, so much for a Students' Council that was responsible to the students it was representing."

"However," Ms. Ito continued,

"she also recognized that she had agreed that the students could have a type of responsible government. She expected some students to be unhappy with the decision and knew that there might be complaints. However, she went along with the decision of the Student Council majority."

"Yes!" Erin gave the thumbs up.

"Finally, some decision-making power!" Dakota nodded.

"How about a celebration snack," Roberto rubbed his stomach.

Brenda smiled, "Only if we get to vote on where to go."

Exploring Further

1. In groups of seven or eight students, role-play the Section V story on pages 182–183.

Questions to Talk About

See "Questions to Talk About" on page 186.

183

Chapter 7
Upper and Lower Canada
(1815–1838)

Overview
Use this Overview to predict the events of this chapter.

1815–1850
The Great Migration brought thousands of new settlers to Upper Canada, Lower Canada, and the Atlantic Colonies.

1821
Rivalry between the North West Company and the Hudson's Bay Company ended in 1821. The new company was called the Hudson's Bay Company.

A thriving timber industry developed in Upper Canada and Lower Canada.

Towns were slowly built.

Most of the new pioneers moved into the forested areas of Upper Canada. Many faced great hardship as they felled the trees and built new homes.

The structure of the government in Upper and Lower Canada was based on the Constitution Act of 1791.

Government of Upper Canada

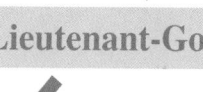

British Government

⬇

Lieutenant-Governor

⬇   ⬇

Legislative Council   Executive Council

Legislative Assembly

⬆

Voters

Lower Canada had the same government structure but had an entirely separate government.

In both Upper Canada and Lower Canada, small groups of powerful and conservative men appointed by the governor controlled the government. They shaped policy and provided favours for their friends.

Executive Council

The ordinary people felt they had little influence in the government. Only property owners had the vote. Bills put forward by the elected assembly (the Legislative Assembly) could be stopped by the Legislative Council or the governor.

Legislative Assembly

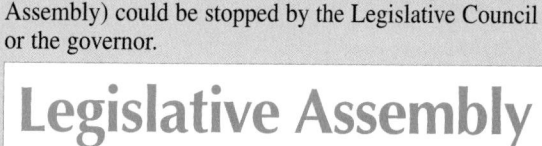

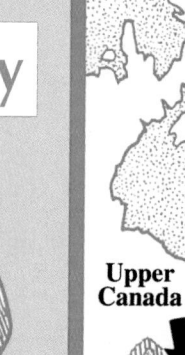

Lower Canada

Upper Canada

1837–1838
Rebellions broke out in Lower Canada and Upper Canada.

Section V Questions to Talk About

Discuss the following questions by referring to the section story on pages 182 and 183. Keep the questions in mind while you read the rest of the chapter. See if there are similarities between the government of Upper and Lower Canada between 1815 and 1838 and Mrs. Cherniak's Special Council at Fairmont School and the changes brought about by Students' Council.

1. In small groups, discuss some criteria for acting in a responsible way. Share your ideas with the rest of the class and compile a master list. What things did the students on the Special Council do that showed they were acting in a responsible way?
2. Discuss the following questions by referring to the story. At first, who participated in the student government at Fairmont School? How were decisions made? Who had the final authority? How did the situation change when Mrs. Cherniak chose her Special Council? Did the first Special Council operate as if it were a government that was responsible to the student body? Who lost some power when the second Special Council was elected by the Students' Council, to be responsible to them? Who gained more power?
3. As a class, draw a diagram to illustrate the type of government the Students' Council had at the end of the story. Use the diagram on page 160 as a guide.

Chapter 7 Focus

Chapter 6 described the United Empire Loyalists, the effects of their arrival on the existing British colonies, and the formation of new colonies. It also explored the War of 1812 and the fur trade. Chapter 7 is about political reform.

It will deal with creating change and resolving conflict in the British colonies, and describe the causes, personalities, and results of the rebellions of 1837 in Upper and Lower Canada. The concepts of power, co-operation, decision-making, and conflict underlie the events of this chapter. The concept of conflict is the focus of Chapter 7.

  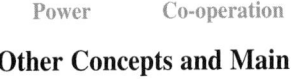 

Power   Co-operation   Decision-making   **Conflict**

Other Concepts and Main Topics
- Changes (population, fur and timber trades)
- Conflict and rebellions in Upper and Lower Canada
- Rural and urban life

Chapter Preview/Prediction

Examine the Overview found on pages 184–185 and briefly look through the chapter, taking note of headings and pictures. Use this information and what you already know to predict what this chapter will be about. Create a three-column chart headed Know, Wonder, and Learn.

In the Know column, fill in everything you know about this chapter. What would you like to know? Add this to the Wonder column. At the end of this chapter, you will check what you have written in your chart and summarize what you have learned in the Learn column.

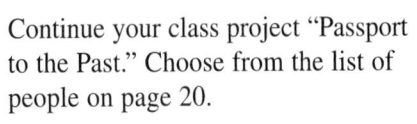 Continue your class project "Passport to the Past." Choose from the list of people on page 20.

Bush Farm Near Chatham. When European and American settlers started farms in Upper and Lower Canada, their first task was to clear away the dense forests. Many of the trees were burned; others provided lumber for homes and furniture.

Changes to Upper and Lower Canada: 1815–1838

There were three major changes in Upper and Lower Canada between the end of the War of 1812 (which you read about in the last chapter) and the rebellions of 1837 (which you will read about in this chapter). Two of these changes, a population explosion and the development of a thriving timber trade, affected both Upper and Lower Canada. The other change, the end of competition in the fur trade, affected only Lower Canada.

Population Explosion

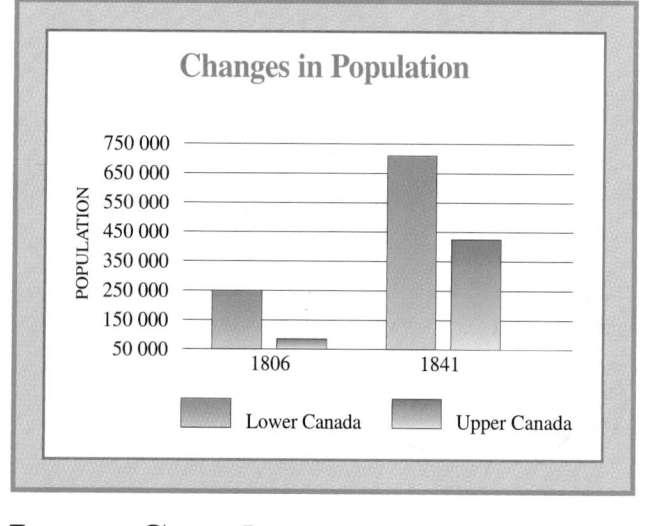

Changes in Population

Lower Canada   Upper Canada

Lower Canada

The population in Lower Canada increased from 250 000 in 1806 to 717 000 in 1841. This population explosion was caused mainly by a very high birth rate among the French-speaking people of Lower Canada. In addition, some British and many American immigrants settled in the Eastern Townships* of Lower Canada. This was an area of Lower Canada that had been set aside for settlement by English-speaking farmers.

Upper Canada

Upper Canada was originally settled by Loyalists leaving the United States during and after the American Revolution; then, until the War of 1812, other American settlers moved there.

After the War of 1812, American settlers were no longer welcome in Upper Canada. A wave of settlers from Great Britain (Ireland, Scotland, England, and Wales) took their

place. Historians call the period between 1815 and 1850 "The Great Migration."

Many tenant farmers in Great Britain were being forced by their landlords to leave their small farms because it was more profitable for the landowners to use the farms for grazing sheep than to rent them to the farmers. Many artisans were finding themselves unemployed because machines were taking over their jobs. In Ireland in the 1840s, many people were starving because of poor crops.

These immigrants came to seek new lives for themselves in British North America. Many of the immigrants bought land and became farmers. Others came to the cities. They often worked as servants, labourers on canals and railways, in the forest industry, or at whatever job was available. By 1860, the majority of English-speaking people in Canada** were of Irish descent.

As a result of British immigration, the population of Upper Canada increased from 71 000 in 1806 to 432 000 in 1841. In 1815, the population was 80 percent American-born. In 1841, almost 50 percent were recent British immigrants.

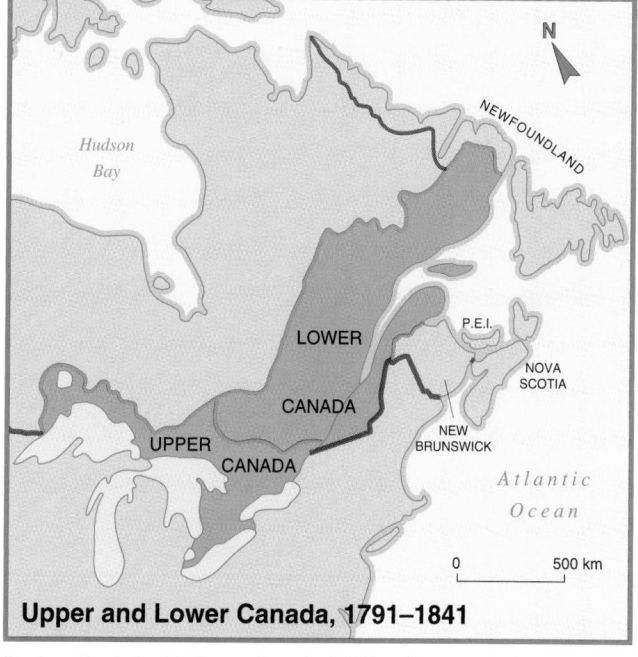

Upper and Lower Canada, 1791–1841

During the late 1700s and early 1800s, the population of both Upper and Lower Canada increased greatly.

---

*The triangle of land in Lower Canada between the St. Lawrence River and the American border

**Sometimes Upper and Lower Canada were called the Canadas or Canada, and the people were called Canadians.

Most British immigrants that came to British North America left behind a life of unemployment and poverty. In spite of having to leave family and friends and most of their possessions behind, they were prepared to venture into the colonies of North America, where their lives could begin again.

Exploring Further

1. Pretend you are one of the people in the illustration below. Write a journal account of your thoughts and feelings (both positive and negative) about leaving your homeland and going to a new country.

Aboard the Immigrant Ship

The sea journey to British North America lasted from 20 days to more than two months. Most of the immigrants travelled in the holds of cargo ships. These ships were not meant to transport people but to carry timber. Living conditions were unsanitary and cramped. The ships were rat-infested. Food was limited in variety due to lack of refrigeration. Food and water had to be taken along. Sea sickness was common because of the many ocean storms. Diseases such as typhus, cholera, and dysentery spread quickly in such close quarters. Many became ill on the long voyage and large numbers died.

In fact, so many people died that the vessels became known as "coffin ships." The first stop for the ships upon reaching British North America was Grosse Isle, an island in the St. Lawrence River just below Quebec City. A doctor would come on board to inspect the passengers. Anyone who was sick was removed to wooden sheds on the island, where they were cared for. Once the ship was given a clean bill of health, it was allowed to sail on to Quebec or Montreal.

Focus On: The Great Migration 1815–1850
continued

An Eyewitness Account:

In many cases in bad weather, they would not go on deck; their health suffered so much that their strength was gone, and they had not the power to help themselves. Hence the between-decks were like a loathsome dungeon. When the hatchways were opened under which the people were stowed, the steam rose and the stench was like that from a pen of pigs.

Some immigrants chose to stay in Quebec or Montreal. Most travelled on to Upper Canada or to the United States. To reach Upper Canada, the newcomers travelled in smaller boats up the St. Lawrence to Kingston and farther. Once in Upper Canada, they tried to find jobs or to search for land. People who bought land received a "location ticket," which described where to find the land. Once they had this, they would travel on foot or in carts through the backwoods to find their new homes.

Exploring Further

1. Continue the journal you started in question 1 on the previous page. Describe the conditions on board the ship and some of the events that happened to you and your family.

2. What groups other than the British immigrated during this time? Why? Write a report or short story about their experiences and contributions.

The Timber Trade

A second major change in Upper and Lower Canada in the early 1800s occurred because the pioneers began to use the forests as a way of making a living. Before that time they had used some trees to build their homes, but most were cut down and burnt in order to clear land for planting crops.

In 1839, wood made up 80 percent of all goods exported from Upper and Lower Canada. It provided jobs for thousands of people in Lower Canada. Much of it was sold to Britain. The United States also bought some. The rest was used in Nova Scotia and New Brunswick in the shipbuilding industry. New Brunswick was a world-leading exporter of timber.

Breaking a Log Jam, P4/3/3, Provincial Archives of New Brunswick

Among the dangers faced by lumbermen were the log jams. The man in this picture is attempting to break up a log jam.

Uses for Trees

Potash made from ashes of trees was used for making soap and glass in Europe. The pioneers could sell potash for a small source of cash income.

Masts made of white pine were needed for the ships of the British royal navy. Until 1815, a supply of new masts was particularly needed, because Britain was involved in European wars.

Square timber was needed in Europe for building. The men would fell the trees, cut off the limbs, and square the trunks. Next, they would lash the timber together in huge rafts that could hold as many as 50 or 60 men and then float the rafts downstream to the ports of Quebec and St. John, New Brunswick. There, the timber was loaded onto large ships and transported to Europe. Sawn lumber was needed for the larger homes that pioneer families wanted as their lives became more settled. By 1854 there were 1618 sawmills in Upper Canada. They produced boards for Europe, the United States, and for local use.

The shipbuilding industry in the colonies of Nova Scotia and New Brunswick required lumber. The ships built in Nova Scotia were for local use, but the New Brunswick ships were exported. By 1800, British North America supplied more ships to Britain than any other region or country did. Nearly 500 ships were built in the peak year of 1875. Most of these ships came from New Brunswick and Quebec.

Philemon Wright (1760–1839)

Philemon Wright was the first lumberman in the Ottawa Valley. He came from the United States. With a small group of pioneers, Wright founded the village of Hull (originally called Wrightstown) in 1800. By 1805, the community was running short of money and Wright came up with a brilliant idea for saving the community.

He knew Great Britain had developed a great need for timber. France had conquered much of Europe at this time and was cutting off Britain's timber supply. If Britain was to keep building ships for its navy, then it would need timber from its colonies.

All one winter, Wright and his men chopped down trees. Next, they lashed the logs together to form a huge raft they called "The Columbo." In June, Wright and three others rode the raft down the swift Ottawa River and the St. Lawrence all the way to Quebec. This proved that timber from the Ottawa Valley could be successfully delivered to market.

The End of Competition in the Fur Trade

The third major change in the Canadas in the early 1800s involved the fur trade.* The fur trade was still an important part of the economy of Lower Canada. The rivalry over the fur trade could have ended in 1763 when the British took control of New France, but it did not. Instead, traders from Montreal returned to the woods and extended the vast fur-trading system even farther than it had gone before.

In 1783, a group of Montreal merchants formed the North West Company to compete for furs with the Hudson's Bay Company. The North West Company proceeded to build trading posts far to the west so that it would be easier for the Native peoples to bring in their furs. (Refer to illustration #3 on page 137.) The Hudson's Bay Company was forced to build posts inland as well. Sometimes the trading posts of the two companies were in sight of one another.

The Hudson's Bay Company had an advantage in that it had posts on Hudson Bay itself and could ship furs and trading goods in and out of the Bay. The North West Company had to use the slower overland route to Montreal. However, the *voyageurs* who worked for the North West Company were so skilled that they provided stiff competition.

The fur frontier was moving farther north all the time. This meant that it was becoming more and more expensive for the North West Company to take their furs to market and to transport trading goods and supplies to the trading posts.

In 1821, the rival companies decided to unite under the name of the Hudson's Bay Company. The new company took over all the trading posts in the West. There would be no more need for *voyageurs* to carry furs and trading goods to and from Montreal.

*Refer to the Fur Trade Timeline pages 172–176.

The Spring Brigade, by Franklin Arbuckle. Fur traders set off from Montreal to go to the fur trading posts in the West.

Shooting the Rapids, by Frances Anne Hopkins. The artist has included herself in the painting.

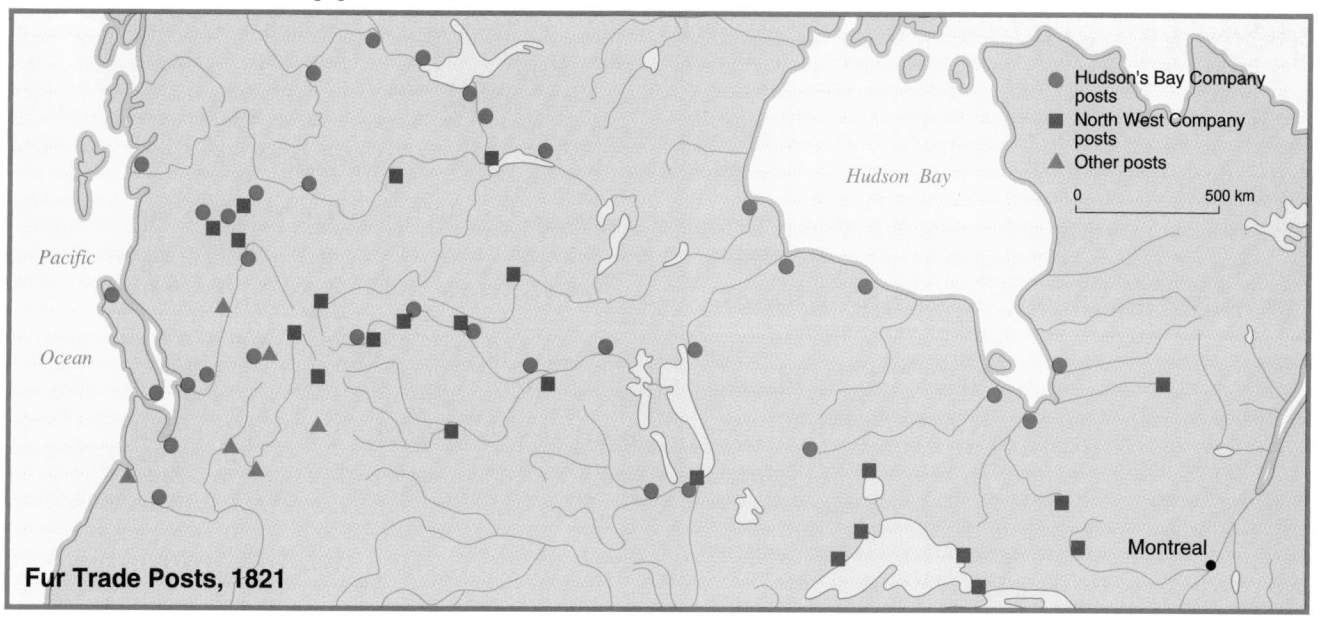

Fur Trade Posts, 1821

- ● Hudson's Bay Company posts
- ■ North West Company posts
- ▲ Other posts

0   500 km

Hudson Bay

Pacific Ocean

Montreal

Life in Lower Canada: 1815–1838

Groups in Lower Canada

There were three major groups in the male-dominated society of Lower Canada at this time. They were the French-speaking habitants, the English-speaking merchants, and the French-speaking professional men.* Each group had special concerns they wanted the government to recognize.

Habitants

The French-speaking habitants continued to live much as they had done for the past 150 years. They worked their long, narrow farms and paid their dues to the seigneur. But change was threatening their lifestyle. Population growth was filling up the available farmland. The narrow farms were becoming even narrower as farmers divided them among their sons. New rows of farms appeared behind the original row fronting on the St. Lawrence, Richelieu, and Ottawa rivers. As available farmland dwindled, young people left to work in the towns or the lumber camps of Lower Canada or they went to the United States.

Extreme poverty was common after 1810. Some faced starvation. The economic situation was made worse by the low prices fetched by wheat at the time, and by the fact that much of the wheat was ruined by bad weather, disease, and insects.

The habitants were anxious over the scarcity of land and the poor economic conditions. The huge number of English-speaking newcomers made them fearful of losing their French language, Roman Catholic religion, and agricultural way of life.

Merchants

Compared to the habitants, the English-speaking merchants were newcomers to Lower Canada. They had arrived following the events in 1763, when New France became a British colony. The merchants were rich and powerful. They had made their money from the export of furs, grain, and later timber. They wanted improvements, such as harbours, canals, and roads, all of which were to be paid for by government taxes.

Professional Men

The French-speaking professionals were the newest group in Lower Canada. This group did not become prominent until after 1800. They were educated people, mostly lawyers and doctors. They wanted to be the leaders of the colony and they believed that they spoke for all the French-speaking people of Lower Canada.

These professional men began to dream of and speak of a separate French-Canadian nation. This nation would preserve the French-Canadian way of life: the French language, Roman Catholic religion, and traditional agricultural lifestyle. They saw the British as a cultural threat. They formed a new political party called the "Parti Canadien."

Louis-Joseph Papineau (1786-1871)

Louis-Joseph Papineau was a wealthy seigneur in Lower Canada. He served as an officer in the militia, defending British North America from the Americans during the War of 1812.

He was elected to the Legislative Assembly of Lower Canada in 1809. He served as the Speaker of the Assembly almost continuously from 1815 to 1837. Papineau was a strong supporter of the Roman Catholic Church and many of the traditional Canadien ways. However, he also advocated changes to government.

As Speaker, Papineau became the leader of the Parti Canadien, which, after 1826, was called the Parti Patriote. In the 1830s, Papineau promoted an American-style, democratic system of government. Papineau and the Parti Patriote wanted **political reform** that would benefit the French in Lower Canada, since they were the vast majority of the population.

---

*Women did not enter the professions (become doctors, lawyers, judges) at this time or become involved in the government. While Native people also lived in the area, they were not involved in the government at this time and are thus not included on this page.

Political reform— changes to make the government better

Government in Lower Canada

The system of government in Lower Canada during this time was that which had been established by the Constitutional Act of 1791.* (See pages 159 and 160 in Chapter 6.)

The power of the elected Legislative Assembly was limited by the governor and the councils. After 1817 the Legislative Assembly controlled revenues in Lower Canada. However, bills recommending how money was to be spent could be vetoed by the Legislative Council and the British-appointed governor. Members of the Legislative Council and the Executive Council were appointed by the governor, so they could not be voted out at election time. Since the governor was English-speaking, the council members appointed by him also usually spoke English. Their interests and concerns were usually different from those of the Canadien habitants and professional men.

Château Clique

One group in Lower Canada held most of the power in the government. This group came to be known as the Château Clique. *Château* means "castle" and *clique* means "a small group unfriendly to outsiders." The Château Clique

- was a small group of powerful people (mostly in businesses) in the colony of Lower Canada

- members were either of British background or wealthy Canadiens who were allied with the British

- believed power should be in the hands of a few capable people (themselves)

- wanted the Roman Catholic Church to stay powerful; in turn the Church supported their political aims

- favoured the British point of view and the British system of government

- wanted more English-speaking settlers in the colony.

Parti Canadien

Many people in Lower Canada wanted to maintain traditional Canadien ways, such as the Roman Catholic religion and the seigneurial system. The Parti Canadien (called the Parti Patriote after 1826) favoured such traditional Canadien ways. However, they also wanted changes to government. They celebrated the granting of representative government in 1791. They pushed to increase the power of the Legislative Assembly and to reform government to make it more democratic. They appealed especially to the Canadien professional elite.

The Parti Canadien was predominately Canadien, but there were a few English-speaking people who took up the cause. The leader of the Parti Canadien was Louis-Joseph Papineau. He was a lawyer and a long-time member of the Legislative Assembly.

Shortly after 1800 the Canadien professional group won control of the Legislative Assembly. Even though the Legislative Assembly had little power they were able to vote against improvements planned by the merchants in the Château Clique, such as canals.

Government Structure of Lower Canada

Governor
(British-appointed)

Legislative Council
(appointed)
- English-speaking merchants and Canadien seigneurs
- usually friends of the governor

Executive Council
(appointed)
- usually English-speaking
- friends of the governor

The Château Clique controlled the Executive Council and the Legislative Council. They dominated the government and business and social life of Lower Canada.

Legislative Assembly (elected by voters)
- controlled by French-Canadian professionals
- led after 1815 by Louis-Joseph Papineau

Voters

→ Appoints
⇒ Elect

---

*Upper Canada had the same government structure but had an entirely separate government.

Unrest in Lower Canada
Points of View

The French-speaking people and the English-speaking merchants wanted different things for Lower Canada. For instance, the merchants wanted to improve canals, harbours, and roads to make it easier to transport wheat and timber to Britain. They suggested that all landowners be taxed to pay for these improvements. The habitants were not interested in these improvements, which they felt would help only the merchants.

Immigration was also causing problems. The Château Clique was encouraging emigration from Great Britain, but the Canadiens looked on the immigrants with dismay. If enough immigrants arrived, the French-speaking inhabitants of Lower Canada could lose their language rights and protection of their Roman Catholic religion. They saw the immigrants settling on land in the Eastern Townships and wondered where their own young people would be able to farm. In June of 1832, an immigrant ship brought a deadly disease, cholera, which resulted in an epidemic in the colony. By September, it had claimed almost 5500 victims.

Another area of concern for the French-speaking people of Lower Canada was the fact that the Executive Council and the Legislative Council were dominated by people who either were English-speaking or supported Great Britain. It was difficult for the Legislative Assembly to get its bills passed into law when the goals and values of the council members and the governor were so different from the members of the Legislative Assembly, the majority of whom were French-speaking.

Appeal to Great Britain

In 1822, the English-speaking merchants asked Britain to unite Upper and Lower Canada. They wanted canals, harbours, and roads to be built. They thought that combining the English vote from the two colonies would increase their power.

In response, Papineau took a protest petition to Britain. He managed to persuade the British Parliament to forget the idea of uniting the two colonies, at least for the time being.

In 1834, the Legislative Assembly put together a list of its grievances, which they called the Ninety-Two **Resolutions**. They decided that they would vote for no taxes until their concerns were resolved. This meant that government workers would not be paid and that the building of roads and bridges would stop.

The British response to the unrest in Lower Canada was to send out Lord Gosford as the new governor in 1835. He had special orders to investigate the grievances in the Ninety-Two Resolutions. He was not well received. Papineau and the Patriotes despised him as a **puppet** of the British. The Montreal merchants were angry with him for trying to please the Patriotes (formerly the Parti Canadien).

Then, as if things were not bad enough, crops failed in much of North America in 1836. Many people in Lower Canada faced starvation.

In January of 1837 Governor Gosford sent a report of his study of the Ninety-Two Resolutions to Britain. In response, the British Colonial Secretary issued 10 resolutions. These were a blow to Papineau and the Patriotes. Britain refused to give the Legislative Assembly any more power. British immigration would continue to be encouraged. It was also decided that if the Legislative Assembly refused to vote for taxes, the governor could simply take from the treasury the money needed to pay his officials.

Then, later in 1837, economic depression hit the United States, Britain, and British North America. Prices dropped and many businesses failed. The situation had a disastrous effect on the rich Canadian timber trade. The Canadiens took out their anger on the English-speaking merchants.

For Your Notebook

1. Who had the power in Lower Canada in the 1820s and 1830s? What role did ordinary people play in making decisions?

Resolution—formal statement of the way a person or group feels; usually written down and sent to one in a position of power and authority; may be followed as a guideline for ruling a group of people
Puppet—leader who is not independent, who does what someone more powerful tells him or her to do

Armed Rebellion in Lower Canada

By the end of November, the Canadiens were ready to fight. Papineau supported the rebellion. The people also followed Wolfred Nelson, another leader, who cried, "The time has come to melt our spoons into bullets!"

The actual rebellion in Lower Canada lasted only a few weeks. It began on November 23, 1837, at St. Denis, where the rebels won a victory.* Following this battle, about 200 of the rebels built a log fort at the village of St. Charles. But this battle was not nearly as successful for them. The British troops fired their cannon, charged, and the rebels fled. Of the Patriotes, 40 were killed, 30 wounded, and over 500 captured. Papineau and other rebel leaders fled to the United States.

The biggest battle took place on December 14 at St. Eustache. Over 1000 Patriotes gathered there and fortified the church and several other buildings. The British attacked the church with cannons and then set fire to it. The rebel leader, Dr. J.O. Chénier, and 70 other rebels died as they tried to escape the flames. The British troops then looted and burned the village. This ended the rebels' hopes for a successful rebellion. A second, small rebellion in November of 1838 was quickly put down.

In the end, 12 of the rebels were hanged and 58 were sent in chains to a prison colony in Australia. The remaining 1200 prisoners were set free. Papineau and others who had fled to the United States were sentenced to be executed if they returned to the Canadas.

After the British attacked the Patriotes at St. Charles, Papineau and other rebel leaders escaped to the United States.

Back View of the Church of St. Eustache and Dispersion of the Insurgents, 1840, by Charles Beauclerk, M4777.6, McCord Museum of Canadian History, Montreal

The Battle of St. Eustache, December 14, was the end of the Rebellion of 1837 in Lower Canada.

---

*The term "rebels" refers to the popular movement known as the Patriotes. Most were French-speaking professionals, merchants, farmers, labourers, and craftsmen. The key leaders were Papineau and Wolfred Nelson. Refer to page 193 under "Parti Canadien" for additional information.

Simulation

A New Home

Behind Bonsecours Market, Montreal (1866), by William Raphael. Many immigrants to Upper Canada stopped in Montreal.

To help you understand better what life was like in Upper Canada from 1815 to 1838, you are to take part in the following four-part activity. Carefully examine the painting above. Imagine what it might have been like to have arrived in Montreal and to wait on the dock before proceeding to your new home in Upper Canada. Throughout this activity you will play the role of the person described on the role card assigned to you. The concluding part of this activity is on page 208. A sample role card is shown on the right.

All Settlers Must Perform the Following Duties:

1. Clear and fence 2.03 hectares for every 40.5 hectares you have been granted.

2. Build a dwelling house, 4.88 metres x 6.1 metres.

3. Clear one half of the road in front of each lot.

These duties must be performed within two years of the date on the location ticket.

continued on page 198

Role Card*

Name	Alex MacIntosh, age 19
Country of Origin	Scotland
Family Information	wife age 17 and daughter age 1
Education/Skills	unskilled, illiterate
Wealth	poor
Religion	Presbyterian

Other All of your family died of cholera on the passage from Scotland. Your wife's family also died aboard the ship.

Month you purchased your lot .... April

Equipment/Supplies you have
1 broad axe, some nails, garden seeds

Location Ticket .... Concession 3, Lot 13

*Additional Role Cards are in the Teacher's Resource Package.

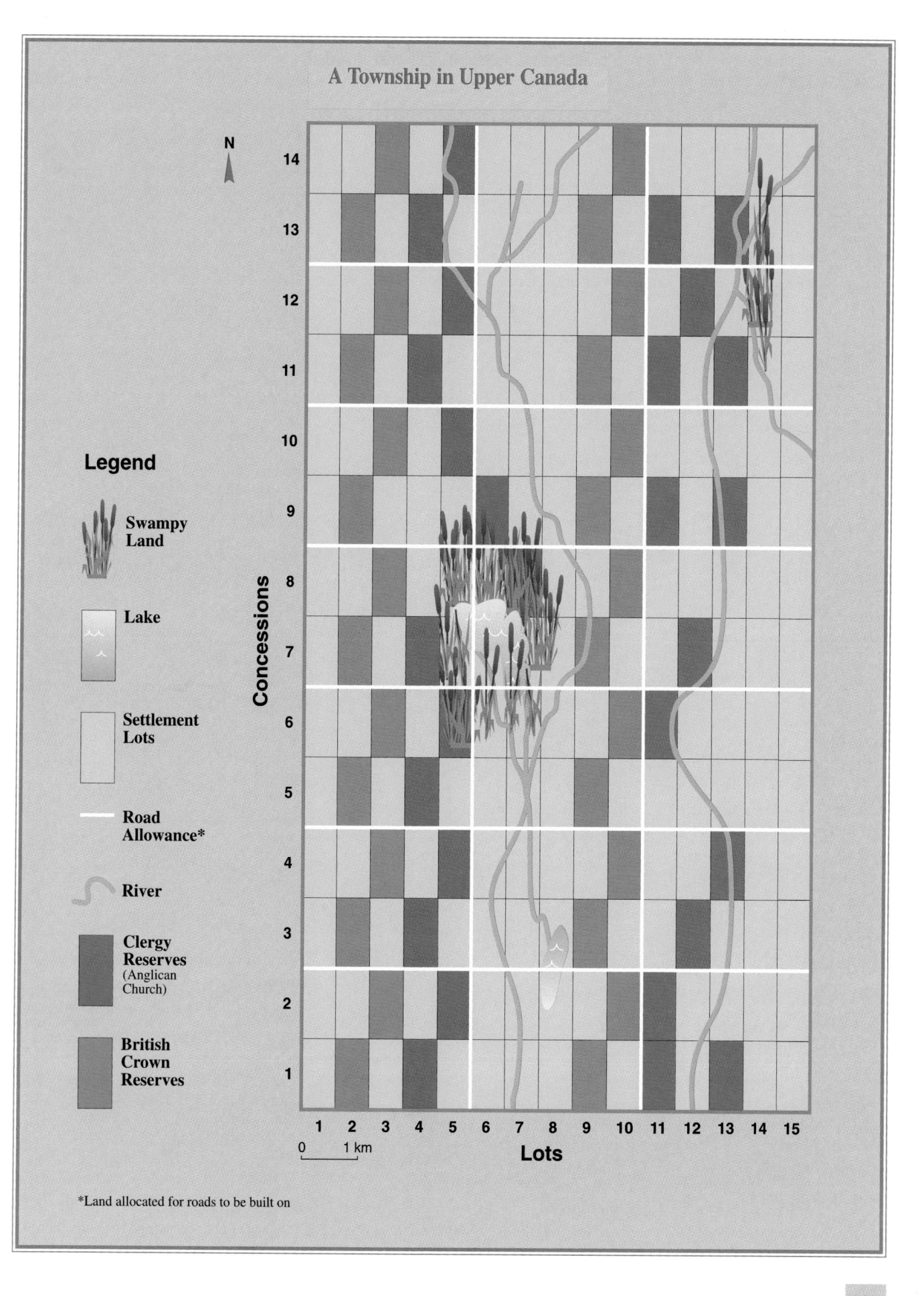

A Township in Upper Canada

N

Legend

Swampy Land

Lake

Settlement Lots

Road Allowance*

River

Clergy Reserves (Anglican Church)

British Crown Reserves

Concessions

14 13 12 11 10 9 8 7 6 5 4 3 2 1

Lots

1 2 3 4 5 6 7 8 9 10 11 12 13 14 15

0   1 km

*Land allocated for roads to be built on

Part 1

As a class, decide on the criteria to evaluate the parts of this assignment. Think about how you can best fulfil the requirements.

a) For Part 1, work with a partner to share and discuss how to deal with your role card. Examine the map provided on page 197. Locate your lot and study the map's legend.

b) Visualize in your mind what the land you have purchased would look like. Imagine yourself walking across the land that you are seeing for the first time. Notice the smells, sights, and sounds around you. Look at the reactions of your family members. Walk around your land and then answer the following questions to describe it.

- Is your land flat? hilly? Is it covered with trees? rocks? water? swamps? What is the soil like? Is it good for growing crops? What is the **drainage** like? What wild animals are in the area? Do you have fresh water available for drinking? Is there a river nearby? Will it be beneficial or harmful?

c) Think about and make plans of what you would do for your first *three months*. Make brief notes of your decisions. Consider these questions:

- What skills do you have?

- What equipment do you have?

- What assistance is available from family members, the religious community, hired help, the Native people?

- What food supplies have you brought with you?

d) Think about and make plans for the next *two years*. (Remember the duties required of you by law before you get the **deed** to your land.)

- How do you plan to survive through the first winter?

- What will you do if someone in your family is injured or becomes sick?

- If you are going to grow a crop, how will you harvest it?

- How do you plan to meet others in your area? Or does the isolation not bother you?

- Do you feel it is important to co-operate with others in your area? If so, how?

- Do you feel a school should be built nearby? A church? If so, who will build it and how?

- Is transportation a problem? What about roads? Waterways? Do you feel you should be involved in building them?

- How do you "pay for" the goods and services you need and use?

- What ways are there for making money?*

- Check back to page 196. Have you completed all the duties required of you?

e) Think about and make plans for the next *five years*. Consider the following questions:

- How will the area in which you live change over the next five years?

- How do you plan on looking after the soil so it does not become depleted of nutrients?

- What will you do if you need more land?

- What industries do you think should be developed in the area?** How should this be done?

- Is there a need for a village or town to be built in your area? Where would it best be built?

- Would you provide assistance to newcomers? If yes, what kind of assistance? If no, why not?

- What problems have you had in keeping the roads in good condition?

- How have the **Crown reserves** and the **clergy reserves** interfered with your building and maintaining of the roads?

- How has the land-granting system encouraged **speculation**?

Drainage—process of water flowing away
Deed—a document legally granting someone ownership
*Making potash (also called "pearl ash" in Upper Canada) was a way for settlers to earn cash after land was cleared. Large hardwood trees were burned in bonfires. The ashes were collected in iron pots and water poured through them. The liquid was boiled until it evaporated. The remaining grey powder (potash) was sold to European factories for use in the manufacture of soap and cosmetics.
**Grist mills for grinding grain and saw mills for planing logs into lumber were needed in pioneer communities. They were located near rivers, as running water was necessary.

Crown reserve—one-seventh of all public land was set aside for the British government by the Constitutional Act of 1791. By 1825 these lands were sold because they prevented compact settlement, making it difficult to complete roads.
Clergy reserve—one-seventh of all public land was set aside for Protestant schools and churches by the Constitutional Act of 1791 (see Chapter 6, page 159).
Speculation—the act of buying or selling land, at some risk, with the hope of making large profits from future price changes

Part 2

You have lived in Upper Canada for years. Write a letter to relatives in Great Britain telling them about your new life. Describe your accomplishments and the hardships you have encountered. You may wish to encourage them to come to Upper Canada by giving them reasons why this is a good place to settle.

Part 3

As a class, brainstorm about the following. Record your contributions on huge chart paper or the chalkboard.

a) What circumstances forced the majority of the immigrants to come to Upper Canada?

b) What problems did travel to Upper Canada involve?

c) What hardships were encountered during

- the first three months

- the first two years

- the first five years?

d) What was the importance of family, friends, and Native neighbours?

e) What geographic features hindered settlement? What other factors hindered settlement? What factors helped settlement? How could settlement of Upper Canada have been carried out more efficiently?

f) How did your area change during the first five years?

g) What cultural groups settled in your township? Is there evidence of a pattern of kinship or cultural settlement? Why did people in history settle in cultural groups? What advantages does this type of settlement have? What disadvantages are there?

h) Suppose that someone from the Legislative Assembly comes to your community. He asks you to fill out a questionnaire on how you have cleared the land, how many animals you own, and other questions. He also asks you to name things you feel prevent the improvement of your township. What complaints or grievances would you give him? List these on large chart paper. Keep this list for later reference.

Note: Part 4 of this activity is on page 208. It is to be done later.

Below: The first task of many settlers was clearing the land.

Focus On: Daily Life on a Pioneer Homestead

Above: Once new roads were built, it became easier to travel.

Right: A pioneer homestead in the early years of settlement was usually a one-room log cabin with a dirt floor.

Below: Fifteen years later, this family had built a larger house with several rooms.

The land the pioneers selected for their homesteads was still in its natural state—an uncleared dense forest. As the pioneers cut trees and drained swamps, the wildlife was forced farther inland, away from the newcomers who were making Upper Canada their home.

Clearing a forested area of thousands of trees and building a new home was a time-consuming and difficult task. But gradually life on a homestead became more comfortable as time went on. The pictures show a pioneer homestead from the early years of settlement, 15 years after settlement, and 30 years after settlement.

The first house of a pioneer family was usually a one-room log cabin with a dirt floor and a wooden chimney. A blanket might be used to divide the room into two for sleeping purposes. These homes were cold and draughty. As the logs dried, they shrank, making the gaps between them even larger. These gaps were filled with mud or lime plaster, which had to be replaced every year.

After a year or two, when there was a little more time, a larger and more comfortable house would be built. It would have several rooms on the main floor, with a loft or attic as well. The fireplace would be stone or brick. Once this house was finished, the old log cabin might be used as a shelter for pigs or other farm animals.

200

Focus On: Daily Life on a Pioneer Homestead
continued

Thirty years after settlement, a pioneer homestead might look like this.

A few years later, the family might add on to the log house, or build a new home of fieldstone or sawn lumber, if there was a sawmill in the district. This house would have glass windows instead of oiled paper or rags, such as covered the windows of the other houses. Glass was expensive because, until 1825, it had to be imported. After that it was manufactured in Upper Canada.

A Summary of Rural Life in Upper Canada in the Early Years of the Nineteenth Century

Most inhabitants:

- lived on the forest frontier

- used physical labour to fell the trees and remove the stumps

- persisted through years of hard work and effort to create a home

- began as **subsistence farmers**

- had to work daily to provide their necessities

- lived a fair distance from their neighbours

- received the little education they had from their parents or a literate neighbour

- visited towns to use the mills to grind their grain or the sawmill to get lumber

- worked together to get big projects accomplished and to have some social activity

- depended on their own ingenuity for their survival.

Above: This man is winnowing—allowing the chaff to blow away so only wheat remains.
Left: These men are threshing to separate wheat from chaff.

Subsistence farmer—only grew enough food for the family; none was left to sell for much-needed cash to buy other products and supplies

201

Focus On: Daily Life in the Towns of
Upper Canada

As more fields were cleared in Upper Canada, more wheat was grown. Farmers could sell wheat for cash. Villages began to grow at places that were convenient for the farmers, like crossroads or mill sites. In the villages the farmers could sell their wheat and purchase goods with the money. A fairly large village could be expected to provide the following services for its local farmers: stores, taverns, shoemaker, blacksmith, miller, carpenter, lawyer, doctor, wagonmaker, tinsmith, tailor, school, church, and newspaper.

Eyewitness Account

Catherine Parr Traill, an early settler, describes the changes that took place in her community over a few years:

When we first came up to live in the bush . . . there were but two or three settlers near us and no roads out . . . . Very great is the change that a few years have effected in our situation . . . .

A village has started up where formerly a thick pine-wood covered the ground; we have now within a short distance of us an excellent sawmill, a grist mill and store, with a large tavern and many good dwellings.

—from The Backwoods of Canada
by Catherine Parr Traill

Kingston

Kingston developed as a British military and naval base for Lake Ontario and was the largest and most important town in Upper Canada for many years.

Eyewitness Account

Here is a description of Kingston, written about 1820:

Kingston, although the largest town in the Upper Province, contains only 2336 inhabitants, most of whom are the descendants of those loyalists who sought asylum in Canada after the revolutionary war.

The rest are English, Irish, and Scotch, with a few Germans and Frenchmen. The streets are laid out with considerable regularity; but the houses, like almost all others in the Canadas, are very irregularly built. In consequence of the neglected condition of the roads in this as well as in every other part of the Province, it is scarcely possible in wet weather to walk out without sticking fast in the mire. The public buildings of Kingston are of such an inferior description as scarcely to be worthy of notice.

—from *Five Years' Residence in the Canadas*
by Edward Allen Talbot

York

The British military began clearing land to build a fort at York in 1793. Governor Simcoe decided to build a capital there. In 1834, it was renamed Toronto.

Despite damage caused by American invaders in 1812, York became more important as new-comers moved westward. It became a business and government centre.

Eyewitness Account

Here is a description of York, written about 1820:

The streets of York are regularly laid out, intersecting each other at right angles. Only one of them, how-ever, is yet completely built; and, in wet weather, the unfinished streets are, if possible, muddier and dirtier than those of Kingston.

—from *Five Years' Residence in the Canadas*
by Edward Allen Talbot

This painting shows King Street, which is still one of Toronto's main streets.

These pictures are from a reconstructed Upper Canada Village.

Right: As communities developed, lumber mills made possible the construction of frame houses.

Below: Weaving of woollen and linen fabrics was one of the early industries.

Below: On winter and summer evenings, travellers were relieved to find food and shelter at an inn. This picture shows the livery stable behind the inn.

Right and below: As soon as the members of the community could afford them, they built schools and churches.

Right: Later there would be a more elaborate centre of government, such as this city hall.

Services Provided in the Towns

In the early 1800s in Upper Canada, town services were few. Running water, natural gas for home heating, sewers to take away water and waste, garbage collection, sidewalks, paved roads, police, and fire protection were not available.

The unpaved roads turned to mud in the rain. People threw their garbage onto roads or into streams and lakes. Many got their drinking water from the same streams where they disposed of their garbage. However, by the 1840s, cities had begun to install sewer systems to take away used water.

Toronto had a water system by 1841, but its main purpose was not to provide clean water for drinking. It was for firefighting. Fire was a serious threat to the wooden buildings of early towns, with their poorly constructed or open fireplaces. There were no paid firefighters. The firefighting was done by the people of the town. By law, every house had to have a water bucket and a ladder on its roof near the chimney. When a fire broke out, people from all around came with their buckets to help fight it. Some towns were lucky enough to have a fire engine that could be pulled by men or horses to the fire. In the 1820s and 1830s towns began to establish volunteer fire departments. This was more effective, since the volunteers received some training.

By the 1840s cities were beginning to have gas lights. Pipes were installed to bring flammable gas to lampposts on streets and to light fixtures in houses. The gas was lit with a flame to produce light.

Mail was delivered by coach in the 1800s.

Transportation in Upper Canada

Walking was often the safest and fastest means of getting around in Upper Canada, since the first roads were often nothing better than wide, muddy footpaths. Even in the towns the unpaved streets turned to mud when it rained. By the 1830s, a few main streets had been macadamized, which meant they were paved using crushed stone or gravel. But most streets remained unpaved. In the countryside, corduroy roads were built. Logs were laid side by side across the road in order to create a hard surface. The result looked like the bumps on a piece of corduroy. These roads were very uncomfortable to walk on or drive over.

Eyewitness Account

Here is one traveller's description of such a road:

... Indeed, "corduroy" is dreadful. When we came to it I tried every thing to save my poor bones—sitting on my hands, or raising my body on them—but it was of little use; on we went, thump, thump, thumping against one log after another, and this, in the last part of our journey, with the bare boards of an open wagon for seats... But we got through without an actual upset or breakdown, which is more than a friend of mine could say, for the coach in which he was went into so deep a mud hole at one part of the road, that it fairly overturned, throwing the passengers on the top of one another inside, and leaving them no way of exit, when they came to themselves, but to crawl out through the window.

—from *Adventures in Canada, or, Life in the Woods* by John C. Geikie

Waterways, as well, were often used for transportation. In the winter, horse-drawn sleighs could travel swiftly over the ice. The rest of the year, many types of boats were used. By the 1820s, steamboats were going back and forth across Lake Ontario, carrying passengers and cargo between the falls of Niagara and the beginning of the St. Lawrence at Kingston.

Government in Upper Canada

In the 1830s the system of government in Upper Canada, as in Lower Canada, remained as had been set out in the Constitutional Act of 1791 (see pages 159 and 160). There was an elected Legislative Assembly, appointed Legislative Council and Executive Council, and a British-appointed lieutenant-governor. As in Lower Canada, the elected Legislative Assembly had limited power. Bills passed by the Legislative Assembly had to be approved by the Legislative Council and the lieutenant-governor. There were two political groups in Upper Canada: the Tories, led by the Family Compact, and the Reformers.

Family Compact

Just as Lower Canada had its elite of powerful people called the Château Clique, Upper Canada also had an elite. This group came to be known as the Family Compact. Members of this group were in the Executive Council and Legislative Council, so they had the power to veto or stop any bills passed by the Legislative Assembly that they did not like. They took for themselves and gave to their friends favours such as jobs, land, and contracts for canal and road work. Most of the Family Compact members were of Loyalist descent, or were British immigrants who had arrived before 1800. They claimed that those who had not proven their loyalty to Britain by fighting against the Thirteen Colonies in the American Revolution and the Americans in the War of 1812 were not true Upper Canadians. They did not want Americans to be part of the government of Upper Canada and some even said that Americans should have their land taken away from them.

The Family Compact

- was a small group of powerful people in the colony of Upper Canada

- along with friends and supporters, were known as Tories

- did not want people from the United States to be part of the government of Upper Canada

- defended tradition (the things that had always been done) and opposed change

- believed power should be in the hands of a few capable people (themselves)

- believed the Anglican Church (Church of England) should be powerful in the colony

- was loyal to Great Britain and to the British system of government.

Government Structure of Upper Canada

Lieutenant–Governor
(British-appointed)

Legislative Council
(appointed)
- members of the Family Compact
- believed in the British system of government
- friends of the lieutenant-governor

Executive Council
(appointed)
- members of the Family Compact
- believed in the British system of government
- friends of the lieutenant-governor

The Family Compact controlled the Executive Council and Legislative Council. They dominated the government and business and social life of Upper Canada.

Legislative Assembly (elected by voters)
- consisted of elected members
- had little power. Bills passed by the Legislative Assembly had to be approved by the Legislative Council and the lieutenant-governor in order to become law.

Voters

Appoints

Elect

Bishop Strachan (1778–1867)

John Strachan was born in Scotland. After he arrived in Upper Canada in 1799, he taught school. His leadership of Upper Canadians and his bravery were noted when the Americans attacked York during the War of 1812, and during his tireless work to help victims of the cholera epidemic of the 1830s.

Strachan was a powerful spokesman for and advisor to the Family Compact. By the 1820s he and his friends in the Family Compact largely controlled the government of Upper Canada.

In 1839 Strachan became the first Anglican (Church of England) bishop of Toronto.

The Reformers

The Reformers in Upper Canada

- opposed the power of the Family Compact

- wanted changes in the government and society of Upper Canada

- were angered by the attitudes of the members of the Family Compact toward the Americans in the colony

- were divided into moderate and radical groups

- included some radicals who later became rebels.

Some of the people represented in the simulation on pages 196 to 199, and in the accounts on pages 200 to 204, were Reformers or shared their values.

Robert Gourlay (1778–1863)

Robert Gourlay arrived in Upper Canada in 1817 from Scotland. He had a plan to bring poor people from Britain over to farm. He said that without land, "no good can be expected of us."

Gourlay sent a questionnaire to farmers in Upper Canada, asking them about their progress in clearing land, the number of animals they owned, and so on. He also asked them to name things they felt prevented the improvement of their township or province.

Gourlay was criticized by members of the Family Compact for attempting to stir up discontent. Farmers began to have meetings to voice their concerns over the land. They felt that the land should be owned by those who lived and worked on it, and improved it. There was a great deal of land in Upper Canada that was not available for farming, between the clergy reserves, the Crown reserves, and the land owned by rich people who did not work it. These land reserves made it difficult to build roads and it took farmers much longer than necessary to get their crops to market.

The Family Compact saw Gourlay as someone who caused trouble. He was thrown in jail and then banished from Upper Canada in 1819.

William Lyon Mackenzie (1795–1861)

Mackenzie was another Reformer. He was born in Scotland and came to Canada in 1820. He began as a shopkeeper, but in 1824 he established *The Colonial Advocate*, a newspaper for which he was publisher, editor, writer, and paper carrier. He used his newspaper to speak out on the land problems, the power of the Family Compact, and the question of who was an Upper Canadian.

A story told of Mackenzie is that on June 8, 1825, 15 young men from wealthy, well-known families of York (now Toronto) smashed their way into the offices of *The Colonial Advocate* and threw the printing equipment into the street. They then tossed the type (letters used for printing) into the harbour. Fortunately for Mackenzie, he was able to turn this disaster into a triumph. He became a public hero. The young men were tried, convicted, and ordered to pay Mackenzie $2450. Before the raid *The Colonial Advocate* had been in financial trouble. Afterwards, he was able to pay off his debts and buy new equipment.

Mackenzie was first elected to the Legislative Assembly in 1828. He used his new position to suggest government changes. He thought that the elected people in the Legislative Assembly did not have enough power and later suggested that Upper Canada adopt the American system of government.

Other members of the Legislative Assembly did not always like Mackenzie's ideas and voted to expel him. Mackenzie was expelled from the Legislative Assembly a total of six times and each time the people re-elected him.

Mackenzie often became very agitated during his speeches. He had lost his hair as a result of a fever and it was a common sight to see him tear his bright red wig off his head and fling it on the ground to make a point.

As the 1830s wore on, Mackenzie became more radical. He decided to resort to armed rebellion in an attempt to destroy Upper Canada's system of government.

Sir Francis Bond Head

Sir Francis Bond Head was appointed lieutenant-governor of Upper Canada in 1835. At first he was welcomed as a friend and ally by the Reformers. He included two leading Reformers among his Council.

When Head ignored his Council's advice, it resigned. The Legislative Assembly decided not to co-operate with him. The Reformers would not vote to pass money bills. As a result, without money, all work on bridges, roads, and docks came to an immediate halt.

The lieutenant-governor called an election in which he personally campaigned on behalf of the Tories.* The people of the colony, worried about their roads and bridges and the pro-Americanism of the Reformers, voted for the Tories. Mackenzie and many other Reformers went down in defeat in this 1836 election. Some **moderates,** like Robert Baldwin, did not support the more **radical** Mackenzie but also felt they could not support Head and the Tories, so they retired from political activity.

Focus On: Elections in Upper and Lower Canada

Strong disagreements, fuelled by alcohol, often turned elections of the 1830s into violent confrontations.

Election violence in the 1830s was very common. There was no secret ballot as there is today. Instead of voting in private booths and then depositing their ballots in a box, the voters shouted their choices for everyone to hear. The choice was often greeted by insults from people who were voting for an opponent. Voters threw stones and even swung clubs at one another. In Montreal in 1832, one candidate hired bullies who threatened and beat anyone who declared his support for the opponent. The resulting riot caused the deaths of three people.

Exploring Further

1. What difference would a secret ballot have made in elections in the 1830s?

2. Compare a Canadian election now with one in the 1830s.

---

*The Family Compact, along with their friends and supporters, were known as Tories. See page 205.

Moderate—a person who does not hold extreme opinions
Radical—holding extreme opinions; wanting fundamental social, economic, and political changes

Simulation Conclusion
(Continued from page 199)

Part 4

Mentally place yourself back into the role you played in the simulation on pages 196 to 199. It is now 1837 and you have lived in Upper Canada for a number of years. You and your neighbours have gathered at a work bee to build a community hall.

People are talking about the recent election and the resulting political unrest. The Reformer William Lyon Mackenzie arrives to try to convince you to join his armed rebellion against the government.

In your role, decide whether you will join Mackenzie or not. Either select one of the decision-making models used in this textbook or design your own model. Working in groups, use that model to decide whether you will join Mackenzie. Be prepared to share your decision-making process and your decision with the rest of the class.

Armed Rebellion in Upper Canada

Mackenzie decided to take advantage of the political unrest. He began to ride around the countryside north of Toronto, stirring up people against the government. Those who became most rebellious were called Radicals. They wanted Upper Canada to have a government like the Americans had in the United States.

On October 9, 1837, news came that Papineau's Patriotes in Lower Canada were ready to spring into armed action. British troops had left Toronto to defend the government of Lower Canada and thousands of weapons were left unguarded in Toronto. Mackenzie decided the time was ripe for armed rebellion.* He suggested to his followers that they seize the weapons, capture Sir Francis Bond Head, the lieutenant-governor of Upper Canada, and proclaim a new government. His followers were not yet ready for armed rebellion. They sent Mackenzie north of the city to collect names of people in favour of the proposed new government, but he was not to speak of armed rebellion. He collected 4000 names on his petition.

---

*At this time, Charles Duncombe also gathered 500 rebels at Brantford. When volunteer militia arrived, they quickly disbanded.

On December 5, Mackenzie, wrapped in several overcoats to keep out bullets, led a group of about 800 men down Yonge Street into Toronto. A few of the men had guns. Others carried pitchforks, clubs, and even carving knives strapped to poles. They were fired on by a small band of defenders, who turned and ran as soon as they fired. In response to the attack, the leading rebel riflemen threw themselves down and returned fire. In the confusion, those behind thought the riflemen had been killed. They turned and fled back the way they had come.

On December 6, with cannon and rifles, 600 of the colony's militia marched up Yonge Street. Before long the rebels were running for their lives. Mackenzie stayed until the bitter end. Then, in spite of the fact that Sir Francis Bond Head had offered a $5000 reward for his capture, he escaped to the United States. There, he tried to raise an army to liberate Upper Canada by offering 120 hectares of free land to anyone who would join him. He was arrested for breaking the legal neutrality between the Province of Canada and the United States and was imprisoned for 11 months.

Two other rebels, Samuel Lount and Peter Matthews, were hanged on April 12, 1838, for the crime of treason.

Mackenzie returned to Canada in 1849. He began another newspaper and was elected to the Legislative Assembly, but he never regained his earlier influence.

During the Rebellion of 1837, radicals were eager to take up arms with Mackenzie.

The Rebellion of 1837 was violent.

Aftermath of the Rebellions

After the rebellion, at least temporarily, Lower Canada ended up worse off than before. The colony's Legislative Assembly was suspended until 1841, and the governor and a Special Council ruled. In Upper Canada, people were afraid to speak out because even moderate reformers were branded as rebels.

Twelve Patriotes were executed after the rebellion of 1837.

The British government was shocked by the rebellions in Upper and Lower Canada. The prime minister sent John George Lambton (Lord Durham) to take over as governor general. Lord Durham was told to investigate the causes of the rebellions and suggest solutions to the problems. (Lord Durham's suggestions and the British response are discussed in Chapter 8.)

Exploring Further

1. Lord Durham was sent by the British to investigate the rebellions in Upper and Lower Canada. Imagine you are Durham. What would you report to the British government about the causes of the rebellions? What possible solutions would you recommend to deal with the unrest in Upper and Lower Canada?

Soldiers captured rebels who spoke out against the government.

Challenge Plus

Points of View

The following documents and primary source* excerpts represent various points of view about the rebellion in Upper Canada. They also represent various times in history—before, during, and after the rebellion. As you read them, keep in mind what you know about the different groups living in Upper Canada at this time, as well as the causes of the rebellion.

 What criteria will be used to evaluate your assignment? Think about how you can best fulfil the requirements.

Before the Rebellion

1. Read the information in the table below. Think about who would agree or disagree with this system.

Land Distribution in Upper Canada**

Recipients	Hectares
Loyalists and their children (refugees before 1787)	1 295 040
Militiamen	295 431
Schools	202 350
Former soldiers & sailors	182 115
Survey Contractors	106 841
Magistrates & Barristers	103 199
Executive Councillors & their families	55 039
Navy & Army Officers	38 659
Legislative Councillors & their families	20 235
Colonel Talbot	19 636
Clergymen (for private use)	14 933
General Brock's heirs	4 856
Clergy Reserves	unspecified

These figures account for nearly 1/2 of the surveyed land in Upper Canada. It is estimated that less than 1/10 of the surveyed land is occupied by settlers.

React to the information given in the table by working with a partner, one student playing the role of a member of the Executive Council and the other the role of a settler. Respond to the following questions:

a) Would you consider the land division (distribution) to be fair? Why?
b) Would you make any changes? What would they be?
c) In what way was the land distribution system in Upper Canada one cause of the rebellion?

2. The following three excerpts were written several years before the rebellion in Upper Canada. All relate to the same man. Are the excerpts about Bishop Strachan, Sir Francis Bond Head, or Robert Gourlay? Use the clues given here and information in this chapter (e.g., biographies) to determine the answer.

Excerpt 1:

[There is]...*a reformer from the United Kingdom, whose declarations in the Provincial Gazettes are...inflammatory amongst [our]... population from the want of Truth, reason and decorum.*

—from a letter written by Samuel Smith, an Administrator of Upper Canada in February 1818

Excerpt 2:

The only building worthy of particular notice is the Jail, which stands about a quarter of a mile out of the town. It is a large two-storey house of brick, very handsome, and is considered to be the finest building in Canada. At present, it holds within its walls the celebrated [Name]....

He is very free in giving his opinion concerning the character of the Governors, and I suspect his greatest fault is speaking too many truths, which are not thought to be seasonable or agreeable.

—from John Goldie's diary entry in July 1819

Excerpt 3:

My Dear Sir:
Since I last wrote I have travelled upwards of a thousand miles through this Province. Everywhere I found the people well disposed to Government, but quite disappointed & dispirited with occurrences which might have been prevented. They see the property of their neighbours in the United States advancing in value while theirs is on the decline; they see everything in motion there, while all is here at a stand: they see the claims of Americans

---

*See Sources on page 269 of the Learning How to Learn Appendix.
**Land Distribution data compiled from *Lord Durham's Report*, 1839. Figures converted from acres to hectares.

who suffered by the War attended to & on the eve of being paid, while theirs are almost despaired of....

—from a letter dated February 7, 1818 (written by the man described in the first two excerpts)

3. Read Mackenzie's handbill for the rebellion, as follows. As you read, think about the message he is trying to give.

BRAVE CANADIANS! ....The law says we shall not be taxed without our consent by the voices of the men of our choice, but a...tyrannical government has trampled upon that law—robbed the exchequer*—divided the plunder—and declared that, regardless of justice they will continue to roll their splendid carriages, and riot in their palaces, at our expense—that we are poor spiritless, ignorant peasants, who were born to toil for our betters....

CANADIANS! Do you love freedom? I know you do. Do you hate oppression? Who dare deny it? Do you wish perpetual peace, and a government ...bound to enforce the law to do to each other as you would be done by? Then buckle on your armour, and put down the villains who oppress and enslave our country.... One short hour will deliver our country from the oppressor; and freedom in religion, peace and tranquility, equal laws and an improved country will be the prize....

Up then, brave Canadians! Get ready your rifles, and make short work of it....

—November 27, 1837

a) What is Mackenzie's message?
b) What colourful words and phrases does he use to make his point? What other devices does he use?
c) Do you think that Mackenzie was successful in getting his point across?
d) Rewrite his message using today's language.
e) What would Bishop Strachan say in response?
f) According to Mackenzie, is this government responsible to the people? Provide reasons.

During the Rebellion

4. A proclamation by Sir Francis Bond Head follows. As you read, think about the people in Upper Canada who would support his views.

To the Queen's Faithful Subjects in Upper Canada.

In a time of profound peace, while every one was quietly following his occupations, feeling secure under the protection of our Laws, a band of Rebels, instigated by a few...disloyal men, has had the wickedness and audacity to assemble with Arms, and to attack...the Queen's Subjects on the Highway—to Burn and Destroy their Property—to Rob the Public Mails—and to threaten to Plunder the Banks—and to Fire the City of Toronto.

Brave and Loyal People of Upper Canada, we have been long suffering from the acts and endeavours of concealed Traitors, but this is the first time that Rebellion has dared to show itself openly in the land, in the absence of invasion by any Foreign Enemy.

Let every man do his duty now, and it will be the last time that we or our children shall see our lives or properties endangered, or the Authority of our gracious Queen insulted by such treachery and ungrateful men....

—by Sir Francis Bond Head, written on December 7, 1837

a) Which of the following people would agree with Sir Francis Bond Head? Bishop Strachan, a British merchant, Robert Gourlay, a settler, a member of the Family Compact, a Tory, a member of the Executive Council, a member of the Legislative Assembly, a Reformer, or William Lyon Mackenzie.
b) Which would disagree?

5. Author Susanna Moodie presents a picture of daily life as she saw it in Upper Canada. An excerpt follows. Think about which point of view she represents (e.g., rebel, Tory, British patriot, or a combination).

Here we found...a copy of the Queen's proclamation, calling upon all loyal gentlemen to join in putting down the unnatural rebellion....

Little sleep visited our eyes that night. We talked over the strange news for hours; our coming separation, and the probability that, if things were as bad as they appeared to be, we might never meet again....

Before the cold, snowy morning broke, we were all stirring. The children, who had learned that their father was preparing to leave them, were crying and clinging round his knees. His heart was too deeply affected to eat; the meal passed over in silence, and he rose to go....

continued on page 212

---

*An exchequer is a department that handles the government's finances.

The honest backwoodsmen...obeyed the call to arms with enthusiasm.... I must own that my British spirit was fairly aroused, and, as I could not aid in subduing the enemies of my beloved country with my arm, I did what little I could to serve the good cause with my pen....

—from *Roughing It in the Bush* by Susanna Moodie, first published in 1852

a) About what circumstances is Susanna Moodie writing in her journal?

b) For which side is this writer's husband taking up arms? Provide evidence.

c) Write the entry that Susanna Moodie might have written following the rebellion.

d) Write a similar journal entry, but from the point of view of a soldier, or the wife or child of a soldier, who is loyal to the other side.

6. Using a dictionary and working with your classmates, read the article that follows. As you read, think about what words and phrases the writer used to get a certain message across.

The manly courage with which two hundred farmers, miserably armed, withstood the formidable attack of an enemy 1200 strong, and who had plenty of ammunition, with new muskets and bayonets, artillery, first rate European officers, and the choice of a position of attack, convinces me that discipline, order, obedience and subordination, under competent leaders, would enable them speedily to attain a confidence sufficient to foil even the regulars from Europe....

As to Sir Francis Head's story of 10,000 men instantly making to the capital to support him, it is a sheer fabrication.... The truth is that thousands were on their way to join us on Thursday evening, that being the regular time for which the towns had been summoned; and they, on learning that we were dispersed, made virtue of necessity, and professed that they had come to aid the Tories!

—from an article written in the *Gazette*, when in exile in New York, May 12, 1838

a) Was the writer a rebel or a Tory? List three words and phrases which helped you to decide whether the writer was a rebel or a Tory.

b) What is the writer's main message?

c) Discuss with your classmates any strategies you can use to figure out the meaning of difficult passages of reading. Record this in the Tools of Learning section of your notebook.

d) Read the last paragraph again. What is "sheer fabrication?" How is Sir Francis Head's version of the events (see page 211) different from the writer's version? Which version is true? Explain. What does this suggest about gathering information from a primary source?

e) Is information gathered from a primary source more reliable than that gathered from a secondary source?

7. Two accounts of the same event follow. The first (a primary source) was written a week after the rebellion. The second (a secondary source) paraphrases the first account and was written when this textbook was written.

Account 1:

During Wednesday large numbers of loyal volunteers were constantly coming in, and most vigourous [sic] measures were adopted for the defence of the city, and for the dispersion of the rebels. The state of public feeling was roused to the highest pitch of indignation on learning that Mackenzie and a band of desperadoes had stopped the mails, and robbed the bags and the passengers of all the money on which they could lay their hands! as [sic] also on learning from various prisoners that were brought in that his plan was to fire the City in various quarters, by force or stealth, and thus reduce it to ashes, and its inhabitants to destitution.... Happily for the rebels, they did not venture to advance on the City. Had they done so, scarcely a man could by any possibility have escaped.*

On Thursday about twelve o'clock a large armed force marched out in three columns to attack the enemy at their head quarters.... After exchanging a few volleys, the enemy fled in every direction.

—from *Christian Guardian*, Toronto, December 13, 1837

Account 2:

On Wednesday, many volunteers joined the militia to fight to defend the city and defeat the rebels. People were very angry to find out that Mackenzie and a group of criminals had stopped mail delivery and had stolen the mail and the money of the passengers who were travelling with the mail. Captured rebels confessed that Mackenzie's

---

*[sic]—the quotation is in its original form. Original spelling and mistakes have been included.

plan was to burn the city to the ground, section by section—either by force or secretly. City residents would be left in extreme poverty. Lucky for the rebels, they didn't dare to come into the city. If they had, hardly any of them would have escaped.

On Thursday at about twelve o'clock, our militia marched in three columns to attack the rebels at their central location. After some gunfire from both sides, the rebels fled in every direction.

—based on an article published in the *Christian Guardian* December 13, 1837 (paraphrased November 1998)

a) From whose point of view is this account written?

b) How closely does the paraphrased version match the original primary source excerpt? Is the meaning the same for both?

c) Which version do you prefer? Why?

d) What are the advantages of the paraphrased version?

e) What are the disadvantages/dangers of rewriting historical documents (primary sources) in new words?

f) If the person paraphrasing a quotation has a particular bias,* what might happen to the meaning of the quotation?

8. How are the two points of view in questions 6 and 7 different? Which one is accurate? Why do points of view of historical accounts about an event differ?

After the Rebellion

9. Following the rebellion, there was some discussion and disagreement about how to treat the rebels. Two points of view follow. Read each excerpt and then answer the questions that follow.

Excerpt 1:

To turn loose upon society, after a deal of expense, those who have disturbed its repose, would be giving a premium for treason, and inciting them on to farther deeds of wickedness. At the same time it would deter the loyal from again entering into the service of the Crown upon the next attempt being made....

—from "Mercy Must Be Dispensed Sparingly," *Gazette*, London, May 19, 1838

Excerpt 2:

....The conduct of the government in respect to the state prisoners here...is...cruel. The most violent partizan admits the injustice, and makes it a pretext for abuse of Lord Durham. Thirty-five prisoners, charged with state offences, are now confined in Hamilton gaol; some of them from last December! Does the government intend they shall rot there?

—from *Mirror*, Toronto, August 18, 1838

a) The first excerpt expressed the concern that being too merciful and gentle with the rebels might be a mistake. What two reasons are given?

b) In the second excerpt, how are the rebels reacting to the imprisonment of other rebels?

10.  Two rebels, Samuel Lount and Peter Matthews, were executed for their part in the rebellion. Ninety-two other rebels from Upper Canada were deported to a British prison colony in Van Diemen's Land, now called Tasmania (a state of Australia). William Lyon Mackenzie was officially pardoned 12 years after the rebellion. Review the primary sources on pages 210–213 for the arguments they present for and against granting **amnesty** to the rebels.

a) Imagine that you are a member of the government of Upper Canada. You must decide whether or not to grant amnesty to the rebels who participated in the rebellion in Upper Canada. Using the decision-making model in the Appendix, work in small groups to discuss the alternatives and prepare your suggested course of action. Present your findings to the other government committees when you meet as a full group.

b) Once each government committee has presented its ideas, work together as a full group to decide upon your course of action.

c) Write the Proclamation which will state your decision, including details about your reasons and future actions to be taken.

*See Learning How to Learn Appendix page 256.
Amnesty—to be pardoned or excused by government for past offences against the government

Review

The icons are your cue to turn to the Learning How to Learn Appendix (pages 256–271) for ideas on how to complete these activities.

 This icon is a reminder to turn to the Research Model (pages x and xi).

 Complete a self-assessment for one assignment from this chapter.

Understanding Concepts

Checking Predictions

1. At the beginning of the chapter, you created a chart with three headings: Know, Wonder, and Learn. In the Know column, you filled in everything you knew about this chapter. Make any changes or corrections needed. In the Wonder column you listed what you would like to know. Write what you have learned in the Learn column.

2. Refer to the Section V story found on pages 182 and 183 and review your answers to the questions on page 186 about the story.
   a) Answer the following questions about the governments in Upper and Lower Canada in 1837:
      • Who participated in government?
      • Who had the power to make decisions?
      • Did majority rule exist?
      • Was the government responsible to the people? Why or why not?
      • What effect did this type of government have on the people? How did they respond?
   b) What would your reaction be to this type of government structure? Would you recommend changes to government?

Recording Vocabulary

3.  Record the following vocabulary in the WordBook section of your notes.

   • potash
   • resolution
   • rebellion
   • treason
   • cause and effect
   • moderate and radical

Conceptualizing

4. Here are some of the main ideas from this chapter.
   • population growth
   • the Great Migration
   • timber trade
   • end of competition in the fur trade
   • French–English conflict
   • political reform
   • rebellion in Upper and Lower Canada
   • rural and urban life

   Do either a) or b).
   a) 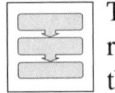 Create a concept poster about one of these ideas. Present your poster to the class.
   b) 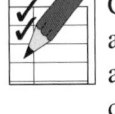 Use a web, mind map, outline, or chart to create a permanent set of notes about one of the above ideas. Explain your work to a classmate.

Working with Information

5.  Review the different examples of conflict found in this chapter. Work with a partner to draw a mind map that organizes these examples on one sheet of paper. Show how this conflict affected the ordinary people's attempts to have more say in governmental decisions. Use simple line drawings and at least three colours.

6. 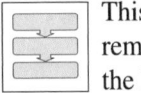 Create a cause and effect chart on either of the rebellions (Upper or Lower Canada).

7. 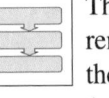 Compare absolute rule decision-making with the type of decision-making used in the governments of Upper and Lower Canada. Look at the Absolute Rule Decision-Making Model on page 51 to guide your comparison.

8. 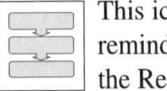 Add up to ten entries for this chapter to your timeline.

9. 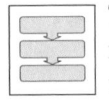 Compare your notebook with that of a partner. Check to see that items are not missing and are in the proper order. Organize your notes.

214

Developing Research Skills

10.  Do research in your school library to investigate in more detail the roles Baldwin and Ryerson played in the rebellion.

11. Investigate the timber trade in Canada in the 1800s. Present your findings to the class.

12. Imagine that you are a *voyageur*. What might you say on a visit to the North West Company office to convince them about your skills?

13. Read about daily life in the towns in Upper Canada on pages 202–204. Imagine that you are seeking work in a town in Upper Canada in the 1800s.
    - What types of positions would be available to you?
    - Which type of position would you choose? Why?

Developing Communication Skills

Reading

14. Read the stories "Shawnandithit" and "Immigration, 1815–1850," found in *Ordinary People in Canada's Past,* Second Edition, by Nancy Sellars Marcotte.

15. Read about the experiences of the workers in the timber industry. Put yourself in the role of a worker in Lower Canada. Write three journal entries to add to the History Journal section of your notebook: the day you made the decision to take your job, after considering its merits over working on a farm; a day during your winter in the woods; and a day during the raft journey downstream.

Writing

16. What role did the ordinary people have in the governments of Lower and Upper Canada before the rebellions?

17. Imagine you are Robert Gourlay. Write and distribute your questionnaire to farmers (fellow classmates) in Upper Canada. Present your findings in a political flyer. Include charts and/or graphs.

18. Reread the information about elections on page 207. Imagine that you have been appointed to improve election procedures in Upper and Lower Canada. Write and post your suggested list of election procedures.

Listening and Speaking

19.  A French-speaking citizen and an English-speaking merchant from Lower Canada are meeting prior to the rebellion. Work with a partner, and each role-play one of the parts. Discuss your needs and concerns with each other. Try to reach a **compromise** about what you will suggest to the government. Share your ideas with the class. As a class, come to a consensus about the best suggestion for the future of Lower Canada.

20.  You are a newspaper reporter interviewing immigrants as they step off their ship in Montreal. Ask them about their reasons for leaving their homeland, their experiences during the journey, and their expectations about life in Canada.

21.  Imagine that you are William Lyon Mackenzie. You are trying to convince someone to sign your petition in favour of your proposed new government. What will you say to them? Ask a classmate to play the role of a citizen.

22.  Work in a group, in which some act as members of the Château Clique and others act as members of the Parti Canadien. Have each side present their **priorities** and proposed actions in a session of government.

23. Conduct a campaign for election to the Upper or Lower Canada Legislative Assembly. Create campaign posters and write a major campaign speech. Deliver your speech to the class. Be prepared to answer questions following your speech.

Compromise—an agreement in which each side gives up some of its demands
Priorities—items ranked according to a certain criterion

Viewing and Representing

24. Design four campaign buttons, one for each of the four political groups discussed on pages 193, 205, and 206. Include symbols, icons, or slogans that represent each group.

25. 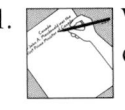 Create political cartoons to represent the four points of view of the political groups discussed on pages 193, 205, and 206.

26. In a small group, create an issue of a newspaper about Upper Canada or Lower Canada devoted to the 1837 Rebellion. Include

 a) articles describing the events of the rebellion
 b) columns analysing causes and effects
 c) columns speculating on what Lord Durham's recommendations may be
 d) letters to the editor
 e) editorial

Applying Concepts

27. Review petitions (page 146). This is one method of promoting change that does not involve violence.

 a) What other non-violent ways to promote change are mentioned in the chapters you have studied? What methods are used in our world now?
 b) As a class, discuss the various ways that people have promoted and created change. Begin a list of ideas on large chart paper.
 c) Create a second chart to list the various ways that people in Canadian history have worked to resolve conflicts.
 d) Post your charts in the classroom. Add to the lists as you continue to discover examples in your study of Canadian history or current events. You will be referring back to your lists at the end of Chapter 8.

28. On page 192 you read about the dreams that French-speaking professionals had of a separate French-Canadian nation. Why did they have this dream? Does this issue relate to more recent events? Discuss this as a class.

29.  On page 205 you read that the Family Compact did not want people from the United States to be a part of the government in Upper Canada.

a) Why?
b) Why are people sometimes unwilling to accept ideas different from their own? Discuss this with your class.

30. 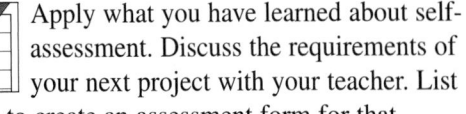 Apply what you have learned about self-assessment. Discuss the requirements of your next project with your teacher. List criteria to create an assessment form for that assignment. Share this with your teacher and make revisions as needed. Have your teacher and/or a classmate complete the assessment. Do a self-assessment. Meet with your teacher to compare and discuss the assessments.

31. Write a modern-day story that includes one of the main ideas or concepts of this chapter.

32. Why have you been studying
 * changes in population of Upper and Lower Canada?
 * political reform?
 * rebellions in Upper and Lower Canada?

33. 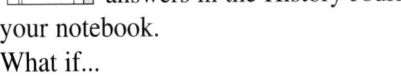 Try to think of as many answers as you can for each of the following. Record your answers in the History Journal section of your notebook.
 What if...
 * the Reformers had been successful in their rebellion in Upper Canada?
 * the rebels had been successful in Lower Canada?
 * competition in the fur trade had increased instead of ending?

34. 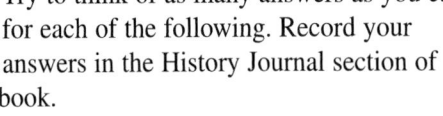 Complete each statement with a paragraph entry.

 a) History Journal: Three things I will remember from this chapter are... because...
 b) Tools of Learning: I can use the learning strategy... outside of school by...

Challenge Plus

35. 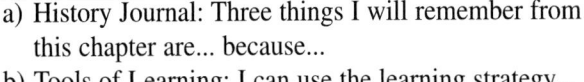 Research the changes in population that occurred between 1663 and 1838. How many people were living in what is now Quebec, Ontario, and the Atlantic provinces? Who lived there? Where did newcomers settle? Show this information in a series of charts, graphs, and maps and share it with your classmates.

36. Research the history of women's right to vote in Canada. Prepare to present your findings to the class.

37. Reread the section about William Lyon Mackenzie on page 206. Although he faced disaster when his printing equipment was destroyed by a group of angry raiders, he was able to turn this disaster into triumph. Terry Fox is an example of another famous Canadian who turned his personal difficulties into something positive for others. Find a recent example of someone who has turned a disaster into triumph. This person may or may not be famous. Create a video documentary or magazine feature about the person's experience.

38. In Montreal, a counter-revolutionary group calling itself the Doric Club wanted to defend the British government by preventing activities which might show disloyalty to the British government. Another group formed in the 1830s was a revolutionary, more radical wing of the Patriotes called the Fils de la Liberté. As a class, discuss the following:
a) What is the purpose of a revolutionary group? A counter-revolutionary group?
b) What does the name Fils de la Liberté mean? What political values and beliefs would a member have?
c) What political beliefs and values would a member of the Doric Club have?
d) How do their beliefs and values oppose each other? Do they have any common beliefs and values?
e) Work together to find a solution for the political differences between the two groups. What compromise might have satisfied both groups?

39. Design a website or history magazine for Section V: Conflict and Change. Decide how to show important people, places, events, and ideas in an interesting way, to assist other students to understand and appreciate Canadian history. Some items you could create include: fact files, visuals (e.g., maps, illustrations, diagrams), samples of students' work, chapter summaries, study guides and practice quizzes, and games. You might also include an interactive part such as an opinion poll or survey (and tables and graphs to show the results), and a "write-in" question and answer column. Provide a list of related websites and resources.

Canada Revisited

William Lyon Mackenzie's printing press in a reconstructed print shop in Mackenzie House, Toronto.

Chapter 8

Planting the Seed of Nationhood (1838–1855)

O v e r v i e w

Use this Overview to predict the events of this chapter.

1838
The British government sent Lord Durham to investigate the rebellions in Upper and Lower Canada. Lord Durham presented his report on the affairs of British North America to the British Parliament; he recommended union of the Canadas and responsible government.

1840s
The British government wanted the colonies to take more control of local matters. Ordinary people were to be given more influence in the government. The British government wished to become less involved in the government of British North America. It also adopted free trade.

Change in Colonial Policy

1841
Union of the Canadas was formally established.

Act of Union 1841

Newfoundland

United Province of Canada

Prince Edward Island

Nova Scotia

New Brunswick

The first steam railway in British North America had been in operation since 1836.

1849
Rebellion Losses Bill

Rebellion Losses Bill

The Rebellion Losses Bill was to pay the people of Canada East for property damaged or destroyed during the Rebellion of 1837. Riots broke out immediately after Lord Elgin, the governor general, signed the bill, and the Parliament Building was set on fire.

1850s
Some cities were beginning to get modern conveniences—gaslight in some houses and, along a few streets, simple sewers to carry away used water.

219

Chapter 8 Focus

Chapter 7 introduced you to the many changes that occurred in Upper and Lower Canada from 1815 to 1838. Chapter 8 will consider the changes that occurred as a result of the armed conflict that took place in both Upper and Lower Canada. For example, the people's wishes became increasingly important in government decision-making after 1839. Power, co-operation, decision-making, and conflict are all important concepts in this chapter. The concept of conflict is the focus of Chapter 8.

| Power | Co-operation | Decision-making | **Conflict** |

Other Concepts and Main Ideas

- Lord Durham's Report
- The Act of Union, 1841
- Rebellion Losses Bill
- responsible government
- political parties
- political deadlock
- life in the Province of Canada
- Underground Railway

Chapter Preview/Prediction

You have had various opportunities to practise your prediction skills throughout this textbook. Recall the purposes and methods for making predictions. What prediction methods have you used? Which was most useful? Which do you prefer? Why? Would you change the methods in any way to make them more suitable for you? Think of one or more new ways to make predictions. Share your ideas with the class.

Next, examine the Overview found on the previous pages. Use the Overview and what you already know to predict what will follow in Chapter 8. You may use any of the prediction methods you have already tried or a method you came up with in your discussion.

Definition Review*

The British Government:

- made the important decisions; had the real power
- appointed the governor to run the colony on its behalf

The Governor:

- was appointed by the British government
- tried to carry out the wishes of the British government
- was very powerful

The Executive Council:

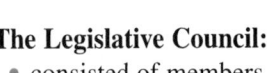

- consisted of members appointed by the governor for as long as he chose to keep them on the council
- advised the governor
- ran the government

The Legislative Council:

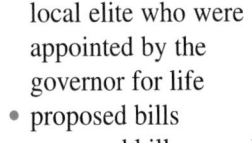

- consisted of members of the local elite who were appointed by the governor for life
- proposed bills
- approved bills passed by the Legislative Assembly

The Legislative Assembly:

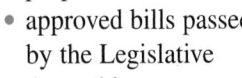

- was elected by the people
- consisted of the representatives of the people
- imposed taxes and proposed bills to serve local needs
- had limited power since the governor and Legislative Council could veto its laws

Legend and Notes

- ▬ Crown (Monarchy)
- ▬ Elite (a small number of powerful citizens)
- ▬ People (whose participation makes this government a democracy)

Note:

- Executive and Legislative Councils were appointed.
- Legislative Assemblies were elected.
- 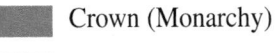 Power was held by the British Government and the local elite.
- When a bill becomes law it is called an Act.

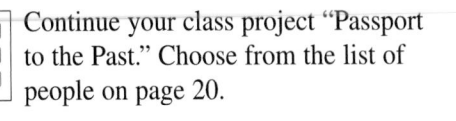 Continue your class project "Passport to the Past." Choose from the list of people on page 20.

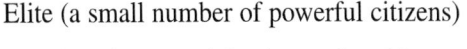
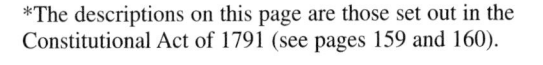

*The descriptions on this page are those set out in the Constitutional Act of 1791 (see pages 159 and 160).

Upper and Lower Canada

Lord Durham was sent by the British government to study the situation in Upper and Lower Canada, investigate the grievances that had sparked rebellions, and search for a solution. Durham stayed only five months in the Canadas. During this time he and his team of experts talked to many people. Upon his return to Britain, he wrote his "Report on the Affairs of British North America," which became known as the Durham Report.

Lord Durham (1792–1840)

John George Lambton, better known as Lord Durham, arrived in Quebec City as governor general of British North America in May of 1838.* He was sent to investigate the causes of the Rebellions of 1837.

Lord Durham was especially interested in educating the poor and giving people more control over the government. He had been nicknamed "Radical Jack" in the British House of Commons because of his **radical policies**.

His most immediate task, upon arrival, was to decide what to do with the Patriotes—those who supported the Rebellions in 1837 in Lower Canada—many of whom were still in jail in Lower Canada. He decided to set most of them free and to **exile** the leaders to Bermuda. Louis-Joseph Papineau and others who had fled to the United States were to be executed if they tried to return to the Canadas.

Durham resigned as governor general toward the end of 1838 because he felt that he was not getting enough support from the British government. He returned to Great Britain and spent two months writing his report. He died soon after, on July 28, 1840.

The Durham Report

Durham made two major recommendations in his report:

1. **The two colonies of Upper and Lower Canada should become one colony called the United Province of Canada.**

Uniting Lower and Upper Canada would place the English in the majority. This was intended as a way of uniting the English-speaking people and giving them a majority in the Legislative Assembly.

2. **The new united colony should have responsible government.**

- British imperial powers would be identified in writing. All other local powers would be held by the colonies.

- On matters involving only colonists, the governor would be advised only by his Executive Council, with no input from the British government.

- The Executive Council members would be chosen by the leader of the largest group in the Legislative Assembly rather than by the governor. This would mean that members of the Executive Council would really be chosen by the people's representatives. This is called responsible government. **

- The governor would not take sides, but would sign into law any bills passed by the Legislative Council and Assembly.

- Members of the Executive Council would keep their jobs only as long as they had the support of more than half the members of the Legislative Assembly, rather than for as long as the governor chose to keep them on the council.

Challenge Plus

1. Look at the diagram of representative government shown on page 160. What change do you think would be necessary to create a responsible government? Write out a model to represent this form of government.

---

*Lord Durham was appointed governor general of all British North America—not lieutenant-governor of Upper Canada and governor of Lower Canada.
Radical policy—plan for extreme changes
Exile—to officially order someone to leave the country
**Under responsible government the government must have the support (confidence) of a majority of the members of the legislature to remain in power. Under responsible government the Legislative Assembly has a great deal of power. This is what happens in Cabinets of the federal and provincial governments today.

The Act of Union, 1841*

Introduction

The British government decided to act on one of Lord Durham's recommendations. The Act of Union of 1841 joined Upper and Lower Canada together as the United Province of Canada. The Act of Union was the first step toward Confederation (the union of the British North American colonies). It was hoped that the English-speaking members (having the majority of votes) would unite and control the Legislative Assembly.

Aim: to unite the two colonies of Canada into a single unit, and to give the English-speaking people control of the newly named colony.

Key Terms

- Eliminate separate governments in Upper Canada and Lower Canada and create a single government with equal representation from Canada West and Canada East, despite the latter's greater population. The system of government was to be the same as in the past.**

- Establish English as the official language of government.***

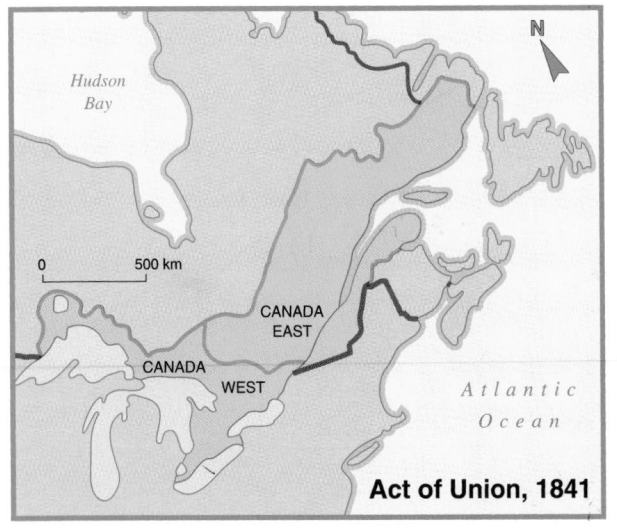

The Act of Union of 1841 joined Upper Canada and Lower Canada to create the United Province of Canada (see pink area on above map).

---

*The Act of Union was passed in Great Britain in 1840 but it was proclaimed in North America in 1841.

**Refer to page 160 to review the type of government in existence before the Act of Union.

***By 1848 the Government of the Province of Canada recognized both English and French as the languages of government. In 1969 English and French became the official languages of Canada.

Act of Union, 1841

British Government
- made the important decisions
- appointed the governor general

Governor General
(British-appointed)
- tried to carry out the wishes of the British government
- very powerful

Legislative Council
(appointed)
- advised the governor
- appointed for life
- proposed bills
- represented the local elite
- approved bills passed by Assembly

Executive Council
(appointed)
- advised the governor
- remained on the council as long as the governor wanted them
- ran the government

Legislative Assembly

Canada West   Canada East

Legislative Assembly (elected by voters)
- made up of the people's representatives from Canada West and Canada East
- imposed taxes; could propose bills to serve local needs; controlled local revenue
- power could be limited because governor and Legislative Council could veto its bills

Voters
(from Canada West)

Voters
(from Canada East)

Appoints   Elect

Colonial Policy in Great Britain

Britain was beginning to rethink its imperial (colonial) policies in the 1840s. After all, the point of having colonies was so that they could provide natural resources for the imperial power. Instead, they seemed to be very expensive to govern. Finally, in 1846, the British government decided to stop giving its colonies special trading protection and to freely trade with all nations. This affected Britain's attitude toward her colonies. It was felt there was no point in being involved in the internal politics of the British North American colonies if they were no longer important to Britain's economic well-being.

Lord Elgin

(detail) *James Bruce, Earl of Elgin*, ca. 1855, by Cornelius Krieghoff, McCord Museum of Canadian History, Montreal

In 1847, James Bruce, the Earl of Elgin, was appointed to be the new governor general of Canada. His instructions were to permit responsible government in British North America.

Rebellion Losses Bill

The first test of responsible government came in 1849, when the Rebellion Losses Bill was presented to the Legislative Assembly. The purpose of the bill was to pay the people of Canada East for property damaged or destroyed during the Rebellion of 1837. The people of Canada West who had suffered losses had already been repaid.

The Tories were strongly opposed to the Rebellion Losses Bill. They did not want any of the rebels to receive payment, because they felt the rebels were traitors. Governor Elgin did not like the bill either, but he was committed to the principle of responsible government, which meant that he must follow the wishes of the majority in the Legislative Assembly. The majority wanted the bill passed.

---

*After a bill received the consent of the Legislative Assembly, Legislative Council, and the Governor, it became law and was called an Act.

Annexation—joining of one territory to a larger political entity

Manifesto—a public declaration of intentions by an important group of people

Reaction to the Rebellion Losses Bill

On April 25, 1849, Lord Elgin signed the Rebellion Losses Bill.* Tory reaction was immediate. There were riots in Toronto and Kingston. But the most violent protest was in Montreal. On the night the bill was signed, an angry mob stormed the Parliament Building and set it on fire. The building was destroyed. The governor was pelted with rotten eggs and stones. Vegetables, dead rats, and garbage were thrown at members of the Legislative Assembly.

After a few months the protests faded away, but the Rebellion Losses Act* remained in effect. In frustration at the Act, and with problems arising from poor economic conditions, some of the English-speaking Tories began to look elsewhere. Three hundred of them signed the **Annexation Manifesto**, which proposed that the Province of Canada drop its ties with Britain and join the United States.

The angry crowd threw rotten eggs and stones at Lord Elgin's coach as he road home on April 25, 1849, the day he signed the Rebellion Losses Bill.

For Your Notebook

1. Compare the decision made by Lord Elgin on this page with the one made by Mrs. Cherniak on page 183.

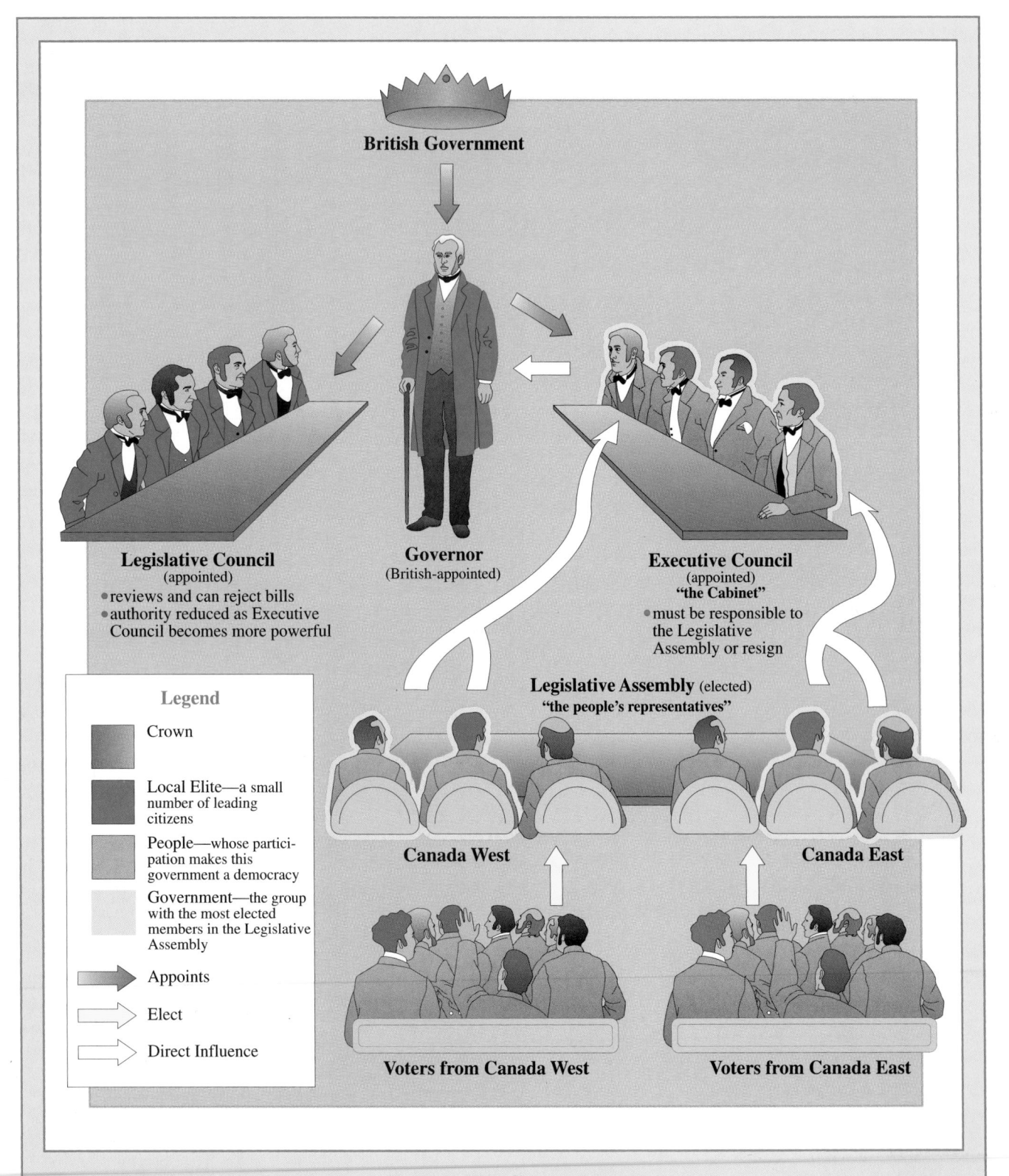

British Government

Legislative Council
(appointed)
• reviews and can reject bills
• authority reduced as Executive Council becomes more powerful

Governor
(British-appointed)

Executive Council
(appointed)
"the Cabinet"
• must be responsible to the Legislative Assembly or resign

Legislative Assembly (elected)
"the people's representatives"

Canada West

Canada East

Legend

Crown

Local Elite—a small number of leading citizens

People—whose participation makes this government a democracy

Government—the group with the most elected members in the Legislative Assembly

Appoints

Elect

Direct Influence

Voters from Canada West

Voters from Canada East

Responsible Government

Members of the Executive Council (today known as the Cabinet) are chosen by the governor from the group with the most elected members in the Legislative Assembly. The most powerful voice in the government is the Cabinet. The Cabinet is thus responsible to the representatives of the voters for its conduct of public business. If the Cabinet loses the confidence of the majority of the Legislative Assembly, it must resign. In other words, the government can function only if it has the support of the Legislature; it is *responsible* to the Legislature.

After the Rebellions

by Nancy Sellars Marcotte

Just now it is late, late at night on April 25, 1849. In the past few hours I have witnessed some of the most perplexing events of my 16 years. When I came to Montreal from Toronto I knew I would hear in the streets a language I do not understand—French. But I did not expect to see Tories acting with violence against the government.

My name is Robert McKinney. I am the son of Douglas McKinney the Reformer, who in 1837 was one of William Lyon Mackenzie's Rebels who marched down Yonge Street on a December night. A few years ago it might have cost my father his life if he had admitted that.

My parents think I was too young to remember the Rebellions of 1837, but I recall as though it were yesterday. I was four years old when my father came home late one night with a bullet hole in the shoulder of his coat. My mother leaned close to the light of a single candle to mend the hole so it would look like part of the shoulder seam.

It is now 12 years later, and that coat is the one I wore to keep me warm on the long trip through the woods of Canada West between Toronto and Montreal.

My father never did publicly admit to being one of the men who marched with Mr. Mackenzie in 1837, although he longed to shout with pride that he had been there. Instead of joining the men in prison, he was the lawyer who defended many of them. I remember my parents being upset when some of the men were exiled, and their tears when Mr. Lount and Mr. Matthews were hanged.

I was too young to realize that another rebellion happened in 1837. It was in Lower Canada, and had many more deaths.

My father was born on a farm north of York—the city we now call Toronto—in 1800. He is now a lawyer in Toronto, and I am his apprentice.

One late afternoon earlier this month—April 1849—I was busy closing up the office for the evening. The fire in the fireplace had died down. I had already put the day's incoming letters away in the desk, and had made a trip to the post office to mail the outgoing letters, the ones I had hand-written so carefully according to my father's instructions. Lawyer's letters could be funny or sad or boring. Somebody in Toronto had better return somebody else's cow, which had wandered into the wrong yard; an employer regretted to inform a family in Queensville that their 12-year-old son had been killed when his arm got caught in some mill machinery; somebody's debts relating to some business had not been paid.

I pulled Father's old grey coat over my shoulders and, as I always did, lightly touched the stitches hiding the old bullet hole. It reminded me of how hard Mr. Mackenzie and his friends had fought for our rights. Then I stepped out onto the wooden sidewalk of Yonge Street. The lamplighter passed me, his long pole swinging over his shoulder. I was glad of the yellow light that he set going in the streetlamp. The streets of Toronto could be very frightening at night. Even though begging could land a person in jail, many a poor person, desperate for a penny to buy some food for himself or his family, would be sleeping in the alleyways of Toronto that night. Some of these people were off the ships from Ireland. People who got too near them sometimes came down with cholera.

No one came near me as I hopped the mud puddles and ditches of the six blocks to our home. However, as I entered the gate of my father's property, a figure slipped out of the bushes. I was startled until I realized that it was my sister Charlotte, who is 13.

"Robbie, did father tell you?" she asked. Knowing that he hadn't, she went on, "Next week he's going to Montreal! Imagine! None of our family has ever travelled so far—except Grandmother and Grandfather when they came here on the ship from Scotland. Father has to go to see about some property that someone here in Toronto has inherited in Montreal. Anyway, Father is taking you to Montreal!"

"Don't be silly, Charlotte," I scolded. "Father wouldn't take me so far. And he certainly won't go to Montreal next week. Why, the ice is barely out of Lake Ontario, and the steamships to Montreal haven't started running yet this spring."

But at dinner that night, over the roast beef and potatoes and carrots,

Father told me sternly that I must pack my travelling box and prepare for a trip to Montreal. Mother started planning out loud the things that she must get ready for our trip.

"I must arrange for the laundress to wash your shirts before the trip. And the cook will pack you some food—although I have heard that many people lose their appetites on that coach. Goodness knows, I would like to see Montreal some time, but I would rather travel by steamer—although there is always the danger of the ship catching fire, or going aground."

"They say that some day we'll be able to travel by railway from Toronto to Montreal," said Charlotte.

"Charlotte, don't be silly," I told her. "They'll never be able to lay railway tracks though the woods of Canada West. Why, in some places, the road disappears into the mud every spring."

I remembered my words the next week as Father and I rode in the stage-coach until the movement made us feel sick. Then we walked. Twice on the first day Father and I had to get out and help push the coach through mud puddles. I remembered the words

Charlotte had hissed at me as we were leaving home: "Be sure to remember every inch of the trip so you can tell me all about it." I would show her a good many of those inches in the mud on my breeches.

At night we stayed in inns along the road. They had only a few rooms for travellers to sleep. We spread our blankets on dirty old mattresses. The food at the inns was little more than bread, potatoes, and salt beef, with

the occasional addition of cheese and pickles. Even so, Father usually paid a dollar each night for our food and lodging.

There was one good thing about the trip. For once Father was not working at his papers, and he talked to me.

"I remember when I was a boy going to a little house in a clearing just like that," he would say. "The woman there grew up in Scotland,

and she could read and write very well. Whenever we could, the children in the neighbourhood would go to her house. It was usually two days a week—Mondays and Thursdays—but not when there was too much snow or at planting time or at harvest. She would teach us how to read and write and do arithmetic."

"And that was probably enough learning for anyone," said a deep voice from the opposite corner of the coach. I jumped. I had forgotten that there was anyone else with us.

A man with huge side whiskers and a very rumpled suit struggled upright. "Have you heard what this man Egerton Ryerson is saying?" he asked. "He's in charge of schooling in Canada West, and he says every child should have schooling, no matter whether the parents can pay or not! He says that the rest of us should pay taxes to support schools, even if we have no children. Furthermore, Ryerson is visiting other countries to see what they are teaching in their schools. Reading, writing, and arithmetic aren't good enough for this man Ryerson, oh no! He says every child should also be learning history, and about government, and drawing and music as well. And not only learning, but also physical exercises to help them be strong!"

The very idea of all this learning seemed to be too much for the rumpled man in the corner of the coach. He slumped back into his corner. Father winked at me. We each knew what the other was thinking. Mother had read a little about what Mr. Egerton Ryerson was hoping to do with the schools of Canada West.

"I would like to be able to hire a nurse for the younger children who could read to them from the Bible," she had said. "And it would be nice to have a cook who could read one of the new cookery books. As it is, I have to read any new recipe to the cook and we make it together until she has learned how to do it. And imagine if the laundress could read. We could deliver the laundry to her house, with written instructions, and not have to see her to tell her anything special we want done."

When we finally arrived at Montreal, after five days of jolting and shaking, we went to the home of a lawyer with whom Father often had correspondence. I found that the lawyer had a son who, like me, was being apprenticed to become a lawyer.

This young man—his name was Peter Sherwin—offered to take me for a walk about Montreal. I was delighted to go, and to talk to him. However, I soon found that Peter Sherwin had some very different ideas than I had. He and his friends were angry about a law that was to be passed in the Legislative Assembly that very day.

"They say that the governor general, Lord Elgin, will sign this new bill, and it will become law," said Peter. "It is called the Rebellion Losses Bill. It will repay people for property that was destroyed in the Rebellion of 1837. Can you imagine? The very people who rebelled 12 years ago will now be paid back for the things they lost!"

"But the old Reformers are now the people in the Legislative Assembly of Canada," I protested. As though I were scratching my shoulder, I reached up and touched the mended bullet hole in the shoulder of my grey coat. "They are our legal government. The governor general is supposed to sign any bills they pass, whether he agrees with them or not. That is what responsible government means. And besides, people in Upper Canada—Canada West—have already been repaid for their losses."

"Well, it isn't right. You don't sound like a good Tory to me," said Peter. "My grandfather left the Thirteen Colonies and came to British North America because he was determined to remain loyal to Britain. He would not support the so-called Patriots in the Thirteen Colonies in 1776. But now in 1849 our taxes have to go to repay those Patriotes in Lower Canada—Canada East—who were traitors to Britain in 1837."

I did not want to be rude to Peter, but I could see that we had very different ideas of how Canada should be governed. I could tell that Peter's family was part of the Château Clique, the wealthy people in Canada East who did not think the colony should be governed according to the wishes of the majority. This was like our Family Compact in Canada West. The Family Compact were the people who controlled the government that my father and Mr. Mackenzie had marched against in 1837. If they had been in Canada East, my father and Mr. Mackenzie would have been with the Patriotes fighting against Peter Sherwin's people, the Château Clique. How embarrassing!

It got worse than embarrassing when we ran into some of Peter's friends. They were so angry that the governor general was about to sign the Rebellion Losses Bill that they went to the Parliament Buildings to wait for the governor general, Lord Elgin, to leave. I think they meant to just shout their anger at him, but one of the Tories threw a rock. Vegetables, eggs, rocks, dead rats—the coach was bombarded with garbage both disgusting and dangerous.

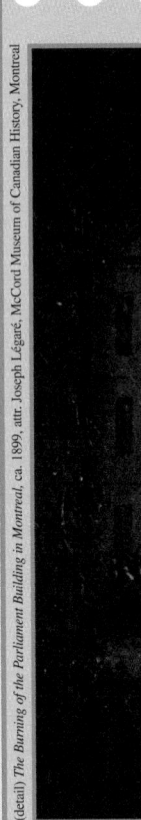

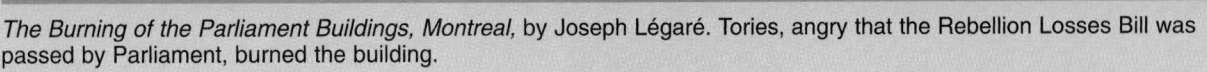

The Burning of the Parliament Buildings, Montreal, by Joseph Légaré. Tories, angry that the Rebellion Losses Bill was passed by Parliament, burned the building.

I hung back, thinking that this would be the end and that soon we would go home. But Peter and his friends continued to walk the streets, shouting their anger that the Patriotes would be paid back for their losses in the rebellion of 12 years ago. Darkness was coming down, and I would have liked to go back to the Sherwins' home to find my father, but I was completely confused by the unfamiliar streets. It was dark when we arrived once again at the Parliament Buildings.

Rocks flew through the air. I found it hard to believe that Tories actually decided to throw rocks at the Parliament Buildings. Then somehow the crowd was surging into the Parliament Buildings. The windows became just shards of glass. Chairs were smashed. I do not believe that anyone decided to set the building on fire. Surely that was an accident, caused by the broken glass lamps.

Just when it seemed that we must escape or be burned, an old man shouted for help. Through the flames he was dragging a portrait of Queen Victoria. Peter and I—Tory and Rebel, who were on opposite sides of this conflict—helped to carry a picture of Queen Victoria out of the flames.

Can you see what has happened in Canada in 12 short years? And not just once, but twice—in both Upper Canada and Lower Canada. Twelve years ago supporters of the rebellion in Upper Canada and the Patriotes in Lower Canada were considered to be traitors. Some of them were exiled or hanged. Now their members are in control of the government.

Together they are one government of the United Province of Canada. They are supposed to meet in the Parliament Buildings in Montreal, but these buildings are now burning in a fire caused by the Tories, the people who used to control the government.

The governor general has signed a law that he didn't agree with because it was passed by the majority of the representatives in the Legislative Assembly. This is responsible government.

Of course, Charlotte will say that we won't really have responsible government until women can vote too. But Charlotte thinks that one day there will be railway tracks from Montreal to Toronto!

Formation of Political Parties

 Once responsible government was in place, members of the Executive Council were chosen from the group with the most elected members in the Legislative Assembly. The members of the Executive Council had to maintain the confidence (support) of the Legislative Assembly or they would have to resign. The Executive Council had to be responsible not only to the Legislative Assembly, but to the voters. It was the voters, after all, who elected the members of the Legislative Assembly from which most of the Executive Council members were chosen.

It made sense for groups with similar beliefs about government to join together in political parties. They could then work together to get their candidates elected as representatives in the Legislative Assembly. Several new parties emerged in the 1850s, as can be seen in the chart.

Political Party

A group of people with similar beliefs about government, who work together to get their candidates elected as representatives.

The New Parties

	Party and Leader	Allies in Legislature	Beliefs	Voter Support
Canada West	**Liberal-Conservatives** John A. Macdonald (later, first Prime Minister of the Dominion of Canada)	• allied with Bleus in 1854	• interested in economic development • wanted co-operation between French and English Canadians	• popular in large towns among people in business
	Clear Grits George Brown (editor of the *Globe* newspaper)	• allied with Parti Rouge after 1857	• wanted "representation by population" because the population of Canada West had now grown larger than Canada East • opposed power of Church in government; opposed Catholic separate schools in Canada West • wanted to acquire the western territories known as Rupert's Land for Canada	• popular in rural districts and small towns
Canada East	**Bleus (Conservatives)** George-Étienne Cartier	• allied with Liberal-Conservatives in 1854	• wanted commercial development of St. Lawrence system through railways • believed that Canadiens needed to co-operate with English Canadians to ensure the survival of their culture and language • wanted to maintain the power of the Roman Catholic Church	• primarily Canadiens • Roman Catholic Church • English-speaking Montreal business interests
	Parti Rouge Antoine-Aimé Dorion	• allied with the Clear Grits after 1857	• French rights; e.g., language, culture • opposed power of Roman Catholic Church in government • in favour of federalism	• supported by urban people such as Liberal Nationalists, working people, and anti-big-business groups in Montreal, and urban nationalists in Quebec City

Political Deadlock

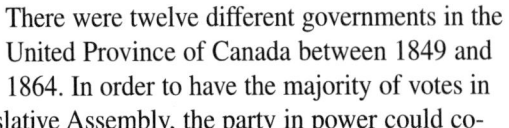

As a result of the Act of Union, the United Province of Canada had one government with equal numbers of elected representatives (in the Legislative Assembly) from Canada West and Canada East. Because no party was Canada-wide, in order to get a majority in the Legislative Assembly, a party from Canada West would have to co-operate with a party from Canada East. The election results and the ability of two parties to work together determined which two parties would form the government. The leaders of these parties would then choose the members of the Executive Council to recommend to the Governor for appointment.

To remain in power, the Executive Council had to maintain the support of the majority (greater than 50%) of members of the Legislative Assembly. Even though members of a political party held similar ideas and beliefs, members of the parties made their own decisions as to how they would vote. The government's own party members could vote against their proposed bills. This increased the possibility that bills proposed by the parties in power might be defeated.

Political deadlock occurred when government decisions (such as the passing of bills) could not be made because the parties in power could not get the support of the majority of the Legislative Assembly.

For Your Notebook

Imagine that in 1850, the government of the Canadas proposed a bill and the bill was defeated. Discuss the following:

1. Explain how this situation relates to political deadlock.

2. Brainstorm for solutions to political deadlock. Which solution is best? Why?

3. What are the positives (pros) and negatives (cons) of each of the following possible solutions for political deadlock?

   a) The government (the two parties in power) resigns

   b) The government reforms itself by adding or dropping members to gain enough support in the Legislative Assembly

   c) The government requests that the governor general call an election

   d) The governor general asks opposition parties to form a new government

4. Which of the above solutions might these individuals or groups prefer? Why?

   a) member of an **opposition** party

   b) member of the Executive Council from Canada East; member from Canada West

   c) governor general

   d) British government

Forming New Party Alliances

There were twelve different governments in the United Province of Canada between 1849 and 1864. In order to have the majority of votes in the Legislative Assembly, the party in power could co-operate with another party so they would not be outvoted. Negotiation before bills got to the Legislative Assembly sometimes helped the government in power to achieve a majority vote on its bills. This helped to prevent political deadlock.

Macdonald, the leader of the Liberal-Conservatives in Canada West, and Cartier, the leader of the Bleus in Canada East, found that they had some similar goals (see chart on page 229). Cartier suggested the French and English Canadians should work together on business-related projects. This was done in 1854.

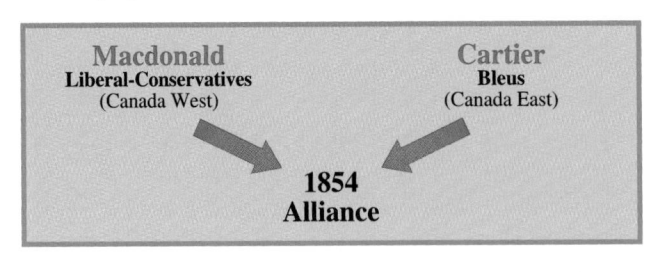

At first, members of the Parti Rouge led by Antoine-Aimé Dorion in Canada East were not interested in joining with a group as strongly against Catholic leadership as Canada West's George Brown and his Clear Grits were. However, in 1857, the Clear Grits allied with the Parti Rouge. They did this to try to keep the Liberal-Conservatives and Bleus out of power and to achieve their similar goals.

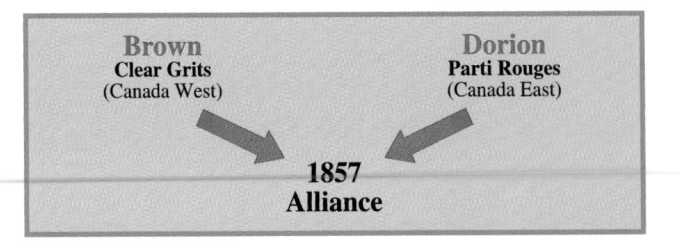

Opposition—the political party or parties represented in the Legislative Assembly but not in power

Choosing a Capital

Part 1: Background Information

Without a majority in the Legislative Assembly, it was difficult to make decisions such as where the capital city should be located. As a result, the capital was Kingston from 1841 to 1844, Montreal from 1844 to 1849, Toronto from 1849 to 1851, Quebec City from 1851 to 1855, and Toronto from 1855 to 1859. This indecision was expensive and inconvenient. It was also an opportunity for criticism and political jokes. For example, William Lyon Mackenzie, a leader of the 1837 Rebellion in Upper Canada, suggested the government... *[get] a steamboat fitted up for the Legislative Assembly, with a nice place for the Speaker's chair, that they might sail up and down the lakes at their pleasure. It would at all events, he thought, be much cheaper than running about the country as they had been doing [with their capital], and were still intending to do.*

—*Toronto Globe*, Toronto, June 7, 1851

In 1857, because no single city could gain a majority in the Legislative Assembly, the members of the Legislative Assembly could not make a decision as to where the capital should be. They asked Queen Victoria to do so. Toronto, Kingston, Ottawa, Montreal, and Quebec were five of the choices. Each city presented its case, in writing, to the queen, who was assisted in making a decision by advisors and the British Prime Minister.

Part 2: Your Task

In this simulation you are being asked to recreate the situation of choosing a capital for Canada. Once you have reviewed the requirements of this assignment, discuss with your classmates the criteria for assessment. Think about how you can best fulfil the requirements.

Preparing and Presenting

1. Divide into six groups, one group for each of five cities (Toronto, Kingston, Ottawa, Montreal, Quebec) and the sixth group to represent Great Britain (Queen Victoria, the British Prime Minister, and their advisors).

   - 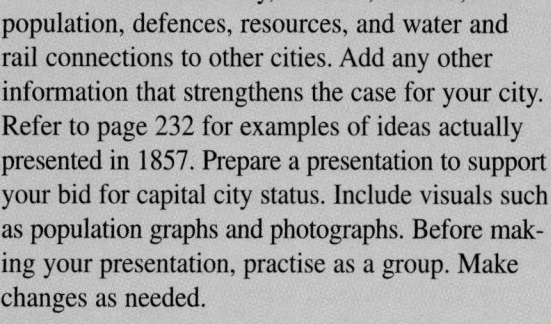 **City groups:** Research your city as it was in the 1850s, examining factors such as history, location, climate, population, defences, resources, and water and rail connections to other cities. Add any other information that strengthens the case for your city. Refer to page 232 for examples of ideas actually presented in 1857. Prepare a presentation to support your bid for capital city status. Include visuals such as population graphs and photographs. Before making your presentation, practise as a group. Make changes as needed.

   - **Queen's group:** Write a detailed list of your expectations for a suitable capital city. Select or design an effective decision-making model to use when selecting the capital city. Refer to the model when evaluating each city's presentation.

2.  Plan to dress in period costume during the presentations.

3. Government officials from each city presented their case to the queen in persuasive letters. Each letter began with a formal statement.

   We, your Majesty's dutiful and loyal subjects of the city of Ottawa, in the Province of Canada, beg leave to approach the foot of the Throne with assurances of our loyalty and fidelity to the Crown of Great Britain, and of our devoted attachment to the person of your Majesty....

   —from a letter, Memorial of the City of Ottawa, May 18, 1857

   The primary source excerpts that follow show some of the topics covered and some of the persuasive strategies used by some of the city groups when they put forth their cases to the queen. If you are a member of a city group, think about these ideas and strategies as you prepare your case.

continued on page 232

Primary Source Materials

Montreal, on the topic of economy and resources

STRATEGY USED: The Montreal group pointed out its strengths by providing examples.

Montreal is the seat and centre of extensive manu-factories, from which all parts of the Province to some extent draw their supplies, and commands within herself an immense hydraulic power, lying, as she does, on the banks of the St. Lawrence, whose rapids above the city furnish her with an inexhaustible supply of water for mill-seats and manufacturing purposes.

—from a letter, Memorial to the City
of Montreal, May 27, 1857

Kingston, on the topic of defence

STRATEGY USED: The Kingston group suggested the weak points of its rivals and emphasized its own strengths.

When the comparative claims of other Canadian cities are considered, the obvious superiority of Kingston appears too great to be passed over. Whilst Montreal would need an enormous expenditure to place it in a state of anything approaching security, the forts, batteries and towers of Kingston already present a formidable barrier against the approach of a foe.

—from a letter, Memorial of the City
of Kingston, June 15, 1857

Quebec, on the topic of past and future

STRATEGY USED: The Quebec group pointed out the area's important history and looked to the future.

The first Europeans who ever visited Canada located themselves at Quebec...no other point between Quebec and the sea offered, to the first colonists of Canada, such a striking position as to induce them to form a permanent establishment.

Talks about uniting the British North American colonies were under way. It was believed this would allow them to strengthen the economy, share resources, and defend against possible American attempts to expand into British territory.

England herself is interested...that a power should exist on this continent to counter-balance that of the great American Republic.... Quebec would be not only the most accessible from the sea, but the most central city of British America.

—from a letter, Memorial of the City
of Quebec, May 25, 1857

*Distances converted from miles to kilometres for this textbook.

Ottawa, on the topic of location

STRATEGY USED: The Ottawa group defended itself against criticism. In 1843, Ottawa's location between Canada East and Canada West had been criticized as being inconvenient for both provinces.

The argument of inconvenience cannot now be urged since the introduction of our railways, which render it easy of access from all parts of the province.

—from a letter, Memorial of the City
of Ottawa, May 18, 1857

Toronto, on the topic of population

STRATEGY USED: The Toronto group used census statistics to make predictions. The mayor presented a table

Population Within			
	80 km*	160 km	240 km
Toronto will have	596 992	1 118 578	1 460 558
Montreal will have	551 667	841 185	1 182 868
Quebec will have	251 262	425 523	897 423
Ottawa will have	234 969	544 242	1 179 810
Kingston will have	180 646	521 383	833 567

of population estimates for areas around each city.

Thus satisfactorily proving that within two years... Toronto will be the centre, not only of the greatest wealth, but of the greatest number of inhabitants....

—from a letter from the mayor of Toronto to the
Right Hon. H. Labouchere, June 15, 1857

Part 3: In Conclusion

Decision-making

- After the presentations, the Queen's group should discuss the case of each city, and use a decision-making model to make a choice.

- The Queen's group should then announce its decision. As a class discuss the quality of the decision. Record your reactions to the process of choosing a capital city in your History Journal.

In History

In 1858, the Queen announced that parliament should be in Ottawa. The Legislative Assembly first rejected this decision, but in 1859 accepted it by a majority of five votes. Parliament was held in Quebec from 1859 to 1865. Parliament was first held in Ottawa in 1865.

Life in the Province of Canada to 1855

Rural and Urban Growth

In 1840, over 80 percent of the men in the Province of Canada worked in either agriculture or lumbering. The lumbering industry provided timber for Europe, as well as timber and sawn lumber for local use. Many farmers burned the trees from their property and made potash to sell. During the 1840s, the cities began installing gas lights, as well as some sewer systems to take away waste water along the main streets. During the 1840s, mail service improved. By the early 1850s, messages could be sent by telegraph to most of the cities of the Province of Canada.

The 1840s and 1850s saw a great population increase. Cities and transportation networks developed extensively.

Canada East

Most of the people of Canada East (formerly Lower Canada) still held their land under the seigneurial system. They worked their long, narrow farms in much the same way as their ancestors had done.

The seigneurial system began to be replaced by the freehold system after 1838. At first the change in land-holding system was optional but by the 1850s it was required. The introduction of the freehold system did not mean that the boundaries of people's land changed. It changed the way the legal title to the land was held and transferred through purchase and sale.

In 1841, the two largest cities in Canada East were Quebec City, with a population of 31 700, and Montreal, with a population of 40 000. Life for city dwellers was showing more signs of change as the cities became centres of business activity.

Canada West

In Canada West (formerly Upper Canada), the main agricultural crop was wheat. From 1843 to 1846, Britain had lower import duties on wheat from British North America than from other countries. This made farmers from Canada West, millers, and other people involved in the wheat trade very prosperous.

By 1841, Toronto had a population of 15 000; Kingston had a population of 3000.

Exploring Further

1. Do research to find out what roles women and children had in the Province of Canada during the 1840s.

2. Investigate the mail system of the 1840s. Trace the route and "experiences" of a letter.

3. What types of fire services were available between 1800 and 1855? How were the challenges of fighting fires different from today?

4. Make a bar graph using the population figures given on this page.

By the mid-1800s along the St. Lawrence–Great Lakes corridor, few of the trees which once covered the land remained. Land had been cleared for roads, settlement, and farming.

Canals

Road travel at this time was slow and difficult. Travel by water was also hazardous because rapids and waterfalls often barred the way. By the 1820s, the government decided to build canals to make it easier to transport people and goods. Canals use a system of locks to move boats up to higher levels and down again. Waterways freeze in winter, but they are efficient during the shipping season.

The Lachine Canal, completed in 1825, allowed ships to bypass the Lachine Rapids on the St. Lawrence River south of Montreal (see map on page 235). The Welland Canal, which opened in 1829, took ships around Niagara Falls and made it possible for them to travel all the way to Fort William, at the western end of Lake Superior.

The Rideau Canal, completed in 1832, provided a safe route along the Ottawa River from Bytown (later called Ottawa) to Kingston. The St. Lawrence River, which was bordered on the south by the United States, was vulnerable to attack by the Americans. The Ottawa River and the Rideau Canal provided a route between Upper and Lower Canada that was completely within British North American territory. Colonel By of the British army was responsible for the Rideau Canal project. He managed to complete the canal in six years, in spite of many problems.

By the 1840s, the Lachine and Welland Canals were so busy that they needed to be enlarged. Other canals were built along the St. Lawrence River at this time, allowing large ships to travel from Lake Huron to Montreal.

The Rideau Canal was used for commercial shipping for a time, but is now used only by pleasure craft. In winter it is a popular skating rink, favoured by many of Ottawa's citizens as a commuter route to their jobs in the centre of the city.

The eight locks of the Rideau Canal at Bytown (later called Ottawa) in 1839.

A boat enters the lock and gates close behind it. Water is drained into the lock from above, raising the boat up to the level of the water it will be entering. Once the water level is equal, the gate at the other end opens and the boat continues on its route. When a boat is travelling in the other direction, the water in the lock drains out to lower the boat.

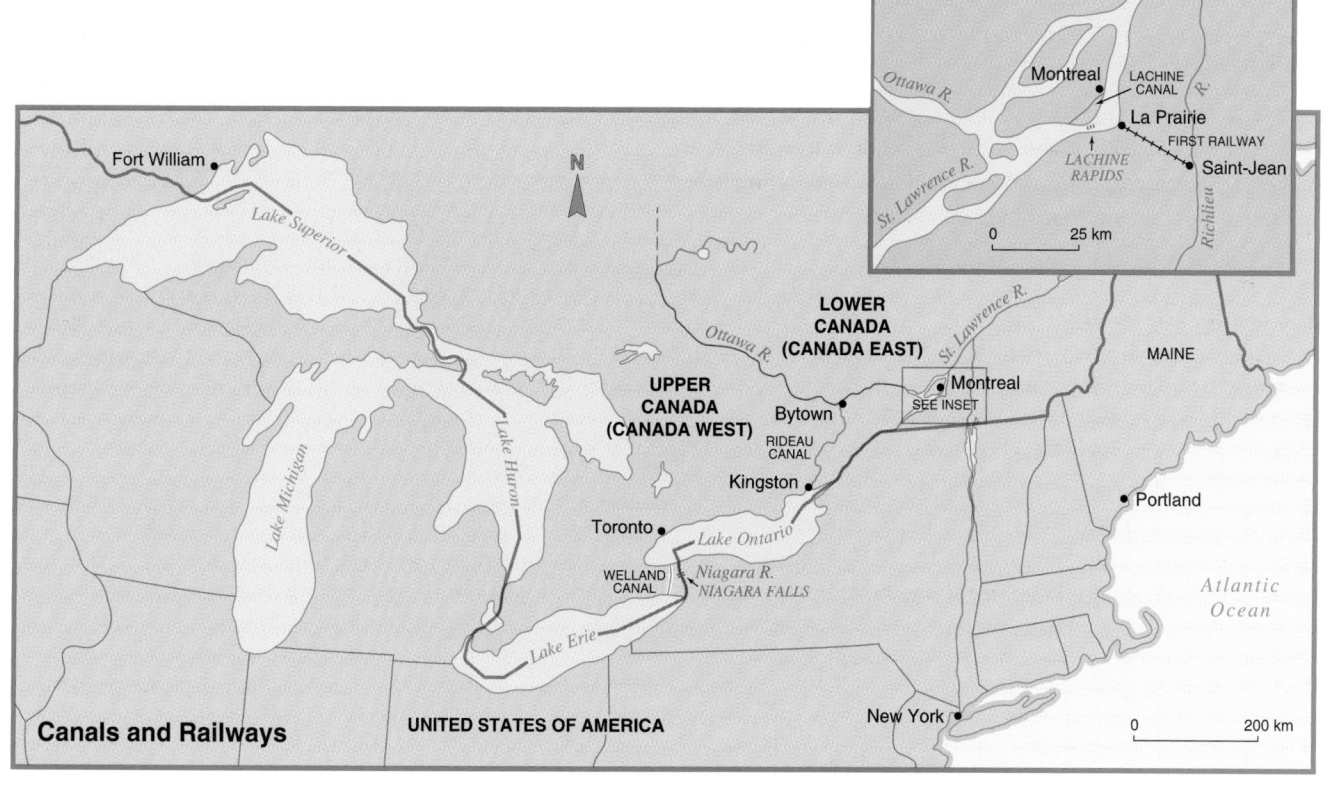

Canals and Railways

UNITED STATES OF AMERICA

Railways

The first railway in British North America was the 24-kilometre line south of Montreal built in 1836. Canada's first locomotive, the *Dorchester*, ran on this route until 1849. Most of the early railways connected waterways. Railways were built because they were cheaper than canals. Fewer than 100 kilometres of track were built in British North America in the 1840s. Throughout the 1850s, about 3200 kilometres of track were built. Several lines

Although many guests were invited to the event, only Governor Gosford and about 30 officials actually boarded the steam train, *Dorchester*, for its first run.

Education

Until the mid-1800s, education was considered to be a privilege for children whose parents could afford to pay for it. In some areas, families got together to build schools. These schools were often little more than log cabins. Sometimes students met in the home of the teacher. Students were expected to bring wood for the school stove, and candles if it was too dark.

Books and paper were rare, so students often wrote on pieces of slate.* Students stayed away from school to help when they were needed at home, particularly at times of planting and harvesting. Even though both boys and girls attended schools, often they were expected to have little contact with each other. Boys and girls often had separate entrances to the school and schoolyards.

By the 1840s, under the influence of Egerton Ryerson, people in Canada West began to think that schools should be supported by the government. When school attendance was made **universal** and **compulsory** in Ontario (formerly Canada West) in 1871, many more teachers were needed.

Egerton Ryerson (1803–1882)

To this day, the person who has had the most influence on education in English in Canada is probably Egerton Ryerson. Ryerson was descended from Loyalists. He believed in many of the goals of the Reformers of the 1820s, but he did not support the radical policies of William Lyon Mackenzie.

Ryerson spent several years as a Methodist circuit rider, riding throughout Upper Canada to preach to people in different places. Later, when he became a newspaper editor, he was able to spread his ideas about education.

From 1846 until 1876, Ryerson was superintendent of education for Canada West (called Ontario after 1867). He visited Europe and the United States to gather ideas about education. He wanted schools to teach more than the basics of reading, writing, and arithmetic. Amongst other subjects, Ryerson wanted to include history, geography, government, art, music, and physical education.

Ryerson saw many of his ideas come into practice when Ontario passed the Schools Act in 1871, making education in Ontario universal and compulsory. Many other provinces have also adopted Ryerson's ideas for education.

Religion and Schools

Many people supported the idea that education should be publicly funded and available to everyone. Many also believed that what was taught need not be exactly the same in every school. They felt that religious and moral teaching was an important part of education. In 1867, a section of the Constitution Act ensured that the law would protect and support Roman Catholic schools in Ontario and Protestant separate schools in Quebec.

Education was once considered to be a privilege for children whose parents could afford to pay for it.

---

* People wrote with chalk on thin slices of blue-gray stone called slate.
Universal—for everybody
Compulsory—required

The Atlantic Colonies

Industry

Fishing and farming were important industries in the Atlantic colonies during the 1840s and 1850s. Lumbering, manufacturing, mining, and trade also employed many people. By this time, shipbuilding had made New Brunswick and Nova Scotia world famous.

The Atlantic colonies relied upon Great Britain for trade. For instance, the shipbuilding industry's survival depended upon the trade in fish and timber within the **British Empire**. Most of New Brunswick's lumber was shipped to Britain and the United States.

Improvements in transportation allowed increased trade. Although most farm products were produced for local use, trade was increasing between the British colonies.

Communication between British North America and Great Britain improved. Samuel Cunard of Halifax started a steamship line in the 1840s, which greatly reduced travelling time between Great Britain and the Atlantic colonies. The mail could now arrive from Britain within fourteen days. The development of stagecoach service also improved mail delivery within the colonies.

Government

 Before Responsible Government

The Atlantic colonies—Prince Edward Island, Nova Scotia, Newfoundland, and New Brunswick—were colonies of Great Britain. Each colony had a governor, Legislative Council, and Legislative Assembly. They all had Executive Councils, except for Newfoundland, which did not get one until 1855.

Executive and Legislative Council members were chosen from upper-class people in the colonies. They were appointed to their positions in government. The Legislative Assembly was elected by the people, but the British government had the final say over any matters under dispute. The government in each of the Atlantic colonies was very similar to the government in the United Province of Canada in 1841, before the idea of responsible government was introduced (see page 222).

By the 1820s there was increasing conflict between the appointed Legislative and Executive Councils and the elected Legislative Assemblies. During the 1820s and 1830s, just as in Upper and Lower Canada, elections became more and more violent, as people tried to prevent others from voting.

British Empire—all of the colonies and countries under Great Britain's rule

Mr. and Mrs. William Croscup's Painted Room, Anon. Canadian, #18688.0. 19 (detail), National Gallery of Canada, Ottawa

Establishing Responsible Government

In the 1840s and 1850s, all four Atlantic colonies would seek and achieve responsible government.

Establishing Responsible Government	
Nova Scotia	1847
United Province of Canada	1849*
Prince Edward Island	1851
New Brunswick	1854
Newfoundland	1855

In Nova Scotia

Nova Scotia was the first of the British colonies in North America to achieve responsible government. This occurred in 1847—two years ahead of the United Province of Canada.

An election was held and the Reform Party, led by J.B. Uniacke and Joseph Howe, won a majority in the Legislative Assembly. The governor of Nova Scotia had been instructed by Britain to choose the Executive Council members from the largest political party in the Legislative Assembly. The governor asked Uniacke to choose them.

Uniacke selected members of the Reform Party. This meant that the Executive Council, now called the **Cabinet**, was made up of men from the group with the most elected members in the Assembly. If the Executive Council did not keep the confidence of the Legislative Assembly, several choices existed. The government could resign or add and drop members to gain enough support in the Legislative Assembly. Or, they could request that the governor call an election. The governor might do so, or call on opposition party leaders to form a new government. Regardless, the Executive Council was responsible to the members of the Legislative Assembly, and therefore, to the voters.

This painting by C.W. Jefferys shows Joseph Howe being carried out of the courtroom by a cheering throng after his 1835 libel case.

Joseph Howe (1804–1873)

Joseph Howe was a colourful politician with a reputation for good **oratory**.

He started work as an apprentice printer in his father's shop at the age of 13. At 24, he bought his own newspaper, the *Novascotian,* and used it to support changes in the government. In 1835 Howe was charged with **libel** after a verbal attack on the Halifax judges. Howe chose to defend himself in court. He gave a six-hour speech to the jury, describing many injustices and pleading for freedom of the press. The jury decided that Howe was not guilty. The victory celebration lasted for two days.

Howe was elected to the Legislative Assembly of Nova Scotia as a Reform candidate in 1836.

---

*Lord Elgin, the Governor, was instructed to permit responsible government in 1847. This was not tested and established until 1849 with the passing of the Rebellion Losses Act (see page 223).

Cabinet—Executive Council chosen from members of the party with the majority in the Legislative Assembly

Oratory—the art of public speaking

Libel—a printed statement or picture that unjustly injures a person's reputation

In Prince Edward Island

In Prince Edward Island, two thirds of the land was owned by absentee landlords who lived in Great Britain or by a few wealthy people in the Atlantic colonies.

In 1832 a land reform party was formed. It won 18 of 24 seats in the Legislative Assembly in the 1838 election. The land reform party tried to bring in new laws which would allow the Legislative Assembly to seize certain lands and tax undeveloped land. They were stopped by the Legislative Council and the British government.

Members of the Legislative Assembly petitioned Britain for responsible government. They declared that until it was granted they would not pass any bills or vote for the money needed to run the government. After a lengthy process of negotiation, Great Britain granted Prince Edward Island responsible government in 1851.

Charlottetown, Prince Edward Island, 1832

In New Brunswick

New Brunswick also had land issues involving the government. Thomas Baillie was one of the owners of the Nova Scotia Land Company. He was also the **Commissioner** of **Crown Lands** and a friend of the Lieutenant-Governor, Sir Archibald Campbell. It was a concern that Baillie, a government official in charge of public lands, might not act in the best interests of the public if he had his own land and profits in mind.

There were rumours that the Lieutenant-Governor's aides were using information they had gained from working with the Lieutenant-Governor. This was seen as an unfair advantage in business and land dealings. People also felt it was unfair that Thomas Baillie was appointed to the new Executive Council, established in 1832.

Colonists began to share their concerns. A Committee of **Grievances** was created. In 1837, the British government granted the Legislative Assembly control of crown

---

Commissioner—a government official who is in charge of a government department
Crown land—land held by the government to be used as it saw fit
Grievance—complaint

lands and the responsibility of managing government money. The Lieutenant-Governor began to choose more members from the Legislative Assembly for the Executive and Legislative Councils. By the late 1840s, all members were being chosen from the Legislative Assembly. These step-by-step changes led to responsible government, officially granted in 1854.

A sawmill in New Brunswick, 1835

In Newfoundland

Political development in Newfoundland occurred more slowly than in the other Atlantic colonies. Great Britain thought of Newfoundland as a source of fish for Britain, rather than a colony like the others. The commander of the British naval squadron acted as the governor. He arrived in the spring with the fishing fleet and returned to Britain with the fleet in the autumn.

It was difficult to travel from the isolated communities to the one city of St. John's. People did not have many opportunities to discuss political matters. However, the people of the colony began to ask for an election. A full-time governor was not appointed until 1817. The colony did not have its first elected Legislative Assembly or Legislative Council until 1832. Newfoundland received responsible government in 1855.

St. John's Newfoundland, 1831

The Underground Railway

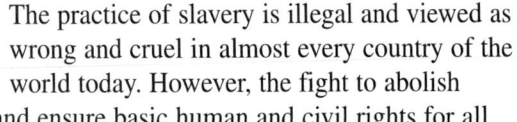

Opposition to Slavery

The practice of slavery is illegal and viewed as wrong and cruel in almost every country of the world today. However, the fight to abolish slavery and ensure basic human and civil rights for all people has been a long and difficult process.

During the 1600s, thousands of people were brought from Africa and the West Indies as labourers for the settlers of the various colonies of North America. Slavery was found throughout the colonies in what is now the United States and Canada. The greatest numbers of slaves were found in the south, where the plantations required large work forces (see page 125). Up to 30 000 slaves were concentrated in that area.

Working and living conditions for slaves varied. Many were mistreated and abused, although there were exceptions. However, all slaves lacked the rights and freedoms that many people take for granted today.

For many slaves, the colonies of British North America were seen as a **refuge**. Many Loyalists migrating north from the Thirteen Colonies brought their slaves with them, and a large number of free Black people also moved there (see page 140). Upper Canada was the first colony to abolish slavery. Lieutenant-Governor Simcoe proposed a bill to gradually end slavery which passed, with some opposition, in 1793.

Some people in the United States who disagreed with slavery tried to abolish it. Others worked just as hard to maintain it. Because slaves were considered to be the property of another person by law, they usually had to escape if they wanted their freedom. Those who assisted them faced fines or imprisonment. Slaves who had been granted their freedom by their owners had to carry papers to prove to others that they were not escaped slaves.

Refuge—place of safety; place to escape from danger

The Routes to Freedom

Many who chose to escape and were able to attempt it, turned to the Underground Railway. It was not a railroad, or even an organization, but a series of routes, workers, and destinations. It was called "underground" because it had to be kept a secret from authorities and "slave catchers."

Word about the routes to freedom and people who would help managed to reach those who were seeking to escape through pamphlets, secret messages, and picture messages for those who couldn't read.

In 1833, Britain ended slavery by law in its colonies, including those in British North America. Slavery was still legal in the United States because it was no longer a colony of Britain. Despite the risks faced by those escaping or those who assisted escaping slaves, the "tracks" or pathways to British North America were well travelled (see map on right).*

"Conductors" included free Black people, former slaves, and **abolitionists** (both White and Black) from all walks of life. Harriet Tubman, who had been abused as a slave, escaped to British North America. Over the next decade, with St. Catharines as her main terminal, she returned to the United States many times to help as many as 300 slaves to freedom. Keeping the operation secret often involved travelling in the dark and in disguise. **Fugitives** walked great distances, or hid on boats, wagons, and trains. "Agents" allowed them to hide in their "stations" —that is, in their homes, cellars, churches, or barns.

Various overland and water routes were taken. "Terminals" included such destinations as Amherstburg, Windsor, Hamilton, Toronto, Kingston, Montreal, St. John, and Halifax. One estimate suggests that over 15 000 escaped slaves reached the colonies of British North America by 1850. A Fugitive Slave Law was passed in the United States in 1850. This gave slave owners the legal right to chase and capture their slaves throughout the United States, including states where slavery was not allowed. Slaves seeking freedom and abolitionists increased their efforts. In total, between 30 000 and 40 000 Black

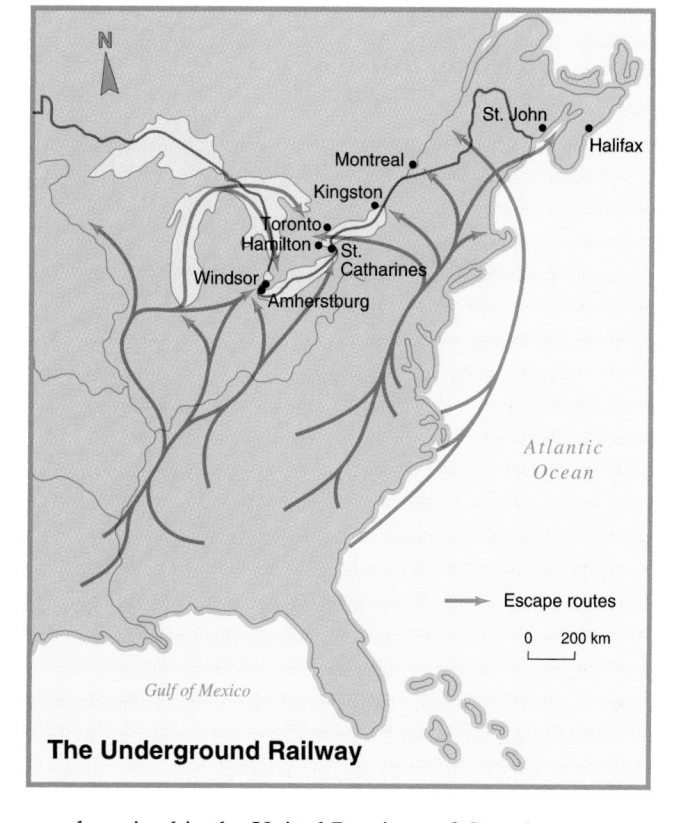

The Underground Railway

people arrived in the United Province of Canada.

A New Life

Once in the United Province of Canada, former slaves faced hardships and adjustments. They were in a new country, with few possessions. The northern climates were colder. They needed homes and jobs. Many had been separated from family and friends. They were not always welcomed or treated well in the communities when they arrived. Over one-half eventually chose to return to the United States; thousands stayed to build new lives.

From 1861 to 1865 the northern and southern states were involved in a Civil War. One of the issues behind the conflict was slavery. In 1863, President Abraham Lincoln signed the **Emancipation** Proclamation which legally ended slavery in some parts of the United States. The 13th Amendment to the American Constitution in 1865 freed all of the remaining slaves.

Harriet Tubman (on the far left) posed with some of the many she helped to escape slavery.

*The escape routes on the map show some general trends as well as some specific destinations.
Abolitionists—those who wished to end slavery
Fugitive—a runaway; a person who is fleeing
Emancipation—freeing from slavery

Review

The icons are your cue to turn to the Learning How to Learn Appendix (pages 256–271) for ideas on how to complete these activities.

 This icon is a reminder to turn to the Research Model (pages x–xi).

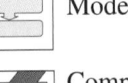 Complete a self-assessment for one assignment from this chapter.

Understanding Concepts

Checking Predictions

1. 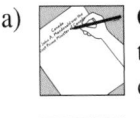 At the beginning of the chapter, using what you already knew and your chapter preview, you made predictions. Now, use what you have learned from studying this chapter. Which items did you correctly predict? Did you use a new prediction strategy? If so, how effective was it for you? Record your ideas in the Learning Tools section of your notebook and share your strategy ideas with a partner.

2. Discuss the following questions by referring to the Section V story on pages 182 and 183. Answer these questions in light of the information you have gained from Chapters 7 and 8.
   a) In what two ways did the Students' Council become more like a responsible government?
   b) Did the Students' Council have more power before or after it became like a responsible government?
   c) Who lost some power when the Students' Council became more like a responsible government?

3. The title of Section V is "Conflict and Change."
   a) Provide examples from Chapters 7 and 8 to show why this title was chosen.
   b) What other titles might you give the Section V story? Share your title ideas with the class.

4. Refer back to the story "Conflict and Change" (pages 182–183) and the diagram of responsible government on page 224. Decide which participants in the story match the participants in the government diagram. For example, which member(s) of government in the diagram does Mrs. Cherniak represent? What other matches can you identify?

5. Recall the four main concepts (power, co-operation, conflict, and decision-making). Show how these apply throughout this chapter of Canadian history. Create a poster or visual display that represents all four concepts.

Recording Vocabulary

6. 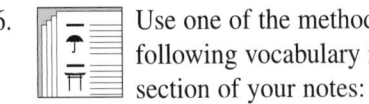 Use one of the methods for recording the following vocabulary in the WordBook section of your notes:
   - radical policy
   - political deadlock
   - political party
   - annexation
   - Underground Railway
   - responsible government

Conceptualizing

7. Here are some of the main ideas from this chapter:
   - Lord Durham's Report
   - The Act of Union, 1841
   - Rebellion Losses Bill
   - political parties
   - obtaining responsible government in the Province of Canada and the Atlantic colonies
   - political deadlock
   - emergence of new towns
   - transportation—canals and railway
   - education
   - emancipation

   Do either a) or b)

   a) 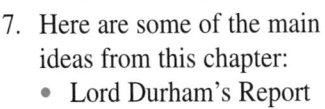 Create a concept poster about one of these ideas. Present your poster to the class.

   b) 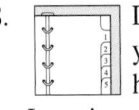 Use a web, mind map, outline, or chart to create a permanent set of notes about one of the ideas. Explain your work to a classmate.

Working with Information

8. 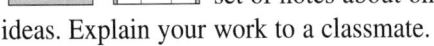 Discuss with your class the various methods you use to review what you have learned in history. Record your ideas in the Tools of Learning section of your notebook.

9. Why are some of the members of the Legislative Assembly and the Executive Council outlined in pink in the responsible government diagram on page 224?

10. On page 223, you studied how people reacted after Lord Elgin signed the Rebellion Losses Bill.
   a) Why do you think people reacted in these ways?
   b) What other ways of responding to Lord Elgin's decision were available to them?

c) How do you think the governor and members of the Legislative Assembly felt?

d) Do you think their actions were fair and reasonable?

e) 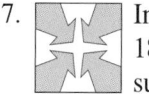 How do you think you would have responded to Lord Elgin's decision had you lived in Upper or Lower Canada? Why? Record your response in the History Journal section of your notebook.

11.  Add up to ten entries for this chapter to your timeline.

12. 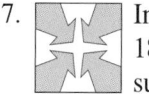 Compare your notes with those of a partner. Check to see that all items are covered and in the correct order. Organize your notes.

Developing Research Skills

13.  Complete your class project "Passport to the Past." Choose from the list of people on page 20.

Developing Communication Skills

Reading

14. Read "After the Rebellions" on pages 225 to 228.

a) With a partner, retell the story using your own words.

b) Could this story really have happened? Explain.

Writing

15. 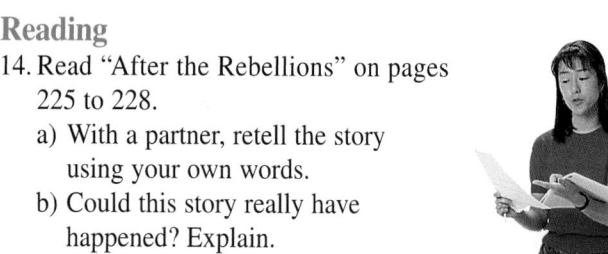 In his report, Lord Durham wrote: *I expected to find a contest between a government and people: I found two nations warring in the bosom of a single state: I found a struggle, not of principles, but of races...*

Record the following in your History Journal.

a) Paraphrase Lord Durham's statement.

b) How did Lord Durham attempt to end the problems in Upper and Lower Canada? Explain your answer.

c) Under "Exploring Further" on page 209 of Chapter 7, you were asked to recommend possible solutions for the unrest in Upper and Lower Canada following the rebellions. Were your suggestions similar to/different from Lord Durham's ideas (shown on

page 221)? Have your ideas changed since the end of Chapter 7? Why?

16.  Refer to "After the Rebellions" on pages 225 to 228. Choose a) or b).

a) Rewrite the story from Peter's point of view.

b) Write the next chapter to this story.

17.  Imagine that you are living in Canada in 1840. Write a letter to the government, supporting either further road construction or canal construction.

Listening and Speaking

18. A Political Forum

 Your teacher will divide your class into five groups. Four groups will each represent one of the four political parties that emerged in the late 1840s. The fifth group will represent the public. The goal of each political party is to present its beliefs and plans to the public in order to gain support. Your teacher will assist you in finding additional information about your political party or you can use the information on the chart on page 229.

a) **Political Parties Prepare**

• Discuss what you know about your party's beliefs. Choose a recorder to list these ideas in point form.

• 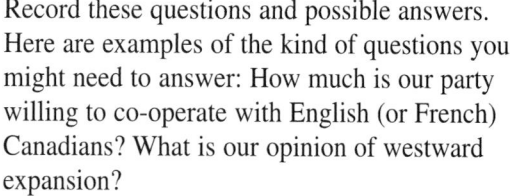 Brainstorm other points you need to know in order to have your leader participate effectively in this forum. Record these questions and possible answers. Here are examples of the kind of questions you might need to answer: How much is our party willing to co-operate with English (or French) Canadians? What is our opinion of westward expansion?

• 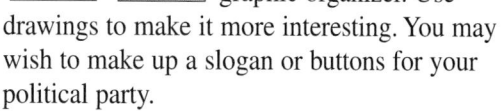 Record your political platform on a wall chart or graphic organizer. Use drawings to make it more interesting. You may wish to make up a slogan or buttons for your political party.

• Choose a party leader from the members of your group. Help your leader to practise answering the questions you prepared earlier. Make suggestions for improvements.

Political forum—a gathering during which representatives of political parties discuss their ideas and answer questions posed by the public

b) **The Public Prepares**
 - Review information about each political party. Consider issues and concerns of the public from various points of view (e.g., British, French, Native). Brainstorm to create a list of questions to ask the political parties. Choose the most important questions to ask each party.

c) **Present the Forum**
 - Choose a moderator from the class. During the forum, each party leader will have a chance to respond to each of the questions asked by the public. At the end of the question period, each leader should give a brief response to the other leaders' statements. Decide on time limits for the responses. Carry out the forum.

d) **Debrief**
 - As a class, discuss and assess the forum.

Viewing and Representing

19. Each student in your class will be assigned a heading or subheading from the chapter. You and your classmates should then organize yourselves into a "human outline" of the chapter. Each person should tell three facts that relate to his or her heading.

20. Create a political cartoon that presents a point of view about the Rebellion Losses Bill.

21. Many slaves and abolitionists risked their lives on the Underground Railway. What values did each group hold that led them to do so? Create a visual to represent these values.

Applying Concepts

22. Create your own political party.
 a) Decide what your platform is. What does your party hope to promote and achieve? How?
 b) Create a billboard promoting your party.

23. In the last chapter, you and your classmates listed the various ways that people

in Canadian history have resolved conflicts. Discuss and update your lists, using what you have learned in Chapter 8. Record answers to the following questions in your History Journal.
 a) How are conflicts sometimes resolved between teams during sporting events? In schools? Between neighbours? Between countries? How is this the same as, and different from, the methods used in Canadian history?
 b) Think of an example of a conflict. This may be real or you may make up an example. What nonviolent method of resolving this conflict would you recommend for this situation? What are the possible advantages or disadvantages of this approach?

24. 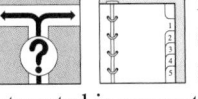 Imagine that you are a member of a local community group for students your age. Your group is interested in promoting positive change in your group and in your community. You and your group have identified areas for possible change:
 - increasing club membership
 - selecting new recreational activities to participate in
 - taking part in fundraising activities
 - promoting community spirit
 - increasing public awareness of the positive contributions of students in your community

In small groups, discuss how you might go about promoting change in one or more of the cases listed above. Share your ideas with the class. Could methods used in Canadian history apply here? What are the advantages and disadvantages of the various methods selected? Record your ideas in the Tools of Learning section of your notebook.

25. Review the information about transportation (e.g., canals and railway) discussed in this chapter.
 a) What were the advantages and disadvantages of transportation systems during this period in history?
 b) How has transportation changed since then?

26. Members of the Legislative Assembly of Prince Edward Island felt petitions were having no effect in their efforts to win responsible government.
 a) What did they do?
 b) Was this a violent or non-violent form of protest?
 c) Think of examples of similar types of protest?
 d) Is this type of protest "harmless"? Explain, using examples.

27.  Try to think of as many ideas as you can for each of the following. Record your responses in the History Journal section of your notebook.

What if...
a) Upper and Lower Canada had not been joined in the Act of Union, 1841?
b) Lord Elgin had not signed the Rebellion Losses Bill?
c) Canada had never achieved responsible government?

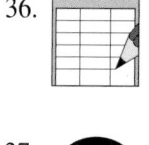

28. Why have you been studying
- political deadlock?
- responsible government?
- the Underground Railway?

29. Complete each statement with a paragraph entry.

a) History Journal: I discovered that...is similar to/different from today.
b) Tools of Learning: My areas of strength are... On future projects I will...

Challenge Plus

30. You have learned that in the 1840s, Britain's attitude toward its colonies changed. Research Canada's relationship and role with the British monarchy since that time. How has it changed over time? What are the effects of these changes?

31. With a partner, create a Venn Diagram to compare representative and responsible governments.

32. Research the historical development of schooling in Canada. Demonstrate to your classmates what schooling was like in the 1800s. Create an interesting lesson, which requires their participation. Also, use the new learning ideas you have gathered while studying Canadian history.

33. Research one of the political parties that exists today. What ideas does it promote? Do you agree or disagree with these ideas? Is it related to any of the parties you learned about in this chapter? How?

34. Read recent editions of your local newspaper(s).
a) What government bills are currently being proposed or passed?
b) What political parties are in the news? What values and beliefs do their current activities suggest?

35. Create a diagram (with visuals and words) to show the many people and events leading to responsible government.

36. Research more to find about the structure of Canadian government today.* Create a chart to compare this to the government structure in 1841.

37. Complete your website or magazine assignment for Section V.

Canada Revisited

The Rideau Canal, completed in 1832, is still in use today.

*Visit the Government of Canada website to find out more at http://canada.gc.ca

In Conclusion

Creating a Bulletin Board

Your study of Canadian history has been divided into five sections: Connecting to Prior Learning (First People and European Explorers), European Colonization, Colonial Government (New France), British North America, and Conflict and Change. To these topics, you have applied four social studies concepts: Power, Co-operation, Decision-making, and Conflict. To review what you have learned, work with your classmates to create a Canadian history bulletin board display.

As a class, discuss what contributes to a meaningful and appealing bulletin board display. Discuss assessment criteria. Keep these ideas in mind as you prepare your part of the display.

Part 1: Prepare to Share

1. You will be assigned one of the four concepts.
2.  Individually, brainstorm for examples from Canadian history that relate to your concept. Think about people, places, events, and ideas. Use the questions on the easel shown on this page as a guide. Write down as many examples as you can.
3. Look through your notebook and the textbook to add to your list of examples.

Part 2: Plan with Your Concept Group

1. Share ideas with students who are working with the same concept. Add new ideas to your list.
2. Brainstorm with the group for effective ways to present these ideas on the bulletin board. Record your ideas.
3. Decide which examples of the concept you wish to display. Who will create the visual/written representation for each example?

4. Decide what materials are needed. Plan a layout. Where will items will be placed and how much space is available?
5. Set completion deadlines. When will you assemble all the parts on the bulletin board? How much time will be needed to do so?

Part 3: Create Your Display

Part 4: Present Your Concept

1. With your Concept Group, discuss how each example on your display represents your concept.
2. Decide how you will explain your display to the class. Practise presenting and answering questions.
3. Tell your classmates about your display.

Part 5: Connect It All Together

1. Discuss how you can apply what you have learned to your lives. Individually, write a paragraph summarizing your ideas in the History Journal Section of your notebook.

Social Studies Concepts

Power: Who held the power? How did this change over time? What impact did power holders have on people and events at the time?

Co-operation: What groups co-operated with each other? How did they show their co-operation? How did co-operation influence people and events?

Decision-making: What types of decision-making were used by government? How did one form of decision-making lead to the next? What impacts did each type of decision-making have on people and events?

Conflict: Who was in conflict? Which methods of conflict resolution were used throughout history? How did each method affect people and events?

246

More Connections

The Passport Tour students and Ms. Ito gathered for a final meeting before returning home. They exchanged addresses and phone numbers and posed for last minute pictures.

"I can't believe we're all going back to different schools. We have to keep in touch!" Brenda tucked her address book into her backpack.

"There are no excuses. After all, we're pretty good at 'making connections' now," Ken pointed out. "I'd never have believed it was possible, but we have actually 'revisited' Canadian history. We've even been 'introduced' to individuals from Canada's past."

Erin looked up from her History Journal. "Now I can see how historical events were often a direct result of people's decisions and actions."

"Those decisions and events really had an impact on the people and their lives," Dakota paused. "And, in many ways, on us," he finished.

Ms. Ito nodded, "Just like our decisions can have an impact on our own lives, and other people and events..."

Roberto finished the thought, "And the future."

Brenda smiled, "All this time, I thought we were studying history! I guess it is fair to say there are connections between then and now, *and* tomorrow."

"All I know about tomorrow is that we will be back to our familiar routines," said Dakota. "You know, Ms. Ito, we're supposed to learn more history next year at school. Why don't we just continue revisiting the past on our Passport Tour?"

The students, all grinning, looked at Ms. Ito.

"Although we are at the end of our tour and I will miss you all and our wonderful adventures revisiting the past, you might be interested to know that there is a program that offers a unique way to study 1850 to 1920," answered Ms. Ito.

The group crowded around her, asking questions all at once...

Glossary

The definitions given in the glossary reflect the specific ways the words are used in this text. Some words have alternative meanings.

A

Abolish—legally end

Abolitionists—those who wished to end slavery

Aboriginal—being the first in a region

Absentee landlord—a landowner who takes an income from his land but does not live there

Absolute Monarch—a leader who has unlimited power over his or her people; a king or queen whose power is not limited or restricted by a set of rules (constitution), parliament, or by groups (such as an aristocracy)

Acadia—included present-day Nova Scotia, Prince Edward Island, and parts of New Brunswick and Quebec

Acadian—a person living in the early French settlements in the Atlantic area of Upper North America (See map on page 40)

Act—a legislative decision; law

Act of Union, 1841—acting on Lord Durham's recommendations, the British government joined Upper and Lower Canada together as the United Province of Canada. The aim was to unite the two colonies and give the English-speaking people control of the new colony.

Administrator—person in charge; official; manager

Advertising—provide information to others orally or in written and visual forms to persuade them to act (e.g., convince someone to buy a product)

Allegiance—loyalty

Alliance—union formed between nations or groups of people based on an agreement that benefits those in the union

Amnesty—to be pardoned or excused by government for past offences against the government

Analyse—to separate a whole into parts and examine the parts

Ancestor—a person from whom one is descended

Annex—to join together

Annexation—joining of one territory to a larger political entity

Anthropology—study of customs, beliefs, and ways of life of different groups of people

Apprentice—a person who works with a skilled craftsperson in order to learn that craft

Archives—a place where historical documents and records are kept

Aristocracy—the ruling class; the nobles of a country

Armoury—a place where weapons are kept

Artisan—worker very skilled in his or her craft

Assembly—an elected group that proposed bills. The Legislative Assembly had little power before Responsible Government, as the governor or Legislative Council could veto its decisions.

Assessment—the act of evaluating or examining work or performance carefully to check achievement level

Assimilation—the process through which one culture is absorbed into another

B

Bastion—section of the fort that extends out to give a better view and aid defence

Bias—a preference which makes a fair judgement difficult; slanting or distorting something (See Appendix page 256)

Biculturalism—two cultures existing side by side in the same country or province

Bill—a proposed law to be debated and voted on. When it becomes law it is called an Act.

Biography—written information about a person's life

Block system of holding land—subdividing land into blocks or squares; also called the square system

Blockade—close off; usually done to a harbour or port in wartime to prevent supplies from reaching their destination

Boycott—refusal to trade with a country or company or to buy its products

Brigade—group of canoes, carts, or dogsleds carrying trade goods and supplies to and from inland posts

British—*see* Great Britain

British Empire—all of the colonies and countries under Great Britain's rule

C

Cabinet—Executive Council chosen from members of the party with the majority in the Legislative Assembly

Canada East—former name for Quebec; previously called Lower Canada

Canada West—former name for Ontario; previously called Upper Canada

Canadiens—French-speaking people born in New France (Quebec); the Canadiens were distinct from the French in Europe.

Cash crop—a crop grown for sale rather than subsistence

Caste system—social system with distinct classes based on differences of birth, rank, position, or wealth

Census—an official count of the people of a country or district to find out the number of people living there

Charter—written permission given by someone in authority who grants privileges

Château Clique—group favouring the British system of government in Lower Canada, composed of men of British background or wealthy French Canadians

Chronological—events in order according to when they happened

Civil law—having to do with private rights of citizens, especially property disputes

Clan—a group of related families that claim to be descended from common ancestors

Clergy reserve—one-seventh of all public land in Upper Canada was set aside for Protestant schools and churches by the Constitutional Act of 1791

Coalition government—temporary joining of political parties to have a majority and be able to form a government

Colonization—settling and controlling new lands

Colony—a new land settled and controlled by citizens of a distant country

Commissioner—a government official who is in charge of a government department

Community—people together in the same general area (e.g., school, town, district)

Community government—a form of local government in the Thirteen Colonies that was also called a town meeting; all free adult males could take part in the decision-making process.

Competition—behaviour in which one tries to do better than another

Compromise—an agreement in which each side gives up some of its demands

Compulsory—required

Concept—a general idea or thought (e.g., colonization, nationhood)

Conceptualize—think about and develop an understanding about ideas or things

Concession—giving up something in order to achieve something

Confederacy—people joined for a common purpose; an alliance

Confederation—the federal union of British North American colonies; the members retained some power over their own affairs and turned some powers over to a central government.

Confiscated—property taken away by someone in authority, usually by a government

Congress—elected members of the Senate and House of Representatives of the United States of America

Consensus—general agreement among all people consulted

Conservative traditions—customs, opinions, and habits that are cautious and opposed to change

Constitutional Act, 1791—Act giving the people of Upper and Lower Canada their own Legislative Assemblies and, as a result, representative government. The aim was to recognize the bicultural nature of British North America by dividing it into the two colonies of Upper and Lower Canada.

Controversial—having several sides or differences; open for dispute or debate

Convert—change someone's religious beliefs to one's own

Corvée—free labour that the habitants owed their seigneurs. In France, this often meant repairing roads at times the habitants should have been farming for themselves. In New France, the habitants spent little time on *corvée* as the St. Lawrence River served as the colony's main road.

Coureurs de bois—French woodsmen, who travelled to the interior for furs; adventurers, expert canoeists, and skilled businessmen

Criteria—standards by which something is judged or categorized

Crown land—land held by the government to be used as it saw fit

Crown reserve—one-seventh of all public land in Upper Canada, set aside for the British government by the Constitutional Act of 1791. By 1825 these lands were sold because they prevented compact settlement, making it difficult to complete roads.

Cultural exchange—objects or ideas passed from one culture to another

Culture—the way of life of a specific group of people; the language, religion, traditions, music, art, and literature of a people

D

Debate—discuss or argue about two sides of an issue

Deed—a document legally granting someone ownership

Demand—want or need for goods and services

Deport—to remove or move away; to force people away from their homes or a country by government order

Development—process or steps to bring about change; e.g., development of natural resources may include extracting them so they can be used for manufacturing products

Dispersed—went in various directions; scattered

Diversity—variety; differences

Dowry—money or property that a woman brings with her into marriage, usually supplied by her father. In the case of "King's Daughters" from France, the state provided it.

Drainage—process of water flowing away

Durham Report—report completed by Lord Durham following the Rebellions in Upper and Lower Canada in 1837. Two major recommendations to the British government were to unite Upper and Lower Canada and to allow the united colony responsible government.

E

Eastern Townships—triangle of land in Lower Canada between the St. Lawrence River and the American border

Economic—having to do with business, expenses, trade, wealth, exchange, and use of material goods

Ecosystem—the system formed by the interaction of all living things in a particular environment with one another and their environment

Elite—special group, usually more educated or richer than others

Emancipation—freeing from slavery

Emigrate—leave one's own country or region to settle in another

Entrepreneur—a business person who invests in a business, hoping for a profit, but risking a loss

Epidemic—disease quickly spreading among many people

Ethnocentric—having a belief that one's own culture is better than everyone else's

Eurocentric—viewing events and issues from the point of view of somone with a European or Euro-Canadian cultural background

Evaluate—assess what something is worth; decide what is best or important; appraise, criticize, rate, defend, or grade

Examine—to look at something very carefully

Excerpt—a piece of writing selected from a larger work; a quotation

Exchequer—a department responsible for the government's finances

Exile—to officially order someone to leave the country

Exploitation—taking advantage or making use of a person or a resource. Unfairness or selfishness is usually implied.

Exploration—seeking new lands and new routes

Export—to sell goods to other countries (or colonies)

Expulsion—being forced to leave; deportation

F

Family Compact—a small group of powerful people in Upper Canada who were loyal to the British system of government; also known as Tories

Fatally—to death

Federalism—a political system in which the provinces or states have certain powers over their own affairs, and certain powers are turned over to a central government

First Nations—includes Native people, the Inuit, and the Metis

First People—includes Native people, the Inuit, and the Metis

Footnote—information at the bottom of the page relating to the text above

Free trade—trade between countries where taxes or tariffs are not involved

Freehold system—to hold the deed or title to a piece of land, with the right to buy, sell, or pass it on to one's heirs

Fugitive—a runaway; a person who is fleeing

Future prospects—expected gains (e.g., profits)

G

Graphic organizer—visual method of arranging information in an orderly way (e.g., diagram, table, chart, graph)

Great Britain—In 1707, with the Act of Union, England and Scotland officially took the name Great Britain.

Grievance—complaint

Grist mill—mill where grain was ground into flour; located on rivers because they were powered by running water

Guerrilla warfare—fighting in small bands, making sudden attacks and ambushes on the enemy

H

Habitant—farmer in New France, and later in Quebec

Habitation—place to live

Hypothesis—a guess about the solution to a problem based upon what you know

I

Icon—a visual representation

Illiterate— able to read or write at a low level of skill or not at all

Immigrant—person who comes to live in a new country

Immigrate—to move to another country to live

Imperial—referring to the monarchy or the empire

Import—to bring goods into a country (or colony)

Independent—acting without help or influence of others

Industry—a business of collecting or manufacturing raw materials, or providing services

Institution—organization or association established for some public or social purpose (e.g., the Church, the family, and the educational system)

Interaction—relationship or involvement between people or groups

Intervention—involvement that is meant to assist or protect

Investment capital—money lent or shares purchased so that businesses have money to fund their day-to-day operations

Isolation—being separated or kept apart

Issue—a problem or question for debate that often does not have one answer; often written as a question using the word "should"

JK

Jesuit—member of a religious order of the Roman Catholic Church

King's Daughters—women who came at the French king's expense to New France to marry and settle there

Kinship—having some of the same ancestors or being related by marriage

L

Landholding—owning or occupying land

Legislative Assembly—a group of representatives elected to the Legislature to represent the people of a colony or province

Libel—a printed statement or picture that unjustly injures a person's reputation

Lineage—a person's descent or place in a line of ancestors

Literate—able to read and write

Lobby—to represent a special interest to the government. A lobbyist tries to get lawmakers to introduce or vote for measures favourable to the lobbyist's interest.

Lower Canada—the southeastern portion of Quebec in 1791 ("down" the St. Lawrence River)

Loyalists—people living in the Thirteen Colonies who remained loyal to Britain, many of whom eventually came to British North America; referred to as Tories

M

Magistrate—judge of a local court

Majority government—the party that receives the most seats in the House of Commons governs the country

Manifesto—a public declaration of intentions by an important group of people

Manufacture—to make raw materials into finished goods

Market—an environment or place where trade, buying, and selling take place

Matrilineal—tracing descent through the mother's side of the family

Mercantilism—an economic theory that called for a country to accumulate wealth in gold and silver

Merchant—business person who buys and sells goods for profit

Metis—people of mixed Native and European ancestry

Migration—movement from place to place, often according to the season

Military rule—government run by the army

Militia—citizens who were not regular soldiers but who underwent training for emergency duty or local defence

Minority government—government that does not have a majority of Members of Parliament

Minutemen—armed men ready to fight at a moment's notice

Mire—mud; wet, soggy ground

Missionary—bringing one's religious teachings to others who do not share them

Moderate—a person who does not hold extreme opinions

Moderator—a person who directs a formal debate

Monarchy—a government ruled by a king or queen

Monopoly—a right granted for one person or group to control buying and selling

Mortar—a cement-like mixture used to hold bricks, stones, or timber together

Mother country—the country where one was born; a country in relation to its colonies

Multicultural nation—one that has people from many different cultural backgrounds

N

Nation—people who live in a certain area, speak the same language, have the same way of life, have the same system of decision-making (government), and usually belong to the same group

Native peoples—includes all Aboriginal peoples (Indians, Inuit, Metis) in Canada. In this book, Native peoples may also be called First People, First Nations, or Aboriginal People.

New France—area along the St. Lawrence River, in what is now Canada, which was colonized by France (See page 58)

Nobility—people with special rank and authority by virtue of birth or title, (e.g., duke, duchess, count, countess, *marquis*, *marquise*)

Nomadic—moving from place to place, usually according to the season, following migrations of game or seeking sources of food

Northwest Passage—a route for ships around the northern coast of North America leading from eastern North America to the Pacific Ocean

Notary—someone trained in the law, but who could not plead cases in court

Nutrient—food for plants or animals; minerals in the soil that provide food and nourishment for plants

O

Oath of allegiance—a promise of loyalty to a country and/or ruler

Occupation—the control of an area by a foreign military force

Opportunist—a person who takes advantage of a situation for his or her own benefit

Opposition—the political party or parties represented in the Legislature but not in power

Oppression—loss of one's freedom; having little power

Oratory—the art of public speaking

Overview—a brief look over or survey

P

Palisade—high fence built of pointed stakes

Paraphrase—to express the meaning of a book, a passage, or a set of words in different words

Parish—district that is the responsibility of a particular church

Parish system—the system of districts having their own churches

Parliament—the law-making body of government

Parti Canadien—people in Lower Canada who supported many traditional Canadien values, practices, and institutions, but also promoted changes to achieve a more democratic form of government; mostly French people; later called Parti Patriote

Parti Patriote—the name for Parti Canadien after 1826

Participatory democracy—when people take part in decision-making

Partnership—co-operating and working together for a shared goal

Patrilineal—tracing descent through the father's side of the family

Patriote—person in Lower Canada who favoured many traditional Canadien ways and also reform to government (See also Parti Canadien)

Patriots—colonists in the Thirteen Colonies who rebelled against British rule; also known as rebels

Pemmican—a food made from buffalo meat, buffalo fat, and berries

Peoples—when more than one group or nation is involved

Persecution—when a person or group is repeatedly mistreated or harmed, often for political, religious, or cultural reasons

Petition—a formal request to a government or authority by a group of people, for a specific action

Plantations—large farms where crops are grown

Platform—the principles and policies of a political party; what the political party feels is important, and what they believe in

Point of view—the way an individual looks at situations and issues; based upon attitudes, beliefs, customs, traditions, goals

Political—providing direction, order, and security to meet group needs

Political deadlock—when government decisions (such as the passing of a bill) cannot be made

Political forum—a gathering during which representatives of political parties discuss their ideas and answer questions posed by the public

Political party—a group of people with similar beliefs about government, who work together to get their candidates elected as representatives

Political reform—changes to make the government better

Poll—voting; results of voting

Potash—grey ash left after trees had been burned. The ash was boiled in a pot until no water was left (also called "pearl ash" in Upper Canada). Potash was sold for making soap and cosmetics.

Prediction—to think about and/or state ideas and events you believe will occur

Pre-history—before events were recorded or written down

Presentation—communication of information in visual, oral, or written forms

Primary source—an account of an historical event by someone who witnessed it or lived during the time of the event; historical evidence from the time (See Appendix page 269)

Priorities—items ranked according to a certain criterion

Privateer—privately owned and staffed armed ship

Proclamation—a formal announcement issued to the public by the government

Proclamation of 1763—a statement issued by the British government to outline what was to be done in Quebec. The aim was to make Quebec British through assimilation. (Also called the Royal Proclamation)

Profit—when more money is taken in than spent in the running of a business

Protest—to object in writing or through action

Provincial rights—the powers maintained by the provincial governments, usually involving cultural, social, and local issues

Puppet—leader who is not independent, who does what someone more powerful tells him or her to do

Q

Quebec Act, 1774—Act passed by the British government to keep the loyalty of Canadiens; aimed to preserve and strengthen the British Empire by allowing both the French and British ways of doing things

R

Radical—holding extreme opinions; wanting fundamental social, economic, and political changes

Radical policy—plan for extreme changes

Rank—position based on importance

Raw material—resource taken from the environment that may be manufactured into a product

Re-annex—to unite with a province or country again

Rebel—person who acts against the government; Patriots in the Thirteen Colonies who wanted to separate from British rule to form the United States of America; Patriotes in Lower Canada and Reformers in Upper Canada were also called "rebels."

Rebellion—a revolt or fight against the government

Rebellion Losses Bill—bill that proposed paying people of Canada East for property lost in the Rebellion of 1837. When Lord Elgin signed the bill, although he did not agree with it, responsible government was confirmed.

Reformers—group seeking change in government and society in Upper Canada

Refuge—place of safety; place to escape from danger

Refugee—person who leaves home or country to seek safety elsewhere

Representation by population—the number of elected members of a Legislative Assembly (the representatives), based on the number of voters (the population qualified to vote)

Representative government—citizens elect people who represent them in their Legislative Assembly (decision-making body). Every voter has a voice in government, but only a small group actually makes the decisions.

Resolution—formal statement of the way a person or group feels; usually written down and sent to one in a position of power and authority; may be followed as a guideline for ruling a group of people

Responsible government—Members of the Executive Council (today known as the Cabinet) are chosen by the governor from the group with the most elected members in the Legislative Assembly. The Cabinet is thus responsible to the representatives of the voters for its conduct of public business. If the Cabinet loses the confidence of the majority of the Legislative Assembly, it must resign. The government can function only if it has the support of the Legislature. It is responsible to the Legislature.

Revenue—income; money coming in

Revolution—a forceful takeover of government

Rivalry—competition

Royal Colony—a colony governed directly by a king or queen in another country

Rural—of, or related to, the countryside

S

Sachem—the appointed representative of an individual clan among certain Native peoples

Secondary sources—information resources created after the time period being studied; often created using primary source information (See Appendix page 269)

Seigneur—a person granted land by the French king to divide into lots and assign to habitants

Seigneurial system—the King of France granted land in New France to seigneurs with the expectation it would be divided into lots to be farmed by habitants; also involved a system of duties and responsibilities

Seigneury—land in New France granted to an individual to be divided into lots and farmed

Seminary—special school for the training of priests

Shaman—a Native spiritual leader

Slavery—a system whereby a person was owned and controlled by another. Slaves had no civil rights. They could be bought and sold as property. Families were often separated, and children of slaves were born into slavery. Many African people were captured and sold as slaves in North America and elsewhere.

Social—having to do with the way people relate to each other in relationships and communities

Social problems—problems concerning life in a community; problems between people that arise in day-to-day living

Sovereign Council—a group of officials appointed by the king of France to make and enforce laws in New France

Sovereign nation—a country that is independent of the control of other governments

Sovereignty—independence; freedom from control by another authority (or government)

Speculation—the act of buying or selling land, at some risk, with the hope of making large profits from future price changes

Statistics—information (facts) in number form (e.g., population)

Status quo—the way things are at the present time

Subsidy—a grant or contribution of money

Subsistence farmer—only grew enough food for the family; no surplus production to sell for cash to buy other products and supplies

Supply—goods and services that are available for use

Survey—to find out the exact boundaries of an area of land by measuring; to study to obtain information (e.g., using interviews or questionnaires)

La Survivance—refers to the French concern for preserving their distinctive culture, including the Roman Catholic religion, French language, and French civil law

Sympathetic—in agreement with

T

Tableau—participants represent a scene by taking positions and not moving. A tableau can be based on a picture, story, or idea.

Tariff—a tax paid to the government on goods brought into a country

Taxation without representation—being taxed without benefit of elected representatives to speak on your behalf

Technology—the knowledge and application of developments in science, manufacturing, business, and the arts

Thirteen Colonies—areas settled by the British along the east coast of what is now the United States

Tithe—originally, a tax of one-tenth of income or produce of one's land, paid to help support the work of the Church

Tories—those in Upper Canada who were loyal to the British system of government (Family Compact); Loyalists; today called Conservatives. A member of the Conservative Party in Great Britain is also called a Tory.

Trade—exchanging goods for money or other goods

Traditional—following customs handed down for a long time

Treason—betrayal of a country or ruler

Treaty—an official agreement between groups or nations

Treaty of Paris—there were two treaties by this name: the treaty of 1763 ended the Seven Years' War; the treaty of 1783 ended the American Revolution.

Tributaries—streams feeding larger streams

U

Underground Railway—an informal network of secret helpers and places of safety by which Black people were helped to escape slavery in the United States in the mid-1800s

Universal—for everybody

Upper Canada—Quebec was divided into two colonies in 1791. Upper Canada was "up" the St. Lawrence River; part of present-day Ontario

Urban—of, or related to, towns and cities

V

Value—a long-established idea on which one's life is modeled

Veto—the right or power to forbid or reject

Viewpoint—the way an individual looks at situations and issues; based upon attitudes, beliefs, customs, traditions, goals

Voyageur—a boatman or canoeman, usually French-speaking, who travelled inland for the early fur-trading companies

WXYZ

War—fighting between nations, groups, or regions within a nation

War Hawks—a group of young men in Congress who wanted war (War of 1812). They believed that the Americans could easily win a war if they invaded the colonies of British North America.

Winnow—to separate grain from chaff

Other Contributions

Text Acknowledgements

33 Excerpt from Carlotta Hacker, *The Book of Canadians*. Edmonton: Hurtig Publishers, 1983. Reprinted with permission.
38 Excerpt from Marie-Claire Daveluy, "Paul de Chomedey de Maisonneuve," in *Dictionary of Canadian Biography*, Vol. I, ed. George W. Brown. Toronto: University of Toronto Press, 1966. Reprinted with permission.
49 Excerpt from The Canadian Press, "321 years later, Bay quits fur trade," Toronto (January 1991). Reprinted with permission.
64 Information from *Historical Atlas of Canada: From Beginning to 1800* (Vol. I), ed. R. Cole Harris. Toronto: University of Toronto Press, 1987. Reprinted with permission.
73 Linda McDowell, *Ordinary People in Canada's Past Teacher Resource Package, Second Edition*. Edmonton: Arnold Publishing Ltd., 1991, 1997.
80 Excerpt from André Vachon, "Marie-Madeleine Jarret de Verchères," in *Dictionary of Canadian Biography*, Vol. III, ed. George W. Brown. Toronto: University of Toronto Press, 1966. Reprinted with permission.
99 Excerpt from "Defender of Acadia," in *Great Canadian Lives: Portraits in Heroism to 1867*, Karen Ford. Scarborough, ON: Nelson Canada, 1985. Reprinted with permission of ITP Nelson.
167 Excerpt from "The Bold Canadian: A Ballad of the War of 1812," from Ontario Historical Society Papers and Records, Volume 23, (1926), pp. 238–239. Reprinted with permission.
202 Excerpt from Catherine Parr Traill, *The Backwoods of Canada*. Toronto: McClelland and Stewart, c1989.
210 Information from G.M. Craig, ed., *Lord Durham's Report*. Toronto: McClelland and Stewart, 1963, pp. 118–119.
164, 210, 211 Excerpts from Dean Fink, *Life in Upper Canada, An Inquiry Approach: 1781–1841*, Curriculum Resource Book Series, ed. Mollie E. Cunningham. Toronto: McClelland & Stewart Ltd., 1971.
211 Excerpt from P.B. Waite (Ed.), *Pre-Confederation*. Canadian Historical Documents Series, Volume II. Scarborough, ON: Prentice-Hall, 1965.
211, 212 Excerpt from Susanna Moodie, *Roughing It in the Bush*. Toronto: McClelland and Stewart Inc., 1989.
212, 213 Excerpts from Colin Read and Ronald J. Stagg (Eds.), *The Rebellion of 1837 in Upper Canada: A Collection of Documents*. Ottawa: Carleton University Press, 1988. Reprinted with permission.
231, 232 Concept adapted from Charles Hou, *Selecting A Capital for Canada 1857*. Adapted with permission. Charles Hou, Burnaby South Secondary School, Burnaby, British Columbia.
231, 232 Excerpts from David B. Knight, *Choosing Canada's Capital: Jealousy and Friction in the 19th Century*. Toronto: McClelland & Stewart Inc., 1977. Reprinted with permission.

Picture Credits

The publisher gratefully acknowledges the assistance of the various public institutions, private firms, and individuals who provided material for use in this book. Every effort has been made to identify and credit all sources. The publisher would appreciate notification of any omissions or errors so that they may be corrected.

Legend

CLG—The Confederation Life Gallery of Canadian History
NAC—National Archives of Canada
NGC—National Gallery of Canada
MTRL—Metropolitan Toronto Reference Library
MMCH—McCord Museum of Canadian History
PA—Phyllis A. Arnold

t	top	mc	middle center
tl	top left	mr	middle right
tc	top center	b	bottom
tr	top right	bl	bottom left
m	middle	bc	bottom center
ml	middle left	br	bottom right

3 (1) Photo: Parks Canada/Shane Kelly/1996; (2) (3) (4) (5) PA **7** (9) *Jules (Ojibwa and Cree)*, by Carl D. Fontaine **8** (11) Corel Corporation Ottawa, Ontario, Canada (This publication includes images from *Corel Gallery 2* which are protected by the copyright laws of the U.S., Canada, and elsewhere. Used under license.); (12) PA **10** (21) Based on C.W. Jefferys/NAC/C-069767 **14** (1) *The Vikings*, Dennis Rose, CLG, Rogers Cantel Inc.; (4) *First British Flag on North America*, J.D. Kelly, CLG, Rogers Cantel Inc. **15** (7) *The Discovery of Canada*, J.D. Kelly, CLG, Rogers Cantel Inc. **17** (9) *Sir Humphrey Gilbert Claims Newfoundland*, J.D. Kelly and H.B. Goodridge, CLG, Rogers Cantel Inc.; (10) mc, mr PA **18** Courtesy of NASA **19** Courtesy of NASA **25** *The Trading Room*, C.W. Jefferys, Photo: Parks Canada/Nathanial Tileston/1998 **26** Courtesy of Massachusetts Archives **27** (detail) C.W. Jefferys/NAC/C-106968 **28** tr *Oeuvres de Champlain (Samuel de Champlain)*, C.H. Laverdiere, MTRL **29** George Agnew Reid/NAC/C-011013 **30** (detail) NAC/C-017338 **32** (detail) C.W. Jefferys/NAC/C-073635 **33** NAC/C-007695 **34** Stamp reproduced courtesy of Canada Post Corporation/NAC **35** Kathleen M. Vanderlinden **36** Photos courtesy of Sainte-Marie among the Hurons, Midland, ON, Canada **37** t, bl Photos courtesy of Sainte-Marie among the Hurons, Midland, ON, Canada; br *Sainte-Marie Among the Hurons*, Vernon Mould, CLG, Rogers Cantel Inc. **38** *The Founding of Montréal*, Donald Anderson, CLG, Rogers Cantel Inc. **39** (detail) NAC/C-004765 **42** mr *An Acadian House*, Belleisle, Nova Scotia, c. 1720, by Azor Vienneau. History Collection, Nova Scotia Museum, Halifax; br *Inside an Acadian House*, Belleisle, Nova Scotia, c. 1720, by Azor Vienneau. History Collection, Nova Scotia Museum, Halifax **43** tr *Trading*, Belleisle, Nova Scotia, c. 1720, by Azor Vienneau. History Collection, Nova Scotia Museum, Halifax; mc *Repairing a Saltmarsh Dyke*, Belleisle, Nova Scotia, c. 1720, by Azor Vienneau. History Collection, Nova Scotia Museum, Halifax; bc Acadians *Cutting Saltmarsh Hay*, Belleisle, Nova Scotia, c. 1720, by Azor Vienneau. History Collection, Nova Scotia Museum, Halifax; br, *Micmac Indians*, Anon. Canadian, #6663, NGC, Ottawa **44** (detail) From a painting by Adam Sherriff Scott, RCA/NAC/C-011237 Reproduced with permission **45** *The English Destroy Port Royal*, 1613, Lewis Parker, from Bold Ventures **46** PA **47** Coat of Arms: Hudson's Bay Company Archives, Provincial Archives of Manitoba, 1987/363-C-43/6 **54** PA **55** PA **56** PA **57** PA **59** NAC/C-005400 **60** *Meeting of* the Sovereign Council, by Charles Huot, photographed by KEDL, 72-266-26, Assemblée Nationale **62** mr Portrait de Mgr François de Laval (detail), (copie d'après une gravure de Claude DUFLOS, 1708), 1995.3480, by Pierre Soulard, Musée de la civilisation, dépôt du Séminaire de Québec **63** ml Portrait de Jean Talon (detail), from Théophile Hamel (attr.), 1991.51, by Pierre Soulard, Musée de la civilisation, dépôt du Séminaire de Québec; tr, br PA **64** tl The Sovereign Council in Session, Lewis Parker, from Bold Ventures; ml Canada's First Shipyard, Rex Woods, CLG, Rogers Cantel Inc. **65** t (detail) C.W. Jefferys/NAC/C-010688 Reproduced with permission; bl Frontenac and the Iroquois, J.D. Kelly, CLG, Rogers Cantel Inc. **66** Lower Canada, 17th Century, Lewis Parker **67** PA **68** PA **69** PA **70** A view of the Château Richer, Cape Torment, Thomas Davies, #6275, NGC, Ottawa **74** PA **77** Lawrence R. Batchelor/NAC/C-011925 **78** Harvest Festival, William Bent Berczy, #16648, NGC, Ottawa **79** (detail) Lawrence R. Batchelor/NAC/C-010520 **80** (detail) C.W. Jefferys/NAC/C-010687 Reproduced with permission **81** tr, mc, ml Arnold Publishing Ltd.; br PA **85** Courtesy: Grey Nuns' Archives, St. Albert Province **88** bl Illustrations by Gerry Embleton (Grenadier) and Michael Roffe (Fusilier) from volumes in the Men-at-Arms Series reproduced by permission of Osprey Publishing Ltd. © Osprey Publishing Ltd. **90** Hudson's Bay Company Archives, Provincial Archives of Manitoba, 1987/363-T-37/14 **91** Kelsey on the Plains, Rex Woods, CLG, Rogers Cantel Inc. **92** PA **93** PA **94** View from a Warship, 1745, Lewis Parker, Courtesy of Fortress of Louisbourg, Parks Canada, 4x5 84 2881 **95** (detail) T. Jeffreys/ NAC/H3/240 (NMC 1012) **96** Le Loutre at Fort Beauséjour (Life Inside The Fort), © Artist Lewis Parker, Commissioned by Canadian Heritage (Parks Canada) **98** Deportation of the Acadians from the Isle of St. Jean, Lewis Parker, Courtesy of Canadian Heritage, Parks Canada **99** La Dispersion des Acadiens (The Dispersal of the Acadians), Henri Beau, 1900, Collection Musée acadien, Université de Moncton, Moncton, New Brunswick **100** Judy Bauer **103** PA **105** t NAC/C-001078; br (detail) Adam Sherriff Scott, RCA/NAC/C-011043 Reproduced with permission **106** tl NAC/C-027665; tr (detail) (Major General James Wolfe), 1759 by George Townshend, M245, MMCH, Montreal **110** Richard Short/NAC/C-000361 **115** (detail) NAC/C-026065 **121** PA **126** PA **130** (detail) George Washington, by Gilbert Stuart, Dover Publications Inc., Mineola, New York **131** Americans Invading Canada at Québec City, Alan Daniel, c.1978, The Reader's Digest Association, Heritage of Canada, reproduced with permission **137** tr C.W. Jefferys/NAC/C-096362 Reproduced with permission; mr (detail) James B. Dennis/NAC/C-000276; br Hudson's Bay Company Archives, Provincial Archives of Manitoba, P-416 **138** Photograph Courtesy of the Delaware Art Museum **141** Henry Sandham/NAC/C-000168 **142** (detail) Richard Short/NAC/C-004293 **144** (detail) Charles Walter Simpson/ NAC/C-013954 **145** Duhamel Du Monceau's 1769 View of Newfoundland /NAC/C-105230 **152** (detail) NAC/C-002833 **153** Thayendanegea (Joseph Brant) (detail), William Berczy, #5777, NGC, Ottawa **156** (detail) George Heriot/NAC/C-000251 **164** tl The Toronto Purchase, J.D. Kelly, CLG, Rogers Cantel Inc.; tr Governor Simcoe Arrives in Newark, J.D. Kelly, CLG, Rogers Cantel Inc.; br (detail) Elizabeth Frances Hale/NAC/C-040137/ C-034334 **165** ml (detail) Henry DuVernet/NAC/C-000608; br Bytown, J.D. Kelly, CLG, Rogers Cantel Inc. **167** tr (detail) Milner/NAC/C-005716; (4) (detail) Henry Louis Stephens/NAC/ C-016404 **168** (5) t (detail) James B. Dennis/NAC/C-000276; (5) m M.G./NAC/C-036181; (6) Canadian War Museum, Robert J. Marrion, The 104th (New Brunswick) Regiment of Foot, CN 75008; (7) Photograph courtesy of the Royal Ontario Museum, © ROM **169** (8) William Heath/NAC/C-000974; (10) C.W. Jefferys/NAC/C-073575; (11) Photograph courtesy of the Royal Ontario Museum, © ROM; (12) (detail) Henri Julien/ NAC/C-003297; (15) John Hewett/NAC/C-000794 **170** ml MTRL, J. Ross Robertson Collection (T16600); tr (detail) NAC/C-010717 **171** mr Courtesy of Parks Canada, Ontario; br Canadian War Museum, Brock's uniform, AN 19670070-009 **177** Old Fort William, John de Visser, Photographer Ltd., Cobourg, Ontario **181** mr Courtesy of Parks Canada, Ontario **186** (detail) Philip John Bainbrigge/NAC/C-011811 **188** Emigrants' Arrival at Cork – A Scene on the Quay, c.1830 (detail), IUV 10/5/1851, p.386, The Illustrated London News Picture Library **189** Emigration Vessel – Between Decks, c.1830 (detail), IUV 10/5/1851, p.387, The Illustrated London News Picture Library **190** Breaking a Log Jam, P4/3/3, Provincial Archives of New Brunswick **191** tr Hudson's Bay Company Archives, Provincial Archives of Manitoba, P-412; mr Frances Anne Hopkins/NAC/C-002774 **192** (detail) Louis-Joseph Papineau, s.d., Livernois, #P560, S2, P300370-992, Archives nationales du Québec à Québec **195** tr (detail) Charles Beauclerk/ NAC/C-000393; b (detail) Back View of the Church of St. Eustache and Dispersion of the Insurgents, 1840 by Charles Beauclerk, M4777.6, MMCH, Montreal **196** Behind Bonsecours Market, Montreal, William Raphael, #6673, NGC, Ottawa **199** (detail) W.P. Kay/NAC/C-000017 **200** tl James Pattison Cockburn/ NAC/C-012632; mr, bl PA **201** tl PA; mr C.W. Jefferys/NAC/C-073396; b C.W. Jefferys/NAC/C-073395 **202** (detail) Thomas Young/NAC/C-001669 **203** PA **204** (detail) C.W. Jefferys/NAC/C-069849 **206** tl MTRL, J. Ross Robertson Collection, #T16969; tr (detail) NAC/PA-001993 **207** (detail) NAC/C-018789 **208** Rebels of 1837 Drilling in North York, C.W. Jefferys, 1898, T-1316#1, Art Gallery of Ontario, Toronto Reproduced with permission **209** t Death of Colonel Moodie, C.W. Jefferys, MTRL, #T13350 (1086) Reproduced with permission; mr (detail) Henri Julien/NAC/C-013493; bl (detail) Michael Angelo Hayes/NAC/C-003653 **217** PA **221** (detail) Sir Thomas Lawrence/NAC/C-005456 **223** (detail) (James Bruce, Earl of Elgin), ca.1855, by Cornelius Krieghoff, MMCH, Montreal **228** (detail) The Burning of the Parliament Building in Montreal, ca.1849, attributed to Joseph Légaré, MMCH, Montreal **233** (detail) National Library of Canada **234** (detail) Henry Francis Ainslie/ NAC/C-000518 **235** From a painting by Adam Sherriff Scott, RCA in the Royal Bank of Canada Corporate Archives **236** (detail) Egerton Ryerson, ca.1875; S 623, Archives of Ontario **237** Mr. And Mrs. William Croscup's Painted Room, Anon. Canadian, #18688.0.19 (detail), NGC, Ottawa **238** tr (detail) C.W. Jefferys/ NAC/C-073708; br (detail) NAC/PA-022002 **239** ml Reproduction of painting by Spencer Macky of Market Day in Charlottetown. Original painting currently hangs in the Council Chambers of City Hall in Charlottetown, PEI. This painting was presented to the city of Charlottetown in April, 1924 by Adam Andrew in memory of his early childhood days in Charlottetown. Courtesy of the Public Archives and Records Office of Prince Edward Island, Accession #2320/5-1; tr (detail) Philip Harry/NAC/C-003552; br (detail) William Eagar/NAC/C-041605 **240** Cincinnati Art Museum, Subscription Fund Purchase **241** © Corbis-Bettmann **245** PA

Appendix
Learning How to Learn
(SKIMM™)

On the following pages you will find a variety of ideas to help you with your assignments. Use these organizers as sample formats. Add to them or delete as needed.

Bias

A bias is a preference based on values and beliefs that can make it difficult to make fair judgements.

Example

If a referee is biased in favor of Team A and against Team B, s/he might call more penalties against Team B.

To make careful judgements about resource materials (to prevent bias), ask yourself these questions:

- Who created this source? What beliefs and values did the creator(s) hold?
- When and where was this source created?
- Under what special circumstances was it created?
- Why was it created? What is its purpose?
- Who is expected to refer to it?
- What is my reaction to this source? What do I think and feel about it?

See also Critical Thinking.

Brainstorming

Brainstorming is a strategy for coming up with as many ideas about a topic as possible. After the ideas have been listed, you can choose the best one(s).

Suggestions for Brainstorming

1. All ideas must be accepted. Do not evaluate or criticize ideas as they are mentioned.

2. Quickly add ideas to the list. Don't concern yourself about whether the idea is "good" or not. Unusual and fun ideas should be added to your list.

3. Sometimes thinking about one idea leads to another. Add to, subtract from, join, and change ideas to come up with new ones. The more you have, the better.

Concept Poster

Concept posters are meant to represent general ideas or thoughts (concepts) in any combination of visual, auditory (sound), and written presentations.

Steps for Creating a Concept Poster

Step 1:
1. Review information about the concept in your textbook and your notebook.
2. List examples of the concept (historical and current, and possible future examples).
3. Brainstorm to decide what the examples have in common. Look for patterns, links, and connections.

Step 2: Plan and create a presentation to represent your ideas and examples about the concept. You could include any of the following: picture (photo, drawing, map, diagram), skit or tableau, music/song/sound effects, words (spoken, on paper), objects/models.

Step 3: Present your concept poster to your classmates. You may either tell them what concept you are presenting or have them guess.

NOTE: Registered™ 1996 Arnold Publishing Ltd. SKIMM™ (Skills, Models, and Methods) Learning How to Learn—the techniques of assigning questions/activities written in a textbook or digital presentation and referring users to an appendix or glossary (print or digital) for suggestions on how to carry it out—has been registered as a trademark by Arnold Publishing Ltd. All copy used in SKIMM™ (Learning How to Learn), including the icons, is protected by copyright. © 1996, 1998 Arnold Publishing Ltd.

An expansion of SKIMM™ (Learning How to Learn) is available on the Arnold Publishing internet site.

Cause and Effect

A cause is something that makes an event or situation occur. The event or situation then leads to an effect (result).

Use a diagram similar to the one below to show cause and effect.

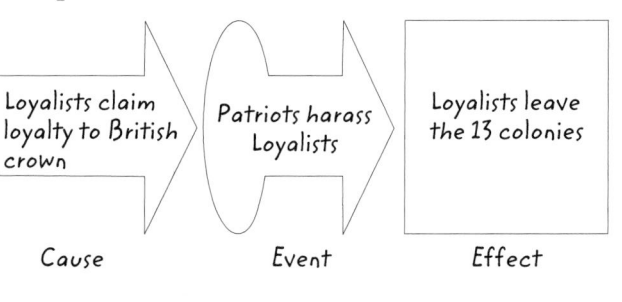

Example

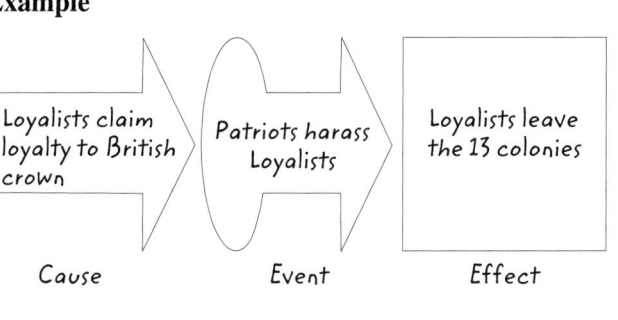

Sometimes there are many causes that lead to an event or situation. There may also be one or more effects.

Example

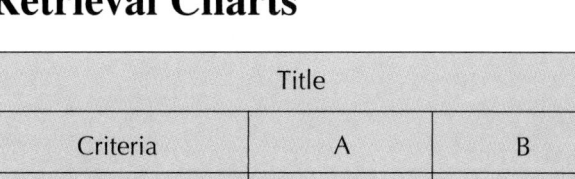
Charts and Graphic Organizers

Charts are also referred to as diagrams, tables, or graphs and are used as a quick way to organize and record information.

Retrieval Charts

Title		
Criteria	A	B

List items or criteria you are describing.

Record important information as it relates to the criteria.

Example

The following retrieval chart organizes some notes on three types of decision-making models.

Decision-making Models

Characteristic	My Model	New France	Coach's Model
1. participants	• •	• King Louis XIV •	• Coach Earnest •
2. power	• •	• King believed power inherited from ancestors • power to be used for well-being of subjects • • •	• we don't know how he got his position (chosen? volunteer?) • believed he knew what was best for team •
3. majority or minority rule	•	•	•
4.			

257

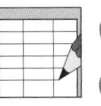

Charts and Graphic Organizers (continued)

Flow Chart

Flow charts are sequential diagrams that show classification, relationships, possibilities, or choices.

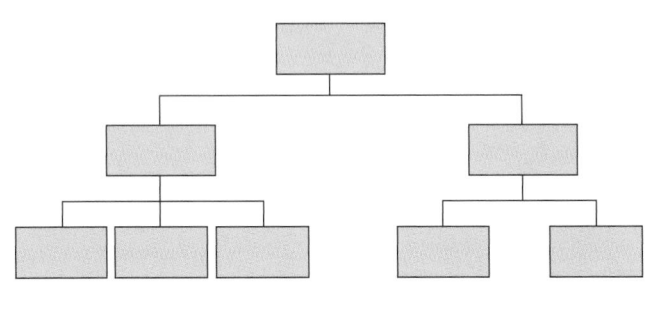

Steps Involved in Classifying

Classification is a commonly used thinking tool. To classify, you gather together ideas, events, or items and arrange them into groups that have common characteristics. Because we each think differently, there are many ways to classify information. The example on this page (the flow chart) shows one way to do this.

1. Randomly list items or examples.
2. Identify and label groups (categories) based on their characteristics.
3. Sort into groups based on similarities.
4. (optional) Record information on a graphic organizer.

Example

The topic is "Responsibilities of Sovereign Council in New France."

Step 1: Randomly list items or examples.

figurehead	hospitals
finances	military plans
churches	Native relations
King's representative	informing King
harmony	schools
day-to-day matters	supervising officials
law and order	missionaries

Step 2: Identify and label groups (categories) based on their characteristics.

GROUP 1	GROUP 2	GROUP 3
Governor General	Bishop	Intendant

Step 3: Sort into groups based on similarities.

figurehead	churches	finances
King's representative	harmony	day-to-day matters
military plans	hospitals	law and order
Native relations	schools	informing King
supervising officials	missionaries	

Step 4: Record information on a graphic organizer.

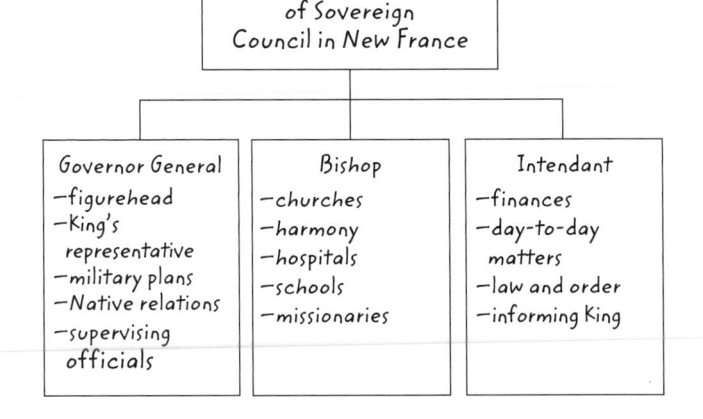

Comparison Chart

This thinking tool is used to show how something is similar to and different from something else. Another style of chart used for comparison is the Venn diagram (see right column).

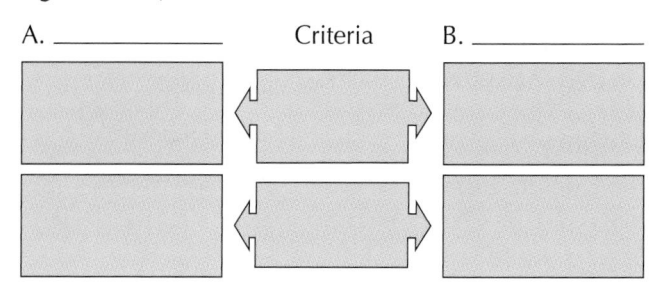

A. _____   Criteria   B. _____

Steps Involved in Comparing

1. Identify what you are comparing.
2. Identify what criteria you are going to use in comparing. The number of criteria will vary depending upon what you are comparing.
3. Show how the items you are comparing are the same and how they are different based on the criteria you identified.

Example
Step 1: Identify what you are comparing.

A. British   FUR TRADE FROM 1670   B. French

Step 2: Identify what criteria you are going to use in comparing.

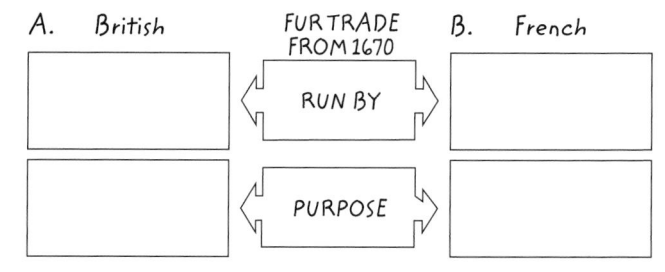

A. British   FUR TRADE FROM 1670   B. French

RUN BY

PURPOSE

Step 3: Show how the items you are comparing are the same and how they are different based on the criteria you identified.

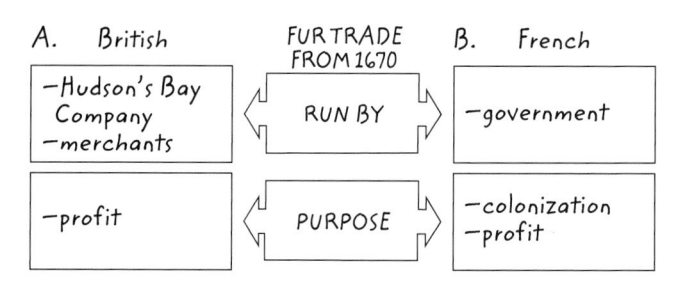

A. British   FUR TRADE FROM 1670   B. French

- Hudson's Bay Company
- merchants   RUN BY   - government

- profit   PURPOSE   - colonization
- profit

Venn Diagram

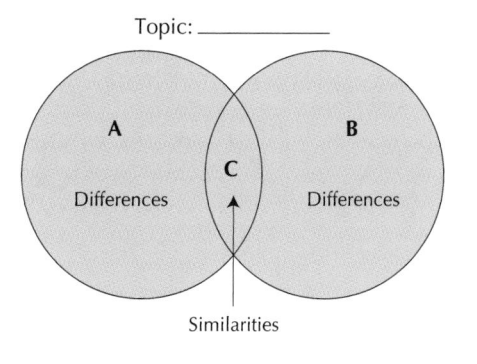

Topic: _____

A — Differences
C
B — Differences

Similarities

Steps for Using a Venn Diagram

1. Identify what two people, places, objects, or ideas (subjects A and B) you are comparing, in relation to what topic.
2. Identify (and keep in your mind) what criteria you are going to use to show differences. In circle A write words or descriptions about subject A according to the criteria you selected. Do the same for subject B in circle B.
3. In the central space C randomly list ways in which A and B are the same.

Example

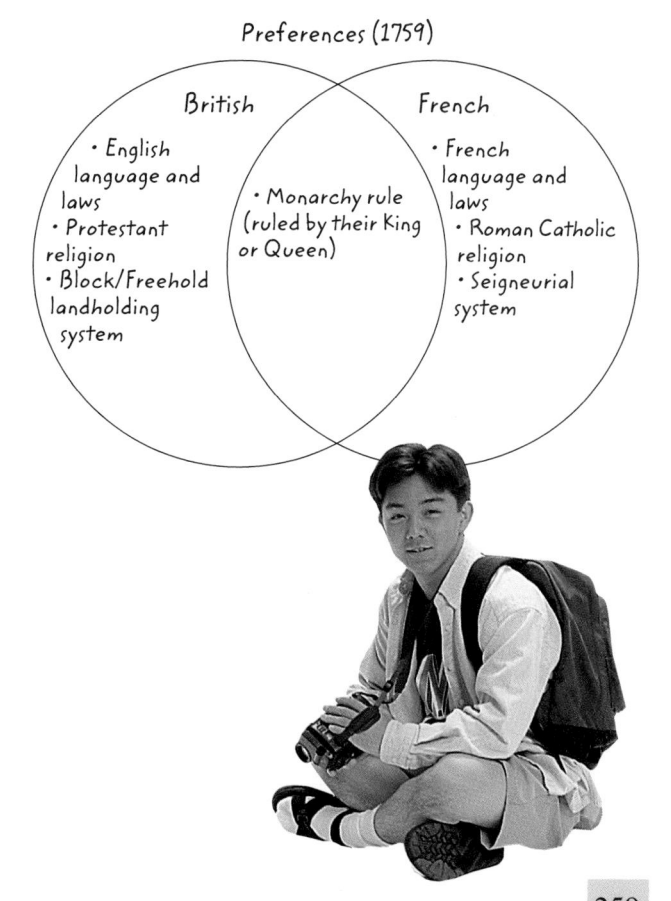

Preferences (1759)

British
- English language and laws
- Protestant religion
- Block/Freehold landholding system

- Monarchy rule (ruled by their King or Queen)

French
- French language and laws
- Roman Catholic religion
- Seigneurial system

 # Critical Thinking

Critical thinking involves

- examining ideas or issues in order to make a judgement about them
- looking at ideas and issues from different points of view
- questioning information as presented
- noticing bias in our own and in others' points of view
- recognizing fact and opinion

Points of View*

Each of us has our own point of view (viewpoint). We have our own ideas, attitudes, beliefs, ways of doing things (e.g., customs and traditions), and priorities and goals. This affects how we look at situations and issues.** This also affects how we behave, solve problems, react to situations, and make decisions.

When thinking critically, you are examining ideas, situations, and statements. You are trying to "step out" of your point of view to look at the situation or issue from the perspective of another person or persons.

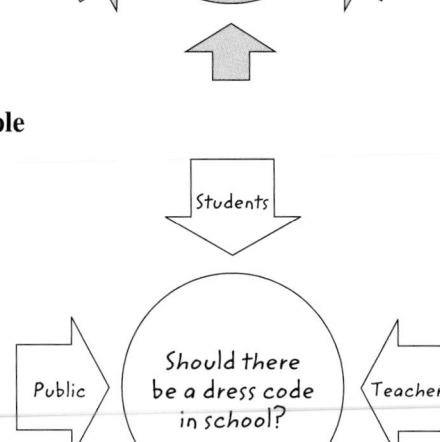

Example

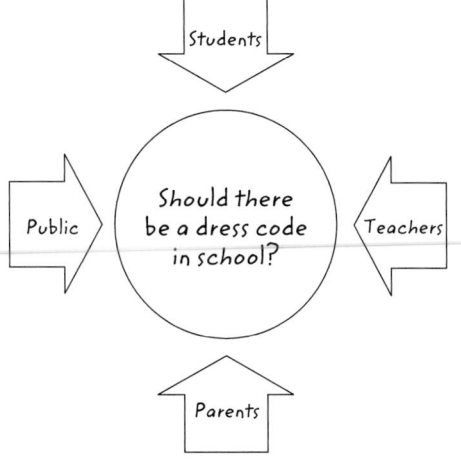

Steps for Critical Thinking

Step 1: Identify the issue and examine the information you already have about this issue.

- Are your facts accurate?
- Are there any inconsistencies? (ideas which do not relate or work together/ideas which go against one another)
- How strong are the ideas and arguments?
- How reliable is the information?

Step 2: Identify the various people who will have different points of view in a situation.

- Who are the various people who would have an interest in and opinion about this issue? (Often these are people that would be affected in some way, depending upon how the issue is resolved.)

Step 3: Try "stepping out" of your own point of view and thinking about what one or more of the other people might think about this issue. To do so, it might help to ask yourself

- why does a person think the way s/he does?
- why does a person think his or her way is best?
- why does s/he choose to do things differently?
- what might a person be feeling to act the way he or she does?
- what might a person be thinking to have certain feelings?

---

*Points of view are represented throughout this textbook, in journal and diary excerpts, eyewitness accounts, quotations, role-plays, and decision-making, critical thinking, and problem solving activities.
**Issues involve a problem or question for debate. Issues are often written as a question that uses the word "should." There is often not a definite answer to an issue. Refer to page 262 under Decision-making for more information about issues.

The diagram below represents the three steps.

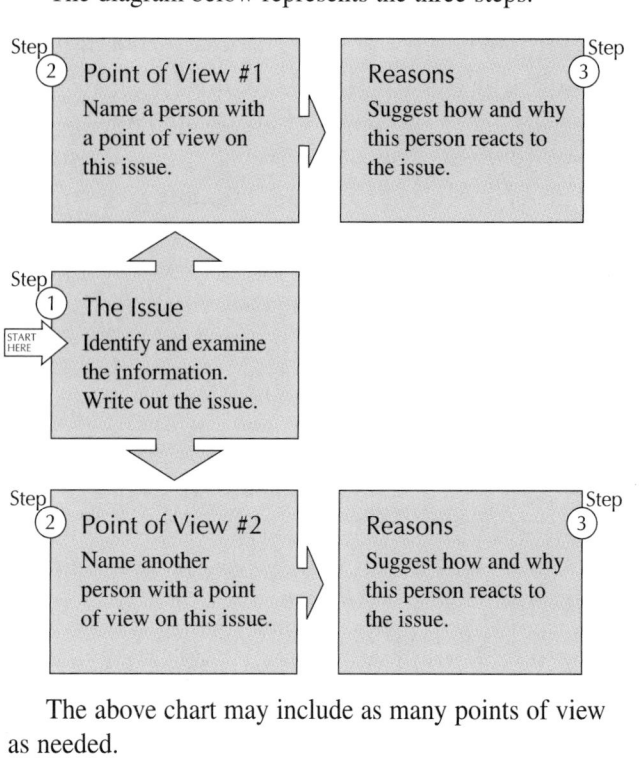

The above chart may include as many points of view as needed.

Example

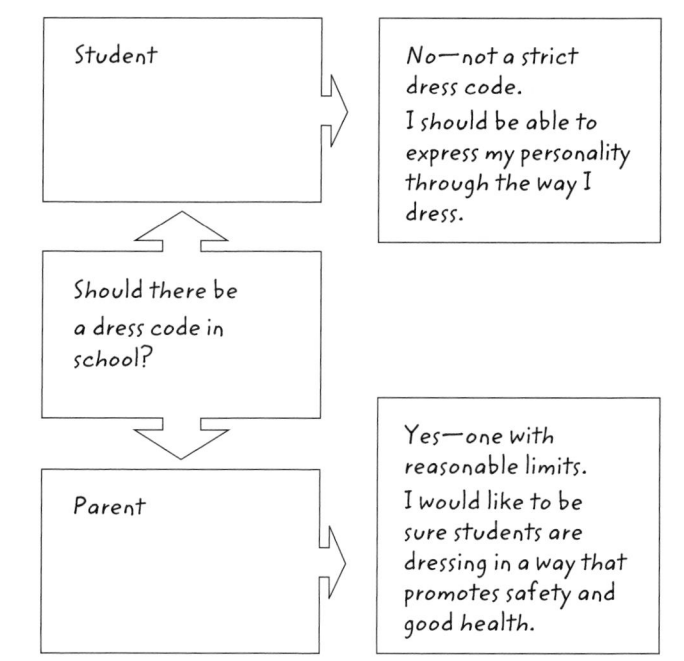

Some Tips

Avoid oversimplifying the situation. If you state an idea or situation as absolute or too definite, you are not recognizing the possibility that additional information could change how you think.

Examples of Absolutes

It should *always* be this way.
It should *never* happen that way.
Everyone did it.
It was *completely* good.
It was *totally* wrong.
He/She is *always* right/wrong.
This factor is the *only* cause.

Use qualifiers like the ones below to remind yourself that you may still not have all the information necessary to make a judgement on an issue. These help us to recognize that there is still some doubt.

Examples of Qualifiers

highly likely	some
most	sometimes
seldom	usually
often	I doubt
probably	not very likely
many	I suspect

Example

Many French people resented the British taking over the colony of New France.
Because the word "many" is used instead of "all," the statement shows that there may also have been some French people who did not mind the British takeover.

Fact and Opinion

Recognize the difference between fact and opinion. A fact represents something "real" and can usually be proven. An opinion involves a judgement about something and may or may not be based upon what is true.

Example

Samuel de Champlain helped to establish settlements in New France. (fact)
This can be verified (proven) using historical records.

Samuel de Champlain was the most important person in establishing New France. (opinion)
This statement might be argued with additional information (e.g., King Louis XIV had ambitious plans for France).

Decision-making

Decision-making is a process used to resolve an issue. Issues involve a problem or question for debate. They are often written as a question that includes the word "should" (e.g., Should students be allowed to bring outside guests to school dances?) There is often not a definite answer to an issue—a person must choose from several alternatives. As a result, opinions and emotions are often involved.

Steps for Decision-making

Step 1: Decide: What is the issue to be solved?

Step 2: Brainstorm for alternatives (choices).

Step 3: Analyse the alternatives by listing the consequences (results) of each (the pros and the cons).

Step 4: Decide what options are best. Try to select the alternative(s) with the most positive and fewest negative results. Organize the alternatives in rank order from the most desirable to the least desirable.

Step 5: What is your decision? Choose the "best" alternative.

Step 6: Evaluate your results by asking yourself
• was this a fair and effective decision? Why?
• what difficulties are expected from this decision?
• what benefits are expected from this decision?
• faced with the same issue again, would I change my decision? Why?
• what changes or improvements might be made to this method of decision-making?

Decision-Making Chart

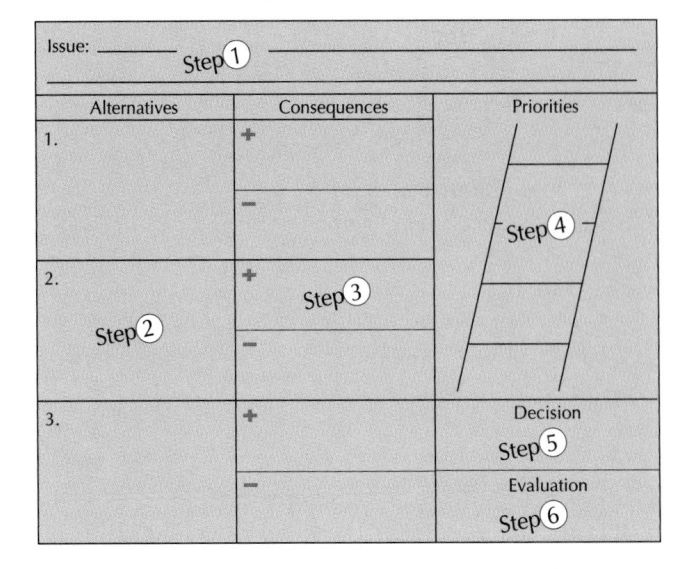

Example

Issue: Should students be allowed to bring "outside" guests to school dances?		
Alternatives	Consequences	Priorities
1. Yes— any time	+ Increased attendance	Most preferred
	− Over-crowded dances	#2
2. Yes— one dance this year	+ Chance to show guests and staff how positive students are	#3 #1
	− Students disagree about which dance this should be	Least preferred
3. No— never	+ Will build school spirit for our students	Decision Yes—one dance this year
	− Some students will choose not to participate	Evaluation

262

Notebook Organization

Your notebook is your record of the material you have studied. It is intended to make your work more manageable and your notes easier to use and study from. Notebooks might include any of the following:

- notes copied from the board
- assignment sheets/handouts
- journal entries
- vocabulary
- information from discussions
- information from group work
- notes about textbook information
- tests
- research notes
- notes about learning (Tools of Learning)
- student reference material (e.g., Research Model booklet)
- visuals (drawings, maps, cartoons, charts, graphs)

It is easier to learn material if it is organized into categories. One method of organizing your notes (four sections: Activities, WordBook, History Journal, Tools of Learning) is outlined on page 23. Your teacher might tell you which categories to use, since s/he is familiar with what you will study. Often, one section for each chapter is used.

Suggestions for Organizing your Notes

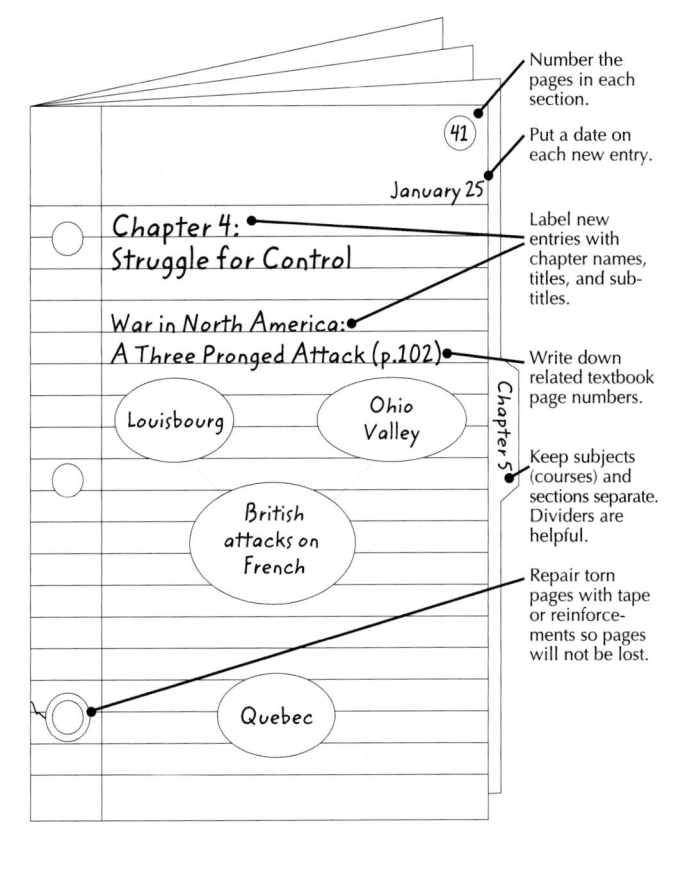

Number the pages in each section.

Put a date on each new entry.

Label new entries with chapter names, titles, and sub-titles.

Write down related textbook page numbers.

Keep subjects (courses) and sections separate. Dividers are helpful.

Repair torn pages with tape or reinforcements so pages will not be lost.

More Ideas

- Create a table of contents to help you see what is covered in each section and locate items quickly.
- Keep the pages in order—add new information to the back of the section.
- Compare your notebook with that of a partner to check for items that are missing or out of order.
- Use colours to underline, highlight, illustrate, and code your notes. Colours help us to learn material.
- Keep your notes neat and readable.
- Update your notes as you go along.

Note Making

Point Form Notes (Rough Notes)

Writing point form notes involves reading a section, thinking about the main or most important ideas, and recording these ideas in your own words (paraphrasing). Your goal is to record only the most important ideas in your own words.

Some ideas

- Use chapter and section headings.
- Under each heading, record only key words/ideas.
- Do not write in complete sentences. Use a dash (–) to begin new ideas.
- Use abbreviations.

Example

(Refer to page 70, Chapter 3)

The Seigneurial System

Land:
- long narrow strips
- began along the St. Lawrence R.*
- King owned
- gave seigneurs right to use it

Seigneurs:
- divide land
- build house & flour mill**
- help provide church
- report to intendant

Habitants:
- use mill, pay miller
- pay dues (produce/money)
- build house
- <u>corvée</u>

Donut

Write the title in the centre and notes in the "donut pieces," one idea per piece. Add to or take away partitions from the donut as needed.

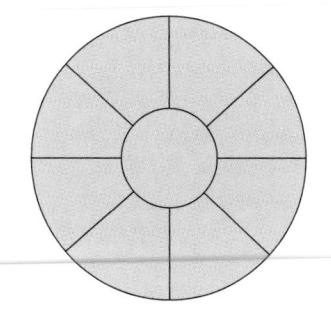

Paraphrasing

This means you are restating in your own words what you have read or heard.

Steps Involved in Paraphrasing

1. Read or listen to a small amount of material. Covering too much at once may be confusing, or you may forget ideas. Covering too little may result in copying word-for-word.
2. Decide what you feel are the most important points. (Imagine how you would summarize the information for a friend.)
3. Write down or say the ideas in your own words.

T-Notes

T-Notes combine written notes and drawings. Use the following format, or design your own.

Main title Write one or two sentences to describe what this section is about.		
Drawing or sketch	Sub-titles	• Write notes in point form here.

Example

(Refer to page 112)

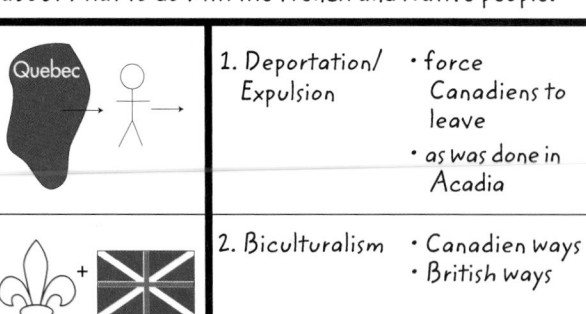

---

*St. is an abbreviation for Saint and R. for River.
**Use symbols like & when writing point form notes. Other symbols include numerals and %, #, +.

Webs

Also called clustering, this type of graphic organizer is used to

- generate ideas, as in brainstorming (see page 256)
- illustrate ideas (by using words and/or drawings)
- link ideas
- take notes

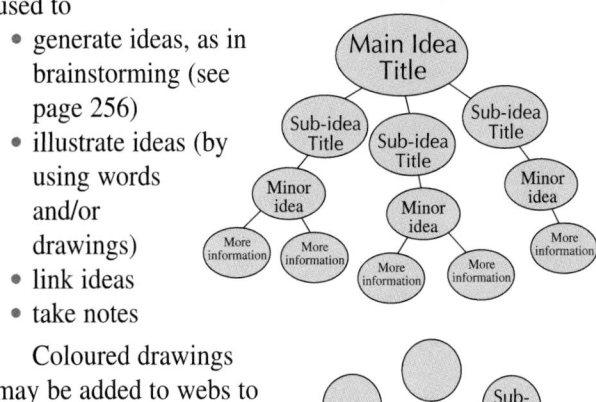

Coloured drawings may be added to webs to aid memory. Either add or take away outer circles as needed.

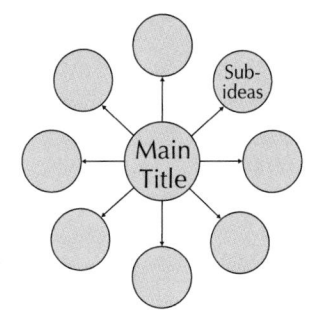

Example

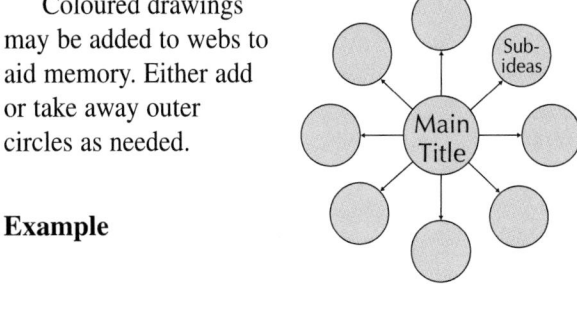

Mind Maps

Mind maps work much like webs. Each idea is placed on a separate line. Each word or idea must be joined by a line or at least one other word or idea. Coloured sketches and pictures are often used to represent words or ideas, since they help us remember.

The mind map shown below is based upon the ideas and concepts covered in Chapter 3.

Example

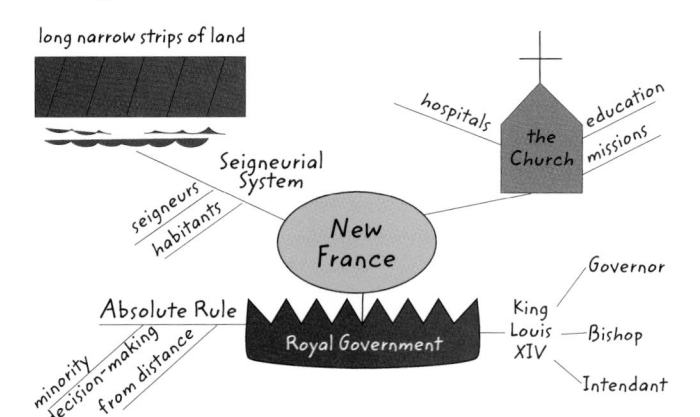

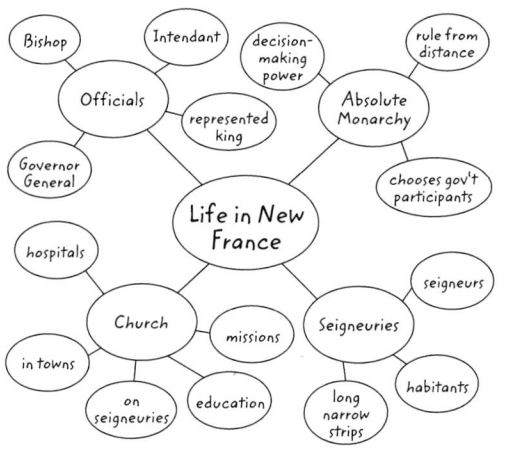

Outline Notes

(also called Outlining and Topical Outlines)

In this textbook title sizes are coded by size in each section to help you create an outline or web. (See page vii.) When a new idea is introduced the largest heading size is used. Title size gets smaller as the idea is explained in greater detail.

Example

In Chapter 3, there are six *main ideas*—Territorial Claims, 1663 (p. 58), A Royal Colony (p. 59), Royal Government (p. 60), Changes to New France (p. 64), The Seigneurial System (p. 70), The Church in New France (p. 78).

Titles are also colour-coded by Section—in Section III (both Chapters 3 and 4), the largest titles are teal.

The six titles represent six main ideas, so they are each assigned a level one title in outline notes—a Roman numeral.

    I. Territorial Claims, 1663
    II. A Royal Colony
    III. Royal Government
    IV. Changes to New France
    V. The Seigneurial System
    VI. The Church in New France

Under New France, 1663, there are no *sub-ideas* (level two titles). Under A Royal Colony there are two sub-ideas—King Louis XIV of France and Colbert. Subtitles are smaller than the main idea title. In Section III they are purple. Ideas supporting the sub-topics are smaller and black. Check each section for its heading colours.

Focus On pages (such as page 93), narratives (see page 76), and activity pages (see page 55) do not follow this system. You are usually not required to make outline notes on these pages.

To make outline notes, you could use a format similar to this one:

    I. Territorial Claims, 1663
    II. A Royal Colony
       A. King Louis XIV of France
          1. Absolute Monarchy
       B. Colbert
    III. Royal Government
       A. Characteristics of an Absolute Monarch
       B. Colonial Government in New France
       C. Important Officials in the Government of New France
          1. The Governor General
          2. The Bishop
          3. The Intendant

When you have made an outline of all the titles, read the textbook and write brief notes under the appropriate titles. For example, under "1. The Governor General," write the main details of the topic covered on page 62.

Role-playing

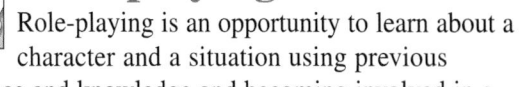

Role-playing is an opportunity to learn about a character and a situation using previous experience and knowledge and becoming involved in a lifelike situation.

This is an excellent activity for using critical thinking. When you place yourself in the situation of one of the individuals you are studying about, you experience an issue from their point of view.

Steps Involved in Role-playing

Step 1: You will be assigned or you can choose a role-play scene. Research the historical time and the person you will be playing in advance.

Step 2: To begin a role-play, the people involved go into "freeze" positions, eyes closed. No one should be moving. Someone from the group (or the teacher) sets the scene by describing for the viewers the setting, the historical time period, and giving some background information on the issue.*

At the agreed-upon signal the group "comes to life" and starts their planned conversation. Although characters are planned and researched ahead of time, you don't memorize lines as you would for a play. You speak and behave as the person you are playing might.

Step 3: After the role-play, discuss what happened. Think about what was learned from the activity by asking yourself
- what did I learn about the issue?
- what did I learn about the points of view of the characters?
- how does this affect my viewpoint about the issue? (Has my viewpoint changed?)
- how can I relate this knowledge to what I am studying?
- can I apply this information to other situations? How?

---

*Dressing in historical costumes or using suitable props may help to make role-play more authentic.

 ## Presentations

Some Presentation* Ideas

advertisement	music
banner	newspaper
booklet	newspaper article
cartoon	oral report
charades	painting
chart	pamphlet
collage	panel discussion
collection	papier-mâché
comic strip	photo album
concept poster	photographs
construction	picture
cooking demonstration	play
dance	poem
debate	poster
demonstration	project triangle
diagram	puppet show
diorama	puzzle
display	questionnaire
drawing	radio show
exhibition	rap
fact file	riddles
fairy tale	role-play/drama
flow chart	scrapbook
game	scroll
graph	sculpture
illustrated poem	skit
interview	slide/tape show
job description	song
letter	speech
magazine	story
map	survey
mask	tableau
mime	talk show
mobile	television show
model	timeline (illustrated)
mosaic	top 10 list
multimedia presentation	web page
mural	written report

Challenge yourself to complete a variety of presentations. Check the Arnold Publishing website at **http://www.arnold.ca/** for information about completing presentations.

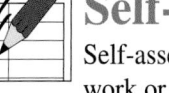 ## Self-assessment

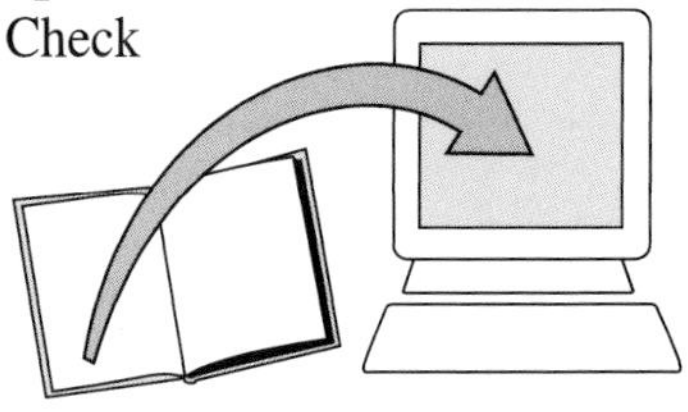

Self-assessment is the act of evaluating your work or performance to decide how well you have met the expectations on an assignment or activity. Consider

- in what situations are you assessed?
- in what situations are you required to assess something?
- what helps assessment to be meaningful and positive?
- what should be avoided when making an assessment?
- what kinds of questions could you ask when assessing something?

Steps for Self-assessment

1. Review the expectations for the assignment.
2. List the criteria you will use to assess your assignment.
3. Decide what you have to do to achieve Level 4 (highest rating) for each of the criteria. What would earn Level 3 (next highest rating) for each of the criteria? What would earn a Level 2? A Level 1?
4. Keep the criteria and rating descriptions in mind as you complete your assignment.
5. You may use the sample assessment format shown below. Change the criteria and descriptions to fit the assignment.

Self-Assessment

Criteria
(Expectations to be decided by the teacher, the student, or both.)

1. _____
2. _____
3. _____
4. _____
5. _____

Personal Assessment   Level   1   2   3   4
(Circle one based on above criteria)

Reasons for circling the number I did: _____

Next time, I would _____

This is what I learned about the way I think and work: _____

Assessment by Teacher   Level   1   2   3   4
(Circle one based on above criteria)

Reasons for circling the number I did: _____

*Presentation, as used in this book, refers to the communication of information in visual, oral, or written forms.

Problem Solving

A problem is a difficult question that requires you to consider a number of possible solutions in order to choose the best solution to a problem. For certain kinds of problems (e.g., a math problem), there is one correct answer. There are also many problems in life that have more than one solution.

Problems ask: Who? What? Where?
When? Why? How?

Steps for Problem Solving

Step 1: Define the problem. Decide what you want to find out.

Step 2: Come up with possible questions and a hypothesis to guide your research. (A hypothesis is a rough guess about the solution based on what you know.)

Step 3: Do research to locate data (information) that supports or disagrees with your hypothesis.

Step 4: Record the data (information) that supports or disagrees with your hypothesis.

Step 5: Evaluate the information you have collected by thinking about how it relates to your hypothesis.

Step 6: Arrive at a conclusion by choosing what you think is the best solution—one that makes sense and solves the problem. Think about whether your conclusion agrees or disagrees with your hypothesis.

Step 7: Share your conclusion.

Problem Solving Retrieval Chart

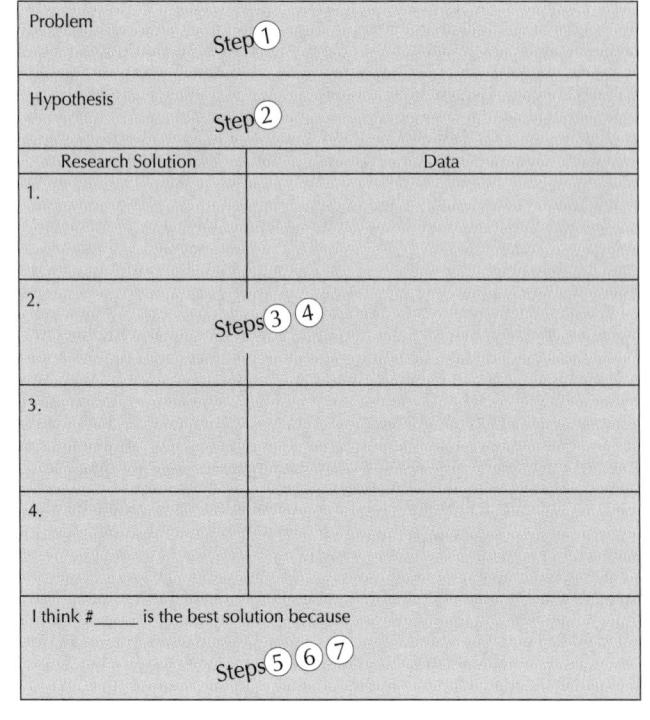

Problem	Step ①	
Hypothesis	Step ②	
Research Solution		Data
1.		
2.	Steps ③ ④	
3.		
4.		

I think #_____ is the best solution because

Steps ⑤ ⑥ ⑦

Example

Problem: How can Students' Council plan an activity that more students will participate in?	
Hypothesis: If students were allowed to choose the activities they would be interested in them and would attend.	
Research Solution	Data
1. Give door prizes	—budget only covers planning and preparing the activity
2. Ask all students for ideas	—some students say they don't like the activities —last year we did this and got 100s of ideas but could not decide
3. Provide students with a list of 5 choices and ask them to rank them	—teachers are willing to allow 10 minutes in class to do the survey —all students will have a say
4. Hold activities after school rather than at lunchtime	—many other activities at lunchtime —many students must catch a bus right after school

I think # 3 is the best solution because:
It will allow us to get student ideas in a way that is manageable, given the time and budget we have.

Sources

Anything that gives you information about a topic you are studying is a source. There are two types of sources:

1. **Primary Sources** are written, visual, or auditory (sound) accounts by someone who witnessed or lived during the time of an event; historical evidence from that time

   ### Examples

   - To study life during your grandmother's childhood, you might refer to the diary she wrote at that time.

   - If you wanted to find out what happened around the world on a particular day, you might look at the news.

   - If you wanted to study Canada in the early 1800s, you might visit the library's **archives** to read news-papers written during that time.*

   This textbook has many **excerpts** taken from primary sources. These include eyewitness accounts. Repro-ductions of historical pictures are also included.

2. **Secondary Sources** have been created after the time period you are studying. Often, secondary sources have been created using primary sources for reference and research. This textbook is a secondary source.

Timeline

A timeline is a way to show events in the order in which they occurred. It can include both words and pictures. (See pages 40–41 for example)

Example

John's Life

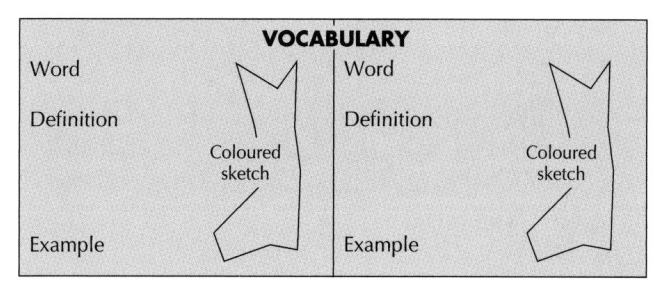

Visit Arnold Publishing's website for more details on timelines.

Vocabulary

Start a section in your notebook called WordBook. Record in it any new words you want to remember. Several strategies for recording vocabulary follow:

Spider Definition

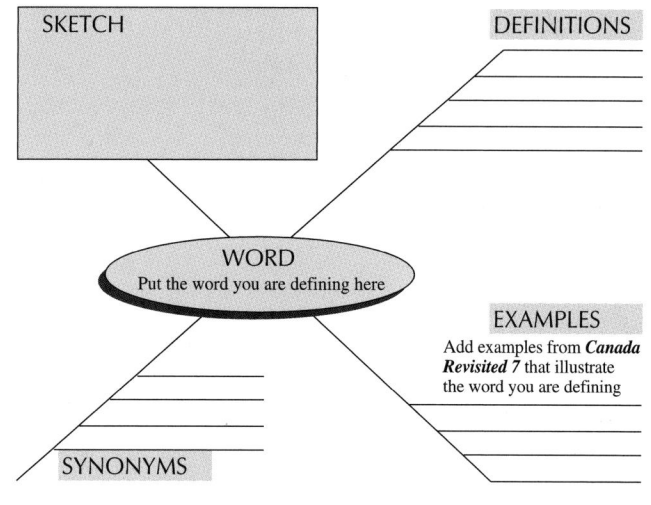

Word Chart

Word Write the new vocabulary term here.		Picture Draw a simple sketch to help you remember the meaning. Colour this sketch. You are not expected to create something artistic and no one will see this drawing unless you want them to.
Meaning Write out the mean-ing in your own words. Use the information in the textbook, in the glossary, or from a dictionary to help you understand the meaning.	Example Write out examples from *Canada Revisited 7* to show how the word is used.	

New Words

VOCABULARY

Word		Word	
Definition		Definition	
	Coloured sketch		Coloured sketch
Example		Example	

Archives—a place where historical documents and records are kept
Excerpt—a piece of writing selected from a larger work; a quotation

---

*A visit to the website of the University of Saskatchewan Archives provides a list of various links to Canadian archives, museums, and special collections. The address is
http://www.usask.ca/archives/menu.html

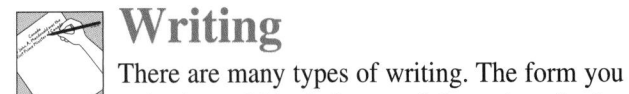

Writing

There are many types of writing. The form you write in could include any of those described briefly on these two pages, or others. Your purpose for writing might include telling, persuading, explaining, reporting, describing. Think about your purpose and your audience so you can choose the most effective form and words. Challenge yourself by writing in a variety of forms.

Storytelling

There are many ways to tell a story about an incident or series of events. Stories may include your personal thoughts, feelings, and ideas. They are often meant to entertain.

1. Biography
   - Written account of someone's life
   - Includes information and events from the person's life so the reader can "get to know them"
   - Will require research
   - An autobiography is a biography told by the person him/herself
2. Diary or Journal
   - Personal account (description) of daily activities and experiences
   - Each entry begins with the date
   - Includes thoughts, ideas, feelings
3. Friendly Letter
   - Tells about events/information of interest to the person who will receive the letter
   - Can also ask questions, congratulate, comment on events, tell entertaining stories
   - Intended for someone you know (e.g., friend)
   - Format includes writer's return address, the date, a greeting, and a closing
4. Hard News Story
   - Describes a current event of some importance to the reader
   - Answers who, what, where, when, why, and how
   - Factual but may include quotations that express opinions
5. Historical Story
   - Story based on historical fact (e.g., people, places, events) but may contain fictional parts (e.g., invented characters)
   - Requires research about people, events, and setting (description of place at the time)
   - See also Short Story (#7)
6. Play
   - A story presented as a dramatic performance
   - Includes title, character and setting description, lines intended to be spoken by actors, direction about costumes, set/stage design, actions and expression of the actors
7. Short Story
   - Includes title, description of characters and setting, conflict (problem)
   - Series of incidents or events take place as characters try to resolve conflicts
   - Climax or point of highest interest comes when the problem is solved. (Note: Problem may be solved in a positive or negative way)
   - Conclusion

Persuading

Persuasive writing is intended to convince your reader to accept your point of view.

8. Advertisement
   - Announcement or written notice for the public
   - Provides information that is meant to persuade people to act in a certain way (e.g., buy a product, vote for a candidate)
   - Words and pictures should catch people's attention
9. Brochure/Pamphlet/Flyer
   - Usually a small booklet or folded sheet providing details (written and visual) that highlight the most appealing features of a place, person, event, idea
10. Editorial
    - An article (short essay) found in most newspapers that expresses an opinion on behalf of the newspaper about a current event or issue in the news
    - Includes related facts that support a point of view and strengthen an argument
11. Letter to the Editor
    - Written to a newspaper to express opinions about current events or issues
    - Includes related facts that support a point of view and strengthen a position
    - May contain emotional and descriptive words
12. Political Cartoon
    - A drawing meant to express opinions about political issues or people (e.g., politicians, public)
    - Many visual clues (e.g., symbols) work together with the words to give a message
13. Review or Critique
    - An evaluation or judgement of a product or performance (e.g., play, movie, artwork, CD, book)
    - Gives information that supports the writer's claims and opinions
    - Can include emotional and descriptive words

14. Speech

- May serve many different purposes (e.g., entertaining, paying tribute, congratulating); often intended to convince (e.g., campaign speech)
- Intended to be spoken to an audience
- Words should be appropriate for the audience and the situation
- Planning and practising out loud is needed so volume, expression, pace, posture, and gestures give added meaning and impact to the words
- Point-form notes (cue cards) may be used when presenting but should not be read

Explaining

This type of writing helps the reader understand how to do something and how/why something works as it does.

15. Instructions/Manual/Directions

- Provide a step-by-step order
- Use clear language that is easy to follow
- Use special terms that relate to the topic and suit the audience (e.g., sifting is a suitable term in a recipe)

Reporting

Reports use knowledge gathered from a variety of sources and provide factual information.

16. Census

- A specific count of the people living in an area
- Might include information about ages, jobs, education, and religion

17. News Report

- See Hard News Story (#4)

18. Magazine/Newspaper Feature Article

- Provides information about people, places, and events that are of interest to the readers
- Usually requires an interview or other research
- Includes visuals

19. Research Report

- Provides detailed information on a specific topic or issue (see Research Model on pages x–xi)
- Can be presented in a number of ways (see Presentations on page 267)

20. Survey/Poll/Questionnaire

- An investigation about a situation or issue
- Includes clear and specific questions intended for a certain group
- Poll should allow for responses that are easily recorded and counted (e.g., Yes/No responses)
- Results may be presented in graphs, charts, tables, or paragraphs

21. Interview

- Meant to gather information from a person
- Questions should help to gather factual information and details about the person's ideas and opinions
- May be a "live" interview or presented in written, taped/visual forms (with the person's permission)

Describing

Describing can be a part of almost any form of writing.

- Includes details that appeal to the five senses (sight, hearing, smell, taste, and touch) to help the reader become involved in the subject.
- Make careful word choices that are suitable to the form of writing (e.g., an instruction manual may need different descriptive detail than a brochure about a tropical resort).

Index

KEY

● map   ■ picture   ▲ chart   ◆ biography

KEY
● map ■ picture ▲ chart ◆ biography

KEY
● map ■ picture ▲ chart ◆ biography

R

S

T

KEY

● map   ■ picture   ▲ chart   ◆ biography

KEY
● map   ■ picture   ▲ chart   ◆ biography

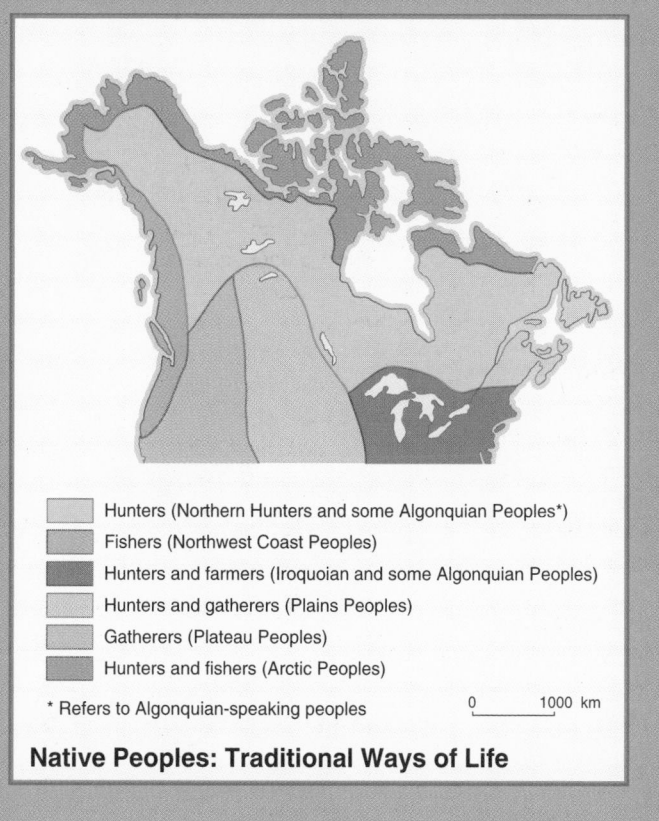

Native Peoples: Traditional Ways of Life

Hunters (Northern Hunters and some Algonquian Peoples*)
Fishers (Northwest Coast Peoples)
Hunters and farmers (Iroquoian and some Algonquian Peoples)
Hunters and gatherers (Plains Peoples)
Gatherers (Plateau Peoples)
Hunters and fishers (Arctic Peoples)

* Refers to Algonquian-speaking peoples

0   1000 km

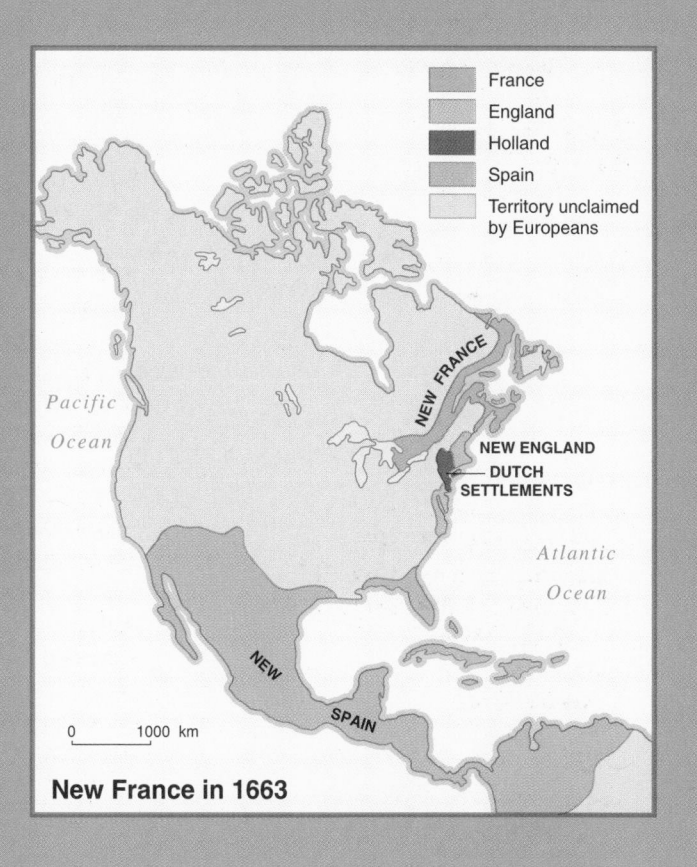

France
England
Holland
Spain
Territory unclaimed by Europeans

New France in 1663

Pacific Ocean

NEW FRANCE

NEW ENGLAND
DUTCH SETTLEMENTS

Atlantic Ocean

NEW SPAIN

0   1000 km

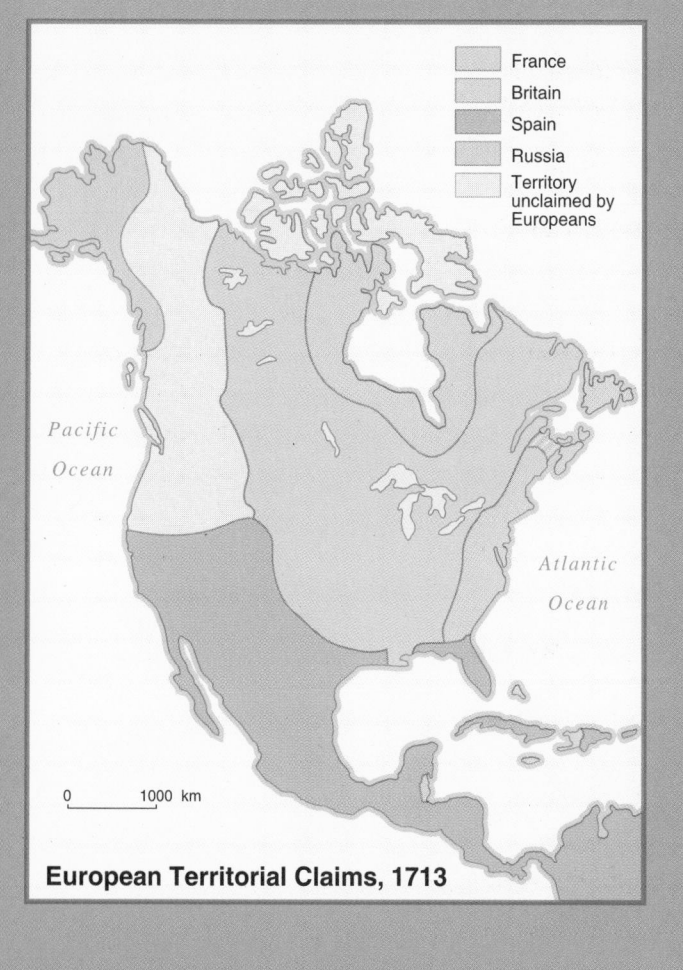

France
Britain
Spain
Russia
Territory unclaimed by Europeans

Pacific Ocean

Atlantic Ocean

0   1000 km

European Territorial Claims, 1713

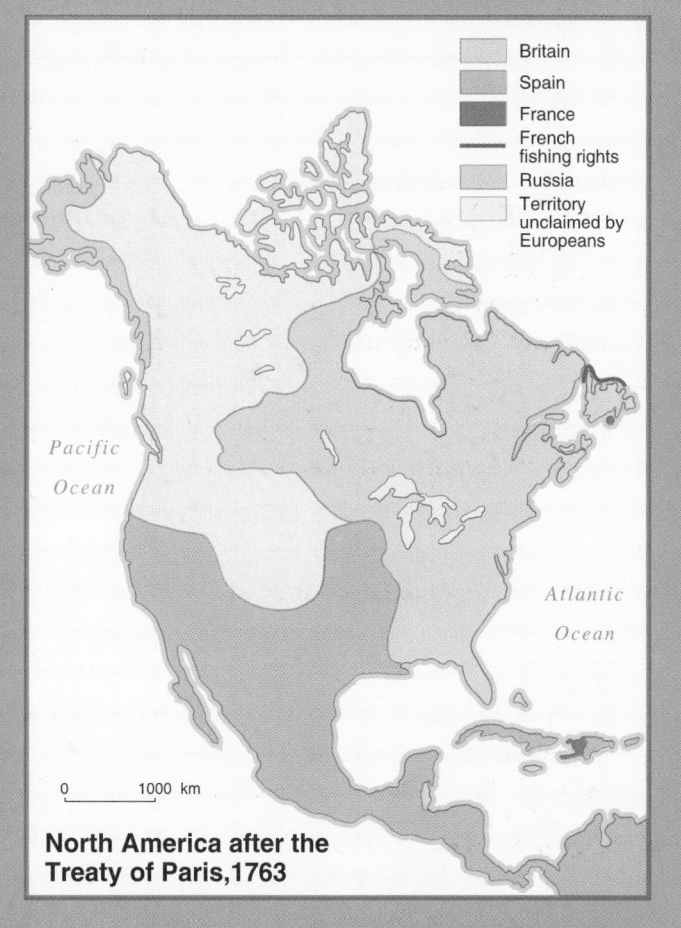

Britain
Spain
France
French fishing rights
Russia
Territory unclaimed by Europeans

Pacific Ocean

Atlantic Ocean

0   1000 km

North America after the Treaty of Paris, 1763

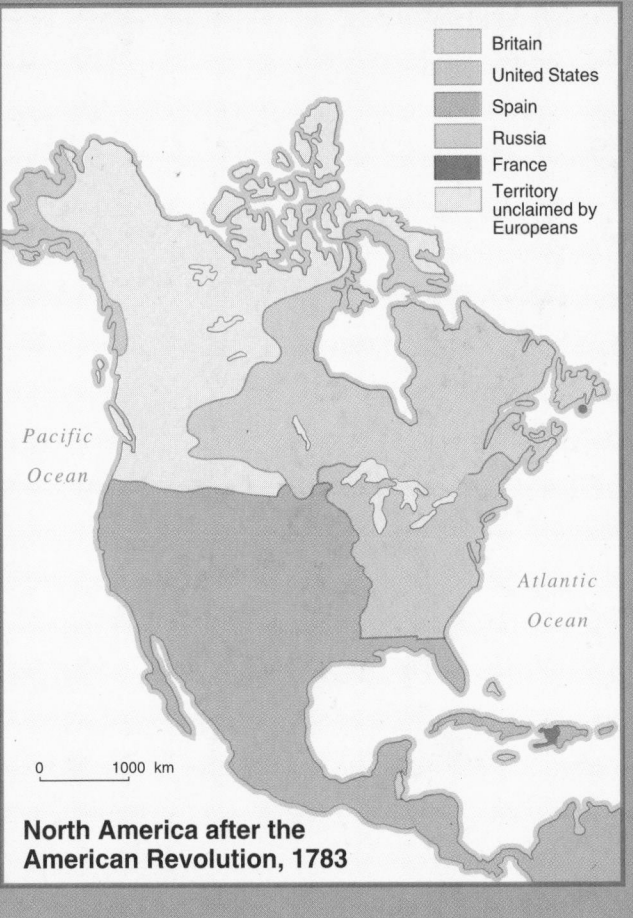

North America after the American Revolution, 1783

Legend:
- Britain
- United States
- Spain
- Russia
- France
- Territory unclaimed by Europeans

Pacific Ocean

Atlantic Ocean

0   1000 km

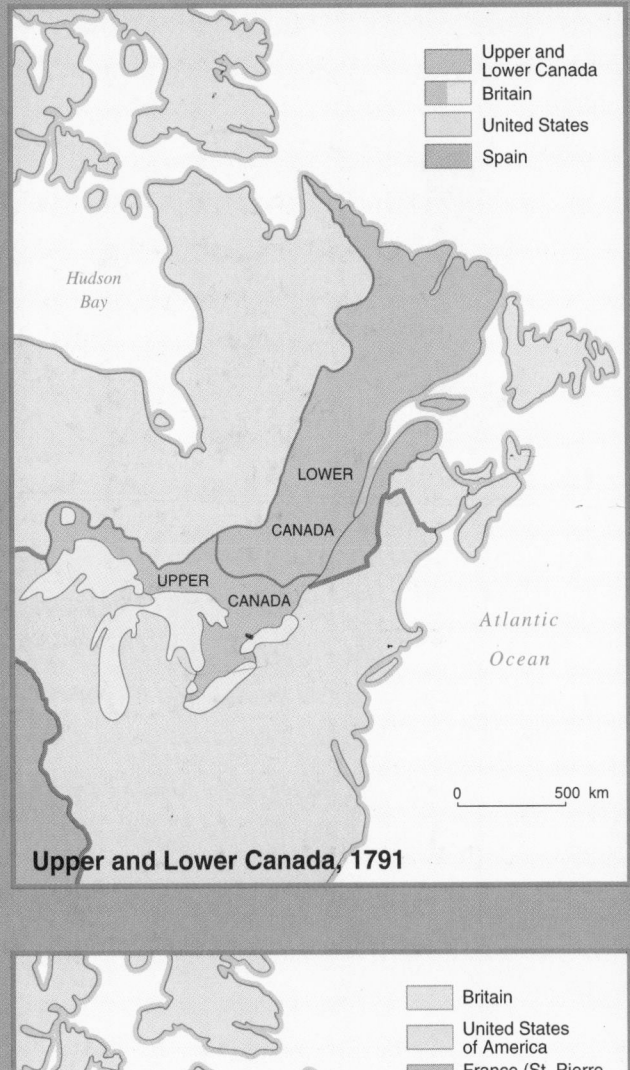

Upper and Lower Canada, 1791

Legend:
- Upper and Lower Canada
- Britain
- United States
- Spain

Hudson Bay

LOWER CANADA

UPPER CANADA

Atlantic Ocean

0   500 km

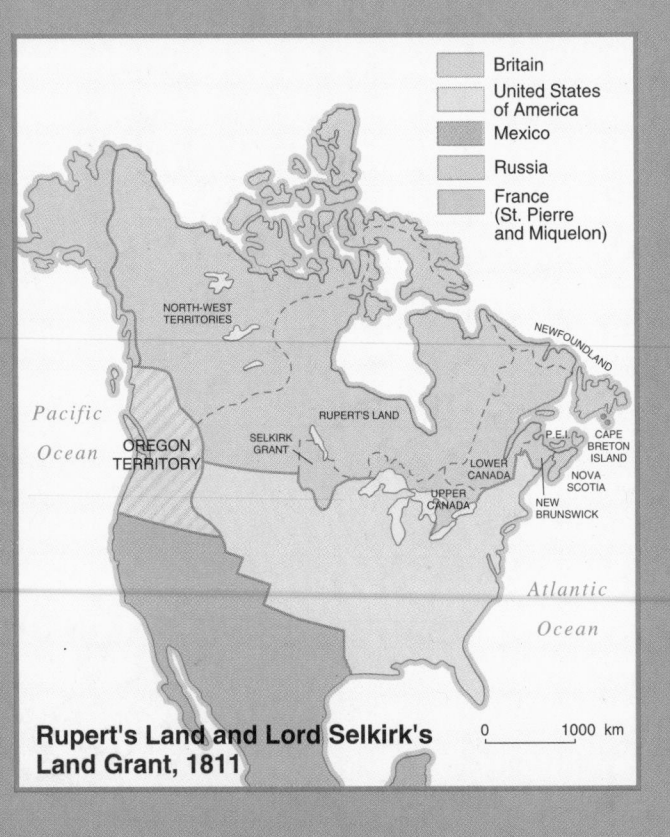

Rupert's Land and Lord Selkirk's Land Grant, 1811

Legend:
- Britain
- United States of America
- Mexico
- Russia
- France (St. Pierre and Miquelon)

NORTH-WEST TERRITORIES

NEWFOUNDLAND

RUPERT'S LAND

Pacific Ocean

OREGON TERRITORY

SELKIRK GRANT

LOWER CANADA

UPPER CANADA

P.E.I.

CAPE BRETON ISLAND

NOVA SCOTIA

NEW BRUNSWICK

Atlantic Ocean

0   1000 km

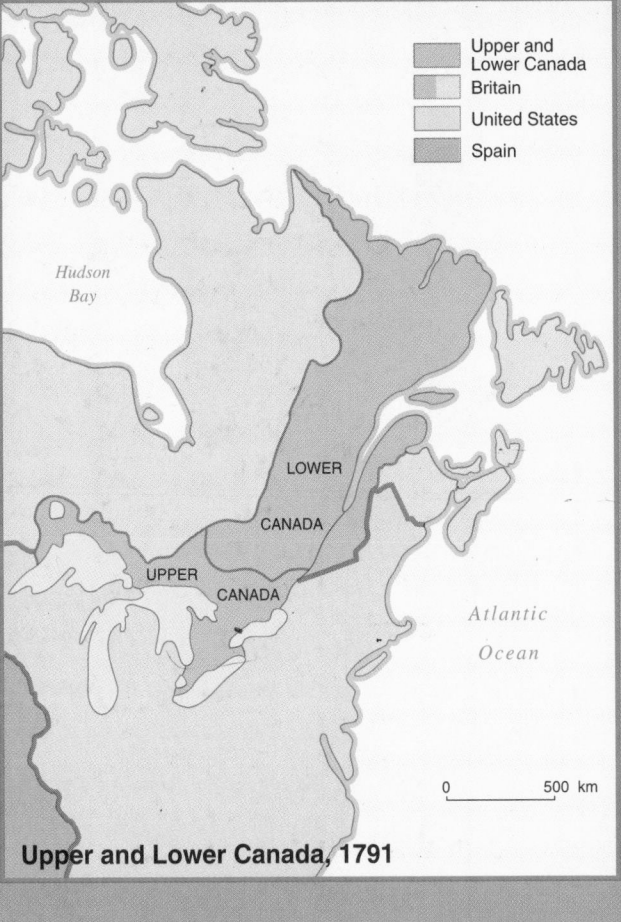

Canada East and Canada West, 1857

Legend:
- Britain
- United States of America
- France (St. Pierre and Miquelon)

Hudson Bay

CANADA EAST

CANADA WEST

Atlantic Ocean

0   500 km